Classroom Techniques:
Foreign Languages
and English as
a Second Language

Classroom Techniques: Foreign Languages and English as a Second Language

EDWARD DAVID ALLEN
The Ohio State University

REBECCA M. VALETTE
Boston College

HARCOURT BRACE JOVANOVICH, PUBLISHERS
*San Diego New York Chicago Washington, D.C. Atlanta
London Sydney Toronto*

Preface

The success of a second-language course depends not only on the quality of the basic program but also on the flexibility with which the teacher uses that program. The aim of this handbook, which is a revised and expanded edition of *Modern Language Classroom Techniques* (published by Harcourt Brace Jovanovich in 1972), is to show the teacher ways of implementing and supplementing existing materials. The suggested teaching procedures may be used with large classes, small groups, and individual students. They may also be used with any method, inasmuch as a special effort has been made to include a variety of teaching approaches.

Classroom Techniques: Foreign Languages and English as a Second Language contains several new features. First of all, the reader will note the inclusion of special techniques for teachers of ESL (English as a Second Language). The emphasis, as before, is on elementary and intermediate language classes, although some of the techniques are applicable for advanced students. Second, all sample items from foreign languages are accompanied by English equivalents, so that readers can understand them more readily. Third, a wide variety of communication activities has been included for all four language skills. Finally, the chapter on teaching culture has been substantially revised to reflect recent trends.

Part One of the handbook presents an overview of the language class. Ways of preparing supplementary materials are briefly reviewed. A variety of procedures for classroom management is suggested.

Part Two focuses on specific techniques for teaching the language itself, its sound system, its grammar, and its vocabulary. For the sake of simplicity we have used traditional grammar terminology. The actual techniques, however, cover a broad range of methods and approaches. All teachers will be able to discover many ideas for varying their instruction, no matter what their teaching situation or basic materials.

v

Part Three of the handbook presents ways of developing the skills of listening, speaking, reading, and writing. The aim of these procedures is to build up the student's ability to use the language as a vehicle for meaningful communication.

The final section of the handbook, Part Four, offers some suggestions for teaching culture, both daily life patterns and general civilization.

The Appendix contains sample lesson plans that show how several different procedures and techniques may be woven into a single class period.

This handbook does not treat the preparation of performance objectives and the use of learning contracts to individualize instruction.* However, teachers planning to adopt performance contracts will discover in this handbook many ways of varying classroom activities and of thereby avoiding the main danger of a poorly planned individualized program: student boredom.

In revising this handbook, the authors have received the encouragement and assistance of a great many people. Special thanks go to Barbara Freed of the University of Pennsylvania for a number of helpful suggestions. We would also like to express once again our appreciation to all those who contributed to the success of the first edition of the handbook: Alfred N. Smith, Lorraine Strasheim, Virginia Garibaldi Allen, Renée S. Disick, and the native speakers who checked the accuracy of the examples: Jean-Paul Valette, Werner Haas, Thérèse Bonin, Joseph Wipf, Jacob Voelker, and Esteban Egea. Once again we would like to thank our editor, Albert Richards, who, as ever, brought his critical eye to the manuscript.

Finally, we wish to express our thanks to our many readers, students, and colleagues throughout this country and abroad who, although not mentioned by name, have helped us in the formulation of our ideas and to whom this handbook is gratefully dedicated.

E.D.A.
R.M.V.

---

*For suggestions in these areas see Rebecca M. Valette and Renée S. Disick, *Modern Language Performance Objectives and Individualization: A Handbook* (New York: Harcourt Brace Jovanovich, 1972), and Renée S. Disick, *Individualizing Language Instruction: Strategies and Methods* (New York: Harcourt Brace Jovanovich, 1975).

Contents

part one
The Language Class— an Overview

outline

one
The Teacher
and the Course

The success or failure of a course in a foreign language or in English as a second language (ESL) may be evaluated by the progress of the students in language acquisition and cultural understanding and in the development of a positive attitude toward language learning. One simple, direct measure is provided by enrollment figures: What percentage of students are continuing with language study? The students themselves, with their aptitudes and their weaknesses, form the given or the point of departure for the evaluation. The key question is, Did the course succeed or fail with respect to the students enrolled in it? and not, Would the course have been more successful had more able students been enrolled?

The success of a course depends on several factors, the most important of which is the teacher. The scheduling of classes, the outward form of the instruction, and the basic program being used are of secondary importance.

1.1 THE TEACHER

The teacher is the key figure in the language course. It is the teacher who sets the tone for the learning activities. In a classical audio-lingual approach, the teacher is an orchestra leader directing a group of apprentices. With a highly student-centered approach, the teacher may simply encourage student activity and answer occasional questions. In either of these cases, as well as in the classroom situations falling between these two extremes, the teacher plays a prime role in effecting student progress or lack thereof.

3

1.1.1   The teacher's competence

It is, of course, desirable that all language teachers be fluent speakers of the language they are teaching. At the same time, however, it is evident that the great majority of foreign-language teachers whose native language is English do not possess near-native fluency in the second language.

Professional foreign-language teachers continually strive to improve their competence in the second and often third language. They try to get abroad at least once every five years, perhaps taking advantage of the low-cost charter flights of the professional organizations (such as MLA, ACTFL, the AATs). They try to get to foreign films, possibly seeing them two or three times, once for entertainment and subsequently as a means of increasing their audio-lingual skills. They subscribe to at least one foreign periodical to keep abreast of current developments in the countries whose language they are teaching. If possible, they listen regularly to radio broadcasts in the foreign language, on shortwave or (in many parts of the country) on local stations. They may even invite (and pay) a willing native speaker residing in their community to visit their language classes from time to time to note any mistakes they make.

Yet, how effective can native Americans hope to be as foreign language teachers? The answer is that they may be highly effective.

First, their own continuing role as students of the language they are teaching is sensed by their students. Students will respond warmly to a person who doesn't pretend to "know it all," but who is truly committed to the learning process.

Second, a recent study has failed to find any definite correlation between teacher language proficiency and student language achievement at the elementary levels.[1] Although there may be many explanations for this lack of significant correlation, it seems plausible that a dynamic language teacher of average-to-low language proficiency who uses tape recordings and a variety of techniques in the classroom might well be more effective than the very fluent teacher who is less responsive to the needs of the students and lacks imaginative teaching methods.

Although techniques in themselves cannot compensate for very poor language proficiency, they definitely enhance the effectiveness of the teacher in the classroom.

If the language course introduces the culture of people who speak the target language, it is evident that the teacher should develop a solid familiarity and understanding of that target culture or cultures. Nothing is as effective as a prolonged period of residence in the target country, but even such an experience must be supplemented with ongoing activities: reading, conversations with visitors from the country, films, recordings, and so on. With the increased

---

[1] See Philip D. Smith, Jr., *A Comparison of the Cognitive and Audiolingual Approaches to Foreign Language Instruction: the Pennsylvania Foreign Language Project* (Philadelphia: Center for Curriculum Development, 1970).

availability of international communications, most countries of the world are in a period of growth and change. The France of 1976, for instance, is not the France of 1956 or even that of 1966.

1.1.2 The teacher's attitude

The attitude of the teacher also influences a student's success. A study among elementary-school students seems to indicate that a teacher's expectancies are self-fulfilling.[2] In other words, if a teacher assumes that half the class is incapable of mastering the German /y/, then many of the students will never learn the sound. If another teacher is confident that all of his or her students can produce the /y/, they all eventually find they can say it. If the teacher feels that modern languages are just for the bright student and that the slower ones will be unable to keep up, then many of the students will drop out at the end of the semester or the end of the year.

Teacher attitude is particularly crucial in the case of ESL students. When students from another culture and/or linguistic group enter an American school, their integration is definitely enhanced if teachers demonstrate a supportive and understanding attitude. Such students not only need help in developing their command of English, but also frequently could benefit from an introduction to American culture, its conventions and its value systems.

A positive attitude on the part of the teacher is essential to success. The many techniques suggested in this handbook will work only if the teacher is personally convinced that the students are capable of learning another language.

1.1.3 Teaching for mastery

The pace of the class may be governed by three things, either singly or in combination: the book or program, the syllabus, and the ability of the students. For some teachers the book is the decisive factor: the First-Year Book, as the title indicates, must be covered in one year, no more, no less. In some school systems teachers are expected to adhere rigidly to a prescribed syllabus, which again makes no allowances for individual differences among classes and students.

Ideally, the pace of a language class, particularly at the beginning and intermediate levels, should be determined by the rate at which the students master the material. High attrition rates in foreign languages are an indication that most classes are paced too fast for the average student. Teaching for mastery means organizing instruction so that all students are given the opportunity to learn what is being taught.

[2] See Robert Rosenthal and Lenore F. Jacobsen, *Pygmalion in the Classroom* (New York: Holt, Rinehart and Winston, Inc., 1968).

Teaching for mastery also implies the creative use of a variety of teaching procedures. Since different students learn in different ways, the introduction of a new technique frequently helps a student overcome a learning problem. If a teacher expects the entire class to master the usage of the subjunctive, then he or she must utilize techniques to help the eye-minded as well as the ear-minded students, to help those who need explanation as well as those who learn best by developing their own generalizations, and to help those who are hesitant to express themselves and thus run the risk of looking foolish as well as those who are eager to try to express themselves and are unmindful of errors.

1.1.4   Classroom behaviors of the outstanding teacher

In a recent research project, Gertrude Moskowitz identified and studied a group of outstanding foreign language teachers in the Philadelphia area. In comparison with a matched group of heterogeneous teachers, the outstanding teachers exhibited the following classroom behaviors and interactions:[3]

1. The target language dominates the classroom interaction, whether or not the teacher or the students are speaking.
2. The teachers have an excellent command of the target language.
3. Even in first-level classes, very little English is used.
4. The teachers have fewer verbal tics.
5. Students use the foreign language to raise questions.
6. The amount of teacher talk is less.
7. The teachers are active nonverbally and use many more hand gestures.
8. The teachers are more expressive and animated.
9. The teachers move around the classroom a great deal.
10. The teachers use more behaviors that encourage and reinforce student participation, whether communicating in the foreign language, English, or nonverbally.
11. The teachers give students more immediate feedback.
12. The climate is warm and accepting.
13. The teachers often smile, praise, and joke.
14. Their praise is longer, more varied, and they use more nonverbal praise.
15. There is more laughter in their classes.
16. The teachers personalize the content more.
17. The students are "with" the teacher, rather than being apathetic or flippant.
18. Students exhibit more outward signs of enthusiasm to participate.
19. Student behavior is very seldom criticized.
20. Less classroom time is devoted to silent reading and written tasks.
21. There is less writing on the board by the teacher.

[3] Adapted from Gertrude Moskowitz, "The Classroom Interaction of Outstanding Foreign Language Teachers," *Foreign Language Annals* 9, no. 2 (April 1976), pp. 156–57.

22. Students speak to the teachers before and after class.
23. The teachers greet students before the class formally starts.
24. There is a greater amount of warm-up questions, review, and focusing on the skill of speaking.
25. There is a greater number of different activities per lesson.
26. The pace of the lessons is generally more rapid.
27. Drills are conducted rapidly.
28. The teachers have excellent classroom control.
29. The teachers exhibit patience.
30. When correcting student behavior, the teachers tend to joke or to maintain eye contact with students.
31. When correcting student errors, the teachers do so gently.
32. Students assist the teachers more in setting up and running equipment.

In an informal way, the teacher may simply read through the above list and determine personal areas of strength and weakness. The list may also be used by students observing foreign language classes, or by supervisors visiting those teaching under their charge. Some teachers may wish to experiment with Moskowitz' more formal system of Interaction Analysis.[4]

1.2   SCHEDULING

School schedules determine the basic arrangement of teaching time. However, no matter which of the following systems is being applied at a particular school, the actual foreign language class is ultimately as flexible or as rigid as the teacher makes it.[5]

1.2.1   Setting up time blocks

1.2.1a   TRADITIONAL SCHEDULING

The day is broken up into periods of forty or fifty minutes in length. Each class meets a certain number of periods a week in the same classroom with the same teacher. Sometimes one or two half-hour periods per week are scheduled in a language laboratory.

Teachers may treat the period as one long period for full-class activity, or they may alternate full-class activity with small-group work or individualized instruction. While they may cut the period up into smaller time segments, however, they can rarely arrange for activities lasting more than one period.

[4] For an excellent introduction to Interaction Analysis, see Gertrude Moskowitz et al., "Interaction in the Foreign-Language Class," in James W. Dodge, ed., *Sensitivity in the Foreign-Language Classroom*, Reports of the Working Committees of the Northeast Conference (1973).
[5] For a more complete treatment of this subject, see Jermaine D. Arendt, *New Scheduling Patterns and the Foreign Language Teacher*, ERIC Focus Report No. 18 (1970). Available from ACTFL Materials Center, 2 Park Avenue, New York, N.Y. 10016.

1.2.1b MODULAR SCHEDULING

The day is divided into modular units or "mods" of twenty minutes each. A French class, for example, might meet for two consecutive mods on Monday, three consecutive mods on Tuesday, two mods on Wednesday, one at 8:30 and the other at 2:30, not at all on Thursday, and two consecutive mods on Friday. Small-group activities, such as a conversation group or several interest groups, could meet during a single mod period. A film might be shown during the longer Tuesday class.

Unfortunately, even in schools having modular scheduling the teachers sometimes fail to differentiate among the time combinations available to them. In other words, teachers have not adapted their techniques to the flexibility offered by the varied class periods.

1.2.1c FLEXIBLE SCHEDULING

Under flexible scheduling, time blocks can be moved as well as increased. For example, on Monday of the first week the German class might have a time block or mod of twenty minutes at 8:30. On Monday of the second week, this same class might meet for three mods at 1:00.

Flexible scheduling allows the teacher to request specific time arrangements to coincide with the week's lesson plan. A long time sequence could be requested, for example, to show a full-length foreign language film. However, since such a system calls for a complex computer program and considerable advance planning on the part of each teacher, the flexible scheduling arrangement often degenerates into the modular scheduling described in the previous section. An effective flexible scheduling arrangement does, however, make it possible to offer a greater variety of learning activities than the straight modular system does.

1.2.1d OPEN SCHEDULING

Open scheduling allows each student to plan the day's activities. This system cannot be implemented unless all courses are fully programmed with special sets of material for every level. The Spanish IV student, for example, can decide at what time he or she wishes to take Spanish and then go to the appropriate carrel, laboratory booth, or working table.

1.2.2 Back-to-back scheduling

With any of the time arrangements mentioned, it is possible to schedule classes *back-to-back*, that is, at the same time. Back-to-back scheduling can contribute to the increase of flexibility of ESL and foreign language classes in several ways.

1.2.2a TRACKS OR STREAMS

If a school offers two or more tracks of a given language course, such as Spanish I, it is advisable to schedule these tracks at the same hour. Then if a student in the faster track or stream falls behind for any reason, he or she may be transferred to the slower track without any shift in schedule. Similarly, if a student in the slower track begins to spurt ahead of the others, he or she may be transferred into the faster track.[6]

1.2.2b BETWEEN-CLASS EXCHANGES: SAME LEVEL

Back-to-back scheduling facilitates between-class exchanges. (The informal grouping of two or more classes is called informal team teaching. See Section 1.3.) One first-year class may prepare a skit for another first-year class. Then for part of a period on the day chosen the two classes can be merged without raising any scheduling problems. Exchanges can be more frequent than this. For example, if both classes are progressing at similar rates, both might use the same set of tests. As a follow-through, one teacher might take those students from both classes who passed the test into one classroom while the other teacher would meet with the rest, who need remedial work, in the other classroom. The extent and variety of this between-class cooperation is limited only by the imagination of the cooperating teachers.

1.2.2c BETWEEN-CLASS EXCHANGES: DIFFERENT LEVELS

Classes of different levels may also benefit from back-to-back scheduling. The faster students of the upper class might be excused at certain times to help tutor students or guide small group conversation or pattern drill practice in the lower class. Students in the upper class who have consistent difficulty with a confusing point of vocabulary or grammar might prepare a presentation on this problem area and give it at the appropriate time in the lower class. The teacher of the upper class might even wish to send those students who, for example, are unsure of the partitive to the lower class on the day that teacher is presenting the partitive to that class. The lower class, on the other hand, might prepare short skits or dialogs for the upper class.

1.2.2d DOUBLE REGISTRATION

Double registration allows gifted students to advance more rapidly than their classmates without requiring additional time from the teacher. If Spanish II and French I are offered at the same time, a gifted Spanish II student might attend

---

[6] See Michael Hernick and Dora Kennedy, "Multi-level Grouping of Students in the Modern Foreign Language Program," in *Foreign Language Annals* 2, no. 2 (December 1968), pp. 200–04.

Spanish class three times a week and French class twice a week. Such a student would do the work and receive credit for both courses.

1.3   TEAM TEACHING

In formal team teaching, two or more persons work with the same group of students and share the responsibilities. The classroom teacher may also work with the assistance of a student teacher, a teacher aide, or an intern.[7] Members of a department may work together in preparing course materials.

Each foreign language teacher or teacher aide has special contributions to make to the program. The beginning teacher can learn much from an experienced and highly trained colleague. The older teacher can profit from some of the new ideas brought in by the beginner.

1.3.1   Formal team teaching

When two or more similar classes are scheduled back-to-back, the teachers can teach the combined classes as a team. This method is particularly effective if one of the classrooms is large enough to hold the combined group. For example, if two teachers are involved, one might meet with two-thirds of the students to present a new grammar point while the other directs remedial work or leads conversation practice. During a chapter test, one teacher may proctor the written part of the test while the other teacher conducts oral interviews.

Since the grouping changes frequently, team teaching allows teachers to vary techniques and approaches to meet the needs of the students. Class size may be varied at will. Such a system does, however, require considerable planning on the part of the teachers concerned. It is most easily introduced in a programmed or partially programmed course.

1.3.2   Grouping within one class

Frequently the teacher may receive assistance in teaching a single class. A student teacher may be working with one group of students in one part of the room while the head teacher is working with a second group. A teacher aide may be administering a speaking test to a third group of students in the language laboratory. In such cases the head teacher plans the lesson in consultation with his or her helpers.

1.3.3   Informal cooperation

Teachers within a department can pool their resources on an informal level. Native speakers in a department may review their colleagues' recombined reading materials, correct stylistic errors, and record supplementary listening

---

[7] An intern is usually a salaried, beginning teacher who holds a bachelor's degree and is in a supervised teacher-training program in order to earn certification.

exercises. In exchange, the non-native teachers might prepare visuals or type ditto masters that they would share with the native speakers. A teacher who has developed a cultural unit with slides and a work sheet for one class might be willing to present the same unit to a colleague's class. The teacher of an intermediate class might let a group of students rehearse an elementary dialog and present it to a beginning class. The teacher who has been abroad might have brochures and realia to share with those who have not.

By pooling and exchanging talents, materials, and ideas, a foreign language department can develop a strong, articulated program.

1.4 THE STUDENT-CENTERED CLASSROOM

In some areas of the country, there is a strong interest in the student-centered classroom. In its most formalized aspect, this interest is translated into individualized instruction. At the course level, it has given rise to mini-courses on topics of student concern. Within the more traditional language classroom, the application of values clarification techniques (Section 1.4.3), encourages student-centered language use. Another variation is the activity-centered classroom.

1.4.1 Individualized instruction

In an increasing number of schools, foreign language instruction is being individualized.[8] Individual pacing plans allow each student to progress through the prescribed material at his or her own rate. Individual instructional plans allow different students to engage in different kinds of activities. In both cases, however, some provision is made for whole-class or group activities. Not only does group work provide communication practice in the language, but the students themselves benefit psychologically from it.

1.4.1a PROGRAMMED MATERIAL

Programmed material makes use of some sort of "teaching machine." This may be simply a book with a grid that covers the correct responses for each frame, or a book plus tape, or a complex piece of hardware with audio-stimulus and looping or branching facilities. Programmed materials are most suited for the teaching of reading and writing, grammar, and vocabulary. Programs in phonetics are also available. Communication and self-expression, however, require at least two people.

---

[8] For a practical introduction, see Renée S. Disick, *Individualizing Language Instruction: Strategies and Methods* (New York: Harcourt Brace Jovanovich, 1975). See also Rebecca M. Valette and Renée S. Disick, *Modern Language Performance Objectives and Individualization: A Handbook* (New York: Harcourt Brace Jovanovich, Inc., 1972).

Students may work on programmed materials in large rooms with little supervision. Teachers are free to meet with small groups of students to practice language skills. Students who work through the program more quickly than others may be assigned special projects according to interest groups: developing a skit, preparing a display, reading sports magazines in the foreign language, and so on.

1.4.1b   INDIVIDUAL LEARNING PACKETS

A *learning packet* is a printed statement that describes the desired outcomes of a unit or lesson: it includes a listing of the objectives, a description of the types of tests, and the sequence of learning activities that the student should follow. Not all of the activities need be individual projects: a learning packet may include full-class presentations, group projects, and small-group conversations.

1.4.2   Mini-courses

A *mini-course* is a short unit of instruction that runs for one quarter or term. Mini-courses are most frequently found at the third- and fourth-year level in the secondary school. Topics may vary from French cooking to Spanish folk dances to reading the VW repair manual in German. The nature of the courses is determined by student interests and teacher competencies.

1.4.3   Values clarification techniques

Values clarification techniques encourage students to talk about their own impressions, opinions, and feelings. When these techniques are adapted to the foreign language classroom, the emphasis usually is shifted from an analysis of student values to the encouragement of self-expression.[9]

1.4.4   Activity-centered classes

In the activity-centered class, instruction is based on areas of interest. For example, an ESL class might develop a unit around a tour of a region of the United States. The activities could include map study, writing letters to the Chambers of Commerce, learning about the tourist attractions of the area and their significance, reading hotel and motel guides, and budget planning. As a component of this activity, students would acquire new vocabulary and master useful structures and phrases.

[9] For an example of this type of adaptation, see Virginia Wilson and Beverly Wattenmaker, *Real Communication in Foreign Language* (Upper Jay, N.Y.: Adirondack Mountain Humanistic Education Center, 1973). Sample techniques are found in this handbook in Chapter Nine.

The activity or activities selected as a point of departure can be varied. They might include the preparation of an original videotape, the making of a film, the planning of a series of bulletin board exhibits, the construction of a simulated cafe or shop, the editing of a second-language newspaper, the recording of a second-language radio program, and so forth. As the students enter into the activity, they are motivated to learn the related vocabulary and structures that will permit more natural communication.

1.5   THE BASIC PROGRAM AND SUPPLEMENTARY MATERIALS

Although teachers generally have a say in the selection of materials, a teacher, especially a new teacher, sometimes finds himself or herself in the position of being handed a program and told to teach it. For this teacher, the program defines the course. The grammar and the vocabulary content of the lessons and their sequencing will determine the content and the sequencing of the teacher's lessons.

The manner in which the content is presented to the students, however, is left to the determination of the teacher. It is possible to take an out-of-print traditional book of the 1930s and with the aid of homemade visuals teach a course stressing conversation and an inductive approach to grammar. It is possible to take an audio-lingual textbook, teach the vocabulary and sentence patterns first, and reserve the dialog itself for comprehension practice at the end of the lesson. It is possible to take a review grammar and prepare individual learning packets so that students can work at their own pace. In other words, through a judicious choice of techniques and classroom procedures, the creative teacher can go beyond the structure of the assigned program.

Supplementary materials in foreign languages are usually available in all schools, even though they are sometimes difficult to find. Old readers may furnish selections that may be mimeographed or put on transparencies. Tapes from a previous textbook series, now no longer used, may provide additional material for listening comprehension. Old workbooks may have suitable grammar exercises for review work. Wall charts and maps can be used for speaking and writing cues. Preview materials from publishers might have new ideas for presentations of vocabulary and structure. Unused foreign language magazines may be cut up for visuals. Short English films, especially films taken in the country under study, could be shown, replacing the English sound track with the teacher's narration in the foreign language. ESL classes might use short films depicting the students' native countries; if desired, the students can help with the English narration by designing their own sound track.

Effective teaching does not mean waiting for the ideal materials to be made available. It means investigating materials presently available and using them to their fullest extent.

outline

two
Preparing
Supplementary
Materials

Many of the teaching techniques described in the latter part of this handbook utilize supplementary materials which have been prepared by the teacher. These materials, visual aids for the most part, can usually be made very rapidly. This chapter gives brief guidelines for the construction of various types of materials and the use of standard classroom teaching equipment.

2.1 GENERAL CONSIDERATIONS

One does not have to be a professional artist or a communications engineer to develop and use a wide variety of supplementary materials in the classroom. Many teachers hesitate to venture beyond the commercial recordings and visuals provided by publishers, but this hesitation is largely based on lack of experience with the broad range of possibilities for creating supplementary materials with available resources.

2.1.1 Hints for nonartists

Even teachers who consider themselves nonartists can prepare fine visuals. Simple line drawings are often even more effective than detailed sketches, because the main function of the drawing is to elicit speech, not to distract the eye.

Students remember symbols very easily, once their significance has been explained in the native language. The teacher might say that an inverted V represents a roof. Then he or she could quickly designate the following buildings:

church

school

bank

train station

bakery

The students may help generate simple drawings to cue vocabulary items.

Sometimes students themselves are willing to make posters and other visuals. Perhaps a lettering class in art could be persuaded, with the consent of its teacher, to prepare charts of grammar generalizations. Perhaps a colleague in another department likes making posters or charts; in exchange for such a service the language teacher would render a service of another kind. Any teacher who has an idea for an effective visual can usually get help in executing it.

2.1.2   Audio-visual equipment

Most schools have a variety of audio-visual equipment, which they encourage their teachers to use.

2.1.2a   SCHEDULING AUDIO-VISUAL EQUIPMENT

Although some language departments have their own audio-visual equipment, in many schools it is necessary to schedule the use of the equipment in advance. Sometimes the red tape seems interminable, but the persistent teacher soon discovers how to obtain the equipment he or she wishes to use. If a teacher uses a piece of equipment several times a week, or every day, most schools eventually allow that piece of equipment to remain in his or her classroom. Students may own cassette recorders that they can bring to class.

2.1.2b   PREPARING TO MEET PROBLEMS

Sometimes the carefully scheduled piece of equipment arrives on time but then cannot be used because some component was not delivered. If the classroom has two-prong outlets, and most of the school's equipment has three-prong plugs, it is wise to keep a three-prong adapter in the desk. If the classroom has an electrical outlet only at the back of the room and the teacher likes to have the overhead projector at the front of the room, it is wise to have an extension cord on hand. If the tape recorder is occasionally delivered without the take-up reel, it is not an expensive matter to keep an empty reel in the room. If the projector screen is not delivered, a well-known substitute is a light-colored classroom wall. It is also a good idea to keep spare projector bulbs on hand.

2.1.2c   ENLISTING THE HELP OF STUDENTS

The teacher who is uncomfortable with a complex piece of mechanical equipment can usually find a student who can run it. If the basic program depends on films or film strips, the teacher may let students take turns running the projector. The responsibility of running a machine that the teacher finds complicated often increases the self-confidence of a student who is having difficulty learning the second language. It may also be possible to allow such a student to be excused from study hall to run the projector for another language class. The double exposure to the same lesson might provide the necessary extra practice to help that student improve his or her language competence.

2.1.3   Classroom library and realia center

A corner of the classroom can be equipped with bookcases to house the library and realia. The contents of such a realia center can be constantly expanded and renewed through the combined efforts of students and teacher. In addition to magazines and newspapers in the target language, the center can contain commercial games, posters, labels from various products, records, coins, stamps, old tickets, maps, theater programs, and the like. The material may be used to provide props for skits, illustrations for the bulletin board, points of departure for guided compositions, and supplements to the basic textbook.

Whenever the teacher or the students (or relatives of students) travel to the target country, they should be encouraged to bring back a variety of new materials: brochures, candy wrappers, ticket stubs, decks of cards, and so forth. In this way the realia center remains up to date.

2.2   NON-PROJECTED VISUALS

The easiest visuals to use are of the non-projected variety: charts, posters, maps, and so on. Frequently the foreign language department or the school possesses several types of these non-projected visuals, including those from commercial materials which have been replaced by newer texts. Often, however, the teacher will want to make additional visuals.[1]

2.2.1   Posters and charts

Posters and charts are usually made of tag board, available from any arts and crafts supply store. This heavy cardboard can be supported on the ledge of the chalkboard or propped on a desk. It comes in a variety of bright colors.

Lines should be broad enough and words large enough to be easily visible from the back of the room. The indelible felt marker, such as the Magic Marker, is an excellent writing tool. The darker colors are the most visible.

---

[1] For a good introduction to visuals and other supplementary materials, see James W. Brown, Richard B. Lewis, and Fred F. Harcleroad, *AV Instruction: Technology, Media and Methods*, 4th ed. (New York: McGraw-Hill, 1973).

2.2.2 Cue cards

Cue cards can be used by both the teacher and the students. They range in size from 3 × 5 to 8½ × 11—occasionally somewhat larger.

Ordinary 3 × 5 index cards may be used for single digit numbers and simple line drawings. The 4 × 6 are more suitable for longer numbers or words. Larger cards, perhaps of heavyweight construction paper or manila paper, may be used to mount magazine pictures.

Again, the teacher must be sure that the cards are easily visible from the back of the room. Letters and digits must be large and legible. Broad-tip felt pens are the most convenient writing tools.

Cue cards that are to be distributed to the students should be marked on both sides. For example, the teacher may have distributed index cards with letters symbolizing Spanish cities (M—Madrid, T—Toledo, B—Barcelona, and so on). He or she might ask Joe in Spanish to hold up his card and then ask another student to tell where Joe lives. All students should be able to read the letter on the card.

2.2.3 Cloth board

The teacher can make an inexpensive cloth board by getting a piece of plywood, heavy cardboard, or artist's canvas and tacking or taping a piece of colored felt or dark flannel to it. It is also possible to hang the felt or flannel directly from hooks above the chalkboard. Pictures or cutouts can be displayed on the cloth board by gluing a small piece of flocking paper, sandpaper, or flannel to the back of the picture or cutout. Cutouts may also be made out of Pellon (a material used in sewing, available in any yard goods department) or from desk blotters. Words may be written on the Pellon or the blotters with felt pens.

Sturdier cloth boards can be made with Velcro. The board is covered with Velcro yardgoods, which have a fine fuzzy surface. The pictures or objects to be displayed are backed with small pieces of Velcro tape, which has a looplike texture. When pressed onto the Velcro board, they will not slip out of position; they must be firmly pulled away.

2.2.4 Magnetic board

Many of the newer chalkboards are magnetized and can be used as magnetic boards. Commercial magnetic boards are also available. One can be made by cutting a piece of light-weight sheet metal to a size of 24″ × 24″. Masking tape can be used to bind the sharp edges. The shop teacher may be able to help with this project.

Magazine pictures and light-weight cue cards are held to the board by magnets. The order of the pictures or cards can easily be varied.

2.2.5 Pocket charts

Pocket charts are available commercially; most elementary school classrooms will have one. A pocket chart may be made very simply by taping the bottom and side edges of four or five narrow strips of oaktag to a larger sheet of oaktag that has been mounted on heavy cardboard or tacked to a bulletin board. These strips form pockets in which flash cards, cue cards, or pictures can be inserted.

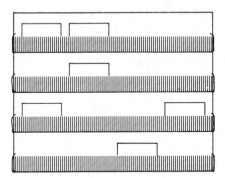

2.2.6 Peg board

A piece of peg board, about three feet by four feet, can be used as a playing board for games like "Jeopardy." Hooks are evenly spaced to hold the question cards. The question cards may be prepared on 5 × 7 index cards, with the question on one side and the response on the other. Each card has a hole punched on the top so that it can hang easily from the hook.

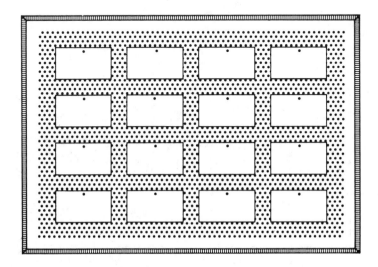

2.2.7 Maps

The frequent use of maps of the country or countries where the target language is spoken helps increase student awareness of the geographical parameters of the foreign culture. Many classrooms have commercial maps that can be hung at the front of the classroom. (Maps may also be projected on a screen with an overhead or opaque projector.)

Often the teacher will simply want to sketch the map of the foreign country on the chalkboard to show a specific part of the country mentioned in the lesson or reading. In such instances, it is useful to be able to draw an acceptable outline map of the country in question. The following illustrations show how to begin with a rectangular grid to produce an outline map. (With practice, the grid may be omitted.)

Figure 1
FRANCE

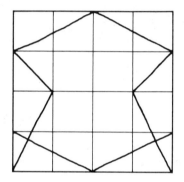 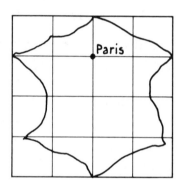

Figure 2
MEXICO

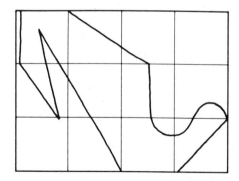 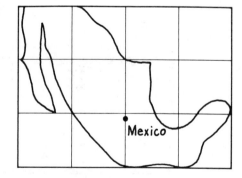

2.3 DITTOS

The most widely used supplementary materials in foreign language teaching are undoubtedly sheets prepared on a spirit duplicating machine such as the ditto.

Masters may be prepared with a typewriter, ball-point pen, or pencil. Errors are easily corrected by scraping the back of the master sheet and then writing in the new form. Clear corrections may be obtained by shifting the top sheet so that an unused portion of the purple backing sheet is directly below the space where the correction is being entered. In addition to the familiar purple, backing sheets are also available in red and green, allowing for more colorful stencils.

The master may also be prepared through a photostatic process using a Thermofax or similar heat-process machine and a typed or printed master. For example, the teacher might wish to have the entire class read a German newspaper article. He or she would cut out the article, edit it if necessary, perhaps type a few questions, and make a Xerox copy of the new page. The Xerox print would be used to prepare a ditto master that would in turn provide copies for the entire class. If the materials to be used are copyrighted, the teacher should first request written permission from the publisher.

2.4 PROJECTED VISUALS

Projected visuals allow the teacher to show the class a large image. Some projected visuals, such as films, require a darkened classroom, but others, such as overhead transparencies, may be used with normal classroom lighting.

2.4.1 The opaque projector

Flat, printed or drawn pictures may be projected with an opaque projector. The picture or illustration from a book is placed on a special carrier that holds the material in place in the machine.

The disadvantage of the opaque projector is that it must be used in a darkened classroom. Therefore, it is most useful in illustrating oral presentations by the teacher or the students: talks on art, architecture, and aspects of the foreign country can be enhanced with pictures from books or postcards.

The opaque projector can also be used as an enlarger to prepare posters:

Step 1: Tape or attach the poster board to the wall or chalkboard.

Step 2: Place the cartoon or illustration on the opaque projector.

Step 3: Project the picture onto the poster board. Move the opaque projector until the image is of the appropriate size and clarity.

Step 4: With broad felt markers, trace the projected image onto the poster board. Add color if desired.

2.4.2   The overhead projector

The overhead projector uses transparencies, which are thin acetate sheets. They can be obtained commercially or prepared by the teacher.[2]

To write or draw pictures on a transparency, the teacher may use a grease pencil or, better yet, a water-soluble Vis-a-Vis pen (broad or narrow tip). The narrow tip is more appropriate for writing. The transparencies can be erased with a paper tissue and reused as often as desired.

If transparencies are to be shown more than once, it is wise to use indelible felt pens. The colors show up brightly on the screen and do not fade with age. Cardboard frames, while not necessary, make the transparencies easier to handle and more convenient to file. These cost approximately ten cents apiece.

Transparencies may also be made from a written or printed master using a Thermofax or other similar duplicating machine. It is essential that the master be on white (or light colored) paper and that the black lines contain carbon. This means that a dark lead pencil, india ink, a typewriter, or a Xerox copy can be used, but not a ball-point pen or a purple ditto sheet. If a typewriter is used, it is advisable to use primer (large) or pica type; elite type is very hard to read, even in a small classroom.

The overhead projector is a versatile machine that lends itself to a variety of presentations.

2.4.2a   THE OVERHEAD AS A CHALKBOARD

It is possible to write directly on the transparency over a lighted projector. The overhead has an advantage over the chalkboard in that the teacher maintains eye contact with the students while writing. A typed quiz or homework assignment may be made into a transparency. When the class is finished, the teacher may fill in the blanks or indicate the correct answers with a grease pencil. He or she may use the transparency again with a subsequent class after having wiped off the correct answers. (The typed questions are permanent and will not be erased.)

2.4.2b   THE OVERHEAD AS A POSTER

A drawing on the overhead may be used as a large poster. Instead of using a pointer, the teacher points to appropriate symbols or pictures with a pencil or a long, thin stick (such as a long Tinker Toy stick sharpened in a pencil sharpener). Here again the teacher can maintain eye contact with the students while cuing their responses with the overhead.

---

[2] See James J. Wrenn, *The Overhead Projector*, ERIC Focus Report No. 19 (1970). Available from ACTFL Materials Center, 2 Park Avenue, New York, N.Y. 10016.

2.4.2c   MASKING TECHNIQUE

A sheet of ordinary paper may be used to mask any part of the transparency. The teacher, however, can still read what is under the paper. For example, one might first expose a question, keeping the answer covered, and then slide down the mask to reveal the answer. In a two-column presentation, the right-hand column might be covered until the students have first read the left-hand column.

2.4.2d   OVERLAY TECHNIQUE

Since acetate is transparent, it is possible to place two or more sheets on top of each other, building more complex drawings or sentences. It is conversely possible to begin with several sheets and remove them one by one to arrive at a simpler drawing or sentence.

For example, the basic transparency might have a table set for dinner with four chairs. The first overlay would put two people in the chairs and food on the table. The next overlay would add two guests. If the negative pattern in French were being presented, the basic transparency might have several sentences in the present tense, with the words appropriately spaced so that the overlay would contain the *ne* or *n'* and *pas* so that they would appear before and after the verb.

The overlay might simply be the figure of a boy or girl cut from cardboard. This figure may be moved along the streets of a map, or from room to room in a house, casting a silhouette on the picture projected from the transparency.

2.4.2e   PUZZLE TECHNIQUE

Acetate transparencies may be cut into smaller pieces. It is possible in this way to shift words or phrases. In teaching word order in German, for example, the teacher might prepare pieces that read as follows: *Ich weiß, daß / er / hat / Geld / sie / ist / nett (I know that / he / has / money / she / is / nice)*. First, *er hat Geld* would be arranged on the overhead. The students would be asked to identify the verb, and the teacher would circle *hat,* using a grease pencil. Next, *Ich weiß, daß* would be put at the front of the sentence and the verb moved to the end. After removing that sentence, the teacher would put *sie ist nett* on the overhead and again have the students find the verb. Last, the teacher would add the piece *Ich weiß, daß* and ask the students where *ist* will go.

2.4.3   Filmstrips

Filmstrips provide a convenient and relatively economical way of presenting information to full classes, groups, and even individuals. Many foreign language departments own some commercial filmstrips: views of the target country, illustrations of architectural styles, contents of well-known museums, and so on. Frequently the social studies department will also have filmstrips on geographical, sociological, or historical subjects that can be integrated into the foreign language class. The filmstrip may have a foreign language soundtrack or a native language soundtrack; in the latter case, the teacher may prefer to describe the filmstrip orally in the target language rather than play the tape.

In using cultural filmstrips, the teacher should always preview the filmstrip before presenting it to the class. In preparation for the filmstrip, the teacher can ask the students to look for specific features in the photographs. As a follow-up, the students can describe what they learned from the filmstrip or narrate the filmstrip during a second showing without the original soundtrack.

Cartoon filmstrips have been developed to teach vocabulary and structures in the target language. Frequently, filmstrips developed for one language may be used in teaching other languages. Cartoon filmstrips of fairy tales, for instance, can be used by all the language teachers in the department.

It is possible to buy reels of a special plastic film, 35 mm in width, that contain the standard sprocket holes. Students can draw their own filmstrips directly on the plastic, using them to illustrate original narratives and dialogs.

2.4.4   Slides

Many teachers have slides taken in the target country. In addition, many language departments have commercial slides showing aspects of the foreign culture. The advantage of a set of slides is that the teacher can select only those which seem appropriate and can rearrange the order of presentation at will. Once a specific slide program has been developed, it is advisable to number the slides and place them in an individual box for easy accessibility at a later date. If the teacher or department has a large collection of slides, students can be allowed to look through the slides to develop their own presentations.

Students could take slides of the school and the town in which they live to illustrate original narrations. Oral reports accompanied by slides encourage more active participation on the part of the other members of the class. Title slides may either be photographed or made by hand by scratching off the color on dark overexposed slides.

If the teacher has access to a 35mm camera and tripod, either directly or through the audio-visual center, it is possible to make slides of illustrations in books, magazine advertisements, advertisements, foreign currency, and so on. While most of these illustrations could be shown with the opaque projector, the making of slides eliminates the manipulation of a series of objects or books; it also allows the illustrations to be projected in a somewhat lighter classroom. Advanced classes can be encouraged to prepare an illustrated report in which all illustrations are transformed into slides; in this way, the teacher will have a growing collection of visual programs.

2.4.5 Movies

Classroom movies fall into two categories: commercial 16mm films and home-made super-8 films. Both types of visuals are usually more expensive than the visuals mentioned above.

Frequently the school or school district has a film library. Social studies films, or even films on topics such as art or history, can be utilized in the foreign language classroom. If desired, the soundtrack can be turned off and replaced with a target language narration by the teacher. Commercial foreign language films are also available.

Students often enjoy preparing short super-8 films as part of a class project. These films may be intended to illustrate a recorded dialog or narration in the textbook. Students may also wish to make films with an original soundtrack or silent films that they will accompany with a live narration. Students in a film class may wish to make an animated film to illustrate a fable or story in the target language.

Teachers may also purchase commercial silent super-8 films of comedies or cartoons. Different groups of students may work together preparing a foreign language sound track for such films.

2.4.6 Television

Many schools have video-tape facilities. Beginning students may produce videotapes of the dialogs or exchanges in the textbook. The tape recording of the dialog provides the soundtrack of the program, while the students silently act out the conversation. More advanced students may wish to prepare and film their own compositions: short skits, TV commercials, news reports, etc. Video-taping is a time-consuming enterprise, and should be considered as an out-of-class activity. Before any video-taping, the teacher should verify the script and the pronunciation so that the end result is linguistically acceptable.

Commercial television programs are frequently an excellent adjunct to second-language classes. ESL students should be encouraged to watch news-casts, dramas, situation comedies, mysteries, and even commercials. If appropriate programs are presented during class hours, they can be watched on a regular school television set. However, if the teacher wants to use a segment of a program or a series of commercials for more intensive study, it is advisable to prepare a videotape recording that can then be replayed at will. Foreign language teachers might also be able to obtain foreign television programs or American series with second-language dubbing.

2.5 RECORDINGS

Commercial recordings accompany almost all of the available foreign language programs. At some point, however, the teacher usually finds it desirable to prepare supplementary recordings.

2.5.1   Editing available materials

Often the available recordings do not completely meet the needs of the class. By using two tape recorders, or a record player and a tape recorder, the teacher can edit an appropriate lesson tape for the language laboratory or classroom. For example, he or she might wish to use two review exercises from a previous lesson and three exercises of the current lesson. The students may even be asked to go through one of the exercises twice. On a new tape the teacher duplicates the commercial recordings in the desired sequence. Using a microphone, instructions between exercises may be added.

2.5.2   Bringing radio broadcasts to the classroom

In most parts of the country it is possible to receive foreign language radio broadcasts. Some of these originate in the larger cities or in regions where there are strong ethnic minorities. Others originate in Canada and Mexico. Some are especially prepared for language students and are broadcast on FM stations at regular times. The widest selection of broadcasts is available on short wave, which can be heard most clearly at night. ESL teachers have a wide choice of materials.

The teacher who has a tape recorder or a cassette recorder can tape these broadcasts and bring them into the classroom. Even beginning German students who are aware of the current news headlines will be able to grasp parts of the previous night's newscast transmitted from Cologne via short wave.[3]

2.5.3   Recording tests and homemade exercises

If the teacher plans to record original materials, several steps must be followed.

A script must be prepared in advance. If the teacher does not possess native fluency, it is advisable to have a colleague read over the script. If the script is a multiple-choice listening test, a colleague should read each item to look for possible ambiguities of interpretation.

Ample time must be allowed for the recording session; it usually takes two and a half to three hours to record an hour of tape. If two voices are required, as in a rejoinder-type item or exercise, the teacher should invite a colleague, or an available native informant, to assist in the recording. The making of a recording usually takes longer than one anticipates. Moreover, it is advisable to listen to the entire recording at the end of the session so that, if necessary, parts can be rerecorded at once.

---

[3] See also Robert J. Nelson, *Using Radio to Develop and Maintain Competence in a Foreign Language*, ERIC Focus Report No. 11 (1969). Available from ACTFL Materials Center, 2 Park Avenue, New York, N. Y. 10016.

2.5.4   Recorded interviews

With the growing availability of cassette players, many teachers and students are able to record informal interviews with native speakers. The ESL students in the United States might be encouraged to record the views of their English-speaking classmates or colleagues. The students should be encouraged to listen to their recordings several times in order to improve their level of listening comprehension. The recordings might then form the basis of oral resumés or written reports.

American students studying one of the ethnic languages of their area should similarly be encouraged to contact native speakers and record their interviews. An excellent source of interviews might be a local old-age home. Elderly immigrants are often delighted to use their native language to talk to young people about their homeland as they remember it.

2.5.5   Classroom recordings

Cassette players can also be used to record classroom activities. Skits, oral exposés, and small group conversations can be recorded so that the participants can themselves evaluate their speech. In intermediate and advanced classes, the teacher might also use the cassette player to record comments, in the second language, on written work and compositions. The students would then have to listen to the teacher's evaluation of their written work and make the necessary modifications before receiving credit for the assignment.

outline

three
In the
Classroom

Time is the element most precious to language teachers: much more time than is available in schools is needed to learn a foreign language well. It is estimated that two and a half weeks of living with a French family are the equivalent of one whole year's instruction in a high school French class. In this respect, the ESL teacher in the United States has a decided advantage over the foreign language teacher, for the ESL students can maintain their contact with the target language through radio, television, and interpersonal communication outside the classroom.

The teacher's primary concern in preparing the lesson and in carrying out class activities is to maximize the amount of learning that takes place, to involve the greatest number of students, and to reduce the amount of time devoted to matters not directly related to the business of acquiring language competence.

3.1 LESSON PLANNING

Careful planning is essential to successful teaching. The teacher must determine the educational aims of the lesson and then select activities that will contribute to the realization of those aims. These activities will vary from class to class according to the needs and abilities of the students concerned.[1]

3.1.1 Setting course goals

Before determining lesson plans and lesson objectives, the teacher must establish a clear view of the goals of the course. These goals may be expressed in terms of percentages. Here is a sample description of a first-year course:

[1] Sample lesson plans for an elementary, an intermediate, and an advanced class are to be found in the Appendix.

70% control of grammar, vocabulary, and pronunciation:
15% oral control of grammar
20% written control of grammar
10% oral control of vocabulary
15% written control of vocabulary
10% pronunciation
30% communication skills:
20% listening, speaking, and conversation
10% reading and composition

In this particular course, over two-thirds of the time is spent on "skill-getting" activities, that is, on the acquisition of elements of the new language. About one-third of the focus is on "skill-using" activities, in which the students develop communication skills.[2]

In setting the course goals, the teacher is also determining the framework in which the final grades for the course will be assigned. The manner of evaluation, however, is not specified: it might consist of quizzes, formal tests, or class participation evaluated informally.

3.1.2 Setting lesson objectives

Lesson objectives should be stated in terms of student behavior, that is, in terms of what the student will be able to do as a result of instruction. It is for the student, after all, that the teacher has been hired and the basic program selected. It may be the teacher's aim to cover a particular unit by a given date, but the lesson objectives must specify the end result in student behavior: for example, the student will be able to answer yes / no questions using the present tense of the -re verbs plus the irregular verbs prendre and mettre.

3.1.2a PERFORMANCE OBJECTIVES

Lesson objectives worded in terms of student behavior are called *perform-ance objectives,* or *instructional objectives,* or behavioral objectives. It is not within the scope of this handbook to describe in detail the preparation and classification of performance objectives.[3]

Briefly, a formal performance objective evaluates skill-getting activities and contains four parts: the purpose of the behavior, the description of the behavior, the conditions under which it is to occur, and the criterion by which it is to be evaluated. A sample item is often included:

[2] The terms "skill-getting" and "skill-using" have been developed by Wilga Rivers. See her book *A Practical Guide to the Teaching of French* (New York: Oxford, 1975), pp. 3–5.

[3] For more information see Rebecca M. Valette and Renée S. Disick, *Modern Language Performance Objectives and Individualization: A Handbook* (New York: Harcourt Brace Jovanovich, Inc., 1972).

(1) Purpose: To demonstrate awareness of number markers in spoken French.

(2) Desired behavior: The student will indicate whether the direct objects (preceded by *le, la, l'*, or *les*) in a series of spoken sentences are singular or plural.

(3) Conditions: He will hear fifteen sentences read aloud by the teacher at classroom conversational speed. Each sentence will be read only once.

(4) Criterion: The student must identify at least fourteen sentences of the following type correctly:

> Teacher: Je cherche les livres.   *I'm looking for the books.*
> Student: Plural.

The objective described might be one of several objectives for a particular lesson.

3.1.2b   ANALYZING THE AIMS OF THE LESSON IN TERMS OF PERFORMANCE OBJECTIVES

In determining the performance objectives of a lesson, the teacher must ask the following questions: What are the essential features of this unit? What must *all* students get out of this unit if they are to continue with the next unit? (The concern here is for *minimum* performance to be required of every student in the class.) The teacher of an audio-lingual program might decide that the aural comprehension of the basic dialog lines, presented in random order, is absolutely essential and insist that the students be able to select the native language equivalents of such recorded sentences with complete accuracy. The teacher of a German class might decide that the students should be able to complete in writing at least nineteen out of twenty sentences with the appropriate form of *haben*, but that he or she will tolerate ten mistakes on a thirty-item test of vocabulary.

The teacher, in other words, decides in advance which features of the unit are to be stressed in class and what degree of proficiency the students must develop with respect to each of those features.

3.1.3   Planning lesson activities

Once the objectives have been determined, the teacher selects appropriate lesson activities in order to attain these aims.

The general nature of the activities will be determined by the objectives themselves. If the students are expected to hear the differences between subjunctive and indicative forms of verbs, for instance, the teacher must provide various types of listening practice.

The specific nature of the activities will correspond to the needs of the students and be determined by their age, their background, their interests, and their abilities. To a lesser extent, the physical classroom setup and the length of the class period must be taken into consideration.

3.1.3a INTEREST LEVEL

Seventh graders might enjoy constructing a Spanish house or making relief maps. Twelfth graders might prefer debating current problems, such as pollution.

All students seem to be interested in developing closer contact with the foreign culture through foreign guest speakers, pen pals, short-wave radio, or films. They are also interested in developing communication skills. Here again ESL teachers in the United States have the advantage of omnipresent linguistic and cultural support.

3.1.3b VARIETY

In order to hold the interest of most students, it is necessary to provide a large number of varied activities. (The sample lesson plans in the Appendix contain seven activities for a forty-minute class period and nine for one of fifty minutes.) Although the numbers are arbitrary, the teacher should strive for a minimum of five activities per standard class period.

Often the teacher thinks that the class activities are varied, but in the minds of the students, there is only one activity repeated over and over again. If, for example, the lesson is on the future tense, a varied lesson might illustrate use of the future tense in a demonstration on the overhead projector, a dictation, a game, and a song.

Variety in the use of equipment and materials is also vitally important: for example, one day, the overhead projector might be used; the next day, the felt board; and the following day, the film strip projector. If one medium, such as the film strip projector, is used for all lessons, the class can become very dull.

3.1.3c TIMING

All activities do not necessarily have to last the same amount of time. In general, intensive drills, such as pattern practice, should be done for only a few minutes at a stretch. Otherwise, the students are likely to become listless and cease to attach any meaning to what they are saying. An activity that requires physical movement, such as "Simon Says" or a physical response exercise, makes time pass quickly. In these cases it is advisable to know when to stop the activity, despite the students' protests to the contrary. It is better to end an activity when interest is high and then introduce it again, perhaps in a varied form at another class meeting, than to let it continue until interest begins to wane.

3.1.4 Modifying the lesson plan in the classroom

It is sometimes necessary to abridge the lesson plan in the course of the lesson. Sometimes an activity takes longer than anticipated, or perhaps a fire drill cuts into the available class time. In such cases, it is usually wiser to eliminate one of the subsequent activities altogether than to try to rush through the entire lesson plan.

If an activity fails to interest the class, even though the teacher has spent a great deal of time planning it, it is best to drop it as quickly as possible and try something else. Often lack of interest is a sign that the class is not ready for the activity and that additional preparation is necessary.

3.2   INDIVIDUAL AND GROUP INSTRUCTION

Any classroom with movable furniture lends itself to a variety of instructional groupings ranging from the full class to individualized activities. Very large classes should frequently be broken down into small groups.

In a classroom where furniture is screwed to the floor, grouping may at first glance seem impossible. However, the combined ingenuity of teacher and students can devise viable solutions, such as having four Spanish conversation groups sit on Mexican blankets in the different corners of the room.

3.2.1   Whole-class instruction

In whole-class instruction the entire class is engaged in the same activity. Most frequently this activity is led by the teacher, who is giving instructions, modelling sentences, using the overhead, asking questions, leading drill, giving a talk on culture, and so on. The larger the class size, the more difficult it is for the teacher consistently to maintain the interest and participation of all the students.

Certain techniques help improve the effectiveness of whole-class instruction.

3.2.1a   ALTERNATING RESPONSE PATTERNS

In the early stages of a language course much repetition and guided response are necessary. The teacher can maintain an element of newness in the classwork by introducing unpredictable response patterns. Nothing is more boring to students than knowing that the teacher will call on each one individually, row after row. Even if the teacher randomly calls on one student after another, the rhythm may become monotonous; it can be broken by occasionally eliciting a response from the whole class, or a specific row, or only the girls, and so on.

3.2.1b   QUESTIONING TECHNIQUE

In questioning students, or in presenting the stimulus of any type of oral work, the teacher should always give the question or stimulus *before* calling out the name of the student. This way all students mentally prepare the correct response, aware that their turn may come next. If the name is called before the question is asked, many other students stop paying attention.

3.2.1c   MOVING THE CENTER OF VISUAL ATTENTION

A stationary object quickly loses its power to attract attention. The teacher seated at a desk at the front of the room is ineffective as a center of attention. Almost as ineffective is a teacher who remains standing at the front of the room during the entire class hour. The effective teacher must move around the classroom.

Visual and aural aids also contribute to varying the center of attention. The students' eyes go from the teacher to the wall map and pointer, from the teacher to the image on the screen, from the teacher to the flannel board, from the teacher to the tape recorder. Having students come to the front of the room to hold visuals brings additional people into the center of attention. Having students talk about cue cards that their classmates are holding up encourages the students to look around the room.

3.2.1d   SPEAKING UP

In any whole-class instruction it is necessary that all students hear what is being said. Not only must the teacher speak so that all can hear, but he or she is responsible for making sure that students speak up clearly. Often a gesture, such as a cupped hand behind the ear, is sufficient to remind a student who is speaking too softly.

3.2.1e   MAINTAINING THE PACE

The pace of the class should not be allowed to drag. If one student hesitates in responding, the teacher should quickly call on another student and then ask the first student the same question once more. Although students should not feel pressured or rushed, they should learn to respond quickly. A slowing of pace is almost always an indication that the teacher has moved through the material too quickly and that the students have not had the chance to assimilate it.

Transition from one activity to the next should be smooth. The teacher who allows long moments of silence while looking for his or her place in the textbook or shuffling through the material on his or her desk to uncover the appropriate visual, quickly loses the attention of the class.

3.2.2   Half-class instruction

The class can be divided in half for debates and contests. Each group prepares for an activity that will later involve the other group. Unless the class is small, however, the half-class groups are often still too large to be assigned projects or conversation practice.

3.2.3   Ability grouping

The typical foreign language class is composed of students who have a wide range of abilities, needs, and interests. This is especially obvious by the time they reach their second year of study. Provision must be made for all students: those who are eager to advance quickly as well as those who enjoy language study but require a slower pace. Ability grouping, however, can engender negative feelings, especially if one group is consistently identified, even though not in so many words, as the "dumb" group. Often it is advisable to alternate pure ability grouping with other types of grouping.

3.2.3a   THREE GROUPS WORKING ON ONE SKILL

The teacher has the entire class prepare a short reading lesson. Group A (the most talented) writes a composition without the teacher's assistance. Group B (average) answers oral questions asked by the teacher. Group C (less talented) does a written completion exercise and a true / false drill on the reading.

3.2.3b   SPECIFIC SKILLS GROUPS

The teacher sets up groups to work on specific skills: listening, speaking, pronunciation, grammar, reading, and writing. A student who reads fluently might have great difficulty with pronunciation, so he or she joins that special group.

3.2.4   Interest groups

Interest groups are most effectively used with third and fourth level classes. The students have acquired basic linguistic notions and may be encouraged to use the foreign language to develop specific interests. Groups may use foreign periodicals to research topics such as aviation, clothing, politics, or pollution. Groups may also decide to write to foreign businesses for sample products, or to particular localities for travel brochures. Students dramatically inclined might like to prepare a short play. Another group might want to make a home movie with a foreign language sound track. One day a week or part of one day a week might be devoted to such interest-group activities.

3.2.5   Small conversation groups

At the second or third level most students can express themselves orally on a certain number of topics. In a whole-class conversation that lasts twenty minutes, for example, each student is allowed to talk for less than a minute. If the class is divided into groups of four, each student can talk for about five minutes. Students quickly become adjusted to the hum of conversation around them.

There are several ways of forming the groups. The teacher can decide on the makeup of the groups or permit the students to form their own groups. As a change of pace, other techniques may be used to form the groups: for instance, the students can group according to zodiac signs, number of siblings, date of birth, etc.

Small conversation groups need initial guidance. The teacher might appoint group leaders and give them lists of lead questions. More advanced classes might read a controversial article and prepare questions they want to discuss. (See Sections 9.6 and 9.7 for other ideas.)

The teacher circulates around the classroom, helping those who have trouble getting started, answering queries, and generally assuming the role of silent eavesdropper. The teacher might make note of errors and take them up at the end of the period or in a subsequent lesson.

3.2.6   Working in pairs

Even first-year language students can work profitably in pairs, especially on oral drills. If a teacher carries out an intensive drill for five minutes, calling on individual students, each student in a class of thirty will be speaking for only about five seconds, and the teacher will be speaking for two and a half minutes. If the drills plus correct responses are distributed to the students, or if the textbook already has the correct responses, then pairs of students can take turns playing the teacher: one holds the text and reads the cue, and the other answers. The end result is that each student is able to speak for two and a half minutes—almost thirty times as much as he or she would have in a whole-class drill. Moreover, the students have not been able to daydream, as they might have done in the language lab, since they have been actively involved in the entire drill. Role-play and personalized exercises are even more effective since the students are using the language in a meaningful way.

It is true that some students will make pronunciation mistakes as they read aloud, but the only way to learn the language is by practicing, and working in pairs does keep students speaking. The alert teacher will catch many of the mistakes as he or she walks around the classroom and can correct errors later, in private. The teacher is also available to answer questions that students were too embarrassed to ask in front of the whole class.

3.2.7   Independent activities

Independent activities at present usually revolve around the skills of reading and writing. Workbooks obviously lend themselves to independent work. Reading programs may be established to let students work on their own. Some programmed materials are available in foreign languages. Contract teaching is also designed to let students advance at their own pace.

The introduction of low-priced cassettes will make possible a greater variety of simultaneous activities in the classroom (see Section 1.4.2).

3.2.8 Mixed grouping

Not all students in a classroom must necessarily be engaged in the same type of activity. Half the class might be working on independent activities while the teacher reviews a grammar point with those students who need remedial help. One group may be listening over headsets while the rest of the class is working in pairs.

3.3 RECORDED SPEECH

Over the past fifteen years the use of recorded speech in foreign language instruction has become widespread. Bringing a variety of native voices into the classroom is a feat that can now be accomplished by the teacher in the most remote school district, thanks to the broad availability of commercial tapes and records.

The United States is far from being a monolingual country: radio and television programs in Spanish may be heard in many areas. Other languags such as French, Italian, and Chinese are also broadcast in many urban areas. The ESL teachers are able to obtain recordings with a broad spectrum of American accents.

3.3.1 The role of the recording

Foreign language recordings may fill one of several roles in the instructional program.

3.3.1a TO PROVIDE A MODEL

This is one of the original roles of recordings in language instructions. The students listen to the basic sentences and basic dialogs which have been recorded with or without pauses. If the teacher has not acquired a near-native accent, the recording allows him or her to present accurate models to the class in spite of these personal deficiencies. The recording also lends itself to identical repetitions of material with no change in tone, pitch, or intonation.

3.3.1b TO PROVIDE CUES FOR ORAL DRILL

The advent of pattern drills paralleled the commercialization of tape recorders and language laboratories. The tape cues a drill and after a pause for the student's answer provides him or her with the appropriate response, thus reinforcing his or her right answer or allowing the student to correct his or her mistake without delay.

3.3.1c   TO PROVIDE SPEECH SAMPLES

The recording allows the teacher to capture a speech sample and bring it to the classroom so that the students may listen to it in a variety of ways. They can hear the entire recording, they can replay sections of it, and they can even replay parts of sentences. The recorded speech samples may be *contrived*, that is, they may be dialogues or readings written to accompany a set of instructional materials and especially recorded at a desired conversational speed. Recorded speech may be simply *controlled;* that is, a specific authentic speech sample, such as an interview broadcast, may be selected for its pedagogical value, edited, and made available to the students.

3.3.1d   TO GIVE INSTRUCTIONS

The recorded voice may take the role of the teacher in giving instruction. Pronunciation tapes, for example, frequently not only provide models for imitation and exercises for practice but also tell the student what to listen for in discrimination drills and what factors to take into consideration in producing certain sounds or sound patterns.

3.3.1e   TO TEST

Recordings can provide the stimulus for classroom tests. The students may write from taped dictation; they may indicate their comprehension of recorded passages by marking a multiple-choice answer sheet; they may check off boxes on a grid to show their ability to discriminate sounds and structural patterns, or they may respond orally to recorded cues. The consistency of the recording increases the reliability of a test that is to be administered more than once.

3.3.1f   FOR ENJOYMENT

Short recordings may be played simply for the enjoyment of the students. These may take a wide variety of forms: popular songs, student-prepared skits, radio commercials, mystery voices (a recording by a classmate or by a well-known public figure), announcements of language club activities, etc. Such recordings may be used in the classroom at the beginning or end of the hour. They may also be used between exercises on cassettes or laboratory tapes.

3.3.2   Physical installations

Speech recordings may be used in the foreign language classroom, in a special room designed for that purpose, such as a media center or language laboratory, or at home.

3.3.2a   THE CLASSROOM

The simplest way to use recordings in the classroom is to play a tape, cassette, or record to the entire class. The students listen to the recording and the teacher leads the learning activities.

In an electronic classroom the teacher's desk becomes a console and the students hear the recording via headsets. Generally the teacher is also able to monitor individual students.

Groups of students or individuals may also work with recordings independently of the rest of the class if a program source and headsets are available. The program source may consist of individual cassette players or of a tape recorder or record player to which are connected several headsets.

3.3.2b   THE STATIONARY LANGUAGE LABORATORY

Many schools are equipped with language laboratories located in a separate classroom. Classes are generally scheduled for the laboratory in advance, usually for two half-hour periods per week. In the simplest installation, the teacher plays a tape from the console, and all the students listen and respond to it. Although most laboratories were designed so that the teacher could individualize instruction by playing one tape for one group and another tape for another group, in practice the unavailability of appropriate commercial tapes differentiated by ability group within a given lesson and the lack of released time for the local preparation of such tapes have limited the activities of the language laboratory. Its possibilities are seldom fully exploited.

In several school districts, schools are installing media centers. These centers generally contain individual learning carrels where students can work with their own cassettes and pace their own instruction.

3.3.2c   AT HOME

Records or cassettes accompanying many textbooks allow the student to practice basic sentences and drills at home. The wide availability of cassette recorders may allow the teacher to assign homework with cassettes and correlated workbooks.

3.3.3   The nature of student participation

For the recording to be effective as a teaching instrument, it must encourage student participation.

3.3.3a   STUDENT RESPONSE

Student response to the recording as it is being played may take one of four forms:

(1) No outward response: The students listen but are not required to show any outward evidence of comprehension as the recording is being played. Perhaps the students will later be required to summarize or answer questions about what they have heard.

(2) Oral response: The students listen and speak. They may either be imitating the model on the tape or responding to instructions or cues.

(3) Written response: The students listen and indicate a response in writing, which may take the form of words (as in a dictation), symbols (as in a multiple-choice exercise), or drawing (as in an assignment that requires completing a scene or tracing an itinerary on a map).

(4) Physical response: The students may go through motions suggested on the tape. In the language laboratory this might consist of opening a workbook to the proper page. In a classroom this might include total physical response, such as standing, walking, or making an appropriate gesture.

3.3.3b   VISUAL SUPPORT

Some recordings have no visual support whatever. The students are expected to put away books, pencils, paper, and simply concentrate on what they hear. This type of listening activity works well with the ear-minded student but often is less effective with the eye-minded student.

In the classroom or language laboratory visual support may be provided by the teacher in the form of a projection of pictures or diagrams using the overhead or slides. The visuals serve to reinforce the meaning of what is being said over the tape.

The textbook, workbook, or a printed ditto sheet may be used to provide visual support in the form of words. Many students at first like to read what they hear and say, and then allow themselves to be weaned away from the support.

3.3.3c   DEGREE OF STUDENT CONTROL

The use of the recordings is controlled either by the teacher or by the student. In using a broadcast, where the tape is played from the console or in the classroom, the teacher controls what is being listened to. Even if the students record their voices for fifteen minutes and then listen to their recordings for the second fifteen minutes, the teacher alone is controlling the pace of instruction. However, if the students can stop their own recordings and listen to parts over again, they are participating in the control of the lesson.

Students exercise the highest degree of control when they pace themselves. This can be done with a language laboratory run on the library system (usually unavailable in secondary schools), or in the classroom with either a tape recorder and earphone jacks (with students running the controls), or with cassettes and cassette players.

3.3.3d INCREASING THE EFFECTIVENESS OF THE LANGUAGE LABORATORY

Much of the negative feeling about the language laboratory can be traced to three sources: the lack of student participation, the absence of visual support for those who need it, and the rigidity of the teacher's control of laboratory activities.

The laboratory can become effective only if the students are actively involved in the scheduled activity. Otherwise students tend to fall asleep, respond unthinkingly, pass notes to their neighbors, or fiddle with the equipment.

The best solution is to use only tape programs that are correlated with lively workbooks or worksheets. The alternate solution is to develop homemade visuals to use with recorded drills and exercises. For example, the teacher may be at the front of the laboratory with an overhead projector and screen visible to all the students. If a drill calls for pronoun substitution, he or she will use a transparency containing drawings for each pronoun (see Section 6.3.1), pointing to the appropriate symbol as the cue is spoken on the tape. Although the teacher cannot hear the students' responses, he or she can watch their eye and mouth movements and check on their performance indirectly.

If the school has a language laboratory that cannot be scheduled on the library system, either because only broadcast equipment is available or because there is a lack of funds and personnel, the students will have to realize that for two half-hours a week they cannot be given the opportunity to pace their own learning. However, if the language laboratory sessions have become somewhat more meaningful, and if opportunity for students to direct learning activities is provided in the classroom, lab periods will nevertheless begin to make a positive contribution to foreign language learning.

3.4 MUSIC AND GAMES

Music and games offer a pleasant change of pace in the lesson. They should be selected primarily for their educational value, however, not as mere distractions or moments of relaxation.

3.4.1 Selecting songs

Songs should be selected so that their lyrics reinforce a point of grammar or pro-nunciation. For example, the song *"Mein Hut, der hat drei Ecken"* (*"My hat, it has three corners"*) might be used to illustrate the normal verb-second word order of German. *"Alouette"* helps the students to remember to use the definite article with parts of the body. For ESL students, "I've been working on the railroad" provides reinforcement of verb tenses. Hit tunes may be used as well as folk songs, as long as the lyrics are appropriate to the linguistic level of the class. Certain songs such as Christmas carols and national anthems may be introduced primarily for their cultural content.

3.4.2 Music in the classroom

The teacher who is musically inclined and likes to sing will have no qualms about leading the class in song. If in addition he or she plays the guitar, the problem will be rather one of refusing to let the class sing every period.

   If the teacher cannot carry a tune, there are two alternate ways of letting the class sing. Perhaps a student plays the guitar or the ukelele and would be will-ing to learn new songs to present them to the class. Records offer another possi-bility. The students can sing along with the recorded song. Moreover, there are programmed albums, often used in the elementary schools, and perhaps avail-able from the school music department, which contain a variety of foreign as well as English songs.[4] First the students hear the entire song sung in the foreign language. Then they hear the first line, followed by the musical accompaniment of the same line, so that they can repeat the line. Then they hear the second line followed by the melody of that line, and so on. At the end of the recording they have the opportunity to sing the song in its entirety.[5]

3.4.3 Playing games

Games should also be selected so that the activity contributes to furthering the linguistic aims of the lesson. Many games are suggested throughout this hand-book.[6]

---

[4] *Exploring Music* (New York: Holt, Rinehart and Winston, Inc., 1967).
[5] See also Olivia Muñoz, *Songs in the Foreign Language Classroom*, ERIC Focus Report No. 12 (1969). Available from ACTFL Materials Center, 2 Park Avenue, New York, N.Y. 10016.
[6] See also Grace Scott, "Games students can play," in Marina K. Burt and Heidi Dulay, eds., *New Directions in Second Language Learning, Teaching and Bilingual Education* (1975). Available from TESOL, 455 Nevils Bldg., Georgetown University, Washington, D.C. 20057.
Helen V. Saunders, *Fun and Games With Foreign Languages*. (Charleston, West Virginia: State Department of Education, 1974) [EDRS: ED 096 857].
Voix et Visages de la France, Games Packet, Level 1 French Program (Chicago: Rand McNally, 1974).

It is important to select a game that retains the interest of all the students who are playing. If only two students are talking while the rest of the students are standing in two lines awaiting their turn, the pace of the game must be very brisk to avoid boring the silent ones. If possible, the teacher should try to select a game in which many persons are active simultaneously.

Games which involve a limited number of people might best be selected group activities rather than whole-class activities. Some games can be played in groups of two or four.

Frequently commercial games can be adapted to classroom use. "Monopoly" in its many language versions encourages students to become more fluent in their handling of numbers. "Lingo," the multi-lingual UNICEF game, helps young children learn the names of foods.

Games developed to teach social-studies concepts can sometimes lend themselves to foreign language adaptations. For instance, "Market: A Simulation Game" has been adapted to French and Spanish.[7]

3.5 HOMEWORK

The primary purpose for assigning homework is to give the students additional practice in developing their language competence. It obviously takes more time to learn a foreign language than the forty to fifty minutes available in the daily school schedule.

However, before giving homework, the teacher should make sure that the particular assignment will help the students attain the objectives of the lesson. If it is not clear that doing the assignment will be of benefit, it would be wiser not to give it.

The difficulty of the assignment must be carefully considered. If the diligent student cannot complete the work with an accuracy level of at least 80%, the assignment should be modified. What will it profit the student to spend an hour of homework time making mistakes in the foreign language? On the other hand, "busy work," such as copying sentences several times each, will be more likely to develop negative attitudes in the students than it will contribute to their progress in the foreign language.

3.5.1 Relating homework to classwork

If possible, the homework assignment should bear directly on the next day's class. For example: "Complete the worksheet on the imperative to get ready for tomorrow's test. The solution to number 4 (horizontal) on the crossword puzzle is the answer to the first question on the test."

---

[7] "Market" is published by the Benefic Press, Westchester, Illinois. For the adaptations, see Nancy McMillan "Le Marché français: a Marketing Game" and Susan W. Madaras and Nancy McMillan, "El Mercado: The Mexican Market Comes to Life in the Spanish Classroom" in the mimeographed publication *Games for the Foreign Language Classroom*. Available from the ACTFL Materials Center, 2 Park Avenue, New York, N.Y. 10016.

Sometimes the actual product of the homework may be used in the activities of the next day's class. Each student in a beginning audio-visual class might be told to find magazine pictures or to make drawings to illustrate each line of the basic dialog. This means that everyone will have to read each line at least once and copy it. The following day, instead of a boring class exercise where everyone reads the dialog from the book several times, the students are encouraged to compare notebooks. The students will be reading the dialog through ten or fifteen times as they discover what kind of illustrations their friends have brought in. Perhaps the class comedian cuts out a picture of a hurricane to illustrate *Il fait beau aujourd'hui* (*It's nice today*). For the next such assignment, students will try to outdo each other in finding crazy illustrations, and motivation to read will even be greater.

Students in a more advanced class might be asked to read a selection (a magazine article, a newspaper clipping, or a textbook page), to note five unfamiliar words or idioms in their notebooks, to use each word in an original sentence, and then to prepare two or three questions on the material that they will ask their classmates to discuss the following day. This type of assignment insures that the students will have prepared the reading that is to form the basis of the classroom conversation. At the same time, since each student prepares questions for the class, he or she will have some say in directing the conversation into areas of particular personal interest.

3.5.2 Assigning homework

It is necessary to make the homework assignment clear. The teacher might announce the homework in the target language, then write the pertinent information in the target language or the native language on a corner of the chalkboard so that all the students are sure to understand. The assignment should never be shouted out to the departing students after the bell has rung. For an advanced class, homework assignments for a week or two could be distributed in ditto form.

The teacher might allow some time at the end of the period for students to begin the homework if it entails a written assignment. In this way help is at hand should any questions arise.

3.5.2a "PIGGY-BACK" HOMEWORK

Any student who so desires may copy another student's homework. Both sets of homework are turned in together. The student who copies receives seventy-five percent of the grade given the original paper. This technique eliminates "cheating," since copying is considered acceptable. It also encourages poorer students to copy only from the better ones, thus giving them experience in writing correct sentences. In practice, few students will turn in "piggy-back" homework, since they can get a higher mark by doing it themselves or as a group. Note the following suggestions:

3.5.2b   GROUP HOMEWORK

Two or more students collaborate in preparing the homework. Each student writes out the whole assignment and the group submits their homework together. If one person has done more work than the others, this fact is noted.

3.5.2c   THE TWO-NOTEBOOK SYSTEM

Each student has two notebooks. The assignments are always written on the right-hand page and the corrections are entered on the left-hand page. If daily homework is assigned and corrected or reviewed by the teacher, this means that every day the student turns in one notebook and gets the other, corrected one back. The two-notebook system is most effective with college classes. It allows the student and teacher to communicate on a regular basis. Moreover, it allows the teacher to make individualized assignments for remedial work or to write out brief explanations of grammar and vocabulary.

3.5.2d   OUTSIDE PROJECTS

Individual students or groups of students are given one or two weeks to prepare a special project. For example, in an elementary language class the students may be asked to research certain cultural aspects of the foreign country in English and either give brief oral reports to the class or prepare a bulletin board display. In more advanced classes students may prepare a panel discussion, a debate, or an oral presentation.

If possible, it is a good idea to have these projects coincide with topics the student is studying in another class. The home economics teacher might let a group of Spanish students prepare a Mexican dish. If the American history class is studying the French and Indian War, some of the French students might prepare a report or display describing the French point of view of the conflict. If the English class is reading a novel by Hesse, the German students might wish to work on a related project. If the biology class is studying the respiratory system, perhaps some interested French students could prepare a brief report on Laënnec and his invention of the stethoscope. If some members of the class are on the school baseball team, they might prepare a poster comparing Spanish and English sports terminology based on items in the sports pages of a Spanish-language newspaper. In ESL classes at the elementary and secondary school levels, the teacher may occasionally work with materials that relate to other courses the students are studying: a social studies topic, a home economics project, a seasonal sport.

This building of bridges between the foreign language class and other areas of the curriculum will help students realize that learning a language is not an isolated endeavor, but that it opens the doors to a wide variety of experiences. Cooperation between the foreign language teachers and their colleagues in other disciplines will also serve to open channels of communication that may have previously been closed. The initial effort to dovetail assignments with activities in other classes may well lead to informal exchanges between teachers. Perhaps the music teacher would be willing to give a brief presentation of Beethoven's music to the German class; in exchange the German teacher might spend fifteen minutes helping the choir improve their pronunciation of German lyrics in a song they are practicing. The economics teacher might be willing to answer questions on the French economy, while the French teacher might be able to provide this colleague with French advertisements for American products. The opportunities for such exchanges are endless and are waiting to be explored.

3.5.3   Correcting homework in class

The major drawback to assigning written exercises as homework is that the correction of such exercises can constitute an enormous waste of precious class time.

Half a class period can be lost when students write homework sentences on the board and sit back as the teacher corrects them. An entire class can fall asleep as students, one by one, read aloud their error-laden sentences for the teacher to comment on. In its most detrimental form homework dominates the language class from beginning to end: today the class laboriously goes over exercises A, B, and C, which had been assigned as homework, and for tomorrow they are to write out exercises D, E, and F, which will be similarly dissected.

3.5.3a   CORRECTING VIA THE CHALKBOARD

The teacher writes the correct sentences on the board, perhaps covering them with a map. The students quickly correct their homework as the teacher reads the sentences aloud. For more objectivity, it is recommended that students exchange papers. This activity should take no more than five minutes.

3.5.3b   CORRECTING VIA THE OVERHEAD

This technique is similar to the one already described. The sentences are written in advance on an overhead transparency. Using a mask, the teacher uncovers the sentences one at a time, reading them aloud. Again, this procedure should take no more than five minutes.

3.5.3c   CORRECTING VIA DITTOS

The teacher distributes dittos with the correct responses. The sentences are read aloud as the students make the corrections.

3.5.3d   READING EXERCISES ALOUD

The teacher may take a few minutes of class time to read the correct sentences aloud. The difficulty with this technique is that many students may not be able to understand by ear alone where their mistakes are. Moreover, although the better students will be able to correct their work, the poorer students—those in the greatest need of guidance—will fail to discover their errors.

3.5.3e   GROUP CORRECTIONS

The class is divided into small groups, and each group corrects the homework. The teacher moves from group to group to answer questions. If desired, one member of each group may be given a copy of the correct responses.

3.5.4   Collecting and grading homework

The collecting and grading of daily homework for four or more classes places a considerable burden on the teacher's time.

3.5.4a   EXERCISES

For beginning and intermediate classes, especially on exercises for which responses are either right or wrong, the teacher may simply use a quick correction technique in the classroom and then enter in the gradebook whether the student completed the assignment or not. From time to time the teacher may want to take a closer look at homework assignments. If time is not available to check all papers, the teacher may choose to read the papers of one class carefully and simply note whether students in other classes have done the assignment. This way the papers of each class get read carefully once a week. It is also possible to spot check at random four or five papers per class.

3.5.4b   COMPOSITIONS

For compositions and other assignments where there is more than one correct form possible and, therefore, where one set of correct answers cannot be made available to all students, the teacher must plan to read each paper. As a general practice, the teacher should insist that each student rewrite the paper incorporating the suggested corrections. Unless the teacher does so, most students look at the red marks, sigh, and throw the paper away.

Some teachers write out the corrections in full and have the students copy the corrected sentences. Other teachers use a set of symbols to cover the most frequent types of errors and have the students make the corrections. Some commonly used symbols are the following: voc—vocabulary, choice of word; g—gender; ag—agreement; wo—word order.

If the classroom has cassette players, the teacher can correct a composition by recording appropriate comments on tape (in the target language, if possible). The grade is given at the end. The student plays back the cassette and incorporates the suggested corrections.

In any case, the teacher should quickly reread the corrected form of the assignment to be sure that the corrections have been understood and incorporated.

3.5.4c GIVING GRADES

Some teachers give actual grades to homework assignments and others just mark whether the work has been done or not. This is a matter of personal philosophy and preference.

3.6 TESTING[8]

For teachers, testing is an important diagnostic instrument. Not only does it allow them to keep track of the progress of their students, but it enables them to measure their own successes and failures in the classroom and lets them know when lesson plans must be modified to meet the students' unforeseen problems.

3.6.1 Norm-referenced tests and criterion-referenced tests

The norm-referenced test is used to rank students. Scores may be given in terms of letter grades, standard scores, percentile rankings, and the like. In other words, the test is often graded on the curve. In giving such a test, the teacher prepares some easy items and some harder items in the hope that the scores will spread out over a wide range. The broader the range, the more certain the teacher is that the letter grades assigned represent real difference in ability. Most teachers are obliged by their school systems to rank their students in some way at the end of each marking period.

The criterion-referenced test is used to determine how many students have attained a given level of mastery. In preparing such a test, the teacher includes only items that measure the behavior defined by the criterion. Let us suppose that the teacher wants to know whether the students can change affirmative sentences (using familiar vocabulary) into negative sentences in writing. He or she would prepare a list of sentences and have the students rewrite them. The objective might be that all students should get at least nine out of ten sentences

---

[8] For a detailed presentation of testing techniques, see Rebecca M. Valette, *Modern Language Testing*, 2d ed. (New York: Harcourt Brace Jovanovich, 1977).

right. If one third of the class misses two or more sentences, then the teacher works with that group and gives them another test to determine whether they can now handle the transformation. This might go on for a third or even a fourth time. Another teacher might decide that the objective in this area had been attained if eighty percent of the students got nine out of ten right. It is up to the teacher to set the level of mastery, but the intention should always be that as many students as possible attain a high score.

These two types of tests may be contrasted as follows. On a norm-referenced test the teacher is upset if everyone gets 100, because the test was too easy. On a criterion-referenced test the teacher is upset if the grades range from 50 to 100, because that means he or she has failed to teach the material; if the whole class scored 100, that would be a sign of success. The norm-referenced test includes some hard questions that only the best students are expected to get right. The criterion-referenced test includes only those questions that everyone is expected to get right—and the teacher will keep teaching for that test until the students *do* get them right.

If foreign language teachers begin defining levels of learning in terms of performance objectives and teaching for mastery through the use of criterion-referenced tests, it will become imperative to establish national standards for Level I, Level II, and so on. The student's record of progress then will not only be in terms of years of study plus grades, but in terms of level proficiency as well.

3.6.2   Formal and informal testing

Much classroom testing is informal in nature. Teachers learn to tell from their students' reactions whether they have understood the meaning of a phrase. They can tell by the fluency and accuracy of the oral responses whether the class has mastered a specific drill.

One question the teacher should *not* ask is, Do you understand? The question serves little purpose, since those who do not understand are usually too shy to show their ignorance and remain quiet. Others have misunderstood but are unaware of their error. The only way to check comprehension is to ask questions or plan activities that allow the students to *demonstrate* whether they have understood or not. For example, if the grammar generalization was about *ser* and *estar*, the most appropriate grammar check is to have students do an exercise where the two verbs are used. When one or more students have difficulty with a specific sentence, the teacher can diagnose the problem area.

Formal classroom tests allow the teacher to form a more precise idea of how much the students have mastered and where their areas of weakness lie. Often a quiet student performs better on a formal test than the teacher would have anticipated, while an alert, out-going student does less well.

3.7   CLASSROOM MANAGEMENT

The matters of classroom management fall into two categories: maximizing available class time and maintaining discipline.[9]

3.7.1   Maximizing available class time

Wasted time may be kept to a minimum through the establishment of routines. Although the setting up of a routine may take a little time at the beginning of the school year, much time will be saved in the long run.

Each teacher will, of course, set up his or her routines as a function of the age of the students, the physical classroom environment, and the aims of instruction. Routines might be established for the following activities:

(1) The beginning of the hour: Students might be correcting homework at their places while the teacher quickly takes attendance. Certain students are assigned to distribute corrected homework and pick up new homework. If a particular arrangement of chairs is necessary, the first students to get to the classroom should be assigned this task so that the class may begin on time. If certain sentences or visuals are to be put on the chalkboard, the teacher should do this before the bell rings.

(2) Assignment to groups: If part of the class hour is to be devoted to group work, the rosters of the groups and their assignments (if appropriate) could be posted on a class bulletin board which students would consult as they entered the room.

(3) Language laboratory or electronic classroom: Procedures and seating arrangements could be made routine.

(4) Handling students' questions: Only a short part of the class hour should be devoted to answering questions, which otherwise might drag out for fifteen or twenty minutes. Students should be encouraged to ask questions privately of the teacher during time scheduled for individual work or small group instruction. Another possible routine to establish is the following: The teacher has a question basket on the desk where students may deposit questions and requests as they come into the classroom. While one student takes roll, the teacher can read over the questions quickly, and if necessary, modify the class plan to cover the points raised. If the homework is done in a two-notebook system, students may be encouraged to write questions to the teacher in their notebooks.

(5) The end of the hour: Routines should be established for replacing furniture, shelving supplementary materials, collecting visuals, and so on. If the class has been using individual cue cards, with names of Paris monuments, for example, the teacher can stand at the door and pick up the cards as the students

---

[9] For additional reflections on classroom management, see Renée S. Disick, *Individualizing Language Instruction: Strategies and Methods* (New York: Harcourt Brace Jovanovich, 1975). Chapter 12.

leave the room. Each student will say a sentence about his or her card: *Je vou-drais visiter les Invalides* (*I would like to visit the Invalides*).

3.7.2 Maintaining discipline

Two situations tend to give rise to discipline problems. The first is the teacher's mental set: if he or she anticipates having difficulties with the students, discipline problems are bound to occur. The second is class activities: if the students are actively involved in a class that is set at their linguistic level and that takes into account their interests and backgrounds, they will be so busy learning the language that discipline will, in large measure, take care of itself.

None but the most docile students will want to look only at the teacher and participate only in teacher-led activities during the entire class period, day after day. Independent work, small group conversations, interest group conversations, student-led drills, all contribute to the smoother functioning of a class. Once the teacher realizes that even beginning students can learn a foreign language *without* constant teacher guidance he or she will experience the challenge of experimenting with different types of instruction and the pleasure of seeing the class take an increased interest in class activities.

part two
Presenting
the Language

outline

four
Teaching
the Sound
System

All foreign languages have sound systems that differ distinctly from that of English. American English is a very relaxed language. Vowels are glided and diphthongs are frequent. Vowels in unstressed syllables are reduced to an /ə/ sound. Consonants at the beginning of a word are forcefully enunciated, such as the consonants /p/ /t/ /k/, for example, which are accompanied by a puff of air (aspirated). Consonants at the end of the word are frequently unreleased.

As the American student learns to speak German, French, or Spanish, he or she must acquire new speech habits. The tension in the speech organs must be increased so that vowels are kept pure, even in unstressed syllables. The puff of air before /p/ /t/ /k/ must be eliminated and the final consonants pronounced distinctly.

Furthermore, the American student must practice new sounds, such as the Spanish /rr/, the French /y/, and the German /x/. He or she must acquire new patterns of rhythm, stress, and intonation in speaking the foreign language. The student must realize that even though words in the foreign language may look like English on paper, they do not sound like English when spoken aloud.

For the student learning English as a second language, the problems of mastering the sound system are just as difficult. Relaxing tension is often harder than preventing glides and aspiration. Furthermore, the student must learn which syllables to stress and which to reduce.

The mastery of a new sound system is one aspect of the process of learning a second language. This chapter will suggest techniques for helping students acquire an acceptable pronunciation in the language they are studying.

4.1 GENERAL CONSIDERATIONS

Most teachers agree that early insistence on correct pronunciation can save many hours of remedial work later on. Bad habits are easily formed and very difficult to change.

The first task is to convince students of the importance of pronunciation. It should be emphasized that failure to pronounce correctly can result in not being understood. The native Spanish speaker who cannot make a distinction in English between *berry* and *very* may have trouble communicating.

The teacher may also wish to point out that poor pronunciation can be unpleasant or comical to the native speaker listening to it. Imitating a thick foreign accent while speaking English or the students' native language can be an effective technique.

In order to achieve the goal of good pronunciation, the teacher needs to insist on it from the outset. The first step is listening practice; it is important to remember that students must be able to hear the target sounds or they will probably never be able to make them. Next, the students may attempt to produce these sounds, most of which will seem very strange indeed. At this point the teacher needs to be fairly indulgent. With encouragement, the students gradually learn to shape the correct sounds.

Constant practice in listening discrimination, pronunciation, and intonation using a variety of drills and exercises can go far in forming good habits of correct speech. However, listening discrimination exercises must be integrated with the various devices for presenting and drilling pronunciation and intonation.

In the succeeding pages an attempt has been made to identify a few of the major problems and to propose techniques for solving them. This chapter is not a treatise on the entire sound system of any foreign language. Such studies are available in other books. However, many of the techniques suggested may be applied to those pronunciation problems that have gone unmentioned here.

4.2 INITIAL LISTENING PRACTICE

Recent research is showing the importance of initial listening practice in language acquisition.[1] Students who receive intensive listening training *before* they begin speaking and repeating tend to develop a stronger command of the second language and a better pronunciation. As students listen to the foreign language, either reacting physically to commands (such as "Open the door") or drawing circles around pictures corresponding to spoken cues, they gradually develop a sense of what that language sounds like. Then, when they begin speaking, they

[1] See, for instance, Valerian A. Postovsky, "Effects of Delay in Oral Practice at the Beginning of Second Language Learning," *Modern Language Journal* 58, no. 5–6 (Sept.–Oct. 1974). See also, Harris Winitz and James Reeds, *Comprehension and Problem Solving as Strategies for Language Training* (The Hague: Mouton, 1975), available from Humanities Press, Inc., Atlantic Highlands, N.J. 07716.

themselves are partly able to monitor what they are saying and do not have to rely entirely on the teacher.

This initial practice does not focus on phonemic differences (such as "ship" and "sheep") but rather uses words and phrases that do not sound similar. For example, in the listening program developed by Harris Winitz, James Reeds and Paul García, the initial words presented are *cat, sun* and *doctor*. After an hour of practice, where each new word or phrase is matched with the appropriate picture, the students are distinguishing between *The doctor is drinking coffee* and *The cat is sleeping.*[2]

If the classroom teacher does not have commercial listening comprehension materials, he or she may adapt some of the techniques suggested in Sections 8.2 and 8.3 in the chapter on listening.

4.3   INITIAL SPEAKING PRACTICE

The first speech samples that the student hears upon beginning his study of a foreign language almost always take the form of sentences: *Buenos días. Comment t'appelles-tu? Ich heiße Fräulein Hof. (Hello. What is your name? My name is Miss Hof.)* Thus, from the very outset, the student realizes that a foreign language is made up of words and phrases, not of isolated sounds.

As the class continues, perhaps after a listening comprehension segment, the student may memorize dialogs, learn sequences of sentences, answer simple questions, or repeat the script of a filmstrip or movie, depending on the type of program used. In all instances, however, he or she will be learning to control a new sound system within the context of phrases and sentences.

4.3.1   Simple mimicry

The students' first steps in learning to speak a second language often entail mimicry. They listen to a model and imitate what they hear.

4.3.1a   THE TEACHER AS A MODEL

The best model is the teacher who has a fluent command of the second language. The teacher can model a phrase as often as necessary. While moving around the room from student to student, he or she can vary the tempo of the sentence to be repeated, saying it more slowly at first and then progressively faster. The sentence can be broken into component parts and then reassembled. The teacher can skip back and forth from new sentences to previously learned sentences.

[2] See Harris Winitz, James A. Reeds, and Paul A. García, *Natural Language Learning* (General Linguistics Corporation, P.O. Box 7172, Kansas City, Mo. 64113), 1975. Available in English, Spanish, German, and Hebrew.

4.3.1b THE RECORDING AS A MODEL

The teacher whose pronunciation is weak can use recordings to model a phrase. The teacher can play the basic sentences on the tape recorder and then walk about the room listening to the students and encouraging their efforts. The teacher can also stay with the tape recorder, playing a sentence once and then stopping the tape so that students may repeat it several times in succession. The tape lets the student hear several voices, but it lacks the flexibility of a live teacher.

The basic tape can be put to excellent use as an aid to the teacher. The unsure teacher should invest in a tape recorder or a cassette player so that sentences in a particular lesson can be played over and over again in the teacher's home until they become second nature. The teacher may not feel fluent in impromptu conversation, but he or she should be able to model the basic sentences with confidence.

4.3.2 Focusing on key sounds[3]

The teacher can use the basic sentences of the lesson to focus on critical sounds. As the students repeat the sentences, their attention is drawn to certain features that may present difficulties for learners.

4.3.2a THE "SEEDED" DIALOG

In some textbooks the initial dialogs or sentences have been built around or "seeded" with certain key sounds. Typically there is a progression from familiar sounds (with new intonation patterns and greater tension) to totally unfamiliar sounds.

The following French example is built on the vowels /a/ /i/ /u/ and consonants that are rather similar to English. The attention of the student is drawn to basic patterns of rhythm, intonation, and stress: *Voici David. Où habite David? David habite Nice.*

The following short German exchange was designed to stress the sound /x/: *Was macht Joachim? Er spielt Schach.*

In an ESL class, the students can be encouraged to glide the final vowels in *Hello, how are you?*

4.3.2b SELECTING SOUNDS TO BE STRESSED

In other textbooks the initial sentences contain most of the sounds of the foreign language. (What "seeding" exists has been determined by grammar and vocabulary, rather than phonetic considerations.)

[3] In the interest of consistency, the IPA transcription will be used throughout this handbook.

First the teacher prepares the dialog or sentences by underlining those sounds that may cause difficulties. As he or she models each line to the class, the teacher is especially alert to the correct pronunciation of the underlined letters:

Ramón, ¿adónde vas ahora? — trilled /rr/: *Ramón* vs. single tap /r/: *ahora*

A la Casa de Música. — pure /a/

¿Vas con Rosita? — /s/ not /z/; see also *casa* and *música*

No, voy con Paco. — nondiphthongized /o/

4.3.3 Treating specific problems

While some students can pick up the sound system of a foreign language by simple imitation, others need guidance in trying to form unfamiliar sounds.

4.3.3a DESCRIBING HOW SOUNDS ARE MADE

The teacher may tell students how to produce certain sounds:

(1) French /i/: Smile broadly, spread your lips, tighten your facial muscles, press the tip of your tongue against your lower teeth and say *qui, ici, fit*.

(2) German /y/: Round your lips, draw them tightly together, pretend you are drinking from a straw, say /i/ and you will really be saying /y/: *fünf, für, Füller*

(3) Spanish /o/: Round your lips, push them forward, tighten your facial muscles and say *mo, no, mono, fo, to, foto*. Hold your lips in this position and keep them from sliding to another sound. As you say /o/, you should feel a vibration in your throat.

(4) ESL /ð/: Touch the tips of the upper teeth with the tip of the flattened tongue and force out a voiced stream of air. Almost bite your tongue as you say: *the, they, mother, bathe*.

4.3.3b USING A MIRROR

The students are asked to bring pocket mirrors to class. The teacher pronounces a difficult sound or contrasts a native language sound with a target language sound. As the students imitate the teacher, they look into the mirror and compare their lips with the teacher's. This technique is especially helpful in eliminating the tendency of Americans to diphthongize vowels at the end of a word. Students are told to freeze their mouth position and not to change it until they have stopped speaking.

The teacher might contrast English *no* with Spanish *no*; English *key* with French *qui*; English *coo* with German *Kuh*.

In ESL classes, on the contrary, students are encouraged to glide these vowels.

4.3.3c GIVING NATIVE LANGUAGE NEAR-EQUIVALENTS

Beginning with familiar words or sounds, the teacher models them so that his or her students pronounce a key sound in the foreign language. Here are examples to be used with English-speaking students:

(1) Spanish /r/: The teacher starts with *pot of tea* and then rapidly pronounces it *pot' a tea*. Gradually he or she shapes the phrase to come to *para ti* and finally the word *para*. Using nonsense syllables, the teacher can also build on *kot' a tea*, *sot' a tea*, and so on.

(2) French /r/: The teacher starts with the name *Bach* and then adds a vowel, such as /i/. The sequence becomes *Bach Bach-i* and finally *Barry*. Similarly, *Pach-i* leads to *Paris*, *Lach-ou* leads to *la roue*, *Kach-é* leads to *carré*.

(3) German /ts/: The teacher begins with *cat soup*. Gradually he or she encourages students to go from *cat soup* to *ca-a-a-at soup* to *ca-a-a-at su* to *ca-a tsu* ending with the word *zu* once the *ca* has been dropped.

4.3.3d BREAKING UP DIFFICULT SOUND COMBINATIONS

Sometimes students have difficulty pronouncing in combination sounds which they have mastered individually. These tricky clusters can be broken up and then rebuilt.

(1) Spanish /r/ plus consonant: In words like *árbol*, the teacher adds a schwa between the /r/ and the following consonant: a /rə/ bol. As the students repeat the word many times, they are asked to accelerate. Finally they say *árbol*.

a /rə/ ma ⟶ arma
a /rə/ te ⟶ arte
a /rə/ co ⟶ arco[4]

(2) German /x/ plus consonants—the choo-choo train technique: In pronouncing the word *sechzig*, the teacher separates the two long syllables with a long pause. Students repeat. Then, as the teacher says the two syllables several times, he or she increases the speed and shortens the pauses. (The accent marker indicates stress.)

nách————ts	séch————zig
nách———ts	séch———zig
nách——ts	séch——zig
nách—ts	séch—zig
nách-ts	séch-zig
náchts	séchzig[5]

[4] Robert L. Politzer and Charles N. Staubach, *Teaching Spanish* (Waltham: Blaisdell Publishing Co., 1965), p. 79.
[5] Eberhard Reichmann, "Tackling Cluster and Juncture Problems in Pronunciation Drill," in *Die Unterrichtspraxis*, I (1968), p. 45.

(3) French nasals—eliminating /n/ or /m/ before a consonant: American students have a strong tendency to insert a nasal consonant between a nasal vowel and the following consonant sound, for example, to pronounce the /m/ of *tomber* or the /n/ of *demander*. The teacher separates the nasal vowel and the following consonant by reversing the order of the syllables and having students repeat them rapidly:

bé—tom—bé—tom—bé—tom—bé—tomber
dé—deman—dé—deman—dé—deman—dé—demander
pression—im—pression—im—pression—impression

(4) Eliminating the /ʃ/ sound: A persistent problem is the American student's tendency to introduce a /ʃ/ into cognates of English words in *-tion*.

Spanish: nación   ci   ci   ci   ción   ción   nación
German: Nation   zi   zi   zi   zion   zion   Nation
French: nation   si   si   si   sion   sion   nation

(5) Eliminating the /e/ before initial /s/: Spanish speakers learning English have a tendency to introduce an /e/ before words beginning with /s/, such as "Spanish." Have the students hiss the consonant /s/, and then lead into the word being practiced: sssssSpanish.

4.3.3e   ELIMINATING ASPIRATION

Americans tend to pronounce /p/ /t/ /k/ with a slight puff of air when these consonants occur at the beginning of a word. Since these same consonants are not aspirated in the combinations /sp/ /st/ and /sk/ in English, these clusters can serve as a point of departure for helping students produce /p/ /t/ /k/ without the air. For example, to get Spanish students to pronounce *pan*, tell them to put an *s* before the word and say *span*. Then have them think the *s*, but not say it.

Students may use one of the following techniques to keep track of their progress:

(1) Hold the back of your hand near your mouth. You should hardly feel any air on it if you are saying /p/ /t/ /k/ correctly.

(2) Put a piece of paper in front of your mouth. As you say the consonants /p/ /t/ /k/, the paper should scarcely move. If you pronounce the consonants the American way, the paper will flutter.

(3) Place a lighted candle or match in front of your lips. The flame will not go out if you pronounce the consonant correctly.

4.3.3f   TAPPING OUT THE RHYTHM

The teacher demonstrates how to tap out the rhythm of a French word and its English equivalent. He or she takes a pencil and taps evenly: *pá-rá-gráphe*

(French), then taps out one long and two short syllables for *pár-a-graph* (English). Then the teacher calls on individuals to tap out other words in French and in English: *Mississippi, impossible, composition, nationalité, correspondance.*

Similarly, the tapping technique can be used to indicate the stressed syllables in English words for ESL students:

difficult ● • • , lesson ● • , announcement • ● • .

4.3.3g   ADOPTING A "FOREIGN" ACCENT

Some students feel silly and uncomfortable speaking a foreign language and compensate by maintaining an American accent, especially when using cognates. Often it is possible to help students over this psychological hurdle by training them to speak English with a heavy French or German or Spanish accent. After the students learn to purify their vowels, substitute one sound for another, and maintain a foreign intonation pattern while speaking broken English, they can then apply this new "accent" to the foreign language:

German: Vee vant to vait here.
French: Eet eez eemposseebla to speak Eengleesh.

4.3.3h   USING HAND SIGNALS

The teacher can use hand and arm motions to make students aware of intonation patterns, raising a hand when the intonation rises and bringing it down when the intonation falls. This is particularly useful in teaching the continuing intonation pattern of French: *Je vais en ville* (arm moves up) *avec Pierre* (arm moves down).

In teaching Spanish, German, and English words where students have trouble accentuating the appropriate syllable, the teacher can develop a hand signal, such as a forward motion of the wrist, with which to emphasize stressed syllables. For example: *au - to - mó* (hand signal) - *vil*; *Kon - zért* (hand signal); *an - ni - ver'* (hand signal) - *sa - ry*.

4.3.3i   DRAWING SYMBOLS ON THE CHALKBOARD

Sometimes a visual representation helps clarify a pronunciation problem.

(1) Sketching mouth positions: A simple side view of the mouth can illustrate the relative position of the tongue and teeth. Here are two French examples:

A To pronounce /i/ and /e/: keep your tongue rounded and hold the tip of your tongue against the lower front teeth. Now say /i/ and round your lips. Do not change the tongue position (result: /y/). Say /e/ and round your lips. Do not change the tongue position (result: /ø/).
B When you pronounce /t/ or /d/, be sure your tongue touches the upper front teeth.

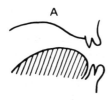 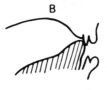

(2) Arrows: A rising arrow is used to indicate a rising intonation. A falling arrow is used to indicate a falling intonation:

Je ne travaille pas.↓

Je ne travaille pas↑   à la maison.↓

(3) Musical notes: Musical notes may be used to indicate intonation and diphthongs:

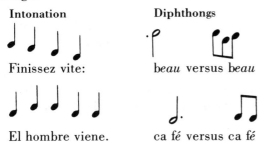

Intonation

Finissez vite:

El hombre viene.

Diphthongs

beau versus beau

ca fé versus ca fé

(4) Contour lines: A continuous line may be superposed on a sentence to show intonation:

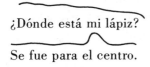

¿Dónde está mi lápiz?

Se fue para el centro.

(5) Marking liaison and linking: Symbols may be used to remind students of sounds that are added or dropped within a group of words.

French: Où est votre ami?

/z/
D'où viennent ses‿amis?

Spanish: para‿escribir

(6) Boxes: The four stress levels of English can be graphically represented by putting the syllables in boxes:

base | ball | play | er

4.4 DEVELOPING LISTENING DISCRIMINATION

Students must learn to discriminate between correct and incorrect pronunciations in learning to speak the foreign language with an acceptable accent. This aural sensitivity is usually developed by means of "minimal pairs." These are words or phrases that differ from each other by one sound or by a general feature such as intonation or stress.

4.4.1 Contrasting the native and the target language

Through discrimination exercises the student is brought to realize that the sound system of the target language differs from that of the native language.

4.4.1a GROUP PRACTICE

The teacher reads a list of words. Some are German and some are English. The students mark G or E on a piece of paper. The list is read a second time and correct responses are given: *Du, die, Lee, day, See.*

Similarly the students mark F or E for French or English as they hear the following list of words: *motor, motor, moteur, moteur, motor, moteur, letter, lettre, lettre, letter, lettre, letter, television, télévision, television, télévision, télévision, television.*

4.4.1b INDIVIDUAL RESPONSES

The teacher reads a random series of English and French words. After each word he or she pauses to point at an individual student who replies either "*anglais*" or "*français*," as appropriate: *feel, ville, mille, meal, sel, sell.*

4.4.1c USING MINIMAL PAIRS

(1) The teacher reads aloud a pair of contrasting Spanish and English words. The students raise their right hand if the first word was Spanish. They raise their left hand if the second word was Spanish: *day—de, lo—low, mi—me.*

(2) In an ESL class the teacher reads words at random from the columns below. Students raise one finger if the word is in column I, and two fingers if the word is in column II.[6]

I /s/	II /z/
Sue	zoo
sewn	zone
sink	zinc

[6] Suggested by Eric Nadelstern, De Witt Clinton High School, New York City.

I /s/	II /z/
racer	razor
price	prize
ice	eyes
niece	knees
peace	peas
place	plays

4.4.1d DETECTING AN AMERICAN ACCENT

The teacher reads a series of words. Students shake their heads if the teacher mimics an American accent. In this example, the teacher randomly switches between an American /r/ and a French /r/. Except for the /r/, the words are pronounced to sound like French: *arrive, garage, parc, Richard, Albert.*

4.4.2 Contrasting words in the target language

In learning a second language, students must be made aware of phonemic distinctions, that is, those differences in sound that change the meaning of a word or phrase. Through exercises of the following types, the students soon realize that in some cases making distinctions between single sounds is necessary for comprehension.

4.4.2a RAISING HANDS

The French teacher reads a series of words containing the vowel /u/ or the vowel /y/. Students raise their hands when they hear the sound /y/: *loup, lu, du, trou, fou, tu, bu, boue.* The ESL teacher could use the same technique with /i/ and /ɪ/: *fit, seat, pill, meal.*

4.4.2b RHYMES

The teacher pronounces groups of three words. As the students listen, they circle on their answer sheets the number of the word in the sequence that does not rhyme. At the end of the exercise, the teacher rereads the list and gives the correct answers: *hem, lamb, jam; look, book, duke.*

4.4.2c SAME OR DIFFERENT

The students listen to pairs of words. Some are the same, others are different. They are asked to mark S (same) or D (different) on their papers.

Here is a Spanish example: *mira—mire, mucha—mucha.*

4.4.2d INTONATION PATTERNS

The teacher prepares a set of sentences including commands, questions, and statements. As the teacher reads each sentence, the students write a period if they hear a statement, an exclamation point if they hear a command, and a question mark if they hear a question: *Carlos, ¡trabaja! María trabaja. ¿Ana trabaja?*

4.4.2e FLASH CARDS

The teacher prepares flash cards, each containing one of the words to be contrasted, for example, *pero* (*but*) and *perro* (*dog*). In the classroom the teacher calls two students forward and gives each a card to hold. He or she then reads sentences that contain one of the two words. If the students hear *pero*, they point to the student on the left who is holding that word. If they hear *perro*, they point to the student on the right. The teacher's sentences might utilize unfamiliar vocabulary, for example, *Pero no bebe leche* (*But she does not drink milk*).

For more advanced students, this exercise can be made more difficult if both words in the minimal pair are the same part of speech: *le dessert* (*dessert*) vs. *le désert* (*desert*). Sample sentence: *Je n'aime pas le désert* (*I don't like the desert*).

4.4.3   Contrasting sentences in the target language

The most important minimal contrasts in a language are those which carry grammatical meaning. While French students should hear the difference between a nasal vowel and a non-nasal vowel plus /n/, this distinction becomes critical if they are to distinguish between *Il vient demain* and *Ils viennent demain*. Similarly German students should hear the difference between *Er kommt zu spät* (*He comes too late*) and *Ihr kommt zu spät* (*You come too late*), and Spanish students should be sensitive to distinctions between *Hablo español* (*I speak Spanish*) and *Habló español* (*He spoke Spanish*). ESL students must distinguish between *I like it* and *I liked it*. In drilling these contrasting sounds, the teacher could ask the students to signal whether they heard *singular* or *plural* (French), *he* or *you* (German), *present* or *past* (Spanish and English).

4.4.3a SPOKEN RESPONSES

The teacher directs the students to listen for a specific distinction and say what they hear. For example, in presenting new vocabulary, the teacher may hold up pictures of nouns and say what each picture represents. Students say whether the noun is masculine or feminine: *Es un gato. C'est une fleur* (*It's a cat. It's a flower*).

4.4.3b PHYSICAL RESPONSES

In this technique students make a physical response to show whether they have heard the sentence correctly.

(1) Fingers: The students raise one finger if the sentence is singular, two fingers if the sentence is plural, and a closed fist if they cannot tell: *Ils finissent demain. Elle aime son frère. Il(s) parle(nt) anglais (They finish tomorrow. She likes her brother. He speaks/They speak English).*

(2) Body movement: (For junior high school students.) The teacher writes across the top of the chalkboard *faire avoir être aller.* A student goes to the front of the room. The teacher reads a sentence containing *font, ont, sont,* or *vont,* for example, *Ils ont deux frères (They have two brothers)* and the student moves to stand under the correct verb, *ont.*

The headings on the board can be varied to suit the type of listening discrimination being practiced. They might be present and imperfect: *nous dansons* vs. *nous dansions;* masculine and feminine: *Mes amis sont américains* vs. *Mes amies sont américaines (My friends are American. My female friends are American);* and so on.

(3) Cards: (For junior high school students.) Students color a blue circle on one index card and a red circle on the other. The teacher reads a set of sentences and students indicate whether they heard *le* (blue card) or *la* (red card): *J'aime la danse. J'aime le théâtre (I like dance. I like theater).*

In Spanish, students could color circles white and black. If the sentence they hear contains a verb in the present tense, they raise the white card. If the verb is in the past, they raise the black card. This exercise measures the student's sensitivity to a shift in stress as indicative of a shift in verb tense and subject: *Estudió español. Hablo bien (He/she studied Spanish. I speak well).*

4.5   PRONUNCIATION PRACTICE

When the students can discriminate among the sound features of the language they are learning, and when they have received specific suggestions about how to produce certain sounds and sound combinations, they must be given the opportunity to practice their pronunciation. The memorization of basic sentences or a dialog already furnishes one of these opportunities, but frequently additional pronunciation practice is needed. Some oral exercises do not lend themselves well to pronunciation practice because their main stress is on structure. In communication exercises the emphasis is on fluency of expression and a teacher's highly critical attitude toward pronunciation may stifle the students' willingness to speak. In the following sections, some further ways of introducing pronunciation practice are suggested.

4.5.1   Tongue twisters

Most students enjoy tongue twisters and do not mind repeating them frequently for practice.

Spanish /rr/:   Erre con erre cigarro,
                Erre con erre barril.
                Rápido corren los carros
                Por la línea del ferrocarril.
French /ʃ/ and /s/:   Un chasseur sachant chasser chasse sans chiens.
German /ʃ/ and /s/, /fr/ and /f/:   Fischer frißt frische Fische.
French vowels: Didon dîna, dit-on, du dos d'un dodu dindon.
ESL /s/ and /ʃ/:   She sells sea shells by the seashore.
     /θ/ and /ð/:   What's this thing he works with? It's a lathe.

4.5.2   Songs

There are many foreign language songs which contain frequent repetitions of difficult sounds.

French /r/:   "Il était un' bergère"
              Il était un' bergère
              Et ri et ron, petit patapon
              Il était un' bergère
              Qui gardait ses moutons -ton -ton.

French /ɔ̃/ vs. /ã/:   "Sur le pont d'Avignon"
                       Sur le pont d'Avignon
                       L'on y danse, l'on y danse
                       Sur le pont d'Avignon
                       L'on y danse tout en rond.

Spanish /rr/:   "Corrocloclo"
                Una gallina con pollos
                Cinco duros me costó
                Corrocloclo, corrocloclo, corrocloclo, corrocloclo
                La compré por la mañana
                Y a la tarde se perdió
                Corrocloclo, corrocloclo, corrocloclo, corrocloclo.

German /r/ and /l/:   "O wie wohl ist mir am Abend"
                      O wie wohl ist mir am Abend,
                      Mir am Abend,
                      Wenn zur Ruh
                      Die Glocken läuten,
                      Glocken läuten,
                      Bim, bam, bim, bam, bim, bam!

4.5.3 Poems

Many teachers have used poetry to practice pronunciation. As students memorize poems, they acquire a feeling for the music of the language. It is not necessary to have students memorize a poem in its entirety; often just a stanza may be introduced.

French /œ/:   Il pleure dans mon cœur
Comme il pleut sur la ville.
Quelle est cette langueur
Qui pénètre mon cœur?
Verlaine

Spanish /rr/ /r/ and /v/ /b/:   "Ñapas"
El cielo está emborregado
¿quién lo desemborregará?
el emborregador que lo ha emborregado
buen desemborregado será.

Tres tristes tigres
comían trigo
en la triga
de un trigal.

De la viña de Valencia
vino el vino
a dar vida
al bien viejo
don Benito.

ESL: "Hints on Pronunciation for Foreigners"

I take it you already know
of tough and bough and cough and dough?
Others may stumble but not you,
on hiccough, thorough, laugh and through.
Well done! And now you wish, perhaps,
to learn of less familiar traps?

Beware of heard, a dreadful word
that looks like beard and sounds like bird.
And dead: it's said like bed, not bead
For goodness' sake don't call it 'deed'!
Watch out for meat and great and threat
(They rhyme with suite and straight and debt.)
A moth is not a moth in mother
Nor both in bother, broth in brother,
And here is not a match for there,
Nor dear and fear for bear and pear,

And then there's dose and rose and lose—
Just look them up—and goose and choose,
And cork and work and card and ward,
And font and front and word and sword.
And do and go and thwart and cart—
Come, come, I've hardly made a start!
A dreadful language? Man alive!
I'd mastered it when I was five.[7]

T.S.W.

4.5.4 Cheers

When there is a forthcoming football or basketball game, some students might enjoy writing and practicing foreign language cheers. For example, an equivalent of *Hit 'em again, harder!* is *Encore—Plus fort!*

4.6 SOUND-SYMBOL CORRESPONDENCES

At some point in a student's language program he or she learns to associate the spoken word with its written form. American students learning a second language in school are almost always literate in English. However, many ESL students lack literacy skills. Many of the techniques suggested in this section may be used with both literate students and those who have not yet learned to read.

This initiation to the sound-symbol correspondences of a second language may begin on the first day of class, or it may be postponed several weeks or months. The teacher may either present sound-symbol correspondences directly, in sequential order, and let students read unfamiliar words aloud (the symbol-to-sound approach) or may select known words containing a given sound and bring the student's attention to the different spelling patterns (the sound-to-symbol approach). First, however, many teachers have their students learn the alphabet in foreign language.

4.6.1 Teaching the alphabet

If students can use the foreign alphabet, the talk about sound-symbol correspondences and about spelling may, at least in part, be carried on in the foreign language. Furthermore, if the teacher uses a deductive approach in teaching sound-symbol correspondences, the sounds of the alphabet may be used frequently as models.

---

[7] From David Mackay, ed., *A Flock of Words* (New York: Harcourt Brace Jovanovich, 1969), p. 237–38.

4.6.1a MEMORIZATION

The alphabet may be memorized chorally in recitation or by song. A common problem is that students who know the letters in sequence often have difficulty thinking of the name of the letter when it is presented in isolation.

4.6.1b GROUPING LETTERS

(This exercise is mainly for junior high school students.) The teacher may prefer to teach groups of letters that sound alike, and then later put together the alphabet in sequence. Each group can also be coded with its own color. Once a group of letters has been taught, the teacher can point to letters and have students name them. The letters can be put on index cards, shuffled, and distributed to students for a variety of oral activities: Who has A? Susie, show me who has D. Joe, trade letters with Dick: What letter do you now have?

French:	B C D G P T V W	F L M N R S Z	I J X Y	A H K
	Q U O E			
German:	B C D E G P T W	F L M N R S Z	I X	A H K
	Q U O V Y J			

4.6.1c INITIALS

To practice the letters of the alphabet, the teacher can dictate initials of famous people, for example J.F.K., and have the students identify these people by name. Initials can be dictated to students placed at the board. Students themselves can dictate initials to their classmates. This type of practice can be turned into a game, and gradually students grow to feel at ease with the foreign alphabet.

4.6.2 The symbol-to-sound approach

The teacher presents sound-symbol correspondences in a step-by-step manner. For example, in teaching French the teacher might explain that the letter *a* usually represents the sound /a/ (the name of that letter in the alphabet). The letter *i* usually represents the sound /i/ (the name of the letter in the alphabet, too). Final *e* is usually silent. Then the teacher lets the students read aloud new words: *salade, Alice, maladie, Annie.* A sentence using these sounds might read: *Annick va à la piscine.* A subsequent lesson might introduce the symbols *ou*, silent *h* and *ch* in sentences such as *Où habite Milou? Il habite la Chine.*

The advantage of this presentation is that the student masters the sound-symbol correspondences in a sequential, cumulative manner. The presentation may be made more inductive if the teacher holds up cards and reads certain key words aloud and then asks students what letter or letters are used to represent the sounds they hear.

4.6.3 The sound-to-symbol approach

The students first practice and control sentences orally. Once they can say them readily, they are allowed to see how these sentences are written. Building on this global approach to reading, the teacher uses known words to present sound-symbol correspondences.

The global approach has the advantage that the student controls certain words and sentences orally before learning to read them. However, since basic dialogs and core sentences are rarely developed around considerations of sound-symbol presentation, the student may encounter dozens of sound-symbol patterns, plus some exceptions, in learning to read one line of dialog.

The following techniques help the teacher build on the student's familiarity with certain sentences and words by focusing on sound-symbol correspondences one by one.

4.6.3a SOLICITING WORDS CONTAINING A GIVEN SOUND

The teacher asks the class for known words containing a given sound. He or she puts these words on the chalkboard or on the overhead and guides the students in discovering which symbols are used to represent that sound. Sometimes there is a one-to-one correspondence, as in the German example below. Sometimes there is a one-to-two correspondence, as in the Spanish example, where both *ú* and *u* represent the same sound. Sometimes the relationship is more complex, as in the French example, where one sound has a variety of written representations.

Teacher: Nennen Sie mir sieben Worter mit /ʃt/.
Class: Strasse, Stein, stoßen, Bleistift, aufstehen, bestellt

Teacher: Denme Vds. una lista de palabras que tienen el sonido /u/.
Class: tu, tú, mucho, música, gusto, azul, busca, lunes

Teacher: Donnez-moi une liste de mots qui contiennent le son /e/.
Class: mes, bébé, thé, café, des, parlez

Teacher: Give me a list of words containing the sound /dz/.
Class: juice, judge, enjoys, agent, rigid, age, edge

4.6.3b FELT BOARD TECHNIQUE

On the left-hand side of the board the teacher places cards with words that contain one particular letter combination, such as *ch: mich, ich, nicht, dich, noch, braucht, euch, nach, acht, Mädchen*. On the right-hand side are placed cards with words that contain a contrasting letter combination, such as *sch: Schiff, schon, schenkt, Schnee, Schier, Schere, schuldet*. The letter combinations under consideration could be underlined, or in capital letters, or in some way made prominent. The teacher asks: What sounds do the letters *ch* represent in the words on the left-hand side of the board? Do the letters *ch* on the right-hand side of the board represent either of these sounds? What letter appears before the *ch* in the words on the right-hand side? What sound do the letters *sch* represent?

4.6.3c   MAGNETIC BOARD TECHNIQUE

On the left side of the board the teacher places a magnet over each of the following cards: *paPEL, capiTAL, aZUL, nacioNAL, hoTEL*. Generalization questions: How do all the above words end? What do you do with your voice when the word ends in an *l?*

Now, on the right side of the board, a magnet is placed on each of the following cards: *FÁcil, HÁbil, autoMÓvil, Ágil*. Generalization questions: These words are not stressed on the last syllable, even though they end in *l*. What difference do you see in how they are written? What must you do with your voice when an accent mark appears over a vowel?

4.6.3d   FLASH CARDS: COLOR CODING

(1) The teacher writes the following words on flash cards. The underlined letters should appear in orange: *qui, café, cinq, d'accord, kilo*. After drilling the pronunciation of each word, the teacher arranges the cards on the blackboard ledge and asks the students to name the different spellings of the sound /k/.

(2) For ESL students, write two sets of cards: one with words containing /u/, the other with /əʊ/. The letters representing /u/ are in green, those in /əʊ/ are in red:

/u/:   too, two, do, blew, blue, through, suit, soup
/əʊ/: boat, soul, sole, dough, throw, pole, go, sew

4.6.3e   CHALKBOARD

The teacher prints two columns of words on the chalkboard, writing the underlined letters in colored chalk. The teacher reads each word as he or she prints it, and the students repeat.

Then the teacher asks: What sound is represented by both *ç* and *c?* What vowels occur after *ç?* Do you see those same vowels after *c?* What vowels occur after *c?* Do you see these vowels after *ç?*

4.6.3f   POSTERS AND WALL CHARTS

(1) One poster shows a penguin and a stork and reads: *El pingüino no puede volar como la cigüeña*. Another poster depicts a guitar and a gourd and reads: *Sé tocar la guitarra y el güiro*.

The teacher points to the pictures and asks: When you hear /gwi/ as in *pingüino* and *güiro*, how do you write it? When you hear /gi/ as in *guitarra*, how do you write it?

Similarly, a poster showing money and ointment and reading: *Pagué por el ungüento* could be used to illustrate /ge/ and /gwe/.

(2) The following poster can remind students of the names of accents in French. Upon putting it up the teacher tells the class: This poor man had an *acute* attack of appendicitis and fell back into his *grave*.

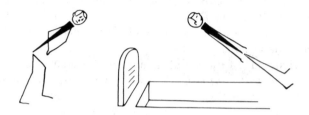

(3) A small poster with the words *hi<u>s</u>* and *hi<u>ss</u>* can serve as a reminder that in French one *s* between vowels represents the sound /z/, whereas a double *s* between vowels represents the sound /s/.

(4) The students pronounce after the teacher and then without the teacher's help:

I		II		III	
/æ/	/eɪ/	/o/	/əʊ/	/ɪ/	/aɪ/
cap	cape	mop	mope	win	wine
fat	fate	cop	cope	rid	ride
tap	tape	hop	hope	slid	slide
pal	pale	not	note	hid	hide
mat	mate	rot	rote	pin	pine

Teacher: Look at the words in each of the left-hand columns. What did we have to add in each case to get the words in the right column?
Class: *e*
Teacher: Yes, by adding *e* we change the vowel from a short to a long form. In your dictionaries this is represented by a flat line over the vowel: cāpe
Teacher: Now repeat the following words and tell me what happens in column IV and column V:

IV		V	
tap	tapping	tape	taping
rid	ridding	ride	riding
hop	hopping	hope	hoping
rip	ripping	hide	hiding
rob	robbing	robe	robing

4.6.4   Phonetic transcription

Some teachers introduce the phonetic alphabet to help their students use foreign language dictionaries to look up the pronunciation of new words. This is particularly useful in the case of French, where the general rules of sound-symbol correspondence are often insufficient for predicting the pronunciation of a word. Other teachers feel that a formal introduction to the IPA alphabet is too time-consuming. ESL teachers sometimes introduce the phonetic transcription used in the classroom dictionaries.

If the teacher does not want to spend time on a formal presentation of IPA symbols, he or she might prepare ditto sheets for independent work by those students who are interested.

4.6.4a   SAME OR DIFFERENT

The teacher can have the students look up the following pairs of words and indicate whether the underlined letters represent the same sound or different sounds: *vers—fils*, *femme—dame*, *examen—lentement*. This could also be a lab drill with printed materials and taped exercises.

4.6.4b   SILENT OR NOT

The teacher can have the students look up the following words and circle those final consonants that are *not* pronounced: *sac, estomac, flirt, vert*.

4.7   REMEDIAL WORK

Once students have acquired bad habits of pronunciation, the process of correction is difficult and very time-consuming. However, with patience and effective teaching techniques, it is possible to attain positive results.

4.7.1   General procedures

The teacher of any language class of second-year level or higher is faced with the general problem of how best to improve the students' ability to discriminate among the sounds of the language and to produce these sounds in an acceptable manner. The problem is compounded by the fact that some students control the sound system better than others, and that each has individual pronunciation difficulties. The following sections suggest some general techniques for doing the necessary remedial work.

4.7.1a LISTENING FOR OTHERS' MISTAKES

The first step in improving one's pronunciation is becoming aware of mistakes. Since another's mistakes are often more noticeable than one's own, the teacher can encourage students to become more critical of one another's speech. If students are giving short presentations, or if pairs of students are reciting a dialog, the rest of the class might note down errors on slips of paper, not indicating students' names. Another possibility is to assign two or three students per day to be "umpires" and listen for mistakes. After all the presentations have been given, the teacher collects the slips and points out the errors without mentioning the individuals who committed them. Throughout these activities the teacher must maintain a friendly and cooperative atmosphere in the classroom.

In a less personal way, the teacher can play a tape recording prepared by another group of students, identified only by number, and have the class pick out pronunciation errors. It is also possible to exchange tapes: Section A criticizes a tape made by Section B, and vice versa.

4.7.1b LISTENING FOR ONE'S OWN MISTAKES

On any recorded listening test or exercise, the students are required to listen to their own recording. Any mistake they catch and note down is scored -1. Any mistake they do not catch, but that the teacher catches, is scored -5. Such a system encourages critical listening.

4.7.1c INDIVIDUALIZED PRONUNCIATION OBJECTIVES

At the beginning of a quarter, the teacher has the students record fifteen sentences containing most of the sound and pronunciation features of the language being taught. The teacher listens to the tape and assigns each student two mistakes to be corrected by the end of the quarter: success in correcting the two mistakes (even if other mistakes persist) is rewarded by an A for that part of the course. This system gives the poorer student a reachable goal and requires the better student to work just as diligently in overcoming less obvious phonological problems. Moreover, the students help each other out, since they are not competing against each other, but rather aiming for a fixed objective.

4.7.1d THE SOUND-A-WEEK SYSTEM

The teacher stresses one sound or phonological feature (such as rhythm or stress) per week. Only mistakes in that area are corrected each time they occur, and only they are counted if spoken activities are graded.

4.7.1e RECORDED SENTENCES: PASS-FAIL

The teacher prepares five sentences containing one or more phonetic features. The students one by one record these sentences (at a tape recorder in the language lab, at the back of the classroom, or at the teacher's desk while others are doing written exercises). The teacher then grades the tape, noting each student's mistakes on a check list. Students making more than one or two mistakes must practice the sentences and then record them again. Only pass marks are recorded.

4.6.1f RECORDED SENTENCES: CLASSROOM EXERCISE

Students record a single sentence one after the other. The sentence contains two or more examples of a critical sound. For instance, *As-tu bu du jus?* The tape is then played back to the students who judge whether the sounds are right or wrong. The teacher is the final arbiter.

Alternate judging technique: Students each have a red and a green card. If they accept the sound, they raise the green card. If they do not accept the sound, they raise the red card. The teacher can tell at a glance if there is unanimity or if the sentence should be played over.

4.7.1g LISTENING DISCRIMINATION DRILLS PREPARED BY STUDENTS

In more advanced classes, the students can take turns preparing a set of listening discrimination sentences (such as those suggested in Sections 4.4.2 and 4.4.3). One student reads his sentences while his classmates mark down, for example, whether they heard the article *ce* or *ces* before the direct object.

4.7.2 Specific techniques

Sometimes a student needs special help in specific areas. Many of the techniques suggested for initial presentation (see Section 4.3) and for listening discrimination (see Section 4.4) may also be adapted for remedial work. In addition, some teachers might want to experiment with the following techniques.

4.7.2a PARTIAL CORRECTION

Many students have difficulty with the German *ü* and the French *u*, for which they substitute the English *oo*. Such students may be encouraged to substitute an /i/ for the /y/. In German, *vier mich* is much more acceptable than *fuhr mich* as a mispronounced *für mich*. Similarly, in French *ti viens* is better than *tout viens* as a substitute for *tu viens*. Since Americans have a tendency to round their lips for the *u* they see on paper, the chances are good that the /i/ sound will gradually come to resemble the /y/.

4.7.2b WORKING WITH COGNATES

Often the worst pronunciation mistakes occur when students are using cognates. The teacher might prepare a tape on the following pattern:

1. (pause) téléphone (pause)
2. (pause) télégraphe (pause)

The student receives a ditto sheet containing the words. The first time she practices with the tape she repeats the French cognate after she has heard it. When she is more sure of herself, she reads the word in the pause between the number and the voice on the tape. She may repeat it a second time after the voice if she so desires.

In speaking Spanish, students tend to transfer the English to pronunciation of cognates. Thus the American is likely, for example, to say *teleFOno* rather than the correct *teLEfono*. A contrastive drill may help the students realize their errors. (This same list may be used with Hispanic ESL students.)

English	Spanish
TElephone	teLEfono
uniVERsity	universiDAD
HOSpital	hospiTAL
PREsent	preSENte
PASSport	pasaPORte
aMERican	ameriCAno
MEXican	mexiCAno
CAnada	CanaDA

4.7.2c UNSTRESSED VOWELS

The introduction of the unstressed vowel, or schwa, into French or Spanish is a very prevalent error. Strong insistence by the teacher on clearly articulated vowels will help students become aware of their mistakes. Whenever the teacher has noted several such mispronunciations in the course of a speaking activity or a small pronunciation test, he or she might have a brief full-class session, proceeding thus: the teacher reads pairs of words; the students repeat the one that is French: *uh-méricain—américain, difficile—diff-uh-cile.* The students know immediately which is the right form and usually cooperate good-naturedly as they recognize the very words they were mispronouncing only a few minutes before.

Very often a student can be helped to make the proper sound if the teacher repeats both the sound the student is making and the proper one. The student often has to hear the contrast modeled by someone else before he or she can produce the sound accurately. This can be a one-second individual correction device as well as a brief full-class session.

4.7.2d STRESSED SYLLABLES AND CHANGE OF MEANING

ESL students need to hear and pronounce words and phrases that carry different stress patterns. If the stress is not correctly placed, there is the problem of being misunderstood; stress placed on the wrong syllable can signal another word and another meaning.

The teacher gives a short definition and the student supplies the phrase just defined while giving the correct stress. Primary stress is written /ˈ /, secondary stress /ˌ/, and tertiary stress /ˆ/.

I /ˆ ´/

Teacher	Student
1. a teacher from England	an Englîsh téacher
2. a house painted green	a grêen hóuse
3. a wonderful father	a grând fáther
4. cream that has been chilled	côld créam
5. a house painted white	a whîte hóuse
6. a brief stop	a shôrt stóp
7. a book that is blue	a blûe bóok

II /´ ˆ/

Teacher	Student
1. a teacher of English	An Énglish têacher
2. a plant nursery enclosed in glass	a grêenhòuse
3. the father of one's father or mother	a grándfàther
4. a cosmetic preparation	cóld crêam
5. the residence of the U.S. president	the Whíte Hòuse
6. a position on a baseball team	a shórtstòp
7. examination booklet	a blúe bôok

4.7.2e STRESS SHIFT AND CHANGE IN VOWEL QUALITY

On a transparency write the words in the two columns below. Make the accent of primary stress red, and the tertiary stress blue. The teacher reads the first column, the students the second. Then the reverse is done.

I /i/	II /ə/	I /e/	II /ə/	I /eɪ/	II /ə/
compéte	còmpetítion	stérile	sterílity	áble	abílity
revéal	rèvelátion	méthod	methódical	stáble	stabílity
repéat	rèpetítion	mélody	melódic	fátal	fatálity
		métal	metállic	procláim	proclamátion
		párent	paréntal	expláin	explanátion

outline

five
Teaching
Grammar:
General
Procedures

Foreign language and ESL teachers, especially teachers of beginning and intermediate classes, spend a considerable portion of their time teaching grammar. The terms may vary: grammar, generalization, sentence patterns, structure, transformations, verb forms, conjugations, declensions, but the basic consideration is the same. Knowledge of vocabulary alone is insufficient for communication.

This chapter presents several approaches to the teaching of grammar. Should the students be presented with a pattern, rule, or generalization and then be given the opportunity to practice it (a deductive approach)? Or should they practice a set of patterns and then be led to derive their own generalization (an inductive approach)? Should the students be guided through a series of pattern drills of increasing difficulty in an effort to form correct language habits (a habit-formation or stimulus-response approach)? Or should they be allowed to apply generalizations and form original sentences in the foreign language (a cognitive or generative approach)? Although these approaches represent different philosophical positions about the nature of learning, the teacher will probably adapt techniques from each of them. Sometimes an approach that works with two-thirds of the class is not as effective with the remaining third, who would learn more readily from a different type of presentation.

Teachers should be encouraged to try out a variety of approaches and discover which work best for them and for their students.

5.1 GENERAL CONSIDERATIONS

The word "grammar" brings to the minds of many high school students a formal and often uninteresting analysis of language. Some students think only of conjugations, paradigms, declensions, and diagraming, all of which appear to be an

81

end in themselves. If, on the other hand, students are eager to communicate their thoughts, and if to do so they must select the proper forms and put them in the correct order, grammar study takes on a new meaning.

Preparing students for a grammar lesson is just as important as choosing the exercises and drills to be used. The teacher who begins the lesson by saying, "Today we are going to study interrogatives," may lose many of the students. If, however, the students are conversing and need to ask questions of their teacher or classmates, they will want to learn the interrogative forms. Let us assume they can use affirmative forms and are able to say *Paul is going to the movies tonight.* If they want to ask Mary if she is going to the movies tonight, they need to learn this new structure. Similarly, in role playing, the student who is at a dinner party and does not have a fork must be able to use the negative when reporting this information to the hostess.

These kinds of situations and many more can serve as a point of departure for the study of grammar.

5.2   SUPPLEMENTING THE TEXTBOOK

The textbook, or basic program, including wall charts, films, or film strips, determines the order of presentation of grammar. Moreover, most textbooks are accompanied by a teacher's manual that gives many suggestions for teaching the grammatical patterns included in each lesson.

However, even the most detailed teacher's manual cannot provide complete guidelines for the teaching of grammar, guidelines that take into consideration differences among students, differences in school populations, differences in teachers, differences in scheduling, and physical environment. The teacher must assume the creative role of bridging the gap between the materials and the students, of teaching those things that the materials fail to present adequately, and of providing supplementary activities where and when needed. The teacher may even discover that the type of presentation suggested in the teacher's manual is not appropriate for his or her particular students and may consequently modify those suggestions.

5.2.1   Determining and checking requisite knowledge

Language learning, particularly at the early levels, is a cumulative process. Students must know the gender of a noun before they can make the article and adjectives agree with that noun. They must know the different forms of auxiliary verbs before they can be expected to produce compound tenses. This kind of basic knowledge is called *requisite learning.*

Although textbooks do present grammar in a sequential manner, they frequently do not have the space to review requisite knowledge before presenting a new point of structure. Recent research has indicated that the student's mastery of requisite knowledge is a greater factor in successful language learning than length and type of practice or the teacher's method of presentation. In other words, if the foreign language teacher wants the students to learn a specific point of grammar, such as the use of the subjunctive after *Pensez-vous que* and *Croyez-vous que,* he or she must first make sure that the students remember the forms of *penser* and *croire* in the present tense, and then that the students can handle the subjunctive forms of the verbs that will be used in the dependent clauses. This time spent for review of requisite knowledge is never wasted. If all students do remember the forms, then the review has built up their confidence and prepared them for the new material. If some students have forgotten certain things, then the teacher is in the position immediately to review the difficult points in the old material before going on to the new lesson.

The following chart gives some examples of requisite knowledge that should be reviewed before introducing the new material:

New Material	Requisite Knowledge
agreement of adjectives	genders of nouns to be used
irregular adjectives	forms of regular adjectives; genders of nouns to be used
direct-object pronouns (accusative)	forms of the direct object (accusative), genders of nouns to be used
position of object pronouns	forms of object pronouns; forms of verbs to be used
French: conditional tense	formation of future stems; imperfect endings or review of imperfect tense
German: prepositions of place	accusative and dative forms of nouns to be used
Spanish: subjunctive forms	imperative
French and Spanish: imperfect vs. preterite, *passé composé*	forms of the imperfect and the past tense
French: *passé composé* with *être*	present tense of *être;* forms of regular adjectives; past participles of *-er* verbs
inverted word order	regular word order; forms of verbs to be used

For each lesson in the textbook, teachers should establish for themselves which previous material the students must master if they are to understand the new material.

The form of the review will vary from lesson to lesson. For example, let us assume the new German lesson will introduce the conversational past with *haben.* The teacher might ask each student to pick up an object and hold it in his or her hand.

Teacher: Was hast du in der Hand?	*What do you have in your hand?*
Student: Ich habe ein Buch.	*I have a book.*

Various question-and-answer patterns will allow a review of *ihr habt, wir haben, er hat, sie hat, sie haben* (*you have, we have, he has, she has, they have*). The review of familiar material has provided a warm-up session in spoken German. The students have been able to demonstrate how fluently they command the verb *haben*, and the teacher has been able to refresh the memories of those students who needed the review. From this positive beginning, the teacher can move on to a presentation of the past tense.

5.2.2 Anticipating areas of interference

Manuals on applied linguistics usually point out areas of interference that may present problems to the second-language learner.

One area of interference is the student's native language. The student of French, for example, will want to pronounce the final *s* on noun plurals, because this is the English pattern. The student of German will want to impose English word order on the German sentence. The student of Spanish will forget to use the *a* with a personal direct object. Some teachers explicitly present the English pattern and contrast it with the foreign language pattern to make students aware of the difficulty. Others prefer concentrating on drill and practice in the foreign language to strengthen the proper foreign language pattern. In the latter case drills containing the areas of interference will need much more practice than those containing patterns which parallel English.

The second type of interference arises within the foreign language itself. Here the textbooks often fail to contrast similar patterns explicitly, and the teacher must introduce supplementary exercises. For example, when beginning French students have learned the present tense of *faire*, they should be given ample opportunity to distinguish between the present tense of *faire* and that of *être*, *avoir*, and *aller*. When they learn the adjectival forms *ce, cet, cette, ces*, they should also review the pronoun *ce*, which becomes *c'* before a vowel sound. In German, <u>der gute Mann</u> should be contrasted with <u>der guten Frau</u> and <u>der Mann, der hier war</u>. ESL students must distinguish between *have* /hæv/ and *have to* /hæftə/, as in *We don't* <u>have</u> *time; we* <u>have to</u> *go now.*

5.2.3 Finding alternate presentations

When the teacher has taught a unit and given the unit test, he or she may discover that not all students have attained the desired level of mastery; some remedial work from alternate sources may therefore be necessary.

5.2.3a   OTHER BOOKS

The department may have other textbooks on hand. Students may be asked to review the presentation of the same grammar points in another book. Often a second, slightly different, presentation seems clearer than the first.

5.2.3b   OTHER TECHNIQUES

The teacher may work with the students who need help while the rest of the class is engaged in another activity. At this time he or she might experiment with another technique, since the first one failed to produce the desired result.

5.2.3c   OTHER STUDENTS

Other students, either from the same class or from a higher class, may work as tutors with those who need assistance. Sometimes another student's explanation is more effective than the teacher's in clarifying a difficult structure.

5.3   PRESENTING RULES: A DEDUCTIVE APPROACH

In a deductive approach, the rules, patterns, or generalizations are presented to the student, and then he or she is given ample opportunity to practice the new feature of grammar. This approach is most effective for the presentation of irregular patterns or exceptions to general patterns, for these by their very nature cannot be discovered through analogy. In the hands of a good teacher, the approach can save class time. There are also some students who prefer having the rule presented and then being allowed to demonstrate their comprehension by applying it to new sentences.

The drawback of the deductive presentation is that it may become dry and technical. The student may feel that he or she is being lectured and stop paying attention. If the examples are too tricky, the student is frustrated in his or her attempts to apply the rule. Learning a second language becomes a purely intellectual exercise instead of being a means to communication. The deductive presentation is most effective when the new sentences are presented in a meaningful context.

5.3.1   Procedure

The deductive presentation of grammar follows this general pattern: 1. Statement of the rule or pattern, 2. Sample sentences that students repeat, 3. Ample opportunity for students to practice the new pattern.

The first presentation is usually made orally. When the students can handle the spoken pattern, they are introduced to the written form. For more complex patterns at the intermediate levels, the teacher may present the written patterns first and then allow for oral practice afterwards.

(1) Teacher: A simple way of turning a statement into a question in French is by beginning the sentence with *est-ce que* and letting your voice go up at the end.↑

Listen: *Paul travaille. Est-ce que Paul travaille?↑(Paul works. Does Paul work?)*

Repeat: *Paul travaille. Est-ce que Paul travaille?↑*

Here is another example: *Marie travaille aussi. (Marie works too.)*

The question: *Est-ce que Marie travaille aussi?↑ (Does Marie work too?)*

Now let us imagine that you doubt everything I say. Whenever I make a statement, you turn it into a question:

Robert travaille. (Robert works.)

What is your response?

Class: *Est-ce que Robert travaille?↑ (Does Robert work?)*

(2) Teacher: Many questions in English begin with *Do* or *Does*. An easy way to change a statement to a question is by starting with *Does* if the subject is singular, and *Do* if the subject is plural. Always keep the main verb in the infinitive form and let your voice go up at the end.

Listen: *Bob goes to school.*
Does Bob go to school?

Repeat: *Bob goes to school.*
Does Bob go to school?

Here is another example: *Bob and Mary go to Florida.*

The question: *Do Bob and Mary go to Florida?*

Now I will make a statement and you turn it into a question: *Mr. Smith sells cars.*

You ask the question.

Class: *Does* Mr. Smith *sell* cars?

5.3.2 Techniques

The teacher may use a variety of techniques to emphasize the essential aspects of the rule or pattern he or she is presenting. The teacher may speak in English or in the foreign language.

5.3.2a FLASH CARDS

(1) The teacher is presenting inverted questions in German. A set of flash cards is prepared:

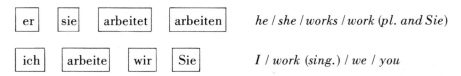

| er | sie | arbeitet | arbeiten | *he / she / works / work (pl. and Sie)*

| ich | arbeite | wir | Sie | *I / work (sing.) / we / you*

As the regular statement is shown, the teacher holds up a subject card and a verb card: | er | | arbeitet | . He or she explains that to turn the statement into a question you just invert, or reverse, the subject and the verb. In saying this the teacher crosses his or her hands so that the flash cards read | arbeitet | | er |

With the other cards additional examples are presented.

NOTE: In a similar ESL lesson, flash cards would also be prepared with *do* and *does.*

(2) The teacher is presenting the singular forms of *count* and *mass* nouns in an ESL class. On each card is written a noun that is either countable or noncountable: book, chair, pencil, money, bread, sugar, shirt, pen, milk, sandwich, etc. The teacher explains that the count nouns will be preceded by *a* and the mass nouns by nothing or by the word *some.* Then the students are told to ask individually for one of the cards by saying, *I'd like* . . . They will say, *I'd like a book* or *I'd like some bread.*

5.3.2b   TRANSPARENCY AND OVERHEAD PROJECTOR

The teacher prepares the following transparency with the present tense of *hablar (to speak).*

> hablar
> hablo
> hablas
> habla
> hablamos
> habláis
> hablan

In class he or she first rapidly reviews forms of *hablar,* using a question-answer technique. Then the teacher puts the transparency on the projector and asks the students to read each form aloud, indicating which syllable is stressed. He or she circles the stressed syllable with a grease pencil (so that the circles may be erased and the transparency reused with another class).

Then the teacher writes (in grease pencil) the infinitive *cerrar* on the right-hand side of the transparency. He or she gives the meaning of the new word and elicits the forms *cerramos* and *cerráis,* which are regular. Then the teacher explains that in these two forms the accent falls on the next-to-last syllable and asks the students to look at the root vowels of *hablar* and *cerrar.* The *a* of *hablar* appears in all the present tense forms. The root vowel *e* becomes *ie* when that vowel carries the accent of the word. An *ie* is written on the board. Therefore we say *Yo cierro.* Then the teacher lets students generate the remaining forms of the new verb.

All the forms of *cerrar* are then practiced orally. Other radically changing verbs that follow the same pattern may be introduced so that the students may apply the pattern to an unfamiliar verb.

5.3.2c PROPS AND CHALKBOARD

The teacher has a boy and a girl come forward, bringing their books with them. The forms of the possessive adjective are reviewed orally:

Teacher: Est-ce que c'est ton livre?   *Is this your book?*
Student: Oui, c'est mon livre.   *Yes, it's my book.*

The teacher asks the question of both the boy and the girl. Then he or she explains that the possessive adjective *son*, which can mean either *his* or *her*, follows the pattern of *mon*. The teacher picks up the boy's book, points to the boy, and says: *C'est son livre—It's <u>his</u> book.* Then he or she takes the girl's book and says: *C'est son livre—It's <u>her</u> book.* Class repeats.

Then the teacher gives the boy and girl each a piece of chalk.

Teacher: Est-ce que c'est ta
craie?   *Is this your chalk?*

Student: Oui, c'est ma craie.   *Yes, it's my chalk.*

Teacher: (Takes back the chalk.)
How would you say
It's her (his) chalk?
Class: C'est sa craie.

The teacher asks a boy to come forward, placing him between the other two students.

Teacher: (To girl)
Est-ce que Larry (stu-   *Is Larry your friend?*
dent's name) est ton
ami?

Girl: Oui, Larry est mon ami.   *Yes, Larry is my friend.*

Teacher: (To class)
How do you say Larry
is her friend?

Class: Larry est son ami.

The teacher continues, with another girl (*son amie*), Larry and the second girl (*ses amis*), two notebooks (*ses cahiers*).

On the chalkboard, the written forms are presented; students may dictate some of the sentences.

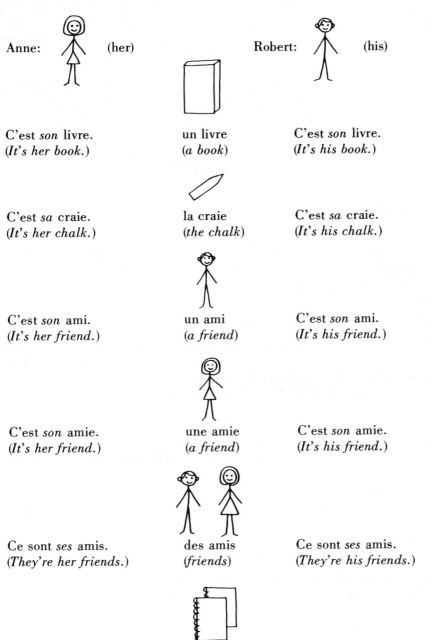

Anne: (her)   Robert: (his)

C'est *son* livre. (*It's her book.*)	un livre (*a book*)	C'est *son* livre. (*It's his book.*)
C'est *sa* craie. (*It's her chalk.*)	la craie (*the chalk*)	C'est *sa* craie. (*It's his chalk.*)
C'est *son* ami. (*It's her friend.*)	un ami (*a friend*)	C'est *son* ami. (*It's his friend.*)
C'est *son* amie. (*It's her friend.*)	une amie (*a friend*)	C'est *son* amie. (*It's his friend.*)
Ce sont *ses* amis. (*They're her friends.*)	des amis (*friends*)	Ce sont *ses* amis. (*They're his friends.*)
Ce sont *ses* cahiers. (*They're her notebooks.*)	des cahiers (*notebooks*)	Ce sont *ses* cahiers. (*They're his notebooks.*)

5.4 PRESENTING RULES: AN INDUCTIVE APPROACH

In an inductive approach, the teacher first gives the students examples of the grammatical structure to be learned. After the examples have been practiced, the students are guided in forming a generalization about the grammatical principle they have been working with. This approach works best with regular grammatical patterns.

The advantage of the inductive approach is that the students participate in the formulation of the grammatical principle. They have been saying or writing sentences using a specific pattern, so that the generalization is meaningful to them in terms of their previous activity. The disadvantage is that it often takes more time than a deductive presentation. Furthermore, some students prefer knowing the generalization before practicing the examples.

5.4.1 Procedure

The inductive presentation of grammar follows this general pattern: (1) Presentation of examples. (2) Oral or written practice. (3) Generalization or rule that grows out of the previous activity. Either the teacher states the rule or the students formulate it. The rule may be in the native or the target language.

5.4.1a SELECTING THE MODEL SENTENCES

The careful choice of examples is the key to success in this approach. Often the use of paired sentences helps to make the grammatical point clear. For example, to teach the past tense in English, the teacher might give a series of examples like the following: *Today I want to play football. Yesterday I wanted to play baseball.*

In selecting sentences for a generalization, it is important to use only those which illustrate the grammatical point of the lesson.

(1) If the lesson had been on the partitive, it would be unwise to include nouns of different gender and number:

Good Choice

Je voudrais du pain.   *I would like bread/butter/sugar/salt.*
Je voudrais du beurre.
Je voudrais du sucre.
Je voudrais du sel.

Here the teacher can ask what the nouns have in common. (They are all masculine.) Then the teacher can ask what word is used to express the idea of "some" before these masculine nouns (*du*).

Poor Choice

Je voudrais du pain.   *I would like bread/meat/carrots/*
Je voudrais de la viande.   *water.*
Je voudrais des carottes.
Je voudrais de l'eau.

Here we have partitives of different gender and number. The way they are grouped makes it difficult to ask simple questions.

(2) For a lesson on the imperative, only regular verbs of the same conjugation should be used:

Good Choice

1. Juan <u>mira</u> la televisión.	*Juan watches T.V.*
Juan, ¡no <u>mires</u> la televisión!	*Juan, don't watch T.V.!*
2. Carlos <u>habla</u> inglés.	*Carlos speaks English.*
Carlos, ¡no <u>hables</u> inglés!	*Carlos, don't speak English!*
3. María <u>toma</u> el libro.	*Marie takes the book.*
María, ¡no <u>tomes</u> el libro!	*Maria, don't take the book!*
4. Carmen <u>compra</u> dulces.	*Carmen buys candy.*
Carmen, ¡no <u>compres</u> dulces!	*Carmen, don't buy candy!*

Here the teacher could ask what the underlined words in the first sentences of each pair had in common. (They all end in *a*.) What kind of sentences are they? (Declarative.) What happens to these underlined words (or verbs) when they are used to make negative commands? (They drop the *a* and add *es*.)

Poor Choice

1. Juan <u>mira</u> la televisión.	*Juan watches T.V.*
Juan, ¡no <u>mires</u> la televisión!	*Juan, don't watch T.V.!*
2. Carlos <u>escribe</u>.	*Carlos writes.*
Carlos, ¡no <u>escribas</u>!	*Carlos, don't write!*
3. María <u>sale</u>.	*Maria leaves.*
María, ¡no <u>salgas</u>!	*Maria, don't leave!*
4. Carmen <u>va</u> a la ventana.	*Carmen goes to the window.*
Carmen, ¡no <u>vayas</u> a la ventana!	*Carmen, don't go to the window!*

These sentences contain both regular and irregular verbs of different conjugations. The only thing they have in common is that they are used in the negative imperative. It would be very difficult to ask any other questions on these groups of sentences.

5.4.1b PROCEEDING FROM KNOWN TO UNKNOWN GRAMMAR

1. Hier ist der Mantel.	*Here is the coat.*
Ich brauche den Mantel.	*I need the coat.*
2. Hier ist der Bleistift.	*Here is the pencil.*
Ich sehe den Bleistift.	*I see the pencil.*
3. Hier ist der Mann.	*Here is the man.*
Ich kenne den Mann.	*I know the man.*
4. Hier ist der Brief.	*Here is the letter.*
Ich schreibe den Brief.	*I write the letter.*

In the first sentence of each pair all the nouns are singular, masculine, and occur in the nominative case. The students must know this information before using the nouns in the accusative case (in the second sentence of each pair). In every case the noun marker changes from *der* to *den*.

1. Je parle français. *I speak French.*
   J'ai parlé français. *I spoke French.*
2. Il regarde la télévision. *He watches television.*
   Il a regardé la télévision. *He watched television.*
3. Nous cherchons le cinéma. *We look for the moviehouse.*
   Nous avons cherché le cinéma. *We looked for the moviehouse.*
4. Tu dînes à sept heures. *You have dinner at 7.*
   Tu as dîné à sept heures. *You had dinner at 7.*
5. Ils étudient l'espagnol. *They study Spanish.*
   Ils ont étudié l'espagnol. *They studied Spanish.*

Before teaching the material in the second sentence of each pair, the teacher should have given a lesson on the verb forms of *avoir,* and he should review the forms of regular verbs in the first conjugation (in the first sentences).

5.4.1c PLACING THE SENTENCES IN A MEANINGFUL CONTEXT

Students are more likely to retain the new structure if it is presented in a meaningful context. It is not always easy to invent a situation in which the key sentences might occur, but it is well worth the effort to find settings for grammatical presentations.

Here is a short example for teaching the use of the imperfect tense in French to describe repeated actions in the past.[1]

Henri is in the hospital after a motorcycle accident. The doctor notices that he has a scar on his back. Henri explains that when he was younger he used to spend his vacations in the Pyrenees and one day he fell. Henri's account is summarized as follows:

D'habitude... *Usually . . .*
J'<u>allais</u> en montagne avec mes cousins. *I would go to the mountains with my cousins.*
J'<u>escaladais</u> des rochers. *I would climb rocks.*
Je <u>faisais</u> attention. *I would pay attention.*
Je ne <u>tombais</u> jamais. *I would never fall.*

Un jour... *One day . . .*
Je <u>suis allé</u> seul. *I went alone.*
J'<u>ai escaladé</u> un rocher très élevé. *I climbed a very high rock.*
Je n'<u>ai</u> pas <u>fait</u> attention. *I didn't pay attention.*
Je <u>suis tombé</u>. *I fell.*

---

[1] Taken from Jean-Paul Valette and Rebecca M. Valette, *French for Mastery, Book Two* (Lexington, Mass.: D.C. Heath, 1975), p. 157.

—Quel temps utilise Henri quand il parle de ce qu'il faisait d'habitude?	*What verb tense does Henry use when he is speaking about what he usually did?*
—Quel temps utilise-t-il quand il parle de ce qu'il a fait un certain jour?	*What verb tense does he use when he is speaking about what he did on a certain day?*

The advantage of the situational presentation is that it allows for quick reference back to a grammatical point. Thus the teacher does not have to ask: "What tense do you use for repeated past actions?" (an abstract question), but can say: "Remember when Henri was telling the doctor about his mountain-climbing accident? What tense did he use to tell about the things he used to do every summer?" (a concrete question).

5.4.1d PREPARING THE QUESTIONS LEADING TO THE GENERALIZATION

The questions on the new structure may focus on the spoken language or on the written language (or both). The questions are so sequenced that almost all students should be able to give the answer.

(1) Spoken language: In French the pattern of the oral forms is often different from that of the written forms. The types of questions that a teacher would ask about the spoken language would reflect this difference. (The IPA transcription used in brackets in the following examples is for the teacher, not for the students.)

Au Café:	*At the cafe:*
Paul et Marc lisent le journal. /liz/	*Paul and Marc read the paper.*
Paul et Marc boivent un café. /bwav/	*Paul and Marc drink a cup of coffee.*
Paul et Marc écrivent une carte postale. /ekriv/	*Paul and Marc write a postcard.*
Paul et Marc partent. /part/	*Paul and Marc leave.*
Paul lit le journal. /li/	*Paul reads the paper.*
Paul boit un café. /bwa/	*Paul drinks a cup of coffee.*
Paul écrit une carte postale. /ekri/	*Paul writes a postcard.*
Paul part. /par/	*Paul leaves.*

The questions for the generalization refer to the spoken forms of the verbs.

The teacher might ask the following questions:

Teacher:	How many boys' names did you hear me pronounce in the first set of sentences?
Students:	Two.
Teacher:	How many in the second set?
Students:	One.

Teacher: What happened to the verb when I used it with only one person?
Students: You dropped off the last sound.

In an oral generalization it is essential that the teacher ask questions about sounds, and not letters.

(2) Written presentation:

holen	Ich	habe	das	Buch	geholt.	*I got the book.*
suchen	Ich	habe	das	Kind	gesucht.	*I looked for the child.*
kaufen	Ich	habe	die	Uhr	gekauft.	*I bought the watch.*
machen	Ich	habe	den	Film	gemacht.	*I made the movie.*
fragen	Ich	habe	den	Mann	gefragt.	*I asked the man.*
bauen	Ich	habe	das	Haus	gebaut.	*I built the house.*
decken	Ich	habe	den	Tisch	gedeckt.	*I set the table.*

In these examples the teacher will need to ask questions: 1. about the presence of the auxiliary and its position in the sentence, 2. about the position of the direct object, 3. about the position and formation of the past participle. Notice that all the verbs selected are weak. In another lesson there could be a list of strong verbs.

Teacher: How many words make up the verb in each sentence?
Students: Two.
Teacher: Which one is the same in every sentence?
Students: *Habe.*
Teacher: Where does *habe* appear in the sentence?
Students: After the subject.
Teacher: Look at the infinitives in the list. What do we do to them when we use them in sentences?
Students: We drop off the *en* and replace it with a *t*. We also add *ge* to the beginning of the word.
Teacher: Where is its position in the sentence?
Students: At the end.
Teacher: Where do we place the direct object?
Students: Before the second verb (or past participle).

5.4.2   Techniques for presenting model sentences

It is possible to use a variety of media in making the generalizations.

5.4.2a   CHALKBOARD

(1) Using only the chalkboard, the teacher presents the Spanish subjunctive. He or she writes the following sentences on the board and covers them with a map until they are needed. As they are uncovered, the same question-and-answer technique just described is used.

1. Vd. *habla* español.	*You speak Spanish.*
Yo quiero que Vd. *hable* español.	*I want you to speak Spanish.*
2. Vd. *termina* el libro.	*You finish the book.*
Yo quiero que Vd. *termine* el libro.	*I want you to finish the book.*
3. Vd. *toma* el dinero.	*You take the money.*
Yo quiero que Vd. *tome* el dinero.	*I want you to take the money.*
4. Vd. *entra* por aquí.	*You enter here.*
Yo quiero que Vd. *entre* por aquí.	*I want you to enter here.*

(2) Writing sentences while students dictate: In this set of sentences the focus is on the written forms of the past participles.

Teacher:	Est-ce que Bob (name of student) est venu en classe?	*Has Bob come to class?*
Class:	Oui, il est venu. (Teacher writes sentence.)	
Teacher:	Est-ce qu'il est allé à sa place?	*Has he gone to his seat?*
Class:	Oui, il est allé à sa place.	
Teacher:	Et Susan, est-elle venue?	*And Susan, has she come?*
Class:	Oui, elle est venue.	
Teacher:	Est-elle allée à sa place?	*Did she go to her seat?*
Class:	Oui, elle est allée à sa place.	
	etc. (Questions continue in the plural with other intransitive verbs.)	
On board:	Ils sont arrivés.	Elles sont arrivées.
	Ils sont partis...	Elles sont parties...
	etc.	

(3) The board plus a prop: To teach the direct object in German, the teacher could use the following technique: He or she writes on the board,

Ich	habe	getrunken.	*I have drunk.*

Holding a glass, the teacher places it in several positions against the board: before the auxiliary, after the past participle, between the auxiliary and the past participle. Then he or she asks, Where must *ein Glas Wasser* (*a glass of water*) be placed? (Between *habe* and *getrunken*.)

(4) The board plus index cards with masking tape or double-adhesive tape: Each card contains either a picture of a drink or the German word: *eine Tasse Kaffee, eine Tasse Tee, ein Glas Milch, ein Glas Wasser, ein Glas Schokoladenmilch, Limonade* (*a cup of coffee, a cup of tea, a glass of milk, lemonade*). One by one the teacher sticks the index cards between *habe* and *getrunken*, for example, *Ich habe Limonade getrunken.* (*I drank lemonade.*)

5.4.2b WALL CHART

A wall chart with drawings may be used to present adjective agreement in Spanish.

(*The boy is tall/short/fat/good.*)
(*The girl is tall/short/fat/good.*)

5.4.2c CLOTH BOARD

The object of the lesson is to teach the dative case with location (German). The teacher cuts out pieces of flocking paper and draws or pastes the following pictures on them: a cat, a car, and a garage.

 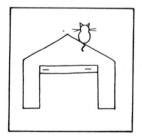

As the cat is placed in various positions on the flannel board, the teacher says:

Die Katze ist $\begin{Bmatrix} \text{auf} \\ \text{vor} \\ \text{hinter} \\ \text{in} \end{Bmatrix}$ dem Wagen.   *The cat is* $\begin{Bmatrix} on \\ in\ front\ of \\ in\ back\ of \\ in \end{Bmatrix}$ *the car.*

Die Katze ist $\begin{Bmatrix} \text{auf} \\ \text{vor} \\ \text{hinter} \\ \text{in} \end{Bmatrix}$ der Garage.   *The cat is* $\begin{Bmatrix} on \\ in\ front\ of \\ in\ back\ of \\ in \end{Bmatrix}$ *the garage.*

5.4.2d OVERHEAD TRANSPARENCIES

(1) A single transparency prepared in advance: This transparency is used to teach Spanish verb endings, present and preterite. The present endings are in blue, the preterite in red.

Hoy	Ayer	*Today*	*Yesterday*
El come	El comió	*He eats*	*He ate*
El escribe	El escribió	*He writes*	*He wrote*
El bebe	El bebió	*He drinks*	*He drank*
El sale	El salió	*He leaves*	*He left*

(2) A prepared transparency with prepared overlays: This set of transparencies teaches the position of object pronouns in Spanish.

Basic Transparency:	El	lee.	*He reads*
Overlay #1:		lo	*it*
Overlay #2:		se	*to him/her/them*

(3) Strips of acetate above a paper grid: This technique can be used in teaching German word order. Take a piece of paper the size of a transparency. Cut four slits in it and place it on the overhead projector.

The slits serve as windows through which various words are made to appear. Then take four narrow acetate strips and print on them the list of words that could be used in each part of the sentence. The loose strips are placed on top of the windows and moved up and down to form a variety of possible sentences. From time to time the teacher may move the strips to different positions making certain that the verb always appears second.

Jetzt	trinkt	Inge	Milch	*Now*	*drinks*	*Inge*	*milk*
Später	bestellt	er	Kaffee	*Later*	*orders*	*he*	*coffee*
Morgen	bekommt	sie	Wasser	*Tomorrow*	*receives*	*she*	*water*
	kauft	Hans			*buys*	*Hans*	

(4) Writing on the overhead in front of the students: The teacher writes the sentence with the noun object, and the students dictate the sentence with the pronoun object.

1. J'ai acheté les fleurs. *I bought the flowers.*
   Je les ai achetées.   *I bought them.*
2. J'ai vu les dames.   *I saw the ladies.*
   Je les ai vues.   *I saw them.*
3. J'ai trouvé les stylos. *I found the pens.*
   Je les ai trouvés.   *I found them.*
4. J'ai perdu les cahiers. *I lost the notebooks.*
   Je les ai perdus.   *I lost them.*

5.4.2e   A PREPARED DITTO SHEET

(1) Each student receives the following sheet:

¡Dé el dinero a los niños!   *Give the money to the children!*
¡Déselo!   *Give it to them!*
¡Dé el retrato a la señora!   *Give the picture to the lady!*
¡Déselo!   *Give it to her!*
¡Dé el lápiz al estudiante!   *Give the pencil to the student!*
¡Déselo!   *Give it to him!*
¡Dé el chocolate a los chicos! *Give the chocolate to the children!*
¡Déselo!   *Give it to them!*

¡Dé la muñeca a la niña!   *Give the doll to the girl!*
¡Désela!   *Give it to her!*
¡Dé la carta al cartero!   *Give the letter to the mailman!*
¡Désela!   *Give it to him!*
¡Dé la propina a los criados!   *Give the tip to the servants!*
¡Désela!   *Give it to them!*
¡Dé la cartera al chico!   *Give the wallet to the boy!*
¡Désela!   *Give it to him!*

The student is asked to draw one line under the direct objects and two lines under the indirect objects, or he or she may underline the direct objects in purple and the indirect objects in orange.

(2) Two-Word Verbs

ESL students receive the following sheet:

Turn on the light.   Turn it on.
Turn off the water.   Turn it off.
Look up the address.   Look it up.
Find out the answer.   Find it out.

I woke John up.	
or	I woke him up.
I woke up John.	
I called Mary up.	
or	I called her up.
I called up Mary.	
I looked my friends up.	
or	I looked them up.
I looked up my friends.	

Students are asked to draw a box or circle around the direct objects in the left-hand column and do the same for the direct object pronouns in the right-hand column.

5.4.2f PROPS

To teach structures such as: "It's made of silk" and "It's a silk dress," the ESL teacher displays several different objects. After supplying the description for a few of the objects, he or she asks the class to use the new structure while identifying the rest.

Teacher	Class
It's made of pearls. It's a pearl necklace.	Repeat
It's made of leather. It's a leather belt.	Repeat
It's made of glass. It's made of plastic. It's made of silver. It's made of cotton. It's made of wool.	It's a glass ashtray. It's a plastic bag. It's a silver spoon. It's a cotton blouse. It's a wool sweater.

5.4.2g WORLD MAPS—PASSIVE SENTENCES

The teacher points to the United States and says: English is spoken in the United States. The class repeats. Then he or she points to other countries and teaches the vocabulary for each nation and language while keeping the passive structure *is spoken* constant, i.e., French is spoken in France, etc.

5.5 ORAL EXERCISES

Oral exercises help the students practice the new grammatical patterns that have been presented. Typically these exercises are conducted as full-class activity, with either choral or individual responses. Most language laboratory programs also contain oral exercises in which the students answer individually and then hear the correct confirmations. Many teachers are experimenting with oral exercises done in pairs or small groups: this type of classroom management allows students to participate more actively in the exercises.

5.5.1 Types of oral exercises

Christina Bratt Paulston classifies exercises or drills into three types: mechanical, meaningful, and communicative, as shown in the following figure.

Figure 3

PAULSTON'S CLASSIFICATION OF DRILLS[2]

	MECHANICAL DRILLS	MEANINGFUL DRILLS	COMMUNICATIVE DRILLS
Expected terminal behavior	Automatic use of manipulative patterns— formation of habits	Automatic use of manipulative patterns— formation of habits still working on habit formation	Normal speech for communication— free transfer of patterns to appropriate situations
Degree of Control	Complete	Less control but there is a "right answer" expected	No control of lexical items—some control of patterns. Answer cannot be anticipated
Learning process	Learning through instrumental conditioning by immediate reinforcement of correct response ANALOGY	Learning through instrumental conditioning by immediate reinforcement of correct response ANALOGY trial-and-error ANALYSIS	Problem solving ANALYSIS
Criteria for selecting response	Teacher	Teacher, situation, readings (knowledge common to the class)	Student himself (new information about real world)

[2] Christina Bratt Paulston and Mary Newton Bruder, *From Substitution to Substance: A Handbook of Structural Pattern Drills* (Rowley, Mass.: Newbury House, 1975), p. 9. Hereafter, this book is cited as *From Substitution to Substance*.

In the *mechanical drill* there is one correct answer and the student can often produce that answer mechanically without knowing what either the cue or the response means. Most traditional pattern drills fall into this category. In the *meaningful drill*, there is also a "right" answer expected, but the student must understand the cue in order to respond. Drills with visual cues and drills with situational context fall into this category. Finally, the *communicative drills* lead the student to use certain grammatical patterns without predicting a specific response.

5.5.2   Mechanical exercises: oral pattern drills

Traditionally the pattern drill is built on rapid oral cues. The teacher reads the stimulus or the tape gives it. The student then responds and the correct response is confirmed.

5.5.2a   KINDS OF PATTERN DRILLS

There are many types of mechanical pattern drills. Briefly, the principal kinds of drills are:

(1) Simple repetition
    Stimulus: Paul sees Mary.
    Response: Paul sees Mary.
(2) Simple substitution
    Stimulus: Paul sees Mary.   Alice.
    Response: Paul sees Alice.
(3) Multiple substitution
    Stimulus: Paul sees Mary.   David. Alice.
    Response: David sees Alice.
(4) Simple correlation
    Stimulus: Paul sees Mary.   Paul and David.
    Response: Paul and David see Mary.
(5) Multiple correlation
    Stimulus: He hurts himself.   They.
    Response: They hurt themselves.
(6) Transformation
    Stimulus: Paul sees Mary. (negative)
    Response: Paul doesn't see Mary.
(7) Joining sentences
    Stimulus: Paul sees Mary. Mary is waiting for a bus.
    Response: Paul sees Mary who is waiting for a bus.
(8) Rejoinder
    Model: Paul sees Mary. That's nice, but I don't see her.
    Stimulus: Paul sees David.
    Response: That's nice, but I don't see him.

(9) Expansion drill
    Stimulus: Paul is buying a house.   New.
    Response: Paul is buying a new house.
(10) Translation drill
    Stimulus: Paul needs Mary.
    Response: Paul a besoin de Mary.

For the teacher who is looking for new ideas for mechanical drills, there are books that contain only pattern drills.[3]

5.5.2b   USING PATTERN DRILLS IN THE CLASSROOM

The success of classroom language drills depends on their implementation. Nothing is deadlier than a difficult drill that bogs down because students are unable to respond quickly. The drill should either be simplified or dropped on the spot.

(1) Tape-cued drills: The teacher plays the tape recorder and points to individuals to respond.

(2) Teacher-cued drills: The teacher reads the cues and points to individuals to respond.

(3) Student-cued drills: A student is asked to prepare and lead a specific drill. This encourages student participation. Moreover, a student can lead a drill with half the class while the teacher is working with the other half.

(4) Working in pairs: One student reads the cue while the other student answers. At the end of the drill the roles are reversed. This method has the advantage of involving the entire class actively in the drill.

5.5.2c   USING DRILLS IN THE LANGUAGE LABORATORY

For suggestions on livening up drills in the language laboratory, see Section 3.3.3d.

5.5.3   Meaningful exercises: drills with visuals

Often drills can be made more meaningful to the students by the introduction of visuals.

5.5.3a   OVERHEAD PROJECTOR

The teacher prepares a transparency showing figures that represent all the subject pronouns:

---

[3] See for example, Mavis Beal, *French Language Drills* (New York: St. Martin's Press, 1967), and James Etmekjian, *Pattern Drills in Language Teaching* (New York: New York University Press, 1966). See also Paulston and Bruder, *From Substitution to Substance*.

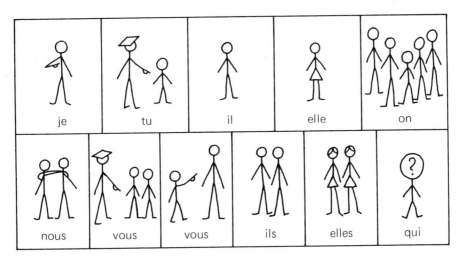

(*I/you/he/she/one*)
(*we/you/you/they/they/who*)

The teacher points to the boy in the transparency and says: *Il lit le livre* (*He reads the book.*) Then while the teacher points to each of the other figures in turn, the class gives the sentence with the various forms of the verb *lire: Je lis le livre. Nous lisons le livre. Vous lisez le livre* (*to read: I read the book. We read the book. You read the book*), and so on.

5.5.3b INDEX CARDS WITH PICTURES

Each index card contains a line drawing of a beverage: milk, water, beer, and so on. This drill is to practice the verb *to drink.*

Teacher: (Holds up a card.)
          Qu'est-ce que tu bois?   *What do you drink?*

Student: Je bois du lait.   *I drink milk.*

5.5.3c INDEX CARDS WITH SYMBOLS

Each index card contains a symbol.

The teacher gives a model sentence in the plural: *Ils font du ski* (*They go skiing*). Then he or she flashes a card with the drawing of one finger. The students say: *Il fait du ski* (*He goes skiing*). The teacher next flashes the card with the question mark. The students say: *Fait-il du ski?* (*Does he go skiing?*) Then he or she shows them the card with the drawing of plural fingers. The students say: *Font-ils du ski?* (*Do they go skiing?*) And then the card with the period. The students say: *Ils font du ski* (*They go skiing*). Finally, the teacher flashes the card with X, meaning negative. The students say: *Ils ne font pas de ski* (*They don't go skiing*).

5.5.3d THE USE OF INDEX CARDS WITH WORDS

The teacher prepares index cards containing German nouns in the nominative. The model sentence is *Ich sehe das Buch* (*I see the book*). The purpose of this pattern drill is to practice the definite article in the accusative case.

| Bleistift | Karte | Schule | Hut | *pencil/card/school/hat* |
| Lehrer | Tante | Mädchen | Rad | *teacher/aunt/girl/bike* |

As the first card appears, the students say: *Ich sehe den Bleistift* (*I see the pencil*). Next, *Ich sehe die Karte* (*I see the card*), and so on.

5.5.3e WALL CHARTS WITH PICTURES

The teacher displays a wall chart with the drawing of a body. The purpose is to practice *le duele. . .* (*it hurts him/her*). The teacher points rapidly to each part of the body and the class says: *Le duele la nariz. Le duele la mano. Le duelen los dedos* (*His/her nose hurts. His/her hand hurts. His/her fingers hurt*), and so on.

5.5.3f WALL CHARTS WITH WORDS

(1) The teacher displays a wall chart with columns containing the elements of the sentence. The teacher points to the words in the last column, and the students give the correct form of the sentence using that word.

| Jean va | au / à l' / à la | épicerie / école / bibliothèque / lac / boulangerie / église / cinéma / restaurant / maison / café | Jean goes to the | grocery store / school / library / lake / bakery / church / movies / restaurant / house / café |

For example, the teacher points to *école*. The students say: *Jean va à l'école* (*Jean goes to school*).

(2) Tag questions—ESL

The teacher forms a few sentences from the words in the following chart, e.g.:
She's going to work, isn't she? They're not going to work, are they? The students
then form many others.

He's		are you?
		aren't they?
I'm		are we?
	going to work,	am I?
She's		isn't he?
		are they?
They're		is he?
	not going to work,	aren't you?
We're		isn't she?
		aren't I?
You're		is she?
		aren't we?

5.5.3g PROPS

(1) The teacher displays a dish containing plastic fruit. He or she picks up one
fruit at a time and the class says: *Pásame la manzana. Pásame el plátano, las
uvas* (*Pass me the apple. Pass me the banana, the grapes*), and so on. The purpose of the drill is to practice the gender of the nouns.

(2) The teacher displays doll clothes. He or she holds up each article of clothing and the class says: *Je voudrais une robe verte. Je voudrais un pantalon noir*
(*I'd like a green dress. I'd like black trousers*), and so on. The purpose of this drill
is to give the students practice in placing the adjective after the noun.

5.5.4 Meaningful exercises: drills with situational context

Just as the students remember grammatical patterns better when they are presented in situational context, so too do they relate more effectively to meaningful
exercises. Drills with visuals obviously carry more meaning than drills with
abstract oral cues. In the drills that follow, the student must understand the
meaning of the cues in order to respond correctly.

5.5.4a CLASSROOM CONTEXT

In the following example, the French version drills direct object pronouns
while the English equivalent drills short answers.

1. Vous voyez les livres?   *Do you see the books?*
   Oui, je les vois.   *Yes, I do.*

2. Vous voyez la chaise?   *Do you see the chair?*
   Oui, je la vois.   *Yes, I do.*
3. Vous voyez l'éléphant?   *Do you see the elephant?*
   Non, je ne le vois pas.   *No, I don't.*

5.5.4b   ROLE-PLAY CONTEXT

Imagine that you are taking a driving lesson. Whenever the teacher tells you
to do something, you insist you are already doing it. Express your impatience.[4]

Start the car, please.   But I *am* starting the car.
Drive slowly, please.   But I *am* driving slowly.
Turn left, please.   But I *am* turning left.
Stay in the right lane, please.   But I *am* staying in the right lane.
Let that other car pass, please.   But I *am* letting that other car pass.
Drive carefully, please.   But I *am* driving carefully.

5.5.4c   IMAGINARY CONTEXT

Friedrich is packing for a vacation in Italy. He is taking summer clothing and
sports equipment, but nothing to remind him of school. Answer the questions
accordingly.

1. Nimmt er seine Bücher?   *Is he taking his books?*
   Nein, er nimmt sie nicht.   *No, he's not taking them.*
2. Und seine Badehose?   *And his swimming trunks?*
   Ja, er nimmt sie.   *Yes, he's taking them.*
3. Und sein Tennisschläger?   *And his tennis raquet?*
   Ja, er nimmt ihn.   *Yes, he's taking it.*

5.5.4d   FANTASY CONTEXT

L'ange et le démon: The angel and the devil.[5] The angel is telling Jean-Paul to
work hard. The devil is telling him to take it easy.

Cue: travailler   *work*
L'Ange: Travaille!   *Work!*
Le Démon: Ne travaille pas!   *Don't work!*
Cue: regarder la télé   *watch TV*
L'Ange: Ne regarde pas la télé!   *Don't watch TV!*
Le démon: Regarde la télé!   *Watch TV!*

In exercises of this sort, half the class can play one role, while the other half
plays the second role. Such exercises may also be done in groups of three students: one reads the cue, one is the angel and one is the devil.

[4] Adapted from Paul Pimsleur and Donald Berger, *Encounters: A Basic Reader* (New York: Harcourt
Brace Jovanovich, 1974), p. 72.
[5] Adapted from Jean-Paul Valette and Rebecca M. Valette, *French for Mastery*, Book One, p. 176.

5.5.5   Meaningful exercises: question-answer techniques

Question-answer techniques enable the students to practice points of grammar and structure by asking questions. The actual questions are often as closely structured as the stimulus lines in a pattern drill. The drill is artificial, in that the students are placed in a situation where they must give a specific response.

Yet, while the question-answer technique has all the qualities of a good pattern drill (intense oral practice, sequential presentation of new elements, and specific desired responses), it has one additional feature in its favor: student involvement.

When Bob goes through a series of drills, *He bought a hat, He bought a coat, He bought a jacket,* all the sentences seem irrelevant. After all, *he* didn't really buy all those things. The question-answer technique introduces an element of role-play, of student participation. For example, the teacher prepares index cards with pictures of items of clothing and distributes them to the students. Then the class is asked *What did Bob buy?* Bob holds up his card, and another student (or the entire class) replies: *He bought a jacket.*

5.5.5a   INDEX CARDS

The use of index cards is the simplest way to implement a question-answer drill. The teacher can walk around the room, holding up cards for all to see and having students exchange cards, thereby introducing an element of movement into the class.

The cards may contain symbols, line drawings, words, or initials. Students may be asked to bring blank index cards to class and prepare their own upon the instructions of the teacher.

(1)   Eliciting the negative

The teacher asks a student who holds a card labeled *math: Do you like English?* The pattern, given by the teacher in a model, requires the student to reply: *No, I don't like English. I like math.*

Students hold cards depicting pastimes. Two boys have cards showing a swimming pool.

Teacher: Are they going to the movies?
Student: No, they're not going to the movies. They're going swimming.

(2)   Change of tense

Students have cards depicting places.

Teacher: Are you going downtown today?
Student: No, I went downtown yesterday.

(3)   Object pronouns

Students have cards depicting objects.

Teacher: Sue, give Jane the record.
              (Student carries out the action.)
Teacher: What did you do with the record, Sue?
Student: I gave it to Jane.

5.5.5b   GROUPING

Roles, or "tags," may be assigned to entire groups. For example, whatever the boys plan to do, the girls will do tomorrow. The boys are given cards depicting sports.

Teacher: What are you doing this afternoon, Jim?
Jim: I'm going to play baseball.
Teacher: And you, girls?
Girls: We're going to play baseball tomorrow.

5.5.5c   DIRECTED DIALOG

The use of groups or cards may also furnish cues for directed dialogue.

Teacher: Jonathan, ask Sally what she's drinking.
Jonathan: Sally, what are you drinking?
Sally: (According to her card.)
           I'm drinking lemonade.

5.5.5d   CHAIN DRILL

The chain drill may also be adapted to the question-answer technique. In the above example, Sally would then turn to her neighbor and ask: What are you drinking?

5.5.5e   MATHEMATICS PROBLEMS: USE OF AGO

The ESL teacher makes statements using dates. The students tell how long ago it happened.

Teacher: Peter has been working here since 1968. When did he start?
Class: [Nine] years ago.
Teacher: John has been playing the piano since 1970. When did he start?
Class: [Seven] years ago.
Teacher: World War II ended in 1945. How long ago was that?
Class: [32] years ago.

5.5.6 Communicative exercises

When the teacher feels that the students can handle a grammatical structure and the vocabulary well in controlled exercises, it is appropriate to introduce communicative activities. In activities of this sort, the students use the language they have mastered to express their own thoughts. Although the situation is structured, the specific student responses cannot be predicted.

5.5.6a PERSONAL QUESTIONS

The teacher asks the students questions using the structures under study. For example: *How many brothers and sisters do you have? How old are they? Do they live at home with you?* The responses of students in the class can be used for further practice: *How many brothers does Maria have? How old are they? Do they live at home?*

5.5.6b SMALL GROUP DISCUSSIONS

The teacher divides the class into small groups and distributes questions for discussion. For beginning students these discussions can be closely structured: Find out how many brothers and sisters each member of the group has. What are their ages? Where do they live? Be prepared to introduce one of the members of your group to the rest of the class.

Further suggestions for small-group communication activities are given in Section 9.6.

5.6 WRITTEN EXERCISES

Students must be given the opportunity to practice new structures in written form as well as orally. Writing, however, is primarily an individual activity, whereas speaking requires two or more people. Written exercises lend themselves well to homework, while spoken exercises are more effectively carried out in the classroom. The following section gives some suggestions for activities designed to develop written control of structures.

5.6.1 Types of written exercises

5.6.1a COPYING

Students copy material from a model. A variation of this activity is unscrambling sentences and rewriting them in logical order. Matching exercises may be developed where the student writes the appropriate caption, selected from among several given possibilities, under each of a group of pictures. Students may also play "Who said what" by selecting a statement and placing it next to the picture of the person who most likely made it.

5.6.1b   DRILLS

Students write the responses to drills. The model may be written on the board, and the teacher may dictate the stimulus sentences. The drills may also be typed on ditto masters.

5.6.1c   QUESTION-ANSWER TECHNIQUE

The students write the answers to the teacher's questions instead of giving them orally.

5.6.1d   DICTATION

The teacher dictates familiar or unfamiliar material to the class. (For examples, see Section 11.3.)

5.6.1e   COMPLETION EXERCISES

The student completes a written phrase by filling in blanks or adding a new word to the sentence.

5.6.1f   GRAMMAR COMPOSITIONS

The students, individually or in small groups, write brief compositions incorporating several examples of a specific grammar point: verb tenses, descriptive adjectives, relative clauses, and so on. For example, students may write about weekend plans (using the future), or they may use the conditional to complete a paragraph beginning with *Si j'étais président* (*If I were president*).

5.6.2   Techniques for utilizing written exercises in the classroom

5.6.2a   INDEPENDENT WORK

Any written exercise which is self-contained, that is, which is based solely on written instructions, may be assigned as independent work. The teacher may wish to let students talk quietly together and help each other with the work.

Written exercises that are correlated with a tape program may be used in the language laboratory. If the recorded material is on cassettes, and if the classroom is equipped with cassette recorders, the students may work individually in the classroom. A group of students may work on this type of exercise together if the classroom has a tape recorder with several headsets.

5.6.2b TEACHER-LED WORK

The teacher can work with a group of students or with the entire class in directing written exercises.

(1) Using the chalkboard: Some students may be asked to put the written work on the chalkboard. The teacher corrects these sentences with the help of the other students while those at their seats correct their own work.

(2) Using the overhead: One student may be given an acetate sheet and a grease pencil. He or she does the written work, a dictation for example, on the transparency. The rest of the class writes the sentences on paper. At the end of the exercise, the transparency is projected on the overhead. The teacher corrects the work and answers questions.

Variation 1: A student may write at the overhead with the light turned on, so that others may immediately see what he or she is doing.

Variation 2: The teacher may prepare a transparency with blanks to be filled in. As the students give the correct answers, the teacher fills in the blanks on the transparency with a grease pencil. A similar ditto is then handed out for homework.

Variation 3: The teacher gives the oral cue to a pattern drill or a question-answer exercise. The students give the oral response and the teacher writes it on the lighted overhead. Students copy the correct written response.

5.6.3 Techniques for correcting written exercises in the classroom

The techniques suggested for correcting homework may be used for correcting written exercises (see Section 3.5.3).

5.7 REMEDIAL WORK

With intermediate and advanced classes the teacher is faced with the problem of remedial work. There are always some students who continually make mistakes with noun-adjective agreements. Others have trouble with irregular verbs, or even regular verbs.

5.7.1 Whole-class technique

Announce the "Error of the Week," for example, subject-verb agreement. When correcting written work that week, the teacher deducts one point for each error, *except* errors in subject-verb agreement, which cost the student five points.

5.7.2 Individualized techniques

Each student is given a personal error to correct over a two- or three-week period. Small groups of students may be allowed to work on the same error.

5.7.2a POSTER

The student makes a poster to illustrate the structure he or she is having difficulty with. These posters may be put up in the classroom. The teacher may also wish to use them with other classes.

5.7.2b DITTOS

Students prepare ditto masters on their errors, perhaps illustrating the correct form with a drawing or cartoon. They may wish to write five or six exercises based on that point of grammar. The teacher will check the ditto masters for accuracy and then let the students run off copies for their classmates. The students give out the dittos to the whole class (or part of the class), and then correct their answers.

5.7.2c TUTORING

The student is asked to tutor a beginning student on his or her particular difficulty. He or she prepares a short test (approved by the teacher). This is given to the tutee when the latter has mastered the structure.

5.7.2d CORRECTING PAPERS

The student corrects exercises for the teacher on the grammar point with which he or she has difficulty. These may be exercises done by a beginning class.

5.7.2e TEACHING

The student prepares a mini-lesson on the grammar point and teaches it to another class or to a group of students. This mini-lesson might also be the joint project of two or three students.

outline

six
Teaching Grammar: Techniques Arranged by Grammatical Categories

This chapter offers a range of techniques for teaching specific elements of grammar. Each technique makes use of media: flash cards, felt board, magnet board, pocket chart, overhead projector, or opaque projector. Games, songs, and crossword puzzles are also included.

The catalog of suggested techniques is far from exhaustive; it is merely illustrative. It is hoped that the teacher will be inspired to apply some of these suggestions to other grammatical problems—that he or she will begin experimenting with a variety of activities and eventually invent new approaches or new variations to old approaches. In other words, the teaching of grammar will cease to be a "grind" and will rather become a challenge to the teacher to express his or her creativity.

In presenting grammar, the teacher should strive to develop meaningful contexts. Once the students have practiced the new forms in a structured format, they should be immediately encouraged to use these forms in communication activities (see Chapters 8 through 11).

6.1 NOUN PHRASES

Noun phrases include nouns as well as determiners (definite, indefinite, and partitive articles, possessive and demonstrative adjectives, expressions of quantity), descriptive adjectives, and adverbs used as intensifiers.

6.1.1 Noun-adjective agreement

6.1.1a COLOR CARDS PLUS WALL CHART

For a French class, for example, prepare a wall chart with line drawings of articles of clothing. The articles of clothing of masculine gender are outlined in blue, while those of feminine gender are outlined in red. Next prepare a stack of

4 × 6 index cards with a colored square in the center of each. For the colors given below add a red superscript on the card: green (*vert*): /t/; white (*blanc*): /ʃ/; gray (*gris*): /z/. The cards for red, blue, yellow, orange, black, brown (*marron*) have no superscripts.

Review the articles of clothing with questions like: *Qu'est-ce que c'est? C'est une jupe (What is it? It's a skirt)*. Then review the names of the colors with the flash cards. Next hold the red card next to the pants and ask: *De quelle couleur est le pantalon? (What color are the trousers?)* Model the response: *Il est rouge (They're red)*. With the card next to a shirt ask: *De quelle couleur est la chemise? (What color is the shirt?)* Model the response: *Elle est rouge (It's red)*. Then vary the questions, using all the cards without superscripts.

When the students can alternate freely between responses with *Il est...* and *Elle est...*, select a card with a superscript, for example, the green card, hold it next to a masculine article of clothing, and ask: *De quelle couleur est le manteau? (What color is the coat?)* Give the answer: *Il est vert (It's green)*. Then ask the class to listen carefully as you say: *De quelle couleur est la robe? Elle est verte (What color is the dress? It's green)*.

Go from one drawing to the next saying: *La jupe est verte. Le pantalon est vert (The skirt is green. The trousers are green)*. The students notice, or the teacher points out, that the red *t* on the green card means that the *t* sound must be pronounced when the adjective modifies a feminine noun (outlined in red on the chart).

Holding up the gray card, he or she asks: *De quelle couleur est la cravate? (What color is the tie?)* Generally the students can give the correct reply: *Elle est grise (It's gray)*, for they notice the /z/ on the gray card.

In a subsequent lesson the students learn how to spell the adjective forms and see the correspondence between the sound /z/, for example, and the spelling "se."

6.1.1b   PIECES OF PAPER

Have the girls in the Spanish class write an A on a piece of paper. Have the boys write an O. Divide the class into two groups, México and Norteamérica. When asked their nationality, the girls answer: *Soy mexicana* or *Soy norteamericana*. Boys give the masculine form. By bringing two boys from the same country together, the teacher can drill *Son mexicanos*. A variety of questions may be asked of the students; for example, *Are you North American? Is María Mexican? Ask Joe if he is North American. Are Pablo and Teresa Mexican? Ask Inez and Carlita if they are North American*. At the end of this oral practice, the students can easily develop the generalization that masculine adjectives end in -*o* and form a plural in -*os* and that the equivalent feminine forms end in -*a* and -*as*.

6.1.2 Definite articles

6.1.2a POSTER

Speakers of French, Spanish, and German use the definite article for parts of the body; speakers of English use the possessive adjective. Draw a picture of a body on the chalkboard.

The teacher points to each part of the body and says:

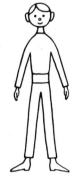

*Jacques s'est cassé la jambe,
   le pied, la tête,* and so on.
*Juan se rompió la pierna,
   el pie, la cabeza,* and so on.

*Jim broke his leg
/ his foot / his head.*

Once the class has mastered the structure, individuals can mimic accidents. Classmates will ask: *Did you break your leg?* and so on. The victim will give an appropriate reply.

6.1.2b OVERHEAD TRANSPARENCY

ESL students learn to use *the* to identify a person or thing just mentioned.[1] They study the examples in Columns I and II, and then compose sentences for the blank spaces in Column II.

I	II
First mention	**Second mention**
I see some boys and girls.	The boys are playing baseball.
I have a pen and a pencil.	The pencil is broken.
There is a dog and a cat in the yard.	
His friend has a Buick and a VW.	
Mr. Smith goes to plays and movies.	

When the students have understood the use of *the,* the class is divided into small groups. Each group is given an illustrated magazine. One student makes a comment about a picture or an advertisement, using an indefinite article. Each of the

---

[1] Jean Praninskas, *Rapid Review of English Grammar* (Englewood Cliffs, N.J.: Prentice-Hall, Inc., 1959) pp. 56–63 (hereafter cited as *Review of English Grammar*).

other students in the group makes an additional statement using the definite article.

6.1.2c   PROPS

The teacher gives each member of the ESL class several objects of the same kind; for example, José receives 4 pencils; Pierre, 5 rulers; Ahmed, 3 magazines; Chang, 6 paperclips; Hiroshi, 3 books, etc.

Teacher: Ahmed, ask José for *the* red pencil.
Ahmed: José, may I have the red pencil?
          (José gives Ahmed the red pencil).
Teacher: José, to whom are you giving *the* other pencils?
José: I'm giving *the* other pencils to Pierre.
          (He does so.)

One by one the students ask for an object, e.g., *the* big paperclip, *the* long ruler, *the* green book, *the* thick magazine, etc. The person addressed complies, and then states to whom he or she is giving the remainder of his or her objects.[2]

6.1.3   Possessive adjectives

6.1.3a   ARTICLES OF CLOTHING

Teach some of the articles of clothing and all of the colors. Say while pointing to your own skirt: *Ma jupe est bleue. Mi falda es azul (My skirt is blue).* The class repeats several times. Then ask individuals: *De quelle couleur est votre jupe? ¿De qué color es su falda? (What color is your skirt?)*

The French examples might be all feminine at first. After a time introduce the masculine form *mon. Ma chemise, ma ceinture, ma jupe, ma cravate; mon pantalon, mon sac, mon pull (My shirt, my belt, my skirt, my tie; my trousers, my pocketbook, my sweater),* and so on.

Plural forms are presented the same way: *Mes chaussures sont noires. De quelle couleur sont vos chaussures? Mis zapatos son negros. ¿De qué color son sus zapatos? (My shoes are black. What color are your shoes?)*

After these forms are mastered, the students could be directed to ask one another the same question. This will require using the familiar forms: *De quelle couleur est ton pull? Mon pull est vert. ¿De qué color son tus zapatos? Mis zapatos son negros (What color is your sweater? My sweater is green. What color are your shoes? My shoes are black.)*

---

[2] Suggested by Sheila Murphy, instructor of ESL at The Ohio State University.

6.1.3b CLASSROOM OBJECTS

English-speaking students confuse the different forms of possessive adjectives in French and German because English uses fewer forms. For practice in the comprehension of the forms corresponding to *my*, *his*, and *your*, the teacher asks individuals to hand objects to one another: *Jean, donnez votre crayon à Pierre. Marc, donnez à Hélène son crayon. Marie, donnez mon crayon à Paulette. Hans, gib Fritz deinen Bleistift! Inge, gib Georg seinen Bleistift! Heinz, gib Karl meinen Bleistift!* (*Jean, give your pencil to Pierre. Marc, give Helen her pencil. Marie, give my pencil to Paulette. Hans, give Fritz your pencil! Inge, give Georg his pencil! Heinz, give Karl my pencil!*)

6.1.4 Demonstrative adjectives

Place objects on the desk in front of you: a green book, a black notebook, a white pencil. Draw on the chalkboard a stick figure of a short boy and a tall boy.

In the back of the room there are objects on a window sill or table: a red book, a blue notebook, a green pencil, a tall boy and a short boy (stick-figure pictures).

While pointing to objects near and far from you, say:

1. Ce livre-ci est vert.	*This book is green.*
Ce livre-là est rouge.	*That book is red.*
2. Ce cahier-ci est noir.	*This notebook is black.*
Ce cahier-là est bleu.	*That notebook is blue.*
3. Ce crayon-ci est blanc.	*This pencil is white.*
Ce crayon-là est vert.	*That pencil is green.*
4. Ce garçon-ci est petit.	*This boy is short.*
Ce garçon-là est grand.	*That boy is tall.*
5. Ce garçon-ci est grand.	*This boy is tall.*
Ce garçon-là est petit.	*That boy is short.*

After these forms are mastered, do the same thing with feminine objects. Draw on the front board a white rose, a yellow apple, a tall girl and a thin girl. Draw on the back board a yellow rose, a red apple, a little girl, and a stout girl.

1. Cette rose-ci est blanche.	*This rose is white.*
Cette rose-là est jaune.	*That rose is yellow.*
2. Cette pomme-ci est jaune.	*This apple is yellow.*
Cette pomme-là est rouge.	*That apple is red.*
3. Cette fille-ci est grande.	*This girl is tall.*
Cette-fille-là est petite.	*That girl is short.*
4. Cette fille-ci est mince.	*This girl is slender.*
Cette fille-là est grosse.	*That girl is fat.*

As a follow-up activity, have each student prepare two statements about objects in the classroom using *this* and *that*. The statements may be true or false. The others in the class determine which are accurate and which are not.

6.1.5   Partitive articles

6.1.5a   PROPS

Use one candy bar and index cards with the following pictures:

The teacher first shows the students the cards on the left while giving the question and the answer: *Qu'est-ce que vous aimez? J'aime le lait, le sucre, le pain, le beurre, la salade, la viande, la glace, l'eau (What do you like? I like milk, sugar, bread, butter, salad, meat, ice cream, water)*. The students then answer the questions individually.

After the genders have been mastered, the teacher shows the cards on the right while giving the question and answer: *Qu'est-ce que vous voulez? Je voudrais du lait, du sucre, du pain, du beurre, de la salade* (*What do you want? I would like milk, sugar, bread, butter, salad*), and so on.

The teacher holds up the candy bar and says: *Aimez-vous le chocolat? Oui, j'aime le chocolat* (*Do you like chocolate? Yes, I like chocolate*). Then he or she breaks off a piece and asks individuals: *Voulez-vous du chocolat?* (*Do you want some chocolate?*) Individual students respond: *Oui, je voudrais du chocolat* (*Yes, I would like some chocolate*).

6.1.5b   CARDS

Place the cards (p. 120) on the chalk ledge. The ESL students ask the teacher to hand them the cards, saying each time, "I'd like some . . ., or I'd like a cup, a bottle, a piece, a dish of . . . ."

6.1.6   Possessive pronouns

6.1.6a   WALL CHART

The teacher displays a wall chart or a transparency depicting many objects of different genders. He or she points to a house and says: *Es para mí* (*It's for me*). Then the teacher says: *Es mía. Es para Juan. Es suya. Es para nosotros. Es nuestra. Es para ti. Es tuya.* (*It's mine. It's for Juan. It's his. It's for us. It's ours. It's for you. It's yours.*) This is done likewise for the masculine forms.

6.1.6b   GAME: BASEBALL

The teacher divides the class into two teams: *Los Rojos* (*The Reds*) and *Los Blancos* (*The Whites*). There are two baseball diamonds on the board—one for each team.

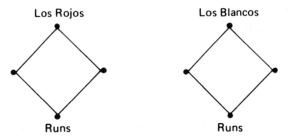

The teacher points to a picture of a hat on the chart (or transparency) and says: *Es para mí* (*It's for me*). Then he or she points to a student on *Los Rojos* team. If the student says *Es mío* (*It's mine*), he or she advances to first base, and the teacher indicates this on the diamond by making a mark with red chalk along the side of the first base. Then the other team has a chance. No one advances if there is a wrong answer.

Runs are scored after a team gets four correct answers, thus arriving at home base. The team having the largest number of runs wins.

6.1.7 Demonstrative pronouns

Index cards, spread along the chalkboard, contain line drawings of people in different colored clothing.

Teacher:	Regardez ces jeunes filles. Qui est la plus grande? (Points to one.)	*Look at these girls. Which is the tallest?*
	Celle en rouge.	*The one in red.*
Class:	Celle en rouge (several times).	*The one in red.*
Teacher:	Qui est la plus petite?	*Who is the smallest?*
Student:	Celle en bleu.	*The one in blue.*
Teacher:	Qui est la plus jolie?	*Who is the prettiest?*
Student:	Celle en vert.	*The one in green.*

The next set of pictures is of boys or men.

Teacher:	(Gives both question and answer. Class repeats.)	
	Qui est le plus grand?	*Who is the tallest?*
	Celui en bleu.	*The one in blue.*
	Qui est le plus beau?	*Who is the most handsome?*
Student:	Celui en vert.	*The one in green.*
Teacher:	Qui est le plus fort?	*Who is the strongest?*
Student:	Celui en noir.	*The one in black.*

6.1.8 Pronouns of negation

The ESL teacher leads the class in a pattern drill to practice changing *nothing* to *not . . . anything* and *no one* to *not . . . anyone.*

Teacher	Class
I'm buying nothing.	I'm not buying anything.
I'm selling nothing.	I'm not selling anything.
I'm doing nothing.	I'm not doing anything.
I'm receiving nothing.	I'm not receiving anything.

She's seeing no one.	She's not seeing anyone.
He's writing to no one.	He's not writing to anyone.
We're giving to no one.	We're not giving to anyone.
They're helping no one.	They're not helping anyone.

When the class is familiar with the pattern, each student prepares two sentences, one with *nothing* and one with *no one*. These statements are the point of departure for a longer exchange:

Paul (reads):	I'm doing nothing.
Teacher:	What did Paul say?
Mary:	He said he's doing nothing.
Teacher (to Bob):	And what about Barbara?
Bob:	Barbara, are you doing anything?
Barbara:	No, I'm not. I'm not doing anything.
or:	Yes, I am. I'm studying.

6.2   VERB FORMS

This section suggests techniques for teaching verb forms and the use of various tenses. Some of the suggestions focus on a rather mechanical manipulation of the new verb forms. Such mechanical exercises should always be followed with more meaningful activities, such as personal questions, original impromptu skits, or small-group conversations based on the new material.

6.2.1   Subject-verb agreement

6.2.1a   OVERHEAD TRANSPARENCY

Draw the stick figures on page 124 on a transparency. Write the pronouns themselves on an overlay, so that they will fall below the figures.

First it may be necessary to clarify the use of the symbols. Put the basic transparency (stick figures minus the words) on the overhead and explain the pronouns. With seventh graders, the concept of personal pronouns might have to be explained in the native language: *The first figure is talking about himself. What pronoun do you use when you talk about yourself?* (*I*). *In German you say* ich. After having presented the pronouns, the teacher can practice them rapidly, pointing to one and having the students give the German equivalent. Finally the overlay may be placed on the overhead so that the students see how the pronouns are spelled.

| ich | du | Sie | er | sie |
| wir | ihr | Sie | sie | sie |

(I / you / you / he / she)
(We / you / you / they / they)

The transparency may also be used from time to time in order to provide cues for verb drills:

Teacher:	Ich gehe in die Stadt.	*I'm going to the city.*
	(Points to *er* [*he*])	
Student:	Er geht in die Stadt.	*He's going to the city.*

6.2.1b LARGE SYMBOLS

The teacher prepares symbols, on 8½″ × 11″ pieces of cardboard, to represent the known verbs:

| aimer | détester | compter | travailler | habiter |
| *to love* | *to detest* | *to count* | *to work* | *to live* |

Five students, each holding up a symbol, come to the front of the class. The teacher has a deck of index cards containing each of the pronoun symbols that have been presented up to that time. He or she holds a pronoun symbol over the head of the student holding the verb card. The class responds appropriately: *Tu travailles. Il compte (You work. He counts).* Short complements should be included for the transitive verbs: *Nous aimons Paris. Nous détestons Paul. J'habite ici (We love Paris. We detest Paul. I live here.)*

6.2.1c FLASH CARDS

The teacher prepares flash cards with infinitives: *entrar, estudiar, hablar, esperar* (*to enter, to study, to speak, to hope*). He or she holds up a card and announces a pronoun. The students give the appropriate verb form.

6.2.1d MAGNETIC BOARD

ESL students have a tendency to omit the verb *to be* in present progressive sentences. The teacher places the following cards in random order on the blackboard with magnets:

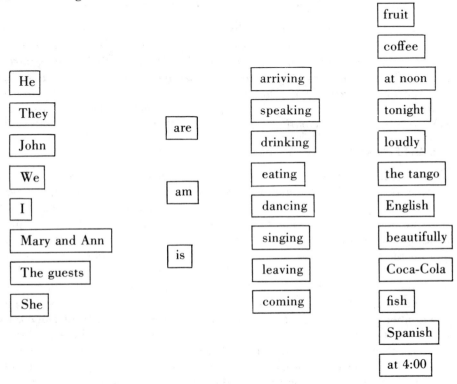

Students go to the board and form correct and meaningful sentences. Then they read aloud what they have composed.

6.2.1e CUE CARDS

The teacher prepares enough cue cards for the entire class. These cards have pictures: a football, a basketball, a baseball, a ping-pong paddle, a volleyball. The cards are distributed and the nouns are reviewed.

Teacher:	A quoi joues-tu?	*What are you playing?*
Student:	Je joue au football.	*I'm playing football.*
Teacher:	Marie et Pierre, à quoi jouez-vous?	*Marie and Peter, what are you playing?*
Student:	Nous jouons au volley-ball.	*We're playing volleyball.*
Teacher:	Et Robert, à quoi joue-t-il?	*And Robert, what is he playing?*
Student:	Il joue au ping-pong.	*He is playing ping-pong.*

This type of conversation drill of verbs is often very effective. The same pictures may also be used to elicit sentences of the type: *J'aime le football. Je déteste le basketball. Je fais souvent du baseball. Hier j'ai joué au football. J'aime faire du volleyball. Je n'aime pas le baseball. Je n'aime pas faire du basketball. Je ferai du volleyball demain* (*I like football. I detest basketball. I often play baseball. Yesterday I played football. I like to play volleyball. I don't like baseball. I don't like to play basketball. I'll play volleyball tomorrow.*)

6.2.1f   GAME: A RELAY RACE

Eight students go to the chalkboard. Each stands under a pronoun: *elles, tu, vous, je, il, nous, ils, elle* (*they, you, you, I, he, we, they, she*). At a given signal each writes a sentence with *être* (*to be*) in the *passé composé*, starting with the pronoun above. As each individual finishes a sentence, he or she moves to the next pronoun and writes a sentence using it. All students keep rotating. The student at the far right of the board takes the place of the student at the far left. After three or four minutes, the teacher says *Halte!* (*Stop!*) and all sit down. Then the teacher, with the help of the class, counts the correct sentences. To add to the excitement, two teams could play, perhaps the boys against the girls.

Variation: All eight students are assigned the same verb and the same tense, for example, *se lever* (*to get up*) in the *passé composé*. The teacher signals *Commencez!* (*Begin!*) and the students each write a sentence. As soon as they are finished, they move to the left and write another sentence. When the teacher calls *Halte!* all sit down, and the number of correct sentences are counted.

6.2.2   Present to past

6.2.2a   CALENDAR

The teacher points to a calendar and says: *Aujourd'hui Paul dîne à sept heures. Hier il a dîné à six heures. Hier, moi, j'ai dîné à six heures et demie* (*Today Paul has dinner at 7:00. Yesterday he had dinner at 6:00. Yesterday, I had dinner at 6:30*).

Then the teacher asks each person: *A quelle heure avez-vous dîné hier?* (*At what time did you have dinner yesterday?*) Individual students respond: *Hier, j'ai dîné à six heures* (*Yesterday, I had dinner at 6:00*), and so on.

6.2.2b CROSSWORD PUZZLE

Change all verbs to the preterite. Then use the "mystery" word in an original sentence.

1. llegan			¹L	L	E	G	A	R	O	N
2. lava				²L	A	V	O	
3. entro	³E	N	T	R	E			
4. ven				⁴V	I	E	R	O	N
5. hablo			⁵H	A	B	L	E	
6. niegan	⁶N	E	G	A	R	O	N	
7. rompe			⁷R	O	M	P	I	O
8. anda			⁸A	N	D	U	V	O

6.2.3 *Passé composé* with *être*

6.2.3a LA PETITE HISTOIRE TRAGIQUE DE JACQUES (JIM'S SAD LITTLE STORY)

Verbs that do not connote motion to or from can be presented by having students memorize: *Jacques est né. Jacques est tombé. Jacques est mort* (*Jim was born. Jim fell. Jim died*).

6.2.3b   WALL CHART OR TRANSPARENCY OF TWO HOUSES

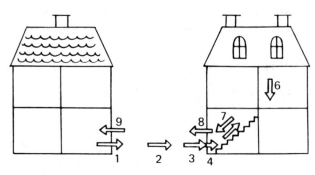

Teacher says while class repeats:

1. Je suis sorti(e) de chez moi.   *I went out of my house.*
2. Je suis allé(e) chez ma grand-   *I went to my grandmother's.*
   mère.
3. Je suis arrivé(e) chez elle.   *I arrived at her house.*
4. Je suis entré(e) dans la maison.   *I entered the house.*
5. Je suis monté(e) au premier   *I went up to the second floor.*
   étage.
6. Je suis resté(e) une heure dans   *I stayed in my grandmother's room*
   la chambre de ma grand-mère.   *one hour.*
7. Je suis descendu(e).   *I went downstairs.*
8. Je suis parti(e).   *I left.*
9. Je suis rentré(e) chez moi.   *I went back to my house.*

When the class is familiar with the sentences, the teacher randomly points to a number and individual students respond.

When the class can control the *passé composé (compound past)*, with the subject *je (I)*, other subject pronouns can be introduced.

Variation: An overlay can be prepared that places the written infinitive next to each number on the basic transparency.

6.2.4   Imperfect versus preterite (or *passé composé*)

6.2.4a   OVERHEAD PROJECTOR

Each transparency has a second one hinged to it so it can be used as an overlay.

The first transparency is of María talking on the phone. The overlay is of her mother entering the room.

Teacher: (showing first transparency)
           María hablaba por teléfono   *María was talking on the phone*
           (adding second transparency)
           cuando su mamá entró.   *when her mother entered.*

Other sentences that lend themselves to similar presentation are: *La mamá preparaba la cena cuando el teléfono sonó. Merendaban cuando empezó a llover.* (*Mother was preparing the meal when the telephone rang. They were having a picnic when it began to rain.*)

6.2.4b CHALKBOARD

Ask a student to stand at the chalkboard holding a piece of chalk high above the ledge. The eraser becomes a train and is moved by the teacher along the chalkboard ledge.

Teacher:	Le train allait à Paris	*The train was going to Paris*
	(continues to move eraser)	
	quand une bombe est tombée	*when a bomb fell on top of it!*
	dessus!	

Student:	(Drops chalk.)

6.2.4c FLASH CARDS

Make flash cards of different actions: boy eating, drinking, reading, writing, and so on. As each card is flashed, the students say: *El comía cuando su mamá llegó. El escribía cuando su mamá llegó. Il mangeait quand sa mère est entrée. Il buvait quand sa mère est entrée.* (*He was eating when his mother arrived. He was writing when his mother arrived. He was eating when his mother entered. He was drinking when his mother entered.*)

6.2.5 Subjunctive

6.2.5a WALL CHARTS OR TRANSPARENCIES

A series of visuals could be used to depict two actions: the first a child behaving in a certain way, and the second, his mother wanting him or her to behave in another way. These could be on wall charts or transparencies with overlays. Teacher points to each visual and says: *Marie ne fait pas la vaisselle. La maman veut que Marie fasse la vaisselle. Le bébé ne dort pas. La maman veut que le bébé dorme. Marc ne va pas chez le dentiste. La maman veut que Marc aille chez le dentiste.* (*Marie is not doing the dishes. Her mother wants her to do the dishes. The baby isn't sleeping. The mother wants the baby to sleep. Marc isn't going to the dentist's. His mother wants him to go to the dentist's.*)

6.2.5b DIRECTED DIALOG GAME

Teacher:	María ¿qué quieres que Juan haga?	*María, what do you want Juan do do?*
María:	Quiero que Juan vaya a la puerta.	*I want Juan to go to the door.*

(Juan must execute this order.)

Teacher:	Carlos, ¿qué quieres que Pablo haga?	*Carlos, what do you want Pablo to do?*
Carlos:	Quiero que Pablo escriba su nombre en la pizarra.	*I want Pablo to write his name on the blackboard.*

(Pablo executes the order.)

Teacher:	Ricardo, ¿qué quieres que Carmen haga?	*Richard, what do you want Carmen to do?*
Ricardo:	Quiero que Carmen se levante.	*I want Carmen to stand up.*

(Carmen executes this order.)

6.2.5c FLASH-CARD DRILL

Teacher holds up a set of cards on which nouns and pronouns appear:

$\boxed{\text{él}}$ $\boxed{\text{tú}}$ $\boxed{\text{ellos}}$ $\boxed{\text{Juan y María}}$ *he / you / they / Juan and María*

The model sentence is *Quiero que ella venga conmigo* (*I want her to come with me*). The class responds chorally and then individually: *Quiero que él venga conmigo. Quiero que tú vengas conmigo. Quiero que ellos vengan conmigo. Quiero que Juan y María vengan conmigo* (*I want him to come with me. I want you to come with me. I want them to come with me. I want Juan and María to come with me*).
Variation: Use index cards with stick figures instead of words.

6.2.6 Conditional with *if*-clauses

6.2.6a GAME

The teacher distributes several slips of paper to each student. He or she then divides the class into two groups. On the separate slips of paper, one group writes only *si*-clauses in the imperfect tense with the subject pronoun *vous*. The other writes only independent clauses in the conditional with the subject pronoun *je*. The teacher writes an example on the board: *Si vous prépariez un repas, je ne le mangerais pas (If you prepared a meal, I wouldn't eat it)*. Then the teacher collects all the pieces of paper and puts them in two separate hats.

Several students are sent to the board and asked to take one of the pieces of paper from each hat. Then they proceed to copy the two clauses and make a sentence. The results can be hilarious. Such combinations as the following are not uncommon: *Si vous étiez le professeur, je vous donnerais une bonne fessée. Si vous étiez riche, je vous épouserais. (If you were the teacher, I would give you a good spanking. If you were rich, I would marry you.)*

The same game can be played in Spanish using the imperfect subjunctive: *Si Vd. fuera el profesor, yo le daría una bofetada. Si Vd. fuera rico, yo me casaría con Vd. (If you were the teacher, I would slap you. If you were rich, I would marry you.)*

A similar game can be played in German: *Wenn Sie Geld hätten, würde ich ein Buch schreiben. (If you had money, I would write a book.)*

6.2.7 *Say* vs. *tell*[3]

Distribute to each student a large card containing one of the following directions:

STOP, ENTER, PUSH, PULL, WALK, WATCH YOUR STEP, DRINK COCA COLA, EAT AT JOE'S, YIELD, RETURN BOOKS HERE, PAY FEES HERE

Then ask individuals, *What does your card say?* The students are to respond, *My card says to stop* (or *to enter, to push*, etc.). Following this drill, ask. *What does your card tell you to do?* The students respond, *My card tells me to stop*, etc.

6.2.7a PAST TENSE

Ask individuals to show their signs to the class and ask: *What did her sign say?* A student responds, *Her sign said to stop. What did his sign tell him to do? His sign told him to enter.*

6.2.7b NEGATIVE STRUCTURES

Distribute the following signs:

DO NOT ENTER, NO RIGHT TURN, NO LEFT TURN, etc.

Teacher: What does your sign tell you to do?

Student: My sign tells me not to turn right.

[3] Suggested by Patrick Roberts, TESOL student at The Ohio State University.

6.3   COMPLEMENTS

This section deals with direct and indirect objects, prepositional phrases, infinitive clauses, relative clauses, and predicate adjectives.

6.3.1   Direct and indirect objects

6.3.1a   MAGAZINE PICTURES

The teacher cuts the following pictures out of magazines and pastes them on index cards: a book, a car, a glass of milk, a house, a loaf of bread, and so on. (Line drawings could also be used, if the teacher can draw.)

As the teacher flashes each card, he or she asks a question and answers it. The students first repeat the answer chorally and then individually.

Teacher:	(Shows picture of book.)	
	Was hat Karl gelesen?	*What did Charles read?*
	Karl hat das Buch gelesen.	*Charles read the book.*
Students:	Karl hat das Buch gelesen.	*Charles read the book.*
Teacher:	(Shows picture of bread.)	
	Was hat Inge gegessen?	*What did Inge eat?*
	Inge hat das Brot gegessen.	*Inge ate bread.*
Students:	Inge hat das Brot gegessen.	*Inge ate bread.*
Teacher:	(Shows picture of glass of milk.)	
	Was hat Helga getrunken?	*What did Elga drink?*
	Helga hat ein Glas Milch getrunken.	*Helga drank a glass of milk.*
Students:	Helga hat ein Glas Milch getrunken.	*Helga drank a glass of milk.*

6.3.1b   OVERHEAD TRANSPARENCY

On a transparency make a series of line drawings with a number alongside each.

The teacher says one of the numbers (from 1 to 10), and individual students respond with either *Je le vois, Je la vois,* or *Je les vois (I see it, I see them).* If he or she says *deux (two),* for example, the answer is *Je le vois (I see it).*

Variation: The first few times, the masculine nouns may be colored blue and the feminine nouns red. If washable ink is used, this color coding may be erased as the students become surer of the genders.

6.3.1c   INDEX CARDS

Draw figures of different people on index cards.

yo	tú	él	ella	nosotros
nosotras	usted	ustedes	ellos	ellas

(I / you / he / she / we)
(we / you / you / they / they)

As the teacher shows each card to the class, he or she uses the English model sentence *He gives it to*_____. If the card depicts the first person singular, the teacher says: *Me lo da* (*He gives it to me*). The class repeats chorally and then individually. The answers will be: *Te lo da. Se lo da. Nos lo da. Me lo da* (*He gives it to you. He gives it to her. He gives it to us. He gives it to me.*)

6.3.1d   SONG

The Spanish song, *"Me gustan todas,"* may be introduced to emphasize the position of indirect object pronouns:

Me gustan todas   (Repeat.)
Me gustan todas en general;
Pero esa rubia   (Repeat.)
Pero esa rubia me gusta más.

6.3.2   Prepositional phrases

6.3.2a   USE OF MAGNETIC BOARD

Most chalkboards are magnetized, especially in the newer school buildings. If not, a regular magnetic board is easily obtainable.

The teacher can cut out pictures from magazines (preferably foreign ones) of a railroad station, pastry shop, bakery, bookstore, restaurant, café, school, church, theater, and so on. He or she places each one on the chalkboard with a magnet. The object is to practice the forms of the preposition plus article.

The teacher points to each object and says: *Je vais au café, au restaurant, au cinéma, au musée, à la bibliothèque, à la boulangerie, à la gare, à l'école* (*I go to the café, restaurant, movies, museum, library, bakery, railroad station, school*), and so on. Then he or she asks individuals: *Où allez-vous?* (*Where are you going?* (Using the same pictures, the teacher can practice: *Je viens de....* (*I am coming from . . .*).

6.3.2b   USE OF CLOTH BOARD

(1) The teacher places on a cloth board photographs of famous landmarks, such as the Eiffel Tower, Big Ben, the statute of Don Quijote and Sancho Panza, the Statue of Liberty, Fujiyama, the Kremlin. (Good sources are *National Geographic* and *Holiday* magazines.)

These visuals can be used to teach *Je vais à Paris, à Londres, à New York, à Madrid; Je vais en France, en Angleterre, aux Etats-Unis, au Mexique, au Japon; Je viens de Paris, de Londres, de New York;* and *Je viens de France, d'Angleterre, des Etats-Unis.* (*I'm going to Paris, London, New York, Madrid;*

I'm going to France, England, the U.S.A., Mexico, Japan; I come from Paris, London, New York; I come from France, England, the U.S.A.)

The teacher asks questions: *Dans quelle ville allez-vous? Dans quel pays allez-vous? De quel pays venez-vous? De quelle ville venez-vous? (What city are you going to? What country are you going to? What country do you come from? What city do you come from?)*

(2) The ESL teacher places cars of different colors on the cloth board (construction paper cutouts with flocking paper or sensitized backing on each object.)[4] Then he or she describes the positions of the car and the class repeats. "The red car is on the left. The green car is on the right. The red car is passing the green car. (Move the car as you say this.) We drive on the right. We pass on the left."

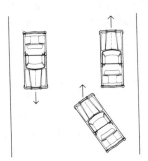

Then the teacher makes statements about the cars and individual students go to the cloth board and arrange the cars accordingly. Finally the students themselves explain how they are arranging the cars.

6.3.2c   PATTERN DRILL

The ESL students practice the following prepositional drill:

Teacher	Students
We went to California by car.	Repeat
train	We went to California by train.
plane	We went to California by plane.
ship	We went to California by ship.
bike	We went to California by bike.
foot	We went to California on foot.
a tour	We went to California on a tour.
horseback	We went to California on horseback.

Then divide the class into groups, giving each group a list of places. The students in each group have to agree on the best means of transportation for each of the places mentioned. For instance: "We are going to class on foot. We are going to Puerto Rico by plane. We are going to the beach by bike."

[4] Jean Praninskas, *Review of English Grammar*, p. 70.

6.3.2d CLASSROOM OBJECTS

The teacher can use a desk and a book to teach the use of the dative and the accusative with German prepositions such as *auf, unter* and *zwischen* (*on, under, between*).

The teacher picks up a book. *Ich habe ein rotes Buch* (*I have a red book*). He or she puts it on the table, saying: *Ich lege das Buch auf den Tisch* (*I lay the book on the table*), then steps back from the table and says: *Jetzt liegt das Buch auf dem Tisch* (*Now the book is lying on the table*).

Other objects may also be used. For example, the teacher shows the class some coins: *Ich habe viel Geld* (*I have a lot of money*). The teacher puts the money in his or her pocket, saying: *Ich stecke das Geld, in meine Tasche* (*I put the money in my pocket*). The teacher holds up his or her empty hands: *Wo ist das Geld? Es ist in meiner Tasche* (*Where is the money? It's in my pocket*).

6.3.3 Infinitive clauses

6.3.3a INDEX CARDS AND MAGNETIC BOARD

The teacher prepares index cards with the following pictures. The cards are then placed with magnets on a magnetic board or the chalkboard.

As the teacher points to each figure, he or she indicates the present, then the immediate future:

1. Jean mange maintenant.   *Jean is eating now.*
   Il va manger ce soir aussi.   *Jean is going to eat tonight also.*
2. Jean écoute la radio main-   *Jean is listening to the radio now.*
   tenant.
   Il va écouter la radio ce soir *Jean is going to listen to the radio*
   aussi.   *tonight also.*
3. Jean étudie maintenant.   *Jean is studying now.*
   Il va étudier ce soir aussi.   *Jean is going to study tonight also.*
4. Jean parle au téléphone main-   *Jean is talking on the telephone now.*
   tenant.
   Il va parler au téléphone ce soir *Jean is going to talk on the telephone*
   aussi.   *tonight also.*
5. Jean joue au tennis maintenant. *Jean is playing tennis now.*
   Il va jouer au tennis ce soir   *Jean is going to play tennis tonight*
   aussi.   *also.*

Then pointing to each of the cards in turn, the teacher asks individuals:

Qu'est-ce que Jean va faire ce soir?   *What is Jean going to do tonight?*

NOTE: All the infinitives in these sentences were from the first conjugation. Later lessons could use verbs from other conjugations as well as irregular verbs. When the students have mastered the phrases about Jean, the questions can be personalized: *Are you eating now? Are you going to eat tonight?*

6.3.3b   POSTER

The visuals suggested in section 6.3.3a may all be placed on a poster. As the teacher points to each drawing, he or she describes the action first in the present and then in the future:

1. Hans ißt jetzt.   *Jack is eating now.*
   Er wird auch heute abend   *He will also eat tonight.*
   essen.
2. Hans hört jetzt Radio.   *Jack is listening to the radio now.*
   Hans wird auch heute abend   *He will also listen to the radio*
   Radio hören.   *tonight.*
3. Hans studiert jetzt.   *Jack is studying now.*
   Er wird auch heute abend   *He will also study tonight.*
   studieren.
4. Hans telefoniert jetzt.   *Jack is telephoning now.*
   Er wird auch heute abend   *He will also telephone tonight.*
   telefonieren.
5. Hans spielt jetzt Tennis.   *Jack is playing tennis now.*
   Er wird auch heute abend   *He will also play tennis tonight.*
   Tennis spielen.

Models may also be presented with the same poster: *Er kann später essen. Er will immer Radio hören. Er soll bald studieren. (He can eat later. He always wants to listen to the radio. He should study soon.)*

6.3.3c OVERHEAD TRANSPARENCY

The ESL teacher shows the class the first pair of sentences on the transparency; a mask covers the remaining pairs. Then the teacher lowers the mask to show sentence 2; the students rewrite the sentence changing the gerund to an infinitive. The mask is again lowered to show the class the new sentence.

1. I've been working in the U.S. for two years.

   I $\boxed{\text{began}}$ to work in the U.S. two years ago.

2. I've been driving a car for ten years.

   I $\boxed{\text{began}}$ to drive a car ten years ago.

3. He's been playing golf for six years.

   He $\boxed{\text{began}}$ to play golf six years ago.

4. They've been speaking English for a month.

   They $\boxed{\text{began}}$ to speak English a month ago.

6.3.4 Relative clauses

6.3.4a CHALKBOARD AND COLOR CODING

(1) The teacher asks the class for a list of noun subjects. As the class dictates them, he or she writes them in yellow on the left-hand side of the board: *la dame, le garçon, les maisons, un homme, une jeune fille, les étudiants (the lady, the boy, the houses, a man, a girl, the students).* Then the teacher takes the first example and writes it in a sentence on the right-hand side. The words *la dame (the lady)* and *qui (who)* are written in yellow, the rest of the sentence in white: *Voilà* la dame qui *parle français. (There is* the lady who *speaks French.)*

The class is then asked to create the remaining sentences using the noun subjects on the left. Possible answers are: *Voilà* le garçon qui *joue au football. Voilà* les maisons qui *sont laides. Voilà* un homme qui *est intelligent. Voilà* une jeune fille qui *sait le français. (There is* the boy who *plays football. There are* the houses that *are ugly. There is* a man who *is intelligent. There is* a girl who *knows French.)*

(2) On another section of the chalkboard the teacher writes the same nouns in purple chalk. He or she then writes a model sentence using the first noun and *que (whom, that)* in purple: *Voilà* la dame que *je connais. (There is* the lady whom *I know.)*

The class is asked to create sentences of the type above using the nouns in purple. Possible answers are: *Voilà* le garçon que *vous aimez*. *Voilà* les étudiants que *nous avons vus*. *Voilà* les maisons que *Paul a vendues*. *Voilà* une jeune fille que *tu devrais inviter*. (*There is* the boy whom *you like*. *There are* the students whom *we saw*. *There are* the houses that *Paul sold*. *There is* the girl whom *you should invite*.)

6.3.4b   USING LINE DRAWINGS PLUS SENTENCES

The teacher places the following drawing and the two sentences on the blackboard or on an overhead transparency. In each sentence the subject and relative pronoun are circled in yellow or purple chalk, as appropriate.

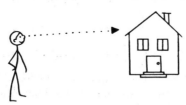

Voilà le garçon qui regarde la maison.
Voilà la maison que le garçon regarde.

There is the boy who is looking at the house.
There is the house that the boy is looking at.

Teacher: What follows *qui?*

Student: A verb (or action word).

Teacher: What follows *que?*

Student: A subject (or noun).

6.3.4c   DITTOS

The ESL teacher distributes a ditto sheet with pairs of sentences. The task is to combine the sentences using the relative pronouns *who, which,* or *that.*

Model: a. The man arrived yesterday. He speaks French.
           The man who speaks French arrived yesterday.

      b. The house is for sale. I saw it last week.
           The house that I saw last week is for sale.

1. The lady is my cousin. She always wears pink.
2. The necklace belongs to Mrs. Johnson. Lucy found it in the street.
3. The doctor will leave for Rome tomorrow. He performs open-heart surgery.
4. The car is in need of repair. My father bought it last year.

When the class is finished, the teacher distributes another ditto sheet with the correct answers.

6.3.5 Predicate adjectives

6.3.5a FLANNEL BOARD: DOLL AND CLOTHES

The teacher puts a cut-out doll on a flannel board and dresses it. As different articles of clothing are placed on it, he or she asks: *¿De qué color es la falda, la blusa, la camisa, el pantalón? ¿De qué color son los calcetines, los zapatos, los guantes? (What color is the skirt, blouse, shirt, trousers? What color are the socks, shoes, gloves?)*

6.3.5b FLANNEL BOARD: "EL CABALLERO DE LA CALABAZA"

The teacher puts a large, cut-out figure of a head on a flannel board. The hair and the eyes are missing. He or she has in hand several cut-out flannel eyes and hair pieces of different colors that are to be placed on the head.

Teacher:	¿De qué color es el pelo?	*What color is the hair?*
Student:	El pelo es rubio (moreno, gris, blanco) *or* Es pelirrojo.	*The hair is blond (brown, gray, white) or He's a red-head.*
Teacher:	¿De qué color son los ojos?	*What color are the eyes?*
Student:	Los ojos son azules, (verdes, negros, café...)	*The eyes are blue, green, black, brown . . .*

6.4 BASIC SENTENCE PATTERNS

This section deals with problems of word order as well as imperative, negative, and interrogative sentences.

6.4.1 Word order

6.4.1a FLANNEL BOARD PLUS CARDS

On the flannel board the teacher places index cards with German words on them. They should be arranged in statement word order.

Adverb	Verb		
immer	trinkt	*always*	*drinks*
morgen	kauft	*tomorrow*	*buys*
jetzt	besucht	*now*	*visits*
später	spielt	*later*	*plays*
manchmal		*sometimes*	

Subject	Complement		
er	Milch	*he*	*milk*
Inge	Fußball	*Inge*	*football*
Hans	ein Buch	*Hans*	*a book*
sie	Wasser	*she*	*water*
	ein Auto		*a car*
	Kaffee		*coffee*
	den Lehrer		*the teacher*
	einen Pullover		*a sweater*
	die Tante		*the aunt*
	Tennis		*tennis*
	ein Kleid		*a dress*
	seinen Freund		*his friend*

The teacher takes one card from each group and forms a sentence: *Morgen spielt Hans Tennis (Tomorrow Jack plays tennis)*. After forming others, he or she puts the cards back and asks for volunteers. The teacher is careful to see that all sentences are correct and make sense.

6.4.1b   LARGE CARDS

The teacher prepares large cards on the following model:

(front)   kauf   t   *buy s*

(back)   hat   gekauft   *has bought*

Four students are called to the front of the class. The middle two students are each given one of the verb cards which they hold so that the present tense is visible. The fourth student holds an object, such as a book.

The teacher explains the sentence: *Hans* (or the name of the first student) *kauft das Buch (Jack buys the book)*.

To form the past tense, the two middle students turn their cards over, and the second of the two walks around to the end of the line. The new sentence reads: *Hans hat das Buch gekauft (Jack has bought the book)*.

6.4.1c   OVERHEAD

See the example of the puzzle technique to teach word order in Section 2.4.2e.

6.4.2 Interrogative sentences

The suggestions below afford practice in the mechanics of question formation. Once the students have mastered the patterns, they should be encouraged to develop original questions for small-group conversations. These questions may be based on a reading or a picture, as well as on topics of general interest.

6.4.2a CHALKBOARD

The teacher writes a sentence on the board. First he or she reads it as a declarative sentence and writes at the end an arrow pointing down. Then the teacher reads it as a question and makes the arrow point upward. Finally individual students are asked to go to the board and write in the arrows.

La maison est jolie. ↓	*The house is pretty.* ↓
La maison est jolie? ↑	*The house is pretty?* ↑
Il est à la maison. ↓	*He's at home.* ↓
Il est à la maison? ↑	*He's at home?* ↑
Juan viene con nosotros. ↓	*John is coming with us.* ↓
¿Juan viene con nosotros? ↑	*John is coming with us?* ↑
Tiene que comprar algo. ↓	*He has to buy something.* ↓
¿Tiene que comprar algo? ↑	*He has to buy something?* ↑

6.4.2b CHALK LEDGE AND CARDS

On separate index cards, the teacher prints verbs, subjects, and complements and arranges them in affirmative sentences on the chalk ledge. (Cards with question marks and periods should be included.) Then he or she switches the subject and verb cards to make the sentences interrogative. Finally, the students are asked to come forward and rearrange the cards to form questions.

Pablo	está	.	
¿	está	Pablo	?
los chicos	llegan	.	
¿	llegan	los chicos	?
vous	lisez	vite	.

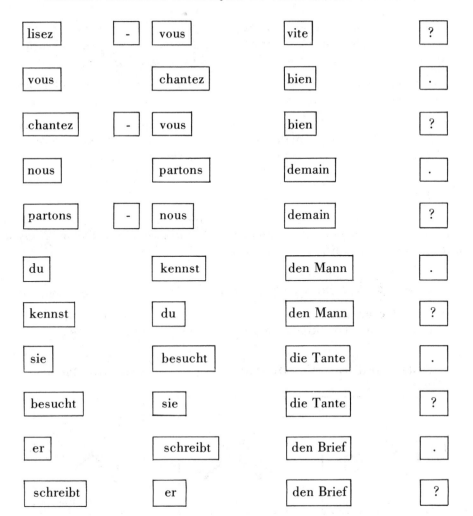

6.4.3 Negative sentences

6.4.3a POCKET CHART

The teacher makes cards containing the following words:

Jean	ne	parle	voit	pas	jamais	plus	personne	français

The cards can be inserted in the pocket chart to form the following sentences:

Jean		parle		français	*John speaks French.*
Jean	ne	parle	pas	français	*John doesn't speak French.*

Jean	ne	parle	jamais	français	*John never speaks French.*
Jean	ne	parle	plus	français	*John no longer speaks French.*
Jean	ne	voit	personne		*John doesn't see anyone.*

The teacher substitutes other cards containing different verbs and subjects. Then the students are asked to come forward and make negative sentences. Other important changes are:

| Jamais | Jean | ne | parle | français | *John never speaks French.* |
| Personne | ne | voit | Jean | | *No one sees John.* |

6.4.3b   SONGS

The teacher can use songs to teach negative word order patterns. For example, in *"Au clair de la lune"* is the pattern *Je n'ai plus de feu,* and in *"Dansons la Capucine,"* *Mais ce n'est pas pour nous.*

6.4.3c   TRANSPARENCY PLUS OVERLAY

The teacher prepares a basic transparency with a picture plus an affirmative sentence. The overlay introduces the negative in a contrasting color.

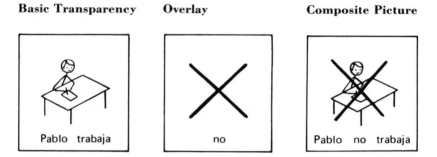

Basic Transparency   Overlay   Composite Picture

Pablo trabaja   no   Pablo no trabaja

Paul works / doesn't / Paul doesn't work

NOTE: In the English version, the overlay must also contain a small "x," which will cover the final "s" of "works."

6.4.4   Imperative sentences

6.4.4a   CHALKBOARD

The teacher writes a sentence on the board, using *vous (you)* as a subject. He or she erases the pronoun to form the imperative sentence.

Vous parlez français.	*You speak French.*
Parlez français!	*Speak French!*
Vous allez dans votre chambre.	*You go into your room.*
Allez dans votre chambre!	*Go into your room!*

6.4.4b MOVEMENTS

The teacher addresses the German class as *Sie.* When he or she makes a statement, the students do not move. When the teacher gives a command, they all obey: *Sie stehen auf.* No one moves. *Stehen Sie auf!* The class stands. *Setzen Sie sich!* The class sits down.

6.4.5 Complex sentences

The ESL teacher prepares a transparency with paired sentences. The students learn to combine the two sentences into one, using the underlined word(s) correctly. The teacher shows them the model and then lowers the mask as the class works as a group on the task.

Model: The student is ambitious. He is learning English.
The ambitious student is learning English.

1.   The north wind is bitter. It will bring snow.
The bitter north wind will bring snow.
2.   The man is weary and old. He cannot work.
The weary old man cannot work.
3.   The young child is very bright. He learns quickly.
The very bright young child learns quickly.

6.4.6 Adverbial clauses

A ditto sheet that is prepared contains paired sentences—one in the future tense, the other with an adverb of time. The ESL students combine these sentences into one. The teacher then distributes a second ditto sheet with the answers.

Model: My friends will arrive.[5] I'll meet them at the airport then.
(future)   (future)
When my friends arrive, I'll meet them at the airport.
(present) (future)

1. I'll go to the airport. Before that, I'll call to check on the time.
Before I go to the airport, I'll call to check on the time.

[5] Worksheet from the English Language Institute, Georgetown University.

2. I'll get to the airport. After that, I'll find out the gate number.
   After I get to the airport, I'll find out the gate number.
3. The plane will land. They'll be happy then.
   When the plane lands, they'll be happy.
4. The plane will come up to the gate. After that, they'll unfasten their
   seat belts.
   After the plane comes up to the gate, they'll unfasten their seat belts.

6.4.7 Passive sentences

To practice word order for passive sentences, students may be asked to un-
scramble sentences.[6] If desired, the shape of the cards can serve as an indication of the appropriate word order:

[6] Taken from Marina K. Burt and Carol Kiparsky, *The Gooficon: a Repair Manual for English*
(Rowley, Mass.: Newbury House, 1972), pp. 49–50.

outline

seven
Teaching
Vocabulary

Words are essential to communication. Little children learn to speak in isolated words and then in chains of nouns and verbs. The child who says "Daddy bye-bye car" is easily understood by English-speaking adults. We expect students of a second language, however, to control the grammatical features of that language as well as its vocabulary.

It is beyond the scope of this handbook to review the research into the role and manner of vocabulary acquisition in first and second language learning. Students who are immersed into a new linguistic setting tend to pick up vocabulary first, and then gradually develop a more accurate structural framework in which to use these words. ESL students in the United States will, therefore, concentrate on vocabulary acquisition and may use pidgin English before mastering standard English. English-speaking students of French or Spanish, on the other hand, will usually go through a course of instruction that focuses at first on mastery of the sound system and selected structures, and subsequently stresses more intensive vocabulary work.

Regardless of the specific target language and the conditions of instruction, vocabulary is an important factor in all language teaching. Students must continually be learning words as they learn structures and as they practice the sound system. This chapter offers suggestions for teaching vocabulary at both the beginning and the more advanced levels.

7.1 GENERAL CONSIDERATIONS

Concrete words are the easiest to learn. Neither younger nor older students have trouble in learning numbers, days of the week, colors, names of objects, and the like. The difficulty arises with using these words in sentences. For this reason, words are generally taught in context.

149

Adverbs and adverbial expressions are difficult to learn. Even intermediate French students, for instance, confuse *souvent* and *surtout*, *tout de suite* and *tout d'un coup*. Much practice with adverbs is necessary in all languages.

Students also tend to forget the inflected forms of nouns, adjectives, and verbs. Unless they learn the gender and plural form of a noun or the correct forms of an adjective, for example, they will be unable to use that noun or adjective accurately in a sentence. Unless they know the forms of a verb, they cannot use the verb properly in speaking or writing. Section 7.3 on improving students' retention suggests ways to help students remember basic forms.

As students progress in their language learning, they discover that words in the target language do not have identical meanings in their native language. Even numbers do not always mean the same thing in different languages. In French, for example, the equivalent of *dozens* of something is *des dizaines* or *tens* of something. The number 36 in French has the additional meaning of *a great many*, an indefinite, large number of things. The question of equivalency or nonequivalency is an even greater problem with cognates.

The final part of this chapter focuses on techniques for vocabulary building.

7.2   TECHNIQUES OF PRESENTATION

In presenting new vocabulary, the teacher must first convey the meanings of the words. Then the students must be taught to use the words properly in full sentences.

7.2.1   Conveying the meanings of new words

Some teachers give native language equivalents of new words. This is often the most direct way to teach adverbial expressions and abstract terms. Other teachers use a variety of techniques to convey the meanings of new words without recourse to the native language. Of course, if the foreign language teacher does not speak the native language of the students the possibility of translation is limited to student use of bilingual dictionaries.

The careful use or complete avoidance of the native language is a matter to be decided by each individual teacher. Some beginning students feel more comfortable when they can mentally assign a native equivalent to a word. They seek the reassurance of a vocabulary in their textbook and will ask friends to tell them what a word means if the teacher refuses to do so. Other students learn more rapidly if the entire class period is conducted in the foreign language. They don't mind feeling a bit unsure about the meaning of a new word, for they know that gradually they can figure out what it means. Some students like to discover the meaning of a new word that has been presented without recourse to the native language and then are so proud of their discovery that they announce the native equivalent aloud to show that they have understood.

In any case, the use of the native language must be minimized in the class-room. Once students know the meaning of a new word, they must use it often and correctly in the target language in order to master the word and make it part of their personal vocabulary.

7.2.1a USING VISUALS

(1) Labels: For a beginning class the teacher can prepare labels for objects in the classroom. For example, in a German classroom the door might have a label reading *die Tür*; above the chalkboard might be a sign saying *die Tafel*.

(2) Magazine pictures: The teacher cuts out magazine pictures that illustrate words in a dialog or basic sentences. These are placed on the chalkboard or on a magnetic board with magnets. The teacher points to the objects and gives their foreign language equivalents: *Das ist die Küche* or *Voici la cuisine* (*This is the kitchen*).

(3) Props: If the lesson is about foods, the teacher could bring to class a basket of plastic fruit.

Teacher:	¿Qué es esto?	(*What is this?*)
Class:	Es un tomate; es una pera; es una naranja.	*It's a tomato; it's a pear; it's an orange.*

In teaching about the house, a doll house with furniture can be used to teach the names of rooms, floors, parts of the house, and articles of furniture.

(4) Classroom objects: The calendar may be used to teach *today, yesterday, tomorrow*, as well as *last week, next week, next month, in two weeks*, and so on.

(5) Slides: Slides furnish an excellent medium for conveying the connotative cultural meanings of ordinary words in a foreign language.

The word *house*, for example, to American students, denotes an American type of house. Even if they live in an apartment, they have seen American houses in the movies and on television and have developed a concept of what a *house* is. The word *casa* to a Spaniard does not evoke an American-style house, but a Spanish-style house. A slide, or several slides, showing what Spanish houses look like can be shown in the classroom to help teach the word *casa*.

Slides of daily contemporary scenes, taken by the teacher on a trip abroad or by students or friends who have traveled in the foreign country, can frequently be used in teaching vocabulary. Items of clothing might be taught first, with the help of drawings or pictures. A slide of several people going shopping provides an opportunity for the students to talk about what the people are wearing. In this way, foreign words slowly absorb the connotations they have in their own culture.

7.2.1b USING MAIL ORDER CATALOGS

For intermediate and advanced classes, the mail order catalog is an excellent source book for vocabulary building. Not only do students learn the names of objects and colors, but they are introduced to clothing sizes and can even learn how to convert their measurements into corresponding measurements and sizes in the target culture.

7.2.1c   USING GESTURES

Gestures may be used to convey the meanings of some words. Certain descriptive adjectives, such as *tall, thin, fat, happy, dumb*, lend themselves to pantomime and gesture. Prepositions of place can also be effectively taught by movements: *Le livre est sur la table. Le crayon est sur le livre. Le livre est sous le crayon. Maintenant le crayon est derrière le livre. (The book is on the table. The pencil is on the book. The book is under the pencil. Now the pencil is behind the book.)*

Action verbs can be acted out: *El profesor come. El profesor bebe. El profesor lee. (The teacher is eating. The teacher is drinking. The teacher is reading.)*

Teacher:	¿Qué hace el profesor? (Teacher pretends to be chewing.)	*What is the teacher doing?*
Class:	El profesor come.	*The teacher is eating.*

7.2.1d   USING KNOWN VOCABULARY

The teacher can use known vocabulary to teach the meanings of new words.

(1) Synonyms and antonyms out of context:

Un sinónimo de *aprisa* es *rápidamente*. ¿Cuál es un sinónimo de *rápidamente*?	*A synonym of* fast *is* rapidly. *What is is a synonym of* rapidly?
Das Gegenteil von *groß* ist *klein*. Was ist das Gegenteil von *klein?*	*The opposite of* big *is* little. *What is the opposite of* little?
Le contraire de *chaud* est *froid*. Quel est le contraire de *froid?*	*The opposite of* hot *is* cold. *What is the opposite of* cold?

(2) Synonyms and antonyms in sentence context: Use the new word in sentences that contain an antonym or contrary expression:

Cette viande est *dure*. Je ne peux manger que de la viande *tendre*.	*This meat is* tough. *I can only eat* tender *meat.*
Pablo era *perezoso* mientras su hermano, Carlos, era *industrioso*. Carlos trabajaba todo el tiempo.	*Pablo was* lazy *while his brother Carlos was* industrious. *Carlos worked all the time.*

Use the new word in sentences that contain a synonym or equivalent expression:

Madeleine était *épuisée*. Solange, elle aussi, était *extrêmement fatiguée*.	*Madeleine was* exhausted. *Solange, too, was* extremely tired.
¡Hombre! ¿Por qué dices eso tan *aprisa?* Los americanos no te comprenden cuando hablas *rápidamente*.	*Man, why are you talking so* fast? *The Americans don't understand you when you speak so* quickly.

(3) Categories: Names of categories can be taught verbally if the students know some names of items that belong within a particular category.

Teacher:	Le café est une boisson.	*Coffee is a beverage.*
	Le Coca-Cola est une boisson.	*Coca-Cola is a beverage.*
	Le thé est une boisson.	*Tea is a beverage.*
	Donnez-moi d'autres exemples de boissons.	*Give me some other examples of beverages.*
Student:	Le lait est une boisson.	*Milk is a beverage.*
Teacher:	El tenis es un deporte.	*Tennis is a sport.*
	El béisbol es un deporte.	*Baseball is a sport.*
	¿Cuál es otro deporte?	*What is another sport?*
Student:	El fútbol es un deporte.	*Soccer is a sport.*

(4) Definitions and paraphrases: Definitions and paraphrases may be given in the target language. Target language dictionaries are useful to the teacher, especially those dictionaries prepared to help foreigners learn the second language.[1]

Un chanteur est une personne qui chante.	*A singer is a person who sings.*
Une fille qui est *moche* n'est pas très belle. Elle est laide.	*A girl who is "bad news" is not very pretty. She is ugly.*

7.2.1e   USING THE NATIVE LANGUAGE

The use of the native language to convey meaning may be direct or indirect, that is, the native language may simply give the meaning of a word or phrase, or it may explain a gesture or symbol that will later be used to evoke the word or phrase.

(1) Direct use of the native language: The question *Quelle heure est-il?* means *What time is it? Wir sprechen Deutsch* means *We're speaking German.*

---

[1] See, for example, Georges Gougenheim, *Dictionnaire fondamental de la langue française* (Paris: Didier, 1958). See also Pierre Fourré, *Premier Dictionnaire en images* (Paris: Didier, 1962). Distributed by Chilton Books, Radnor, Pa. For English as a Second Language, see the *Oxford Advanced Learner's Dictionary of Current English* (London: Oxford, 1974).

(2) Indirect use of the native language—gesture: A beckoning of hands means *repeat: répétez, répétez*. A hand cupped behind the ear means *listen: écoutez, écoutez*. Subsequently, when the teacher wants to tell students to listen, he or she will simply say *écoutez* and, if necessary, accompany the word with the gesture to reinforce the meaning of the command.

(3) Indirect use of the native language—symbols: The teacher can give the meaning of written symbols quickly in the native language and subsequently use the symbols to teach the new words in the second language. Students readily remember the meanings assigned to simple drawings.

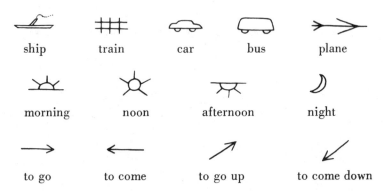

| ship | train | car | bus | plane |

| morning | noon | afternoon | night |

| to go | to come | to go up | to come down |

7.2.2 Teaching series and word sequences

Some of the words taught in elementary language courses occur naturally in sequences, such as numbers, names of months, days of the week. Students readily memorize the series, but they then have difficulty using the words out of sequence. The following techniques help students practice elements in a series.

7.2.2a FLASH CARDS

The items, or abbreviations of the items (days of the week and months of the year), can be put on flash cards. For example, all the letters of the alphabet are put on cards. The teacher shuffles the cards to present the letters out of sequence for drill,

7.2.2b CLOCK FACE

Using a toy clock, or a face of a clock drawn on the board, the teacher randomly points to the numbers 1 through 12 while the students say them aloud. The numbers 13 to 24 may also be added.

7.2.2c CHALKBOARD

The teacher writes the first letter or the abbreviation of each day of the week across the chalkboard. After teaching the new words, the teacher points to the letters on the board in random order, eliciting the days of the week from the students.

7.2.2d TRANSPARENCY

The teacher prepares a transparency with the abbreviations of the months of the year. Once the names of the months have been taught, the teacher randomly points to an abbreviation, and the students name the corresponding month.

7.2.3 Student-initiated vocabulary acquisition

Frequently the students themselves are interested in learning specific words or phrases. Motivation is a strong factor in all aspects of language learning, and such desire on the part of the students should not be shunted off simply because the requested vocabulary items do not form part of the lesson. At the same time, however, the teacher is normally bound to follow a specific syllabus or course curriculum.

Students could keep individual vocabulary notebooks. Here the students would enter the expressions or phrases they wish to learn. (They should be encouraged to write down items they are interested in, rather than to interrupt class to ask for new words.) At designated times, for instance, before class, students could ask for the foreign language equivalents of words they want to learn. Students could also be encouraged to use dictionaries. Beginners can use monolingual picture dictionaries designed for children who speak the language natively. More advanced students can learn to use dictionaries, phrase books, and illustrated catalogs.

To earn extra credit, students must add a specific number of new words to their vocabulary and demonstrate their comprehension by using these words in a brief written or oral exposé.

7.3 IMPROVING STUDENTS' RETENTION

The presentation of new words is only the first step in the process of language learning. The students must subsequently remember these words and make them part of their own vocabulary. Retention is a product of frequent practice. The following techniques suggest ways in which students' retention can be improved.

7.3.1 Color coding

Learning the gender of nouns is a problem for students learning inflected languages. Eye-minded students remember gender more easily if they mentally associate gender with color, for example, blue—masculine, red—feminine, green—neuter. This association may be reinforced in a variety of ways.

7.3.1a CONSTRUCTION PAPER

Pictures of masculine objects are mounted on blue construction paper. Pictures of feminine objects are mounted on red construction paper. Pictures of neuter objects are mounted on green construction paper.

7.3.1b COLORED DISCS

A blue disc is pasted in the corner of a magazine cut-out of a masculine object. Similarly, a red disc codes feminine, and a green disc codes neuter.

7.3.1c COLORED SYMBOLS AND LINE DRAWINGS

Homemade drawings or symbols are used on flash cards, cue cards, posters, and overhead transparencies. Use blue felt pens for masculine objects, red for feminine, and green for neuter.

7.3.1d COLORED CHALK

In writing sentences on the board in which noun and adjective agreement is being stressed, use blue chalk for the masculine forms, red (or pink) chalk for the feminine forms, and green chalk for the neuter forms.

7.3.1e DITTOS AND STUDENTS' NOTEBOOKS

Students who have difficulty with gender should be encouraged to color code nouns (and related forms such as articles, adjectives, and past participle endings) on homework and handouts. This may be done with crayons, colored pencils, felt pens, or water-soluble felt markers. Colored ditto masters may also be used.

7.3.2 Grouping

Many textbooks present vocabulary items in random order. Some books have alphabetical lists of new words. In either case, new words may be further grouped to point out similarities and differences among them. Bright students do this automatically, but often the slower students experience difficulty precisely because they do not notice the obvious groupings.

The teacher can prepare ditto handouts that group words to help students remember them more easily.

(1) Nouns: Nouns can be grouped by gender. In German, the groups could be further subdivided by how the plurals are formed. For more advanced classes, nouns may be grouped by endings to bring out gender patterns (for example, -tion words are feminine, -age words are usually masculine in French).

(2) Verbs: Verbs can be grouped by conjugation patterns. The general groupings may be further refined to group similar irregular forms together (stem-changing verbs, compound tenses formed by *to be* or *to have*, forms of the past participle, and so on).

(3) Adjectives: Adjectives can be grouped according to the way the feminine and plural forms are generated.

(4) Pairs of words: Synonyms and antonyms can be grouped. Root words may be paired with forms using prefixes or suffixes.

7.3.3 Asterisks

Asterisks are sometimes used in dictionaries to show specific types of irregularities (the aspirate *h* in French). Visuals and lists likewise might carry the asterisk. For example, a picture of ice hockey would be coded blue and carry an asterisk: *le *hockey*.

7.3.4 Type face

In Spanish, German, and English, students often stress the wrong syllable of a word. In dittoed lists, the stressed syllable could be lettered in heavier writing, or in capitals, or underlined. Students who tend to mispronounce words by shifting stress could be required to underline the stressed syllable on all written assignments.

7.3.5 Drawings

Drawings illustrating vocabulary may be hung around the classroom. These are especially effective if they illustrate points where learning problems tend to occur.

Ils sont en class.
(*They are in class.*)

Ils vont en classe.
(*They go to class.*)

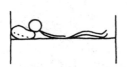

He is lying on the bed.

He is laying the coat on the bed.

7.3.6   Prepared visuals by students

Students should be encouraged to prepare visuals for words or expressions which they find difficult. These visuals can then be displayed in the classroom or integrated into language learning activities. If a second- or third-year student still mixes up some basic vocabulary words, he or she might prepare a visual plus a "mini-lesson" and be asked to teach those vocabulary words to some students in a lower class.

These visuals may take the form of posters, flash cards, ditto handouts, and so on. An art student might like to make a mobile with vocabulary forms.

Students should also be encouraged to put their problem words into sentences. A drawing of a fat person eating several ice cream sundaes could carry the caption *Er hat Eis* besonders *gern* or *Il aime* surtout *la glace* (*He* especially *likes ice cream*). Such drawings help students remember adverbs which often present difficulty.

7.4   COGNATES

The presence of many cognates in the target language facilitates the learning of vocabulary.

7.4.1   Cognate "fit"

The "fit" between cognates refers to the similarity that exists between the native language word and the target language word.

7.4.1a   FIT IN MEANING

For those cognates whose fit is near-perfect, usually scientific or technical terms such as *mathematics = les mathématiques*, the student has no trouble learning the meaning of the new word. The more common words, however, often have slightly different ranges of meaning in the two languages: *voyage* means any kind of trip in French, but in English it refers to a trip by boat. Here the new word should be presented in a variety of different sentences to show its range of meaning.

In false cognates the meanings of the two words are completely different. These words are especially hard for students to learn. Making visuals often helps them learn the differences between words that look alike but have different meanings.

7.4.1b   FIT IN SPELLING

Cognates are sometimes spelled differently. Spelling changes can be made more obvious to the students by underlining the letters that differ in the native and the target language.

7.4.1c   FIT IN PRONUNCIATION

Even cognates that look exactly alike *never* have exactly the same pronunciation in the two languages. Students must be given ample opportunity to practice spoken cognates.

7.4.2   Recognizing written cognates

Students readily recognize obvious written cognates. The average student, however, needs help in learning to recognize cognates that have undergone some spelling modification. Teachers may prepare lists of cognates that follow a similar pattern and present these to the students.

7.4.2a   PREFIXES

Before class begins, write the following list of French words on the board and cover them with a map:

décharger	désagréable
décourager	désenchanter
dédain	déshonorer
défaveur	désorganiser

Ask the class what English prefix *dés-* and *dé-* correspond to. Ask which French prefix is used before a consonant sound (left column) and which is used before a vowel sound (right column). You might also point out that sometimes the French prefix *dé-* corresponds to the English prefix *de*, as in *détacher, déplorer, décider, délivrer, déléguer*.

7.4.2b   SUFFIXES

Show the following list of words on the overhead projector:

curiosidad	brutalidad
humildad	dignidad
oscuridad	familiaridad
responsabilidad	prosperidad

Ask what letters all the words end in. What suffix does this correspond to in English? Say the words in English.

7.4.2c   PREDICTABLE SPELLING CHANGES

(1) For French, prepare a cue card like the following:

Explain that the circumflex accent frequently means that an *s* was dropped over three hundred years ago and that English still has the *s*. Let students give the meanings of words, such as *la bête, la fête, le mât, de la pâte, honnête*.

(2) For German, prepare a transparency indicating a sound shift: | t → d |

Then show flash cards with words that exemplify the sound shift and have students provide the English equivalents of *Gott, das Bett, der Ritter*.

7.4.3 Recognizing spoken cognates

Students who recognize written cognates often fail to recognize the same cognates when they hear them spoken. Since most commercial programs offer little practice in the recognition of spoken cognates, teachers must develop their own exercises.

7.4.3a INDIRECT EXERCISES

Cognates may be used in listening exercises designed to develop students' awareness of structural signals. As the students listen for gender markers, number markers, tense markers, and the like, they will indirectly become aware of what the cognates sound like.

(1) Indicate on your worksheet whether the noun is masculine, feminine, or neuter:

(tape)		
1. Da ist der Bus.	*There is the bus.*	
2. Da ist der Fisch.	*There is the fish.*	
3. Da ist die Garage.	*There is the garage.*	

(worksheet)

	der	die	das
1.	○	○	○
2.	○	○	○
3.	○	○	○

(2) Indicate on your answer sheet whether the verb expresses past time or near future:

1. Paul va inviter sa soeur.   *Paul is going to invite his sister.*
2. Nous avons autorisé cette action.   *We have authorized this action.*
3. Vous allez observer cette classe.   *You are going to observe this class.*

As the sentences are read a second time, and the correct answers announced, the printed sentences are projected on the overhead screen. This allows the students to see the written cognates and helps them understand the words they did not get the first time they heard them. (All the verbs are cognates unfamiliar to the students.)

7.4.3b   DIRECT EXERCISES

The students are given a ditto sheet with ten native language words (or the written target language cognates) in alphabetical order. They then hear ten sentences, each containing one of these words, and write the number of the sentence in which the word appeared next to the word. At the end of the exercise, each sentence is read again, followed by the word in isolation. Then the sequence of the ten numbers is read. Example: *Sa grand-mère s'occupait de son éducation. Education. (His grandmother took care of his education. Education.)*

7.4.4   Generating written cognates

Producing cognates is more difficult than understanding them. Even when the students know the basic patterns cognates follow, there is the chance that they will generate a nonexistent word. This does not mean, however, that the students should be prevented from trying to form cognates. To help them, the teacher should teach the basic transformations and then the exceptions, that is, those native language words which do not have predictable cognates in the target language.

7.4.4a   DEVELOPING AN AWARENESS OF WRITTEN PATTERNS

Whenever the students are given a reading assignment to prepare, they can be given one cognate assignment:

1. Make a list of all words in the passage beginning with *mé-* and give the English cognates where appropriate.
2. Make a list of all words in the passage ending in *-ción* and give the English cognates where appropriate.
3. Make a list of all words in the passage ending in *-ty* and give the Spanish cognates where appropriate.

These lists can be used in class the next day for cognate study.

7.4.4b   PREDICTING GENDER

In inflected languages it is not enough simply to predict the form of a noun cognate. The proper gender must also be predicted. Students should be taught those cases where gender patterns are regular and should be put on their guard for those words where gender varies unpredictably:

English words in -*em* often have French cognates in -*ème*, Spanish cognates in -*ema*. These cognates are masculine: *system—le système—el sistema*.

1. It's a good system.
   C'est un bon système.
   Es un buen sistema.
2. It's a big problem.
   C'est un grand problème.
   Es un gran problema.
3. It's a difficult theorem.
   C'est un théorème difficile.
   Es un teorema difícil.

Students write the French or Spanish sentences, some at their seats and some at the chalkboard. The teacher then corrects the sentences on the board, and students correct their own work at their seats.

7.4.4c WRITING COGNATES: BASIC FORMS

The teacher prepares a list of English cognates that are related in a predictable way to French cognates. As he or she dictates the English word, the students write the French equivalent:

English verbs in -*ate* frequently have French cognates in -*er: operate—opérer.* English verbs in -*cate* have cognates in -*quer: syndicate—syndiquer.* Remember: the letter *e* in English when followed by one consonant or by another vowel is usually *é* or *er* in French: *cooperate, indicate, penetrate, celebrate, ventilate, initiate, marinate, generate, liberate, educate.*

When the students have written the cognates, the teacher places the correct forms on the overhead projector.

Variation: Students do the homework on ditto sheets and then correct their own papers, using an answer key provided by the teacher.

7.4.4d WRITING COGNATES: IN CONTEXT

The teacher prepares a set of sentences in which cognates have been left out. The students supply the appropriate form of the cognate. It is better to give the entire English sentence, rather than just the single cognate, so that students notice that there is not a word-to-word correspondence between the other elements of the sentence:

Many English verbs in -*ish* have French cognates in -*ir*. Remember: a single *e* in English is usually written *é* in French.

1. The Indians perished.
   Les Indiens _____.

2. They are demolishing that wooden house.
   Ils _____ cette maison en bois.

7.4.5 Generating spoken cognates

Before students can generate spoken cognates, they must first learn how to pronounce known cognates accurately. (See also Section 4.6.2.) Once they command the sound system of the foreign language, they may be introduced to
spoken cognate exercises.

7.4.5a LEARNING EXERCISES

At first the teacher guides the students in the pronunciation of cognates:

Teacher:	Répétez après moi: *nation, action, émo- tion, condition, éduca- tion, destruction.*	*Repeat after me*
	A quel son /sjɔ̃/ corre- spond-il en anglais?	*What sound in English corresponds to /sjɔ̃/?*
Student:	/ʃən/	
Teacher:	Bien. Maintenant, je vais vous donner un mot en anglais et vous allez le prononcer en français: *nation, station, deco- ration, munitions.*	*Good. Now I am going to give you an English word and you will pro- nounce it the French way.*
Teacher:	Pronuncien: *perfect— perfecto, active— activo, future—futuro, service—servicio.* Where do we put the stress on the English words we just pro- nounced?	*Repeat*
Student:	On the first syllable.	
Teacher:	Correct. And on the Spanish words?	
Student:	On the next to the last syllable.	

Teacher: Correct. Now I shall give you a list of English words. You are to put them into Spanish. Remember, the Spanish words end in -o: *absolute, modest, human, ordinary.*

7.4.5b   PRACTICE DRILLS

Once the students are aware of the patterns, they need much practice:

Teacher: Comment dit-on *receive* en français?

How do you say receive *in French?*

Student: On dit *recevoir.*

You say recevoir.

Teacher: Comment dit-on *conceive* en français?

How do you say conceive *in French?*

Student: On dit *concevoir.*

You say concevoir.

Teacher: ¿Cómo se dice *explosion* en español?

How do you say explosion *in Spanish?*

Student: Se dice *explosión.*

You say explosión.

Teacher: ¿Cómo se dice *expression* en español?

How do you say expression *in Spanish?*

Student: Se dice *expresión.*

You say expresión.

7.4.5c   FREE CONVERSATION

In free conversation practice (see Section 9.7) students tend to use cognates to express themselves. As the teacher listens to the students speaking with each other, he or she makes note of mispronounced and incorrect cognates. This list of errors forms the basis of cognate study at the end of the conversation hour.

7.5   VOCABULARY BUILDING

As students advance in their study of the foreign language, they must continue to build their vocabularies. Some helpful techniques for vocabulary expansion are given in this section.

7.5.1   Word families

If the students learn to recognize the key parts of words, they will increase their comprehension of unknown vocabulary items and spend much less time thumbing in the glossary or dictionary.

7.5.1a   COMPOUND WORDS

Students of German must learn to form compound nouns.

(1) Put the following chart on the board:

der Mittag	der *Vor*mittag	*noon*	*forenoon*
der Mittag	der *Nach*mittag	*noon*	*afternoon*

Ask students how Germans create the words for forenoon and afternoon.

Teacher: If you know *der Tag,* how would you say *the day before?*
Student: Der *Vor*tag.
Teacher: If you know *der Weg,* how would you say *the way* (to) *home?*
Student: Der Nachhauseweg.[2]

(2) Nominalized verbs often form compounds with other verbs or nouns:

Auto fahren—to drive a car	das Autofahren—(the) driving of a car
einkaufen gehen—to go shopping	das Einkaufengehen—(the) shopping
Kuchen backen—to bake a cake	das Kuchenbacken—(the) baking of a cake
Wasserschi laufen—to waterski	das Wasserschilaufen—(the) water-skiing
zu Mittag essen—to eat lunch	das Mittagessen—(the) lunch, dinner

(3) An adjective and a noun are often combined to form a compound noun:

deutsch + das Land: Deutschland—Germany
gross + der Unternehmer; der Grossunternehmer—big-businessman
fett + der Druck: der Fettdruck—boldface type

ESL students must also learn to recognize compound words.

(4) The teacher distributes dittoes with compound words. The students separate them with boxes or circles.

---

[2] *A-LM German: Level III* (New York: Harcourt Brace Jovanovich, Inc., 1964), p. 191.

(5) Using different colored pencils, connect the following compounds.[3]

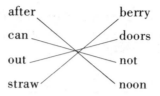

7.5.1b   NOUNS FROM ADJECTIVES

The teacher makes a transparency with the following words:

schön	schwierig	*beautiful*	*difficult*
krank	wirklich	*sick*	*real*
gesund	billig	*healthy*	*cheap*
echt	freundlich	*genuine*	*friendly*
beliebt	ähnlich	*beloved*	*similar*
schwach	gemütlich	*weak*	*peaceful*
dunkel	selig	*dark*	*holy*

With a grease pencil the teacher writes *die Schönheit* after *schön*, explaining that *die Schönheit* is the noun based on the adjective *schön*. He or she does the second example also, unless students already want to generate *Krankheit* from *krank*. As the students dictate, the teacher writes on the board the nouns made by adding *-heit* to the adjectives in the first column.

Then the teacher uncovers the second column and asks the students to listen as he or she reads the series of adjectives aloud. He or she asks what sound all the adjectives end in. The teacher explains that the suffix added to adjectives ending in *-ig* and *-ich* is not *-heit*, but *-keit*, which is easier to pronounce; for example, *Schwierigkeit* is much easier to pronounce than *Schwierigheit* would be. He or she writes *Schwierigkeit* on the transparency. Students dictate the other nouns according to the model.

7.5.1c   WORDS BUILT ON A COMMON ROOT

Once students are able to recognize the roots of compound words, they will find that their recognition vocabulary will increase measurably. Even in a language like Russian with an extensive vocabulary seemingly unrelated to English,

---

[3] Nila Barton Smith, *Reading Instruction for Today's Children* (Englewood Cliffs, N.J.: Prentice-Hall, 1964), p. 552.

a study of the common roots and their variants will significantly simplify the process of vocabulary building.[4]

The following exercise in French demonstrates a technique that leads students to identify the meanings of words based on recognizable roots.[5] Note that such exercises do not lend themselves to equivalent forms when translated.

Students work in pairs on the following ditto. Then they check their answers against the answer key on the teacher's desk.

L'ensemble de toutes les feuilles d'un arbre s'appelle le *feuillage*. Un arbre qui a beaucoup de feuilles est *feuillu*. Arracher les feuilles d'un arbre c'est l'*effeuiller*.	*The ensemble of all the leaves of a tree is called its foliage. A tree that has many leaves is called leafy. To take the leaves off a tree is to defoliate it.*
1. *Feuillu* veut dire *qui a des feuilles*.	Leafy *means* that has leaves.
Que veulent dire les mots suivants:	*What do the following words mean:*
a. barbu	*bearded*
b. chevelu	*with much hair on the head*
c. poilu	*hairy*
2. *Feuillage* veut dire *une collection de feuilles*.	Foliage *means* a collection of leaves.
Que veulent dire ces mots:	*What do the following words mean:*
a. branchage	*many branches*
b. plumage	*plumage*
c. herbage	*herbage*
3. *Effeuiller* veut dire *enlever les feuilles*.	Defoliate *means* to remove the leaves.
Que veulent dire les mots suivants:	*What do the following words mean:*
a. ébrancher	*to debranch*
b. effruiter	*to remove the fruits*
c. écrémer	*to skim the cream*

7.5.1d PREFIXES

The teacher prepares the following transparency and lowers a mask to reveal the first two or three examples. The students figure out the rest.

Prefix	Meaning	Word
un	not happy	unhappy
re	write again	rewrite

[4] See Catherine A. Wolkonsky and Marianne A. Poltoratzky, *Handbook of Russian Roots* (New York: Columbia University Press, 1961).
[5] Adapted from L. Seibert and L. Crocker, *Skills and Techniques for Reading French* (New York: Harper and Row, 1958), pp. 13–14.

pre	view before	preview
anti	against busing	antibusing
dis	not like	dislike
mis	apply incorrectly	misapply

Prefix (re)

Root	(Il répète son action)	
I fait ses devoirs.	Il refait ses devoirs.	*He does his assignments.* *He does his assignments again.*
Il commence à lire.	Il recommence à lire.	*He begins to read. He begins to read again.*
Il met son chapeau.	Il remet son chapeau.	*He puts on his hat. He puts on his hat again.*

Prefix (des)

Root	(El contrario de...)	
Obedece.	Desobedece.	*She obeys. She disobeys.*
Conoce.	Desconoce.	*She knows. She doesn't know.*
Aparece.	Desaparece.	*She appears. She disappears.*
Hace.	Deshace.	*She does. She undoes.*

7.5.1e SUFFIXES

The teacher prepares a ditto with a blank section in the middle for the correct word to be written in. The first two examples serve as models.[6]

art	art*ist*	one who practices art
organ	organ*ist*	one who plays an organ
balloon		one who flies a balloon
real		one who thinks realistically
harp		one who plays a harp
humor		one who has humor
special		one who specializes in something
journal		one who writes for a journal

persona que vende	un vend*edor*	seller
persona que compra	un compra*dor*	buyer
persona que trabaja		worker
persona que pesca		fisherman
persona que cultiva		cultivator
persona que mata		killer
persona que corre		runner
persona que labra		worker

[6] Nila Barton Smith, *Reading Instruction for Today's Children* (Englewood Cliffs, N.J.: Prentice-Hall, Inc., 1964) p. 553.

7.5.1f   PREFIXES AND SUFFIXES

The teacher gives one root word to each student. The students go to the board and make a list of all related words they can think of, using known prefixes and suffixes.

Here is an English example:

play   player
          playing
          playful
          replay
          underplay

7.5.2   Paraphrasing

In paraphrasing, students realize that there are frequently several ways of expressing roughly the same idea in the foreign language.

The students complete sentences by furnishing a synonym or equivalent of an underlined term:

(1) This exercise provides practice in using *por* and *para*. After the students have completed the exercise, pass out a sheet with the answers, or put them on the overhead projector.

En los ejercicios que siguen reemplace las palabras subrayadas con *por* o *para*.[7]	*In the following exercises replace the underlined words with* por *or* para.
Modelos: El avión salió <u>en dirección a</u> México. El avión salió <u>para</u> México.	*The plane took off in the direction of Mexico.*
Los mexicanos cruzaron en balsa <u>a través</u> del río. Los mexicanos cruzaron en balsa <u>por</u> el río.	*The Mexicans crossed the river on a raft.*
1. <u>A cambio de</u> dinero, Judas vendió a Cristo. _____ dinero, Judas (Por) vendió a Cristo.	*In exchange for money, Judas sold Christ.*

[7] Poston, Jr., Lawrence, et al., *Workbook Accompanying Continuing Spanish II* (New York: American Book Company, 1967), pp. 7–12.

2. Salió de la clase <u>a fin de</u> pegarle   *He left the class in order to strike*
   a Tom.   *Tom.*
   Salió de la clase _____
   pegarle a Tom.   (para)

(2) Review orally the synonyms in this exercise before asking the students to fill in the blanks. Each blank in the second part must contain a paraphrase of the words in the first part.

Sylvie et Nicole sont <u>chez</u> Jacqueline. Jacqueline parle trop <u>rapidement</u>, mais tout le monde la trouve <u>gentille</u>. Sylvie ne dit <u>pas un mot</u>, mais elle est <u>extrêmement</u> jolie. Les trois <u>camarades</u> regardent la télévision. Nicole dit, "Je <u>déteste</u> les films de guerre. A <u>quelle heure</u> est-ce que le western commence?" Jacqueline répond, "<u>Immédiatement</u>."

Sylvie and Nicole are at Jacqueline's house. Jacqueline speaks too quickly, but everyone considers her nice. Sylvie doesn't say a word, but she is extremely pretty. The three friends are watching television. Nicole says: "I hate war movies. At what time does the western begin?" Jacqueline answers, "Right away."

Sylvie et Nicole sont _____ Jacqueline. Jacqueline parle trop _____, mais tout le monde la trouve _____.
Sylvie ne dit _____, mais elle est _____. Les trois _____ regardent la télévision. Nicole dit, "Je _____ les films de guerre. _____ est-ce que le western commence?" Jacqueline répond, "_____."

7.5.3 Techniques of inference

Students should be taught to infer the meanings of new words from the context in which they are used.

7.5.3a MULTIPLE CONTEXT

The new word is used in several different sentences.

Put the following sentences on the overhead projector. Tell the students to try to guess the English equivalent of the word *trabaja*. Ask them not to call out the meaning, but to wait until everyone has had a chance to read the sentences and figure it out.

1. El profesor *trabaja* en la escuela.	*The teacher works in the school.*
2. El presidente *trabaja* en Washington.	*The president works in Washington.*
3. El agricultor *trabaja* en su rancho.	*The farmer works on his ranch.*
4. El gato no *trabaja*; él duerme mucho.	*The cat does not work; it sleeps a lot.*
5. El caballo *trabaja* mucho; él transporta a personas y mercancías.	*The horse works a lot; it carries people and merchandise.*
6. El estudiante que *trabaja* mucho recibe una A. El estudiante que no *trabaja* recibe una F.	*The student who works hard receives an A. The student who doesn't work receives an F.*
7. El inválido no *trabaja*; es físicamente imposible.	*The invalid does not work.*

7.5.3b   SINGLE CONTEXT

Prepare sentences for the overhead projector or write them in grease pencil while the students watch. Then ask questions about the sentences.

	Hier soir j'ai entendu un rossignol. Sa chanson était très belle.	*Last night I heard a nightingale. Its song was very beautiful.*
Teacher:	Vous ne savez pas ce que c'est qu'un rossignol. Mais qui peut me dire ce qu'un rossignol peut faire?	*You do not know what a nightingale is. But who can tell me what a nightingale can do?*
Student:	Il peut chanter.	*It can sing.*
Teacher:	Oui, et il a une belle voix. Maintenant je vais vous donner encore une phrase à lire.	*Yes, and it has a lovely voice. Now I will give you a sentence to read.*
Teacher:	(Writes, or lowers mask on prepared overhead.) Je ne pouvais pas le voir, mais il était probablement dans l'arbre près de ma fenêtre. Maintenant,	*I could not see it, but it was probably in the tree near my window. Now can you guess what a nightingale is?*

	pouvez-vous deviner ce que c'est que ce rossignol?	
Student:	C'est un oiseau.	*It's a bird.*
Teacher:	Oui, très bien. En anglais nous appelons cet oiseau un *nightingale.* On le trouve en Europe mais pas aux Etats-Unis.	*Yes, that's right. In English we call this bird a* nightingale. *It is found in Europe but not in the United States.*

7.5.4 Vocabulary lists

7.5.4a LISTS PREPARED BY THE TEACHER

New vocabulary may be presented in list form. This method of presentation (or review) is most effective when the words all relate to a topic that the class is studying.

For example, if the students are given an assignment to describe their bedroom, a vocabulary list would contain the words and expressions they might need to use. The list is most useful if the words are given in all their basic forms and then included in sample sentences.

Vocabulary lists might also be distributed for debate topics and prepared oral conversations.

7.5.4b LISTS PREPARED BY STUDENTS

(1) Whenever a student looks up a word in the end vocabulary, he or she enters a checkmark by the word. When a word has three checkmarks, the student copies that word in a notebook and uses it in a sample sentence. All students are encouraged to try to memorize the words they have listed in their notebook.

(2) For each reading assignment, the students select five words or idioms they are unsure of and consider useful. They write these in a notebook and use each word in an original sentence.

7.5.5 Game: Jeopardy

The TV game "Jeopardy" may be adapted for foreign language classes.[8] It gives the students practice in using their newly acquired vocabulary in varied contexts. The teacher, or the class as a whole, selects four or five categories. Students then write questions and answers for these categories.

[8] Adapted from Clarice Ritthaler and Donna Gregory, "Jeopardize Your Foreign Language Classes," *Show-Me, News and Views (Missouri Foreign Language Newsletter)* 2, no. 2 (February 1971), p. 18.

The questions are grouped in order of difficulty, from simple questions worth ten points each to hard questions worth fifty points each. There should be five questions for each category. The answers are written in columns on the board and covered with large pieces of manila paper that carry the numbers 10, 20, 30, 40, and 50.

Students compete in teams. The first student on a team picks a category and a value. He or she is then shown the answer and must supply a question.

Category: Geografía
Answer: La capital de Missouri
Question: ¿Qué es Jefferson City?

If the student gives the correct question, that team gains the designated number of points. If the student misses, the points are deducted from the team's score.

7.6   PROBLEM AREAS

Vocabulary problems arise when words in the native language and the target language do not cover the same range of meaning. The most troublesome cases are those where the target language makes distinctions that the native language does not make, for the students must learn to reorganize their way of viewing reality. It is also essential that students become aware of the cultural meanings of words. For example, in teaching the names of animals, the French teacher can point out that camels, rather than skunks—which do not exist in Europe—are used to designate unpleasant people: *quel chameau!*

Although it is beyond the scope of this handbook to treat the many problem areas that exist, techniques are suggested for teaching three difficult points.

7.6.1   *Ser* vs. *estar*

Using the two forms of *to be* correctly in Spanish always creates difficulties for American students. Prepare a transparency or wall chart with the figures on page 174.

The teacher points to each figure and describes him:

(A) El muchacho *es* alto, pequeño, inteligente, americano, gordo, flaco. *The boy is tall, small, intelligent, American, fat, thin.*

(B) Hoy el muchacho *está* enfermo, feliz, triste, sentado. *Today the boy is sick, happy, sad, sitting down.*

While it is true that in several of these situations either *ser* or *estar* could be used, one way to present the concept is by contrasting permanent with transitory characteristics.

A pattern drill of the following sort might follow the presentation:

Teacher	Students
El muchacho es alto	El muchacho es alto.
gordo	El muchacho es gordo.
triste hoy	El muchacho está triste hoy.
enfermo hoy	El muchacho está enfermo hoy.
americano	El muchacho es americano.
sentado	El muchacho está sentado.

7.6.2 *Savoir* vs. *connaître*

The teacher can explain that *savoir* means *to know* in the sense of to have learned or to know by heart, whereas *connaître* means *to know* in the sense of to be acquainted with. (NOTE: a similar pattern exists in Spanish and German.)

The distinction between the two verbs becomes clearer, however, if the students see that certain complements *require* one or the other verb. This can be shown on a wall chart.

connaître	savoir

une personne
  (*a person*):
  Monsieur Blot
un endroit (*a place*):
  Paris
un object (*a thing*):
  le "Penseur"
  (*the Thinker*) } je le connais (*I know him/it*)
	infinitif (*infinitive*):
	  nager (*to swim*)
	que (*that*) . . .
	comment (*how*) . .
	pourquoi (*why*) . .
	quand (*when*) . . .
	où (*where*) . . .
	si (*if, whether*) . . } je le sais (*I know that*)

connaître ou savoir une chose qu'on apprend: une réponse, une leçon (*something that one learns: an answer, a lesson*)	

7.6.3   Limited vs. unlimited verbs

The difference in time span between limited and unlimited verbs in English can be conveyed through a diagram:[9]

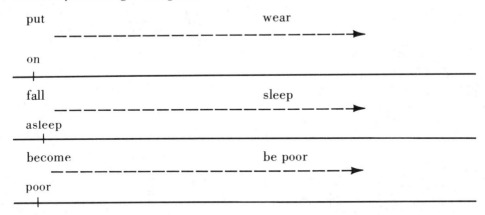

It is also possible to have students act out the limited verb: for example the students can *put on* their jackets and once they have them on, they *are wearing* them.

[9] Taken from Marina K. Burt and Carol Kiparsky, *The Gooficon: A Repair Manual for English* (Rowley, Mass.: Newbury House, 1972), pp. 78–79.

part three
Developing
the Skills

outline

8.1 GENERAL CONSIDERATIONS

8.2 UNDERSTANDING INDIVIDUAL WORDS

    8.2.1 Numbers
    8.2.2 New vocabulary
    8.2.3 Minimal pairs

8.3 IDENTIFYING AND UNDERSTANDING SENTENCES

    8.3.1 Giving a physical response
    8.3.2 Using visual cues
    8.3.3 Giving native language equivalents

8.4 HEARING STRUCTURE SIGNALS

    8.4.1 Listening for number
    8.4.2 Listening for gender
    8.4.3 Pronouns
    8.4.4 Verb tenses
    8.4.5 Identifying subject and object

8.5 LISTENING TO UNFAMILIAR MATERIAL

    8.5.1 Identifying the language
    8.5.2 Anticipating sentence completion
    8.5.3 Listening to stories
    8.5.4 Listening to newscasts

8.6 UNDERSTANDING SHORT ORAL PASSAGES

    8.6.1 Passages prepared by the teacher
    8.6.2 Commercially recorded passages

8.7 UNDERSTANDING COLLOQUIAL SPEECH

    8.7.1 General comprehension
    8.7.2 Paraphrasing rapid speech or regional variants
    8.7.3 Written transcriptions
    8.7.4 Foreign-language movies

8.8 UNDERSTANDING EXTENDED PASSAGES

    8.8.1 Keeping a log
    8.8.2 Preparing discussion questions
    8.8.3 Taking notes

eight
Listening
Comprehension

The teaching of listening comprehension as a separate skill is a recent innovation in language teaching. Even at present most commercial language programs do not focus on a sequential and methodical development of the listening skill. Listening is simply considered as an adjunct of speaking. Tape programs contain models for repetition, cues for spoken drills, and recordings of reading selections. Only a few programs, however, contain exercises for listening discrimination, and even fewer contain listening comprehension selections, which appear only on tape (and not in the student's book).

This chapter presents techniques for the development of the listening skill, arranged in order of increasing difficulty.

8.1 GENERAL CONSIDERATIONS

Developing the ability to understand the spoken foreign language is a long, continuous process. It is a skill that must be taught and that does not happen automatically. One of the teacher's most important tasks is to provide a variety of purposeful listening activities throughout the entire language course.

The students must be given a reason for listening to one another. If the teacher requires individuals to respond to each other, the students will make an effort to listen more carefully for the information requested. In order to accomplish this, the teacher must insist that everyone speak up.

It is also important that teachers not repeat their questions and comments. Those teachers who repeat each utterance a dozen times find that their students stop listening altogether. Even more boring is the teacher who repeats each student's response or question. Obviously the teacher cannot react in silence to a student's utterance, and repeating what has just been said is an easy but unfortunate way to say something. The alternative is for the teacher to develop a large repertory of responses to students' utterances. Even the not-too-fluent teacher can practice a list of possible rejoinders in the foreign language, such as: Great. Wonderful. That's better, but not quite perfect. I see you've been practicing at home. Hey, you got it right. Now if I hear you make that mistake again you have no more excuses. Say that once more. That was perfect.

At the intermediate and advanced levels, the teacher must make the effort to find suitable taped material for listening activities. It is not enough for students merely to listen to each other and the teacher. They must also have frequent opportunities to listen to a variety of different speakers talking at a normal conversational speed.

8.2 UNDERSTANDING INDIVIDUAL WORDS

One of the first things that the language student learns to understand is individual words, either in isolation or more usually in the context of sentences.

8.2.1 Numbers

Numbers are taught early in the language course, yet even advanced students have difficulty understanding them. Page numbers and line numbers in the textbook should always be given in the target language to reinforce listening comprehension.

8.2.1a NUMBER DISCRIMINATION

Repeat the number that is larger.[1]

Model:	tres, cuatro—cuatro	*three, four—four*
1.	dos, uno	*two, one*
2.	cinco, ocho	*five, eight*
3.	doce, quince	*twelve, fifteen*

8.2.1b BINGO

The standard Bingo game is a stimulating way for younger students to improve their comprehension of numbers from 1 to 75.

8.2.1c FLASH CARDS

An easy way to drill numbers is with flash cards. The teacher reads off ten cards, previously shuffled. The students write down the numbers, in digits. Then the teacher rereads the cards one by one, showing the card to the students so that they can correct their list.

[1] Adapted from Edward D. Allen, Lynn A. Sandstedt and Brenda Wegmann, *¿Habla Español?* (New York: Holt, Rinehart & Winston, 1976), p. 35.

For advanced classes, the teacher can prepare forty or fifty index cards with three- and four-digit numbers. These are shuffled, and every day the teacher dictates ten numbers to the students at the beginning of the class hour.

8.2.2 New vocabulary

The teacher uses magazine cutouts, cue cards, or whatever visuals have been prepared to teach the new vocabulary (see Chapter 7).

8.2.2a FOLLOWING INSTRUCTIONS

The teacher prepares large cards that depict the topical vocabulary of the lesson, for instance, the buildings in a city.

Teacher: This is the post office. Who wants the post office? . . . Pablo, here is the post office. (to the class) Who has the post office?
Class: Pablo does.
Teacher: This is the drugstore. Who wants the drugstore? (etc.)
Anna, give the grocery store to Pedro.
Pablo, bring me the post office. (etc.)

As the students manipulate the cards, they learn to understand the new vocabulary. It is frequently much more effective to have students learn vocabulary via listening comprehension before asking them to repeat the new words in the target language.

8.2.2b CHECKING COMPREHENSION: TRUE-FALSE

The teacher says a word and holds up or points to a visual. If the word identifies the visual, the students mark *true* on their papers. If it does not, they write *false*. The teacher says each word only once.

Then he or she goes through the list once more, pausing after each word. The class responds *true* or *false*. If the answer was *false*, the teacher asks a student to identify the visual properly.

By calling for a quick raising of hands, the teacher can check whether the students understood the words or whether they need more oral listening practice.

8.2.2c CHECKING COMPREHENSION: IDENTIFICATION

The teacher lines all the vocabulary cards up along the chalkboard. He or she then writes an identifying letter above each card, beginning at the left with "a."

The teacher then reads a series of sentences in which the new vocabulary words are imbedded, and the students write the letter that corresponds to the appropriate visual. For example: This morning the post office is closed. Mother asked me to go to the drugstore for her.

The students may not understand the entire sentence. (In fact, the teacher may even want to use sentence constructions that are unfamiliar to the class). The point of the exercise is to force the student to listen for the new vocabulary item and identify it properly. When the class understands the new words, it is appropriate to begin speaking practice.

8.2.3   Minimal pairs

Intermediate and advanced students often mix up words that sound almost alike, even though the same students could probably identify the words in written form.

To check this kind of listening comprehension, the teacher distributes sheets on which there are line drawings of objects or events. As he or she pronounces one in each pair, the students identify it with A or B.

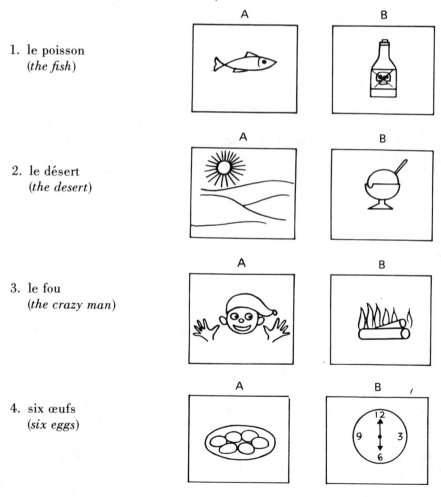

1. le poisson
   (*the fish*)

2. le désert
   (*the desert*)

3. le fou
   (*the crazy man*)

4. six œufs
   (*six eggs*)

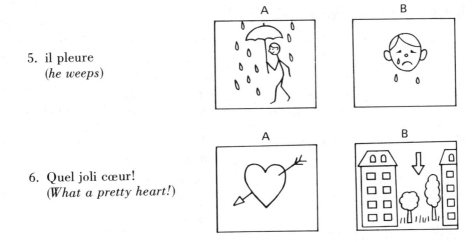

5. il pleure
   (*he weeps*)

6. Quel joli cœur!
   (*What a pretty heart!*)

In the French example, the possible confusions are le poisson—le poison; le désert—le dessert; le fou— le feu; six oeufs—six heures; il pleure—il pleut; Quel joli cœur!—Quelle jolie cour! Similar items in ESL might match pen—pan; he's washing—he's watching; ship—sheep, etc.

8.3 IDENTIFYING AND UNDERSTANDING SENTENCES

Students quickly learn to recognize sentences, especially if they are required to demonstrate their comprehension. (On the other hand, it is possible for students to memorize sentences and forget what these sentences mean if comprehension is not regularly checked and reinforced.)

8.3.1 Giving a physical response

Students carry out some kind of action to show that they understand the meaning of the sentence.

8.3.1a EXECUTING ORDERS

The teacher gives a series of rapid commands to the entire class. The students perform each act as rapidly as possible: *Levez-vous. Levez la main droite. Baissez-la. Levez le pied gauche. Baissez-le. Tournez-vous. Asseyez-vous.* (*Stand up. Raise your right hand. Put it down. Raise your left foot. Put it down. Turn around. Sit down.*)[2]

---

[2] This type of exercise forms the basis of the initial phases of the "total physical response" technique. See James J. Asher, "The total response approach to second language learning," *Modern Language Journal* 53, no. 1 (January 1969), pp. 3–7.

8.3.1b DRAWING PICTURES

The teacher calls on individuals to draw pictures on the board. The other students practice at their seats:

Jean, allez au tableau. Dessinez une maison avec six fenêtres.	*John, go to the board. Draw a house with six windows.*
Marie, dessinez un arbre à droite de la maison.	*Mary, draw a tree to the right of the house.*
Marc, mettez une cheminée sur le toit de la maison.	*Mark, put a chimney on the roof of the house.*

Variation: Students can draw pictures on the overhead projector with the light on.

8.3.1c PANTOMIME

In this audio-motor unit, a series of directions are recorded on tape, preferably by a native speaker. The teacher plays the tape and acts out the instructions. Then the tape is played again, and this time the class does the pantomime.

8.3.1d USING THE MAGNETIC BOARD

The teacher puts various cutouts of buildings on the board with magnets. The students listen to the directions and move the buildings around:

Paco, la biblioteca queda detrás del banco.	*Frank, the library is behind the bank.*
María, la peluquería queda enfrente del banco.	*Mary, the barber shop is in front of of the bank.*
Carlos, el cine queda a la izquierda del banco.	*Charles, the movie theatre is to the left of the bank.*
Juana, la iglesia queda a la derecha de la biblioteca.	*Joan, the church is to the right of the library.*

8.3.1e USING THE FLANNEL BOARD

(1) On the left-hand side of the flannel board are several objects; the right side is bare. The teacher asks individuals to come forward and put various objects from the left side to the right:

Pierre, mettez la chaise sur la table.	*Peter, put the chair on top of the table.*
Monique, mettez la jeune fille sur la chaise.	*Monica, put the girl on top of the chair.*
Claude, mettez le balai dans les mains de la jeune fille.	*Claude, put the broom in the hands of the girl.*

| Claire, mettez une souris devant la table.[3] | *Claire, put a mouse in front of the table.* |

(2) On the left side of the flannel board are the following objects: a cup, a hat, a dog, a pair of shoes, a table, the frame of a house, a chair and a bed (scattered about haphazardly). The right side of the flannel board is bare. The teacher calls on individual students to come forward and make the following pictures:

Ich habe meine Tasse auf den Tisch gestellt.
(*I placed my cup on the table.*)

Ich habe meinen Hund ins Haus gebracht.
(*I brought my dog into the house.*)

Ich habe meinen Hut auf den Stuhl gelegt.
(*I laid my hat on the chair.*)

Ich habe meine Schuhe unter das Bett gestellt.
(*I placed my shoes under the bed.*)

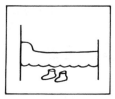

8.3.1f   GAME: SIMON SAYS

Commands are given to the entire class. Students obey commands that are preceded by "Simon says" and do not move when the simple command is given. Students who make the wrong movement or who move at the wrong time are sent to the back of the room, where they continue to participate. The game continues until only one student is left in the front:

| Simon dit: "Les mains sur la tête." | *Simon says: "Put your hands on your head."* |

[3] *Le Tableau de Feutre dans la Classe de Langue Vivante,* Bureau Pour l'Enseignement de la Langue et de la Civilisation Françaises à L'Etranger (Paris: Librairie Istra, 1969).

Mettez les mains sur les épaules.	*Put your hands on your shoulders.*
Simon dit: "Mettez les mains sur les épaules."	*Simon says: "Put your hands on your shoulders."*

At first the teacher carries out all the actions, so that the students can concentrate on the absence or presence of the phrase *Simon dit.* When the class knows the parts of the body well, the teacher can give a command to touch the knees while the teacher touches his or her own head. Students who fail to touch their knees are eliminated.

Variation: The teacher addresses individuals:

Marta, ¡levántate!	*Martha, get up!*
Carlos, Simón dice, "¡levántate!"	*Charles, Simon says, "Get up!"*
Carlos, ¡siéntate!	*Charles, sit down!*
Carlos, Simón dice, "¡siéntate!"	*Charles, Simon says, "Sit down!"*
Roberto, ¡abre tu libro!	*Robert, open your book!*
Ricardo, ¡cierra tu cuaderno!	*Richard, close your notebook!*

8.3.1g CHARADES

This game may be played boys against girls. The scorekeeper at the board marks a point for each person who correctly acts out the statement made by the teacher:

Teacher: J'ai froid.
        (Points to first boy on
            team.)
(Boy shivers.)
	I'm cold.

Teacher: J'ai mal à la tête.
        (Points to first girl on
            team.)
(Girl rubs her head.)
	I have a headache.

Teacher: J'ai faim. (Boy rubs his stomach.)	*I'm hungry.*
Teacher: J'ai sommeil. (Girl yawns.)	*I'm sleepy.*

8.3.1h FOLLOWING LONGER INSTRUCTIONS

(1) The teacher gives a long, rather complicated set of directions to various individual students to develop their listening comprehension. Each attempts to execute the commands:

Hans, stehe auf, gehe an den Tisch, setze dich hin, nimm den	*Jack, stand up, go to the table, sit down, take the red pencil and write*

roten Bleistift und schreibe das
Wort *gut* auf das Papier! Dann
falte es, und stecke es in dein
Buch![4]

the word "good" on the paper!
Then fold it and put it in your
book.

(2) The teacher distributes maps of a city. He or she then gives a series of directions in the foreign language and asks students where they have ended up on their maps:

Teacher: Trouvez l'église. Vous y
           êtes? Ecoutez bien.
           Vous sortez de l'église
           et vous tournez à
           droite. A la rue Na-
           tionale vous prenez à
           gauche. Vous continuez
           tout droit. Puis vous
           prenez la deuxième
           rue à droite. Quel
           bâtiment se trouve
           immédiatement à
           votre droite?

Find the church. Did you find it?
Listen carefully. You go out of the
church and turn right. At National
Street you make a left turn. You
continue straight ahead. Then you
take the 2nd street on the right.
What building is located directly
to your right?

Students: Le bureau de poste.

The post office.

8.3.2   Using visual cues

Students can also demonstrate their ability to understand sentences by indicating their reaction to visuals.

8.3.2a   DIALOG POSTERS

The teacher recites a line of dialog and points to a picture on the poster. Students indicate whether or not the line corresponds to the picture.

8.3.2b   CUE CARDS

The teacher makes a statement about each cue card. The students reply *yes* or *no* to indicate whether the statement is appropriate or not:

Teacher: (Holds a picture of a tall
             boy.)
           El chico es alto.

The boy is tall.

[4] Based on James J. Asher, "The Learning Strategy of the Total Physical Response Approach: A Review," *The Modern Language Journal* 50, no. 2 (February, 1966), pp. 79–84.

Students:	Sí.	*Yes.*
Teacher:	(Holds a picture of a fat boy.)	
	La chica es gorda.	*The girl is fat.*
Students:	No.	*No.*

8.3.2c   WALL CHARTS

The teacher puts up a wall chart showing different kinds of weather. The teacher asks a question and points to a picture. The students answer *yes* or *no:*

Teacher:	(Points to a snow picture.)	
	Regnet es?	*Is it raining?*
Students:	Nein.	*No.*

8.3.2d   CLOCK WITH MOVABLE HANDS

The teacher moves the hands of the clock and then asks if it is a certain time. Students respond *yes* or *no:*

Teacher:	(Moves the hands of the clock to 2:15.)	
	Il est deux heures moins le quart, n'est-ce pas?	*It is 1:45, isn't it?*
Students:	Non.	*No.*

8.3.2e   PICTURE SETS

The student hears a sentence and sees a set of three pictures. The student then indicates which picture portrays the action described on the tape.[5]

(Tape): Ella está tomando su leche.   *She is drinking her milk.*
(Pictures): girl drinking hot chocolate, girl drinking milk, boy drinking juice

8.3.2f   SEQUENCING EVENTS: DRAGNET

The teacher reads an adaptation of the detective serial *Dragnet*. Eleven events occur in the story. The class must remember the sequence of events. Then the teacher distributes dittoed sheets on which there are eleven sketches depicting

---

[5] Taken from Harris Winitz, James A. Reeds and Paul A. García, *Natural Learning: Spanish* (Kansas City, Mo.: General Linguistics Corporation, 1975). Address: P.O. Box 7172, Kansas City, Mo. 64113.

each of the events. The students are asked to write the numbers of the pictures in the correct order:

1. Ich kam bei Fritz an.   *I arrived at Fred's house.*
2. Ich ging die Treppe hinauf.   *I went upstairs to see him.*
3. Ich ging in sein Zimmer hinein.   *I entered his room.*
4. Ich sah Fritz auf einem Stuhl sitzen.   *I saw Fred sitting in his armchair.*
5. Ich näherte mich ihm.   *I went up to him.*
6. Er richtete eine Pistole auf mich.   *He pointed a pistol at me.*
7. Ich erfaßte die Pistole und warf sie aus dem Fenster.   *I grabbed the pistol and threw it out the window.*
8. Fritz lief auf die Tür zu.   *Fred ran to the door.*
9. Ich lief ihm nach.   *I followed him.*
10. Er fiel die Treppe hinunter.   *He fell down the stairs.*
11. Am Fuß der Treppe saß ich auf ihm bis die Polizei ankam.   *At the bottom of the steps, I sat on him until the police arrived.*

8.3.3   Giving native language equivalents

Students can also show their comprehension by giving a native language equivalent. (This is limited, of course, to classes where all students speak the same native language and where this language is shared by the teacher.)

The advantage of a quick translation is that the teacher can check immediately whether all members of the class have understood a difficult phrase or sentence. Oral translation also forces the students to go beyond understanding the "gist" of a sentence and focuses their attention on the interrelationships among all the components of the sentence.

Oral translation should, however, be used sparingly. It is the means to an end, and that end is listening comprehension without the need for recourse to the native language.

8.4 HEARING STRUCTURE SIGNALS

Students are often so busy listening for content words and trying to determine "who is doing what" that they fail to listen to structure signals. They might identify a scene as occurring in a restaurant because they have heard key vocabulary items, but they do not know whether the couple has just ordered, whether they are planning to order, or whether they have already finished eating.

While intermediate and advanced students often fail to listen for verb tense or for whether the conversation has shifted from the formal *you* to the familiar *you*, beginning students often need much practice even in recognizing verb subjects, singular-plural markers, and case differences.

The teacher may easily prepare exercises that help students listen for structure signals. In class, the teacher reads aloud ten sentences containing the structural feature while the class mark their responses on a piece of paper. Then the ten sentences are read again, and answers are corrected. Such exercises may also be recorded and used in the language laboratory.

Advanced students may be asked to prepare their own sets of sentences. At the beginning of the class, one student is assigned to read the ten sentences he or she has prepared and then to correct the answers of the others.

The following examples show some types of exercises that can be devised. When possible, these exercises could be framed in a situational context.

8.4.1 Listening for number

8.4.1a NOUN MARKERS

The teacher reads a series of sentences. As the students hear the plural, they raise their hands or mark their papers:

1. Le garçon parle français.	*The boy speaks French.*
2. Les filles parlent français.	*The girls speak French.*
3. L'homme parle français.	*The man speaks French.*
4. Les enfants parlent français.	*The children speak French.*

8.4.1b VERB FORMS

The teacher reads sentences with *il* or *ils* as a subject. The students determine whether the sentence is definitely singular, definitely plural, or whether it could be either.

You will hear statements about Robert and Chantal. Listen carefully, and decide whether the speaker is talking about only Robert, about Robert and Chantal, or whether you cannot tell. Then, place a check mark (√) in the proper column.

Robert	Robert and Chantal	cannot tell
☐	☒	☐
☒	☐	☐
☐	☒	☐
☐	☐	☒

1. Ils boivent du lait.   *They drink milk.*
2. Il essuie les verres.   *He wipes the glasses.*
3. Ils partent.   *They leave.*
4. Il(s) découvre(nt) le trésor.   *He (or they) discover the treasure.*

8.4.2 Listening for gender

8.4.2a NOUN MARKERS

(1) The teacher reads a series of sentences. The students write on their sheets M for masculine and F for feminine:

1. Es un animal.   *It's an animal.*
2. Es una canción.   *It's a song.*
3. Es una radio.   *It's a radio.*
4. Es una amiga.   *It's a girl friend.*

(2) For the German exercise the students write M, F, or N (for neuter):

1. Ich habe ein Auto.   *I have a car.*
2. Ich habe eine Kamera.   *I have a camera.*
3. Ich habe einen Hut.   *I have a hat.*
4. Ich habe ein Rad.   *I have a bicycle.*

(3) Some of the sentences describe Simon, and others describe Nathalie. The students raise their hand when they hear a sentence describing Nathalie.

1. Mon ami est petit.   *My boy friend is small.*
2. Mon amie est intelligente. *My girl friend is intelligent.*
3. Mon amie est grande.   *My girl friend is tall.*
4. Mon ami est méchant.   *My boy friend is bad.*

(4) The students listen to a series of sentences. On their papers they have two columns—one marked José, the other María. As they hear the adjectives, they put a check mark in the proper column:

	José	María	
1. ¡Qué simpática es!		√	*How nice she is!*
2. ¡Qué alto es!	√		*How tall he is!*
3. ¡Qué bonita es!		√	*How pretty she is!*
4. ¡Qué linda es!		√	*How beautiful she is!*

(5) The teacher reads sentences from a conversation between Alain and Claire on the telephone. The students are told to listen to the adjectives in order to find out who is talking—Alain or Claire. On their papers the students write A for Alain and C for Claire:

1. Maman dit que je suis trop grande pour cela.   *Mama says I'm too big for that.*
2. Mon ami me dit, "Que tu es méchante!"   *My boy friend tells me, "You are really mean!"*
3. Dis-moi où tu es; je suis très curieux.   *Tell me where you are; I'm very curious.*
4. Moi, parresseuse! Tu es fou!   *Me, lazy! You're crazy!*
5. Papa croit que je suis malheureux.   *Papa thinks I'm unhappy.*

8.4.3   Pronouns

8.4.3a   PERSONAL PRONOUNS

The teacher reads a series of sentences. The students have a paper with groups of three pronouns for each item. They circle the correct one:

1. Voy a casa.   (yo)   tú   él   *I'm going home.*
2. No estudias mucho.   yo   (tú)   él   *You don't study much.*
3. Sale temprano.   yo   tú   (él)   *He's leaving early.*
4. Necesito una blusa.   (yo)   tú   él   *I need a blouse.*

8.4.3b   OBJECT PRONOUNS

(1) The students hear a series of sentences with the object pronouns *le, la, les.* On their papers they have three columns: *le cadeau, la radio, les skis.* They are to put a check mark under the column that refers to the object mentioned.[6]

1. Je ne le vois pas. (le cadeau)   *I don't see it. (the gift)*

---

[6] Based on *A-LM French, Level One, Teacher's Edition*, 2d ed. (New York: Harcourt Brace Jovanovich, Inc., 1969), p. T73.

2. Elle ne les trouve pas. (les skis)   *She doesn't find them. (the skis)*
3. Il ne la porte pas. (la radio)   *He isn't carrying it. (the radio)*
4. Tu ne le prends pas. (le cadeau)   *You're not taking it. (the gift)*

(2) ESL

The students hear a series of sentences spoken at normal speed with the typical American tendency to reduce *him* to "m," *her* to "er" and *it* (with an unreleased *t*). On their papers they have three columns: a girl, a boy, a book. They are to put a check under the column that refers to the object mentioned.

1. I can't see'm.
2. They don't see'er.
3. I'll buy it.
4. Do you want to sell it?
5. She'll find'm.
6. We'll tell'm.
7. They'll visit'er.
8. Will you call'er?

8.4.4   Verb tenses

The teacher asks the class to raise their hands when they hear a sentence in the immediate future:

1. Il va partir.   *He's going to leave.*
2. Nous venons de manger.   *We just ate.*
3. Elles vont venir.   *They are going to come.*
4. Je viens de déjeuner.   *I just had lunch.*

8.4.5   Identifying subject and object

The students hear a sentence. On their paper they see two nouns. They mark S beside the noun that was the subject of the sentence and O beside the noun that was the object:

Voice:	Den schwarzen Hund wird der Mann nicht kaufen.	*The man will not buy the black dog.*
Paper:	Hund O Mann S	*dog (O) man (S)*
Voice:	Die Mutter wird einen Kuchen backen.	*The mother will bake a cake.*
Paper:	Mutter S Kuchen O	*mother (S) cake (O)*

8.5   LISTENING TO UNFAMILIAR MATERIAL

In most language classes students get little opportunity to listen to difficult and totally unfamiliar material. Many do not know what to do when they suddenly hear an onslaught of the foreign language—on a standardized listening test, for example, or when traveling abroad.

The following activities introduce the student to foreign speech that he or she is not expected to understand.

8.5.1   Identifying the language

Even beginning students should be taught to identify the foreign language when they hear it spoken and not to mix it up with other unknown languages.

8.5.1a   USING LESSON TAPES

The foreign language department in a school can make composite tapes containing snatches of material from the French program, the Spanish program, the Italian program, the German program, and so on. Sample publisher's tapes for languages not offered in the school also have foreign speech samples.

As students hear short snatches of a foreign language, they pick out samples of the language they are studying. A ditto sheet may be prepared to read as follows:

	French	not French
Selection 1	○	○
Selection 2	○	○
Selection 3	○	○

8.5.1b   USING RADIO BROADCASTS

The teacher uses a portable tape recorder to record snatches of foreign language broadcasts. In Spanish class the students raise their hands when the language is Spanish and keep their hands down when some other language is being played.

8.5.2   Anticipating sentence completion

Students become more involved in listening comprehension activities if they themselves are called upon to predict how the speaker will complete the sentence or what word he or she will use next.

The teacher plays a recorded sentence or part of a dialog and then stops the tape before a predictable word:

Voice 1:	Kennst du das Buch?	*Do you know the book?*
Voice 2:	Ich habe es gestern gekauft, aber ich habe es noch nicht _____.	*I bought it yesterday, but I haven't _____ it yet.*
Students:	gelesen, angefangen. . . .	*read, begun. . . .*
Voice 1:	Tu veux aller au cinéma ce soir?	*Do you want to go to the movies this evening?*
Voice 2:	Il y a un bon _____.	*There's a good _____.*
Students:	film, western. . . .	*film, western. . . .*

Then the teacher rewinds the tape to the beginning of the sentence and plays the entire sentence.

8.5.3   Listening to stories

From time to time, the teacher should give the students practice hearing stories in the foreign language. Although the students will not understand much of what they hear, they will catch a few words here and there, and they will be getting a feel for the foreign language.

8.5.3a   USING VISUALS

The teacher uses a flannel board or line drawings as an aid in telling a familiar story, such as "Goldilocks and the Three Bears," in the foreign language.

8.5.3b   USING AN ILLUSTRATED STORYBOOK

The teacher tells a story in the foreign language, pointing to the illustrations in a book to help the students in their comprehension of what is being said.

8.5.3c   USING GESTURES

The teacher tells of a personal incident that happened over the weekend. Maybe he or she parked his or her car in a tow zone and came back to find it missing. As the misadventures are told, he or she uses gestures to help convey meaning.

8.5.3d   READING ALOUD

At the time of a Christian holiday that is celebrated in the country where the foreign language is spoken, the teacher can read aloud the corresponding passage from the Bible.

Sometimes commercial products have labels or instructions printed in several languages. For example, in a German class, the teacher might bring in and read aloud the German instructions to a Lego construction set. A French teacher might bring in a French book on origami and explain in French how to fold a paper bird. The Spanish teacher might get a Spanish TV guide and read the write-up of a popular TV program as it appears in Spanish.

8.5.4   Listening to newscasts

The teacher records the previous night's foreign language newscast (over local radio or shortwave) and brings the tape to class. Since the students are aware of current events, they can understand much of the foreign language newscast, especially when place names and the names of prominent people are mentioned.

8.6   UNDERSTANDING SHORT ORAL PASSAGES

Students at all levels of instruction need much practice in listening to short passages that recombine known vocabulary and structures with occasional unfamiliar expressions.

8.6.1   Passages prepared by the teacher

Teachers can prepare short passages similar to the ones that follow. Several teachers can work together to develop and record such paragraphs for use in the classroom or in the language laboratory. It is also possible to prepare a script and read the passages aloud to the class.

8.6.1a   PANTOMIME

The teacher reads the directions for a short play. The students who have been assigned the various parts act them out in pantomime. They are not to speak.

Here is an ESL example:

What's the difference?[7]
Characters: Mr. Wilson; the man at the bank window; the bank robber, a policeman

Directions:
Mr. Wilson is at his desk. He gets up from his desk. He goes to another room to get some tea.
The bank robber comes into the bank. He walks to the man at the teller window. He gives a piece of paper to the man at the window.

[7] From Jean N. Dale and Willard D. Sheeler, *The Whistler*, Reading and Exercise Series, Book One (Portland, Oregon: ESL International; and New York: Oxford University Press, 1973, 1975), pp. 38–39.

The man at the window reads the piece of paper. He thinks, "What am I going
to do?"
He gives the robber all the money.
The robber leaves the bank.
The teller runs to get the policeman.
The policeman runs after the bank robber.
Mr. Wilson comes into the room. He sits down at his desk. He doesn't know about
the robber. He thinks, "There's nothing interesting in this bank."

8.6.1b DEFINITIONS

After hearing the definition, the student is expected to furnish the correct
answer:

(1) Je pense à un animal qui a de
longues oreilles et une petite queue.
Il aime beaucoup les carottes, les
choux et la laitue. Qu'est-ce que
c'est?

*I'm thinking of an animal that has
long ears and a little tail. It loves
carrots, cabbage, and lettuce.
What is it?*

(2) Es un artículo de ropa que se
lleva cuando hace frío. ¿Que es?

*It's an article of clothing that is worn
when the weather is cold. What is
it?*

(3) Ich kenne ein kleines Land in
Europa. Dort findet man viele hohe
und schöne Gebirge. Die wichtigsten
Sprachen dieses Landes sind:
Deutsch, Französisch und Italien-
isch. In diesem Lande werden sehr
gute Uhren hergestellt. Die Haupt-
stadt heißt Bern. Das Land heißt

_____.

*I know a little country in Europe.
You find many high, beautiful
mountains there. The most important languages of this country
are German, French and Italian.
Very good watches are made in this
country. The capital is Bern. The
country is called* _____.

(4) Damit kann man über den
Ozean reisen. Die Reise dauert
mehrere Tage. Es gibt sehr gutes
Essen. Abends kann man trinken,
tanzen und singen. Wir reisen auf
einem _____.

*You can travel across the ocean on it.
The trip lasts several days. They
serve very good food. In the evening you can drink, dance, and
sing. We are traveling on a*

_____.

8.6.1c EAVESDROPPING

Students are expected to infer certain information from what they hear:

(1) Listen to the following comments made by teachers in a French school.
On your paper, indicate which subject each one teaches:

1. Je ne sais pas pourquoi la pro-
nonciation de mes élèves est
si mauvaise. J'ai pourtant de
très bons disques américains
que je leur fais écouter en
classe.

*I don't know why my students' pro-
nunciation is so bad. After all, I
have very good American records
which I have them listen to in
class.*

2. Mes élèves ont mauvaise
mémoire. Ils oublient toujours les dates les plus
importantes.

*My students have bad memories.
They always forget the most important dates.*

3. Il faut que je donne à manger
à mes rats. Les élèves n'ont
rien mis dans leurs cages.

*I have to feed my rats. The students
didn't put anything in their cages.*

(2) Listen to the following statements spoken by German salesclerks. Indicate
on your papers what product each person is selling:

1. Wollen Sie nicht ihrer Freundin einen herrlichen Rosen-
strauß kaufen?

*Don't you want to buy your girl
friend a beautiful bouquet of
roses?*

2. Nehmen Sie zwei von den roten
Tabletten, eine um acht Uhr
morgens, die andere acht
Uhr abends!

*Take two of the red tablets, one at 8
in the morning, the other at 8 in
the evening.*

3. Wenn Sie einen Volkswagen
kaufen, können Sie viel
leichter durch den Verkehr
kommen.

*If you buy a Volkswagen, you can get
through traffic much more easily.*

4. Herr Schmidt, das ist das echte
Schwarzbrot, das wir hier
verkaufen.

*Mr. Schmidt, that's genuine black
bread that we sell here.*

5. Frau Köhler, diese Bratwürste
sind gerade angekommen.
Sie sind frisch und billig.

*Mrs. Köhler, these sausages just
arrived. They are fresh and inexpensive.*

8.6.1d PROVIDING TITLES

The teacher reads a short narrative while the students listen and try to retain
the details. Then the students are asked to give possible titles to the selection.
This exercise reveals their understanding of the passage:

(1) Les habitants du village se
demandent s'ils ne devraient pas
essayer de pénétrer dans cette
maison. Voilà cinq ans que l'on ne
voit personne entrer ou sortir de

*The inhabitants of the village wonder
if they shouldn't try to get into that
house. It's been five years since
anyone has seen a person enter or
leave the ancient Dufour residence.*

l'ancienne demeure des Dufour. C'était une famille qui n'aimait pas la société et qui n'invitait jamais.

Récemment un voisin a entendu des cris terrifiants qui semblaient venir de la tour.

They were an unsociable family who never invited anyone.

Recently a neighbor heard terrifying screams that seemed to be coming from the tower.

(2) A Paris quand il n'y a plus de place dans un autobus le conducteur met sur la porte du véhicule une affiche qui porte le mot COMPLET. Cela veut dire qu'aucun voyageur n'a le droit de monter.

Un touriste américain, ignorant cette coutume, croyait que COM-PLET était le nom d'une ville importante puisque tous les autobus qui y allaient étaient pleins. Alors il courait après tous les autobus qui portaient ce nom dans l'espoir de visiter cette ville importante.

Le malheureux a dû retourner en Amérique sans avoir jamais découvert COMPLET.

In Paris when there's no more room on the bus, the driver puts a sign on the door of the bus which reads "Complet" (Full).

An American tourist, unaware of this custom, thought that "Complet" was the name of an important city since every bus that went there was full. So he ran after every bus that posted this sign in the hope of visiting this important city.

The unfortunate man had to return to America without ever having discovered "Complet."

8.6.1e GUIDED LISTENING

Before playing the recorded passage, or before reading it aloud, the teacher tells the students what to listen for:

(1) Questions in English

You are going to hear about Juan. Find out how many people are in his family, where he lives, and what sport he enjoys:

Hoy es domingo. Juan no va a la escuela. Después de la comida del mediodía, Juan va con sus dos hermanos a un partido de fútbol. A los jóvenes mexicanos les gusta mucho este deporte.

Today is Sunday. John does not go to school. After the midday meal, John goes to a soccer match with his two brothers. Young Mexicans like this sport very much.

(2) Questions in the foreign language

Ecoutez bien ce paragraphe. Je vous demanderai combien de

Listen carefully to this paragraph. I'm going to ask you how many

garçons il y a dans la famille d'Henri, où il habite, et quel sport il aime:	*boys there are in Henry's family, where he lives, and what sport he likes.*
C'est aujourd'hui dimanche. Le dimanche les enfants ne vont pas à l'école. Après le déjeuner, Henri et ses deux frères vont à un match de football. Les jeunes Parisiens aiment beaucoup ce sport.	*Today is Sunday. On Sunday the children don't go to school. After lunch, Henry and his two brothers go to a soccer game. Young Parisians like this sport very much.*

8.6.1f LISTENING FOR COMMUNICATION

In the listening for communication exercise, the student tries to extract the essential information from the recorded text. The focus is not on understanding the entire passage but on picking out the main points.

(1) Taking a telephone message[8]

You are living in Germany with a German family (the Schmidts) for the summer. The whole family has gone out of the house and you are left alone. The telephone rings, you answer the phone, and, after appropriate greetings, the party on the line wants to talk to Frau Schmidt. You try to tell her she is not there, but she insists on giving you a message. Listen carefully and take notes in English. Then write up the message.

Ich bin die Nachbarin, Frau Müller. Ich wollte Frau Schmidt sprechen. Würden Sie ihr bitte sagen, dass ich morgen um 8 Uhr vorbeikomme und dann können wir zusammen einkaufen gehen. Sie hat mir gestern gesagt, dass ich mit meinem Auto fahren soll, aber das kann ich jetzt nicht. Ich möchte wissen, ob wir mit Frau Schmidt's Auto fahren können. Sagen Sie ihr, dass sie mich heute abend um 10 Uhr anrufen soll.	*I am the neighbor, Mrs. Müller. I wanted to speak to Mrs. Schmidt. Would you please tell her that I will come by tomorrow at eight and then we can go shopping together. Yesterday she told me that I should drive my car, but I won't be able to now. I would like to know whether we would go in Mrs. Schmidt's car. Tell her that she should phone me tonight at ten.*

(2) Listening to a recorded announcement

The students listen to a recorded telephone announcement. For instance, if they listen to a weather announcement, they should try to understand what the weather will be like the next day. If they listen to the announcement of a movie house, they should listen for the names of the films and the show times.

---

[8] Example taken from Walter H. Bartz, "A Study of the Relationship of Certain Learner Factors with the Ability to Communicate in a Second Language (German) for the Development of Measures of Communicative Competence" Ph.D. diss. (The Ohio State University, 1974), pp. 154–55.

(3) Taking directions

Each student receives a copy of a street map, either of their home town or of a city in a target language country. All students are given the same starting point. The students then hear directions on how to reach another point on the map. They trace the route as they understand it, and mark an "X" on what they presume to be the destination.

8.6.2   Commercially recorded passages

Most language textbooks have some supplementary dialogs and passages that are available in recorded form. The most useful passages for teaching listening comprehension are those which the student has not had the opportunity to read in advance. If the dialogs are in the students' textbooks, have the students keep their books closed.

A fine source for listening comprehension passages are the tapes that accompany programs that were previously used in the school but that have been replaced by new materials. Students should be encouraged to guess at words and expressions they do not know. The teacher can present a few unfamiliar key words before playing the passage if he or she feels that this would improve the students' comprehension.

Another advantage of the commercial tapes is that the teacher can usually obtain a copy of the tape script. (In previously used series, the script is the textbook.) From the script the teacher can prepare the types of activities suggested here:[9]

8.6.2a   ORAL QUESTIONS

The teacher plays the tape and then asks oral questions about the content of the passage. In the Holt series, for example, the recombined conversations are accompanied by questions.[10] The teacher can also formulate his or her own simple questions.

If students are not able to answer all the questions, the teacher plays the tape for them once more.

8.6.2b   WRITING QUESTIONS ON THE BOARD

Write the questions on the board or put them on an overhead transparency. Have students read the questions aloud. Play the tape to the class. Call on students to answer the questions orally. Then play the tape a second time and have

[9] Adapted from a talk by Frederick Bourassa, Calgary Annual Teacher's Convention, Calgary, Alberta, February 28, 1970.
[10] Dominique Côté, Sylvia Levy, and Patricia O'Connor *Ecouter et Parler* (New York: Holt, Rinehart and Winston, 1968).

the students raise their hands when they hear the answer to the first question. When the hands go up, stop the tape. Repeat the question aloud and have students give the answer according to what they have just heard on the tape.

Variation: A writing exercise may be introduced at this point by having the class write out the correct answers.

8.6.2c   TRUE-FALSE STATEMENTS

The teacher prepares a series of true-false statements on the listening passage. The following options may be used:

(1) The true-false statements are written on the board (or placed on an overhead) before the tape is played. They are read aloud in advance. Then the students listen to the passage. When the tape is finished, the students answer the questions.

(2) The true-false statements are shown after the tape has been played.

(3) The true-false statements are not written down for the students to read. The teacher reads each statement aloud once the tape has been played. Students answer by writing true or false on their papers.

After the students have answered the true-false questions, the teacher replays the tape, stopping it at appropriate points to indicate the correct answers to the quiz.

The following true-false questions were prepared to accompany Conversation No. 4 in Lesson 9 of *Ecouter et Parler:*[11]

1. Pauline n'a pas de travail à faire ce matin. oui
    Pauline doesn't have any work to do this morning. yes
2. Marie veut aller à la bibliothèque. non
    Marie wants to go the library. no
3. Il fait plus chaud qu'hier aujourd'hui. oui
    It's hotter today than it was yesterday. yes
4. Pauline va demander à son père si elle peut accompagner Marie. non
    Pauline is going to ask her father if she can go with Marie. no
5. Plus tard, elles vont aller au cinéma. non
    Later they are going to go to the movie. no
6. Marie préfère les films d'aventure. non
    Marie prefers adventure films. no
7. Elles vont se retrouver vers trois heures. oui
    They are going to meet each other around three o'clock. yes

[11] Ibid., p. 123.

8.6.2d MULTIPLE-CHOICE QUESTIONS

The teacher prepares brief multiple-choice questions on the listening passages. These may be presented to the students in one of the following ways:

(1) The teacher writes the multiple-choice questions on the board (or on an overhead transparency). He or she lets the students read them and then covers the questions up. The teacher plays the tape, stops the tape, and then lets students answer the questions.

(2) The teacher writes the multiple-choice questions on the board, but lets the students see them only after they have heard the tape.

(3) The teacher writes only the answer choices on the board. He or she plays the tape and then reads the questions aloud while students select the appropriate options.

(4) The teacher plays the tape, then reads both the questions and the options. When students have answered the multiple-choice questions, he or she plays the tape again. It is stopped at appropriate points to indicate the correct answers.

The following multiple-choice questions were prepared to accompany Conversation No. 2, Lesson 9 of *Ecouter et Parler:*[12]

1. Guillaume téléphone à _____.	*William telephones*
a. Richard	*Richard*
b. Martin	*Martin*
c. Robert	*Robert*
d. Henri	*Henry*
2. Guillaume lui demande _____.	*William asks him*
a. s'il a du travail	*if he has any work*
b. s'il doit aider son professeur	*if he has to help his teacher*
c. s'il aime le français	*if he likes French*
d. quel travail le professeur leur a donné	*what work the teacher gave them.*
3. Guillaume lui demande cela parce qu'il _____.	*William asks him that because*
a. l'a oublié	*he has forgotten it*
b. est libre ce soir	*he is free this evening*
c. y a de bons programmes à la télé	*there are good programs on the T.V.*
d. ne va pas bien	*he isn't feeling well*
4. Un des garçons va téléphoner à _____.	*One of the boys is going to telephone*
a. Lisette Bernier	*Lisette Bernier*
b. Jeannette Benoît	*Jeannette Benoît*
c. Paulette Renier	*Paulette Renier*
d. Claudette Fournier	*Claudette Fournier*

[12] Ibid., p. 120.

5. Guillaume demande à son ami
de lui téléphoner à _____.
  a. cinq heures moins le quart
  b. six heures et quart
  c. six heures et demie
  d. six heures moins le quart

*William asks his friend to telephone
him at _____.*
4:45
6:15
6:30
5:45

8.6.2e RECORDED QUESTIONS AND ANSWERS

If the listening passage is accompanied with recorded questions and answers, the following approach is possible:

Play the conversation. Then play the first question and stop the tape. Ask students for possible short answers to the question. Then play the answer (often longer) as given on the tape. Stop the tape again and have the entire class repeat the recorded answer. Continue in like manner for the remaining questions.

8.6.2f DITTOED WORKSHEETS

Simple questions, true-false statements, and multiple-choice questions may be prepared in ditto form. These dittos may be used in the language laboratory or for individual work with tapes or cassettes in the classroom. The teacher prepares the tape to accompany the dittos in the following manner:

1. Voice on tape tells students to record the name and number of the recorded exercise.
2. Teacher plays the recorded conversation once (or twice).
3. Voice on tape tells students to answer the questions.
4. Teacher gives the correct answers.
5. Teacher plays the recording one last time.

8.7 UNDERSTANDING COLLOQUIAL SPEECH

The aim of instruction in the listening skill is to bring the student to a point where he or she can understand colloquial speech, with its muffled or missing sounds and its fused vowels and consonants. The true test of listening comprehension occurs when the student goes abroad and hears people all around him or her speaking another language.

In the classroom the teacher must go beyond textbook recordings. Most textbook recordings are not appropriate for listening practice at this colloquial level, for the speakers enunciate too clearly and speak too slowly. The best types of materials are recorded interviews, either radio broadcasts or records of conversations with famous persons. Speeches, songs, radio plays, and newscasts are also usable, even though the speech is often stylized.

8.7.1 General comprehension

The teacher can check on the general comprehension of students by asking questions about the recording, by having students give titles to the passage, or by letting the students themselves ask questions about what they have heard.

In the following example the teacher prepares questions on a short-wave newscast he or she has recorded at home. The questions are distributed before the newscast is played.

1. ¿Qué ciudad fue atacada?
2. ¿Qué partido salió victorioso?
3. ¿Cuánto tiempo duró la operación militar?
4. ¿Cuántos muertos hubo?
5. ¿Cómo dejaron la ciudad?
6. ¿Qué les pasó a los habitantes?

Which city was attacked?
Which party was victorious?
How long did the military operation last?
How many deaths were there?
How did they leave the city?
What happened to the inhabitants?

Ahora, ¡escuchen Vds.!

Now, listen!

Las victoriosas tropas federales acaban de entrar en la ciudad de Córdoba. Después de tres días de batallas sangrientas, perdimos doscientos soldados. Según los cálculos oficiales el número de muertos enemigos serían tres mil.

Los reporteros dicen que la mitad de la ciudad fue destrozada y que hay incendios por todas partes. Los habitantes ya empiezan a refugiarse en las montañas.

The victorious federal troops have just entered the city of Córdoba. After three days of bloody battle, we lost 200 soldiers. According to official estimates, the number of enemy dead must be 3000.

Reporters say that half of the city was destroyed and that there are fires everywhere. The inhabitants are already beginning to take refuge in the mountains.

8.7.2 Paraphrasing rapid speech or regional variants

Eventually the student must be introduced to rapid speech and to the regional variants of the language he or she is learning (Austrian German, Provençal French, Castilian Spanish, Cuban Spanish).

The objective of instruction is that the student understand other types of speech, even though he or she is not expected to imitate them. The most appropriate comprehension check is paraphrasing the speech sample into standard speech.

8.7.2a ORAL PARAPHRASING

The student hears a sentence in rapid speech or a dialect, for example, *i'vient pas, chaps nicht, woncha come?* The teacher then asks the students to give the standard equivalent of what they have heard: *Il ne vient pas. Ich habe es nicht. Won't you come?*

This type of exercise may be done with a full class where the teacher either imitates the rapid speech or regional variant, or where he or she plays recorded samples on a tape recorder and then stops the tape to let students paraphrase the sentences.

A taped exercise may be prepared on the same model to allow students to work individually. The student hears the rapid speech sentence, and in the pause that follows tries to give the standard equivalent. Then he or she hears the voice on the tape confirm the standard equivalent and repeat the rapid sample once more.

8.7.2b WRITTEN PARAPHRASING

The standard speech equivalents may be prepared in written form.

(1) Overhead transparency: The teacher prepares an overhead transparency with the standard sentences. The sentences are masked. The teacher says or plays the first sentence of regional speech. The students try to give the standard equivalent and then the teacher lowers the mask to show the written form.

(2) Ditto: Students are given a ditto to work with independently. They are told to mask the sentences with another piece of paper and to look at the written paraphrase only after they have listened to the recorded sentence and tried to understand it.

8.7.3 Written transcriptions

Advanced students should be allowed to listen to a recording several times to try to understand every word that is being said. As they listen, they write out what they hear, that is, they make a written transcription of the selection.

8.7.3a TYPES OF TRANSCRIPTIONS

(1) Full transcription: The student writes down the entire selection.

(2) Partial transcription: The student is given a ditto sheet in which difficult parts, garbled sections, and the like are written out. He or she fills in the remaining text.

(3) Graded transcriptions: The best students do a full transcription. Good students get a ditto on which several very difficult parts are written out. Average students get a ditto on which all difficult parts are written out.

8.7.3b   USING THE TRANSCRIPTION IN CLASS

(1) Before class, each student puts a sentence of his or her previously written transcription on the chalkboard. The teacher has the first student read his or her sentence aloud. Then the others are asked if they have any corrections or additions. As the sentences are being reviewed, the teacher may use the errors as a point of departure for brief grammar explanations. Students correct their own papers. They are told to listen to the recording once more after class. (The teacher may wish to play the recording to the entire class.)

(2) A student is asked to read aloud the first sentence of his or her transcription. The teacher writes on the board, or on a transparency, those parts of the sentence which are correct. He or she calls on other students to fill in the blanks. Gradually the entire transcription is reconstructed. Students correct their own work.

(3) The teacher brings a tape recording to class and plays the selection. Then he or she goes back to the beginning, plays the first part of the first sentence, and asks students to relate what they have heard. The teacher writes the difficult parts on the board. If students have not understood every word, he or she replays that segment until they understand it.

If the teacher has difficulty understanding conversational French, similar transcription exercises may be done with short excerpts from recordings of plays or books. In this way, the teacher has a written copy of the recording, even though the students do not. Often record albums of foreign language songs provide copies of the lyrics. The teacher can use these texts to make dittos for partial and graded transcriptions.

8.7.4   Foreign-language movies

Students should be encouraged to go to foreign-language movies as often as possible. To improve listening comprehension, they should see the same movie at least twice. The first time, they are involved with the plot. The second time, they can visually notice cultural differences while listening to the language more attentively. They should be instructed to ignore the subtitles and listen only to the foreign language. The best test of listening comprehension is the ability to follow the dialog with eyes closed.

8.8   UNDERSTANDING EXTENDED PASSAGES

Intensive listening practice may be termed "audio-immersion." Here the students listen to extended passages: recordings of speeches, radio plays, dramas, even songs and children's story records.

The benefits of audio-immersion should not be underestimated. In a recent experiment with advanced ESL students at the University of Giessen (West Germany), Edward Sittler compared a control group, which took the standard language sequence (conversation, composition, grammar review) with an experimental group, which did not go to class but spent an equivalent amount of time listening to recordings. The students in the experimental group did not write papers or discuss what they had been listening to; they simply listened to whatever cassettes intrigued them: Kennedy speeches, "Dragnet," BBC dramas, recorded novels, and so on.

At the end of the year, the experimental group scored significantly higher than the control group on measures of grammar, vocabulary, and reading comprehension, and had made significant gains on their TOEFL (Test of English as a Foreign Language) scores.[13]

The key to audio-immersion activities is to encourage the student to engage in extensive listening practice. If possible, recordings should be available on cassettes so that students can take them home and listen at their leisure.

8.8.1   Keeping a log

The students are expected to keep a log of which recordings they have listened to, and their reactions. Was the recording easy to understand? Difficult? Would they recommend the recording to a classmate? These evaluations help the teacher catalog the recordings for future use.

8.8.2   Preparing discussion questions

The students listen to a group of people discussing an important issue, or they listen to a speech by a well-known person. They are asked to write out two or three discussion questions related to what they have heard. These questions are then used as the basis for small group work the next day.

8.8.3   Taking notes

The students listen to a radio play and take a few notes to help them situation the action. In class, groups of students are asked to act out impromptu skits relating what happened in each segment of the story.[14]

---

[13] For a description of this project and other related research, see Edward Sittler, ed., *Die Logik des Hörens: Besser Hören = Besser Lernen* (Düsseldorf: Pädagogisches Institut, 1975), Schriftenreihe, Heft 26.

[14] A variety of action-packed recordings, such as "Suivez la piste" in French, are available from EMC, 180 East Sixth Street, Saint Paul, Minn. 55101.

outline

nine
Speaking

earning to speak a second language is a lengthy process. First students must carefully repeat models and imitate the teacher. They may memorize basic sentences to gain confidence in their ability to speak the second language. They may practice sentences and do oral drills. These activities are all preliminary to actual conversation. In a sense, these activities may be termed vocalizing.

Students are truly speaking only when they are generating their own sentences. Students who say *Répétez, s'il vous plaît* are using the new language to communicate what they want to say.

In the classroom the teacher should try to allow for some true speaking activity, either guided conversation or, at later stages, free conversation in every unit. Foreign language is one course in the curriculum where students should be encouraged to talk a great deal in class and to express their own ideas, not simply what the teacher tells them to say.

9.1   GENERAL CONSIDERATIONS

After the basic dialog or list of sentences is learned, and after the guided conversation or directed dialog is practiced, the real work begins. It is at this point that true speaking activity can take place. The teacher should ask numerous questions and elicit responses from comments he or she makes. For example, if the dialog sentence is about buying a blue dress, ask individual girls if they own a blue dress or if they have bought one recently. If one of the basic sentences is about disliking spinach, ask individual students whether they dislike spinach and what vegetables they prefer.

As the students begin to learn to speak the foreign language, the teacher plays the role of umpire. He or she can tell the students whether they are pronouncing the new language accurately and whether they are using correct forms.

211

Gradually the teacher guides the students to a point where they can begin to judge whether they are producing the new sounds correctly and whether they are using appropriate sentence patterns. When this point is reached, the teacher's main concern is no longer primarily to correct, but rather to encourage the students to practice speaking the foreign language as frequently as possible.

Speaking a language differs from writing it in an important way. When students can judge how accurately they spell and how well they use the sentence patterns they have learned, they usually produce rather accurate written compositions. They have the time to reread what they have written and to correct their own work. But when students are speaking freely, they tend to make mistakes they would not make in writing. Frequently they notice their mistakes right after they have said them, but it is too late to correct them. *Only through much free speaking practice will students improve their command of the spoken language.*

It is the responsibility of the teacher to assume two roles. First, he or she must be a meticulous judge and correct mistakes in the initial language-learning stages. Second, at the more advanced stages he or she must be a coach who encourages and reviews performance. Most frequently the teacher will be shifting from one role to the other.

9.2   INITIAL PRESENTATION: DIALOG TECHNIQUE

The elementary lessons in many foreign language courses begin with a dialog. Traditionally, the student is expected to memorize the dialog and to recite it fluently before practicing structure drills and making grammar generalizations. The lesson may either contain one longer dialog followed by the grammar presentation, or several shorter dialogs, each followed by a section of the grammar presentation.

Should the student memorize the dialog? Memorization can lead to greater fluency and less hesitancy in speaking. The memorization of dialog sentences helps the student acquire correct intonation patterns and offers him or her a model of natural, colloquial speech.

If too much class time must be spent on memorizing the dialog, however, the activity will have a negative effect on the students. The good students will get bored and the slower learners will be frustrated by the difficulties they are experiencing. Moreover, the memorization is simply a point of departure for the teaching of grammar and vocabulary and for the development of language skills. A great deal of time spent memorizing dialogs will mean proportionately less time devoted to language-learning activities.

The teacher must judge how best to utilize the dialogs. If one class memorizes material readily and enjoys doing so, then memorization is a worthwhile activity. If another class balks at this type of rote learning, the dialogs could be used for listening comprehension or reading aloud. In either case, the teacher must go beyond simply teaching the dialog if he or she expects his or her students to develop language skills.

The following sections contain suggestions for enlivening the learning of dialógs.

9.2.1   Presenting the dialog

Some teachers present the dialog first in English, then in the foreign language. Others use the foreign language exclusively. The following techniques are designed to establish the meaning of the dialog lines, either with or without the use of English.

9.2.1a   CUE CARDS

The teacher places cue cards on the chalkboard ledge and points to them as he or she says the line in the target language. The class repeats the French in chorus, by groups or rows, and finally one by one.

Tu veux aller au cinéma ce soir?
(*Would you like to go to the movies tonight?*)

Non, il faut que j'étudie.
(*No, I have to study.*)

Alors, je vais y aller avec Anne.
(*Well, I'll go with Ann, then.*)

9.2.1b CHALKBOARD DRAWINGS

1. Wohin gehst du jetzt, Helga?[1]
   (*Where are you going, Helga?*)

2. Ich gehe nach Hause.
   (*I'm going home.*)

3. Warum fragst du?
   (*Why do you want to know?*)

4. Trinkst du eine Limonade mit mir?
   (*Would you like a lemonade?*)

5. Dort drüben ist ein Stand.
   (*There's a stand.*)

6. Gut. Ich trinke Limonade gern.
   (*Sure, I like lemonade.*)

9.2.1c FLANNEL BOARD

The teacher can use commercial figurines and felt tape or draw his or her own on flannel. The sentences are pronounced either by the teacher or a recording.

---

[1] *A-LM German Level One,* 2d ed. (New York: Harcourt Brace Jovanovich, Inc., 1969), p. 7.

1. ¿Dónde está Tomás?[2]
   (*Where is Thomas?*)

2. ¿Está enfermo?
   (*Is he sick?*)

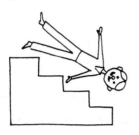

3. No, se cayó en la escalera . . .
   (*No, he fell down the stairs.*)

4. . . . y se rompió un diente.
   (*. . . and broke a tooth.*)

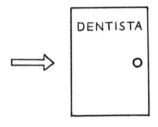

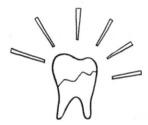

5. ¿Fue al dentista?
   (*Did he go to the dentist's?*)

6. Sí, tuvo que ir. Le dolía mucho.
   (*Yes, he had to go. It hurt so much.*)

9.2.1d IDEOGRAMS

Ideograms are sets of symbols which are used to depict a sentence. Students can help make their own symbols.

Où habite Jean-Michel?
(*Where does John live?*)

[2] Gregory G. LaGrone, et al., *Entender y Hablar*, Teacher's Ed. (New York: Holt, Rinehart, and Winston, 1965), p. 278.

Il habite près de l'église.
(*He lives near the church.*)

Et toi?
(*And you?*)

Moi, j'habite près de l'école.
(*I live near the school.*)

9.2.2   Drilling dialog lines

9.2.2a   CUE CARDS

Cue cards for each dialog line can be homemade or prepared by a publisher:

(1) The teacher places cue cards on the chalkboard ledge and writes a number above each one. As he or she says *Quatre (four)*, the teacher points to a student, who answers: *Vraiment? Moi, je déteste les films de guerre (Really? I hate war movies)*. In addition to individual responses, the teacher can use choral drills, half-class drills, boys and girls, teacher and class dialog practices.

(2) The teacher puts cue cards in a stack and remembers which one is on top. Then the teacher holds the stack behind him or her so that the students cannot see them. The students then guess which card is on top. This gives them practice in saying all the lines. (This exercise is for young junior high school students.)

9.2.2b   WHO SAYS WHAT?

The teacher speaks a certain line and asks which character says it:

Teacher: ¿Quién dice, "¿Por qué no me llamaste anoche?"   *Who says, "Why didn't you call me last night?"*

Student: Pedro dice, "¿Por qué no me llamaste anoche?"   *Peter says, "Why didn't you call me last night?"*

9.2.2c   DIRECTED DIALOG

Directed dialog practice is difficult for the students. It should be carefully prepared, so that the students know what to do. Both the questions and answers should be taught and drilled before this exercise begins:

Question: John, are you going to the movies tonight?
Answer: No, I am not going because I have homework to do.

The difficulty lies in the question: Paul, ask John if he is going to the movies tonight. Many pupils tend to answer: John, if he is going to the movies tonight? Much practice is necessary with this exercise:

Teacher:	Carlos, pregúntele a María si va a la fiesta.	*Charles, ask Mary if she's going to the party.*
Carlos:	María, ¿Vas a la fiesta?	*Mary, are you going to the party?*
Teacher:	María, contéstele que sí, que Ud. va a la fiesta.	*Mary, tell him sure, you're going to the party.*
María:	Sí, voy a la fiesta.	*Sure, I'm going to the party.*

9.2.3 Going beyond the basic dialog

Once the students have memorized the dialog, the teacher can use the sentences as a basis for additional speaking practice.

9.2.3a YES/NO QUESTIONS

The teacher puts cue cards on chalkboard ledge and asks questions to be answered by *yes* or *no* plus a statement:

Teacher:	Est-ce que Guillaume téléphone à Valérie?	*Is Bill phoning Valerie?*
Student:	Non, Guillaume télé-phone à Sylvie.	*No, Bill is phoning Sylvia.*
Teacher:	Ist Heinz im Garten?	*Is Hank in the garden?*
Student:	Nein, Heinz ist im Wohnzimmer.	*No, Hank is in the living room.*

9.2.3b EITHER/OR QUESTIONS

The teacher puts magazine cutouts on the chalkboard with magnets and asks questions such as the following:

Teacher:	¿Le gusta más el café o la leche?	*Do you like coffee or milk better?*
Student:	Me gusta más la leche.	*I like milk better.*
Teacher:	Préférez-vous le football ou le tennis?	*Do you prefer soccer or tennis?*
Student:	Je préfère le football.	*I prefer soccer.*

9.2.3c   WHY—BECAUSE QUESTIONS

Teacher: Répondez à toutes les   *Answer all the questions with*
           questions avec *parce*   because.
           que.

           Pourquoi est-ce que   *Why did Jim break his leg?*
           Jacques s'est cassé la
           jambe?

Student: Parce qu'il est tombé.   *Because he fell.*

9.2.3d   WHO DOES WHAT?

The teacher puts dialog on overhead projector and asks questions about it:

Teacher: Was macht Hans?   *What is Jack doing?*

Student: Hans spielt Tennis.   *Jack is playing tennis.*

Teacher: Que fait Bernard?   *What is Bernard doing?*

Student: Il regarde un film   *He is looking at a detective film.*
           policier.

9.2.3e   HOW (ADVERB) QUESTIONS

The teacher dramatizes each action before he or she asks a question about it:

Teacher: (Sings "La Cucaracha"
             off key.)
           ¿Cómo canta Isabel?   *How does Isabel sing?*

Student: Isabel canta mal.   *Isabel sings badly.*

Teacher: (Speaks rapidly.)
           Comment est-ce que   *How does Claude talk?*
           Claude parle?

Student: Claude parle vite.   *He talks fast.*

9.2.3f   VARYING DIRECT OBJECTS

The teacher puts flannel or felt tape objects on chalkboard ledge. He or she asks individual students to come forward, pick up an object, answer the question *Was bringt Fritz nach Hause? (What does Fred bring home?)* or *¿Qué trae Paco a casa? (What does Frank bring home?)* and put the object on the flannel board. Example: *Fritz bringt eine Katze nach Hause. (Fred brings a cat home.) Paco trae un bote a casa. (Frank brings a boat home.)*

9.2.3g VARYING INDIRECT OBJECTS

On each flash card there is a magazine cutout of a person; some represent professions: doctor, engineer, teacher, and so on. The teacher holds up the cards, and the class says: *Je dis bonjour à la dame, au professeur, au médecin, à la jeune fille.* (*I say hello to the lady, to the teacher, to the doctor, to the girl.*)

9.2.3h PERSONAL QUESTIONS BASED ON DIALOG

¿De qué color es el coche de su padre?	*What color is your father's car?*
¿Cómo se llama la última película que vió Ud.?	*What is the name of the last movie you saw?*
Quel est votre programme préféré à la télévision?	*What is your favorite television program?*
A quelle heure avez-vous dîné hier soir?	*What time did you have dinner last night?*
Wie oft gehen Sie ins Kino?	*How often do you go to the movies?*
Welcher Film gefällt Ihnen am besten?	*What film do you like best?*

9.2.3i PRACTICE USING DEPENDENT AND INDEPENDENT CLAUSES

The teacher should supply most of the information that the students are to use in their answers to his or her question. If the pattern is established, the student needs to furnish only the last two or three words; each of his or her sentences begins with *Si j'étais riche* or *Si yo fuera rico* [a] (*If I were rich*).

Teacher:	Si vous étiez riche, où iriez-vous?	*If you were rich, where would you go?*
Student:	Si j'étais riche, j'irais à Paris.	*If I were rich, I would go to Paris.*
Teacher:	Si vous étiez riche, quelle voiture achèteriez-vous?	*If you were rich, what car would you buy?*
Student:	Si j'étais riche, j'achèterais une Cadillac.	*If I were rich, I would buy a Cadillac.*
Teacher:	Si Ud. fuera rico (a), ¿adónde iría Ud.?	
Student:	Si yo fuera rico (a), iría a Paris.	

Teacher: Si Ud. fuera rico (a),
¿qué clase de coche
compraría Ud.?

Student: Si yo fuera rico (a), compraría un Cadillac.

9.2.4 Using audio-visual programs

Audio-visual programs provide a film or sound filmstrip to accompany the dialog or basic presentation. Many of the techniques of presentation suggested for dialogs may also be adapted to audio-visual programs.

Moreover, the visual part of the program may be used without the sound portion to cue the lines. Individual students may be called upon to play the role of the people on the filmstrip or in the movie.

The filmstrip or the movie is a fine means of presenting parts of a lesson. But like any technique, overuse can lead to boredom. As a change in pace the teacher might wish to present one of the dialogs using posters or cue cards. Later the film can be shown to reinforce what the students have already learned.

As a further change in pace, discontinue using the visual aids in drills. This will serve to check students' ability to perform without the "crutch."

9.3 INITIAL PRESENTATION: CONTEXTUAL SENTENCES

The basic presentation of a lesson might consist of sentences that do not form a dialog. If the sentences are in a sequence, perhaps the teacher will want them memorized. If the sentences form mainly questions and answers, perhaps the teacher will simply insist that the students learn to answer questions fluently.

9.3.1 Physical movement

The basic sentences of the unit may form a Gouin series, that is, a sequence of activities that lend themselves easily to dramatization.

The teacher acts out each activity as he or she models the sentences. The students repeat the sentences as some of them take turns performing the actions: *J'ouvre la porte. J'entre dans la salle de classe. Je ferme la porte. Je vais au tableau noir. J'écris mon nom.* (*I open the door. I go into the classroom. I close the door. I go to the blackboard. I write my name.*)

The teacher can vary the activities by having one student do the actions. *Tu ouvres la porte;* or a pair of students, *Vous ouvrez la porte.* (*You open the door.*)

9.3.2 Question-answer technique

In the question-answer presentation, the teacher, using props or visuals, teaches the basic sentence patterns of the lesson. Using questions, the teacher cues the students' responses. Students are gradually led to say sentences that they have never heard modelled.

The advantage of this type of presentation is that from the first day of instruction the students are using the language creatively to answer questions. They move from the simple repetition of new sentences to individualized responses. In the next step of instruction, which might even take place on the same day (depending on the class), the students learn to ask the questions of each other in a sort of directed dialog.

The limitation of this technique is that not all spoken communication takes the form of questions and answers. The drill may be expanded in the following way: the initial presentation of the lesson material (basic nouns, verbs, adjectives, adverbs, prepositions) could take the form of questions and answers. Once the students control this material orally and can use it in their own sentences, they can be introduced to the lesson dialog or reading selection. Since they have been taught the new material already, they will be able to understand most of the dialog they hear. They can be led to infer the meaning of expletives and conversational fillers. Some students may present the dialog as a skit. Others may prefer reading it aloud.

9.3.2a SELECTING SENTENCES TO BE TAUGHT

The question-answer technique may be used with any set of teaching materials. The teacher selects the questions and answers.

(1) The first step is to determine the basic material of the lesson, both grammar and vocabulary. Let us assume that a given French lesson teaches the verb *aller (to go)*, certain names of places, and the contractions of the definite article with *à*. The students have already learned the verb *être (to be)* and the use of the definite article.

(2) The second step is to determine the order of presentation:

1. New vocabulary: Voici le théâtre. Voici le cinéma. Voici le stade.

   Here's the theater. Here's the movie theater. Here's the stadium.

2. Familiar question: Où est Michel?

   Where's Michael?

   Introduction of *au:* Il est au cinéma.

   He's at the movies.

3. Introduction of *va:* Michel va au cinéma.

   Michael is going to the movies.

4. Introduction of *vas* and *vais:* Où vas-tu? Je vais au stade.

   Where are you going? I'm going to the stadium.

5. New vocabulary: Voici l'église.
   Voici l'école. Voici la
   piscine. Voici la gare.

   *Here is the church. Here is the
   school. Here is the swimming pool.
   Here is the station.*

6. The form *à l'*: Il va à l'église.
   Il est à l'église.

   *He is going to church. He is at
   church.*

7. Introduction of vont: Où vont-
   ils?

   Where are they going?

8. Introduction of *à la, allez,* and
   allons: Où allez-vous? Nous
   allons à la piscine.

   *Where are you going? We are going
   to the pool.*

(3) The third step is to determine the types of materials to be used. The above sentences might be taught by using line drawings on the chalkboard to designate places, stick figures on index cards, and index cards of the places to distribute to the students.

9.3.2b   SAMPLE PRESENTATIONS

The question-answer technique lends itself readily to the use of visual aids. These contribute to the "realness" of the exchanges, for both teacher and student are talking about specific objects and actions.

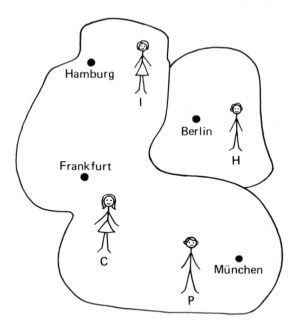

(1) The overhead projector: The teacher prepares a transparency with a line map of Germany and adds dots for a few major cities, such as Berlin, Hamburg, München, Frankfurt. Then he or she places the first letter of each city next to the dot that represents it.

The teacher points to the outline of Germany and says: *Das ist Deutschland* (*That's Germany*). The class repeats. The pattern is repeated for *Das ist Berlin, Das ist Hamburg, Das ist München, Das ist Frankfurt* (*That's Berlin, that's Hamburg, that's Munich, that's Frankfurt*). The teacher then calls on the class and eventually on individuals to answer the question: *Was ist das?* (*What's that?*)

The teacher draws a stick figure of a boy on the transparency next to Berlin and asks: *Wer ist das?* (*Who is that?*) He or she teaches the answer: *Das ist Hans* (*That's Hans*). As the class repeats the sentence, the teacher writes a small H under the drawing. Similarly he or she teaches (and adds to the transparency): *Ilse* (*Hamburg*), *Peter* (*München*), *Christl* (*Frankfurt*).

When the students can handle these sentences, the teacher goes around the class pointing to students and asking: *Wer ist das?* The others give the name of the student indicated.

The teacher introduces a new question: *Wo ist Hans?* (*Where is Hans?*) and a new response: *Hans ist in Berlin* (*Hans is in Berlin*). The teacher continues with *Ilse, Peter,* and *Christl.*

When the students can handle the new pattern, the teacher divides the classroom into four sections, representing the four cities. (If desired, the teacher may write the name of each city on a sheet of typing paper and give the "name" to each of the sections.) Questions and answers are now personalized, using the names of the students.

If the class responds easily, the teacher may also wish to introduce: *Wo sind Anna und Ilse: Wo bist du? Ich bin in Hamburg.* (*Where are Anna and Ilse? Where are you? I am in Hamburg.*)

(2) Cue cards: The teacher prepares enough cue cards for the entire class. For example, if there are twenty-four students in the class, the teacher makes six index cards with milk, six with wine, and so on. (Masculine nouns may be drawn in blue and feminine nouns in red.)

The teacher takes one from each pile and explains he or she is thirsty and is going to drink some coffee. The teacher pretends to drink the coffee on the card and says: *Tomo café* (*I take coffee*). Students repeat. The teacher introduces the three other nouns: *¿Qué tomo? Tomo leche.* (*What do I take? I take milk.*)

Then the teacher calls a student forward and gives him or her a card. He or she models and the class repeats: *Juanito toma leche. ¿Qué toma Juanito? Toma leche.* (*Johnny takes milk. What does Johnny take? He takes milk.*) The student keeps the card and goes to his or her seat. Other students come forward and are given cards while the teacher asks questions and elicits responses. Then the remainder of the cards are distributed.

Students are taught to ask each other: *¿Qué tomas?* (*What do you take?*) and to answer *Tomo. . . .* (*I take . . . .*)

The pace may be enlivened by alternating types of questions and by having the students exchange cards.

If time allows, the plural forms of the verb may also be taught. Two students holding the same card stand up. The teacher asks: *¿Qué toman Marta y Carmen?* (*What do Martha and Carmen take?*) The students are taught the reply: *Marta y Carmen toman Coca-Cola.* (*They take Coca-Cola.*) Only ten or fifteen minutes should be devoted to this activity. Otherwise, this kind of exercise can become long and drawn out simply because too much time is consumed in movement and too little time is left for actual language practice.

9.4 PRACTICING SENTENCE PATTERNS

Once the students have been presented with the basic patterns, they need ample opportunity for practice. This practice can be stimulating if techniques are varied frequently and if visual aids are introduced.

9.4.1 Magazine cutouts

The class is studying the partitive. Students bring to class as many magazine cutouts of foods as they can find. When called on, they offer them to their neighbors:

Student 1:	Voulez-vous de la viande?	*Would you like some meat?*
Student 2:	Merci, je n'ai plus faim.	*No, thank you, I'm not hungry any more.*
Student 3:	Voulez-vous des haricots?	*Would you like some string beans?*
Student 4:	Oui, s'il vous plaît.	*Yes, please.*

9.4.2 Flash cards

One card is flashed at a time:

| Mann | | Schwester | | Frau | | Mädchen | man / sister / woman / girl |

Teacher: Use the sentence *Ich gebe dem Mann das Geld* (*I give money to the man*), and make the necessary changes.

Students:	Ich gebe der Schwester das Geld.	*I give money to the sister.*
	Ich gebe der Frau das Geld.	*I give money to the woman.*
	Ich gebe dem Mädchen das Geld.	*I give money to the girl.*

9.4.3   Transparencies

1. El	2. Ellos	3. Nosotros	4. Yo	5. Tú
(*He*)	(*They*)	(*We*)	(*I*)	(*You*)

Teacher:	Yo digo, "*Cuatro*".	*I say, "four."*
	Uds. dicen, "*Saldré para México*".	*You say, "I'll leave for Mexico."*
	Yo digo, "*Dos*".	*I say, "two."*
	Uds. dicen, "*Saldrán para México*".	*You say, "They'll leave for Mexico."*
	¡Empiecen! "*Cinco*".	*Begin: five.*
Students:	Tú saldrás para México. (And so on.)	*You'll leave for Mexico.*

Following this drill, there are sentences like: *Haré un viaje. Pondré un telegrama. No podrán salir. Vendré mañana.* (*I'll take a trip. I'll send a telegram. They won't be able to leave. I'll come tomorrow.*)

9.4.4 Props

The teacher should teach the names of articles of clothing first:

Teacher:	Ma chemise est blanche. De quelle couleur est votre chemise?	*My shirt is white. What color is your shirt?*
Student:	Ma chemise est bleue.	*My shirt is blue.*
Teacher:	Marie, de quelle couleur est votre jupe?	*Mary, what color is your skirt?*
Marie:	Ma jupe est verte.	*My skirt is green.*
Teacher:	Sylvie, de quelle couleur est votre blouse?	*Sylvia, what color is your blouse?*
Sylvie:	Ma blouse est blanche.	*My blouse is white.*

After drilling all the feminine articles, the teacher proceeds to the masculine articles.

Teacher:	Mon pantalon est marron. De quelle couleur est votre pantalon?	*My trousers are brown. What color are your trousers?*
Georges:	Mon pantalon est noir.	*My trousers are black.*
Teacher:	Anne, de quelle couleur est votre sac?	*Ann, what color is your purse?*
Anne:	Mon sac est rouge.	*My purse is red.*

After drilling all the masculine articles, he proceeds to plurals:

Teacher:	De quelle couleur sont vos chaussures?	*What color are your shoes?*
Paul:	Mes chaussures sont noires.	*My shoes are black.*
Teacher:	De quelle couleur sont vos chaussettes?	*What color are your socks?*
Pierre:	Mes chaussettes sont bleues.	*My socks are blue.*

9.4.5 Executing commands

Teacher: Hans, geh an die Tafel!   *Jack, go to the board!*
(Hans executes command.)
      Hans, was hast du getan?   *Jack, what did you do?*

Hans: Ich bin an die Tafel   *I went to the board.*
            gegangen.

Teacher: Hilde, was hat Hans   *Hilda, what did Jack do?*
            getan?

Hilde: Hans ist an die Tafel   *Jack went to the board.*
            gegangen.

9.4.6 World map

Indicate with a pointer the countries and cities that Henri goes to or comes from:

Teacher: (Moves pointer from New
            York to Paris.)
            Où va Henri?   *Where's Henry going?*

Student: Henri va à Paris.   *Henry's going to Paris.*

Teacher: (Moves pointer from
            Mexico to the U.S.)
            D'où vient Henri?   *Where is Henry coming from?*

Student: Henri vient du Mexique.   *Henry is coming from Mexico.*

9.4.7 Chalkboard frieze

Before class a few artistically talented students draw a series of pictures on the top section of the chalkboard around the classroom. Each picture depicts two people or objects of visibly different characteristics. This frieze is kept for several days. (In picture 1 the new car is blue, and the other is green.)

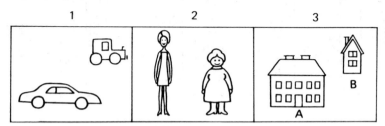

Teacher: ¡Miren Uds. el cuadro   *Look at picture #1. Alice, compare*
            uno! Alicia, ¡compare   *the two cars.*
            Ud. los dos coches!

Alicia:	El coche verde es más viejo que el coche azul.	*The green car is older than the blue car.*
Teacher:	Sí, ¿otra respuesta?	*Yes. Is there another answer?*
Juan:	El coche azul es más moderno que el coche verde.	*The blue car is more modern than the green car.*
Teacher:	¡Miren Uds. el cuadro dos! Enrique, ¡compare Ud. las dos muchachas!	*Look at picture #2. Henry, compare the two girls.*
Enrique:	La muchacha a la izquierda es menos gorda que la muchacha a la derecha.	*The girl on the left is thinner than the girl on the right.*
Teacher:	¡Muy bien! ¡Miren Uds. el cuadro tres! Eduardo, ¡compare Ud. las dos casas!	*Very good! Look at picture #3. Edward, compare the two houses.*
Eduardo:	La casa A es más grande que la casa B.	*House A is larger than House B.*

9.4.8 Large cards

Prepare large cards with the following pictures. Place the cards on the chalkboard ledge:

1	2	3	4
		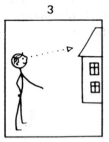	

1. Jim enters first.   *Who* enters first?
2. Jim looks at Louise.   *Whom* does Jim look at?
3. Mark sees the roof.   *What* does Mark see?
4. The book is on the table.   *What* is on the table?

Teacher:	Regardez les images. Je vais décrire ce qu'il y a sur chaque image. Posez la question correspondante.	*Look at the pictures. I am going to describe what is in each picture. Ask the corresponding question.*

1. Jacques entre le premier.
   Student: Qui est-ce qui entre le premier?

   Jim comes in first.
   Who comes in first?

2. Jacques regarde Louise.
   Student: Qui est-ce que Jacques regarde?

   Jim looks at Louise.
   Who(m) is Jim looking at?

3. Marc voit le toit de la maison.
   Student: Qu'est-ce que Marc voit?

   Mark sees the roof of the house.
   What does Mark see?

4. Le livre est sur la table.
   Student: Qu'est-ce qui est sur la table?

   The book is on the table.
   What is on the table?

9.4.9 Game: "¿Quién soy yo?" (*Who am I?*)

Practice using adjectives with only a few nouns permitted. The persons described are all T.V. stars. Boys will be male personalities; girls, female personalities.

One girl leaves the room while the others decide who she will be. When she returns, she asks questions of one student after the other: *¿Soy joven? ¿Soy cómica? ¿Soy bonita? ¿Soy alta? ¿Soy americana? ¿Soy cantatriz? ¿Soy famosa? ¿Soy bailarina? (Am I young? Am I funny? Am I pretty? Am I tall? Am I an American? Am I a singer? Am I famous? Am I a dancer?*)

9.4.10 Direct to indirect discourse

When the students are learning how to form indirect discourse, the teacher may place dialogs from earlier lessons on an overhead transparency for class practice. The students take turns transforming the lines of dialog into indirect speech:

Richard:	Ich will ins Kino gehen.	*I want to go to the movies.*
Student 1:	Richard sagt, daß er ins Kino gehen will.	*Richard says he wants to go to the movies.*

Student 2:	Richard sagte, daß er ins Kino gehen wollte.	*Richard said he wanted to go to the movies.*
Patrice:	Je veux aller au cinéma.	*I want to go to the movies.*
Student 1:	Patrice dit qu'il veut aller au cinéma.	*Patrick says he wants to go to the movies.*
Student 2:	Patrice a dit qu'il voulait aller au cinéma.	*Patrick said he wanted to go to the movies.*

9.4.11　Paired speaking drills

If the teacher prepares ditto sheets for speaking practice, the students can work in pairs (see Section 3.2.6). One student of the pair has a ditto sheet and initiates the exercise. He or she also prompts his classmate if the latter has trouble responding. When the exercise has been completed, the students exchange papers and run through it once more. This time the roles are reversed. The advantage of this type of speaking practice is that all the students are actively engaged in listening and speaking. Furthermore, the teacher is free to walk around and help individual students.

(1) The first student takes the ditto sheet and the second student opens his text to a map of the French-speaking world:

Student 1:	(Reads.) Montrez-moi Québec.	*Show me Quebec.*
Student 2:	(Points to Quebec.) Voici Québec.	*Here's Quebec.*
Student 1:	(Reads *Voici Québec* on his ditto sheet, and acknowledges that the answer was correct by continuing with the next sentence.) Montrez-moi Fort-de-France.	*Show me Fort-de-France.*
Student 2:	Voici Fort-de-France.	*Here's Fort-de-France.*

(2) The first student reads the description of the scene:

You don't like your younger sister. Each time I say something nice about her, you say that the opposite is true.

| Student 1: | Ta sœur est jolie. | *Your sister is pretty.* |

Student 2:	Mais non, elle est moche.	*No, she's ugly.*
Student 1:	(Reads.) Elle est gentille.	*She's nice.*
Student 2:	Mais non, elle est in-supportable.	*No, she's unbearable.*

9.4.12 Traffic signals

The teacher holds up line drawings of international traffic signs (no left turn, etc.) and asks the class what they mean.

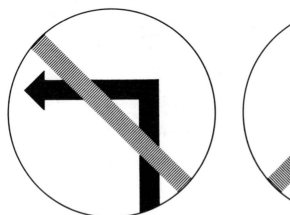

In ESL classes, the traffic signs may also be used to practice modals:

When you see this sign, what must you do? (stop sign)
When you see this sign, what should you do? (yield sign)
What can't you do when you see this sign? (no passing)

9.5 GUIDED CONVERSATION

In dialog presentations and sentence practice, the student is required to respond according to a fixed pattern. This groundwork is essential to the development of the speaking skill. However, conversation by its very nature means that the students themselves decide what they want to say. In guided conversation, the students are given a framework within which to build their sentences, but the actual choice of what they will say is left up to them.

Some work in guided conversation should be provided even for beginning students. Only in expressing their own thoughts will they realize that the foreign language is a viable means of communication.

9.5.1 Mini-exchanges

In a mini-exchange, two students participate, each saying only one line. Although exercises of this sort are not true conversations, they encourage beginners and timid intermediate students to express themselves.

Here is a Spanish example:

Excusas, Excusas[3]

People sometimes give very strange excuses in response to questions or accusations. Each of the following pairs of people is composed of an authority figure and a subordinate. Your task is to imagine a one-line question or accusation the authority figure might say, and a likely—or not so likely!—one-line excuse that the subordinate might give. You may enjoy doing this activity in small groups and then comparing the responses of each group.

Sargento: ¿Por qué no usa Ud. el rifle?
Soldado: Porque no me gusta el ruido.

Sergeant: *Why don't you use a rifle?*
Soldier: *Because I don't like the noise.*

Parejas:

1. un jefe y un empleado
2. un clérigo y un miembro de la iglesia
3. un maestro y un alumno
4. una madre y un hijo
5. un policía y un conductor de coche

Pairs:

a boss and an employee
a priest and a parishioner

a teacher and a pupil
a mother and a son or daughter
a policeman and a bus driver

9.5.2 Mini-conversations

A mini-conversation is an exchange of at least four lines. All too frequently the teacher asks a student a single question and then goes on to another student without developing the conversation. A conversation is a longer exchange between two people.

9.5.2a IMPROMPTU ORAL QUESTIONS

In a mini-conversation the teacher asks two or more related questions of the same person: 1. *Hast du einen Bruder? Wie heißt er? Ist er älter oder jünger als du? Hast du ihn gern?* 2. *Quel sport préfères-tu? Avec qui joues-tu au _____? Où jouez-vous?* 3. *¿Qué clases tiene usted este semestre? ¿Cuál le gusta más? ¿Y menos?* (Do you have a brother? What's his name? Is he older or younger than you? Do you like him? What sport do you like best? With whom do you play _____? Where do you play? What courses do you have this semester? Which do you like most? and least?)

[3] From Marty Knorre et al., *Cara a cara* (New York: Holt Rinehart Winston, 1977), p. 95.

Variation: To maintain pace, the teacher might ask several students one question each and ask the next student three consecutive questions which are related to one another. Information questions are more effective than yes/no questions.

9.5.2b PREPARED QUESTIONS

Distribute dittoed sheets of a one-sided conversation. Leave blanks for the other person's part. Give students a few minutes to think of what they will say when called on.

Situación: Ud. ha perdido algo importante y tiene miedo de contárselo a sus padres:	*Situation: You have lost something important and are afraid of telling your parents about it.*
Yo: ¡Roberto! ¿Por qué esa cara tan triste?	*I: Robert, why such a sad face?*
Ud.: _____	*You:* _____
Yo: ¿Dónde lo has perdido?	*I: Where did you lose it?*
Ud.: _____	*You:* _____
Yo: ¿Cuánto vale?	*I: What is it worth?*
Ud.: _____	*You:* _____
Yo: ¿Por qué no compraste otro?	*I: Why didn't you buy another one?*
Ud.: _____	*You:* _____
Yo: ¿A quién vas a contar lo que ha pasado, a tu mamá o a tu papá?	*I: To whom are you going to tell what happened, your mother or your father?*
Ud.: _____	*You:* _____
Yo: ¿Porqué?	*I: Why?*
Ud.: _____	*You:* _____
Yo: ¿Tus padres te darán el dinero que necesitas?	*I: Will your parents give you the money you need?*
Ud.: _____	*You:* _____
Yo: Entonces, ¿qué vas a hacer?	*I: Well, what are you going to do?*
Ud.: _____	*You:* _____

9.5.3 Role playing

Two or more students come before the class to act out an impromptu conversation. If the class is large, the students may be divided into three or four groups, each carrying out their own role-playing activities in a corner of the room.

9.5.3a PREPARING THE STUDENTS

The success of role-playing activities depends on careful preparation. The students must have learned the needed sentence patterns and vocabulary in advance. The situation should be carefully described so that even an unimaginative student has something to say. At the same time, leeway must be allowed for the creative student to express himself or herself in unexpected ways.

(1) SHOPPING

¿Cuánto vale ese vestido:	*How much is that dress?*
¿Cuánto vale esa camisa?	*How much is that shirt?*
¿Cuánto valen esos zapatos?	*How much are those shoes?*
Se lo dejo por diez pesos.	*I'll let you have it for ten pesos.*
Se la dejo por doce pesos.	*I'll let you have it for twelve pesos.*
Se los dejo por veinte pesos.	*I'll let you have them for twenty pesos.*

(2) DOCTOR'S VISIT

Où est-ce que vous avez mal?	*Where does it hurt?*
J'ai mal à la tête.	*I have a headache.*
J'ai mal à l'estomac.	*I have a stomach ache.*
Qu'est-ce que vous avez mangé hier soir?	*What did you eat last night?*
Montrez-moi votre langue.	*Show me your tongue.*

(3) TELEPHONING: AN INVITATION

Invitations

Veux-tu aller au cinéma avec moi dimanche après-midi?	*Do you want to go to the movies with me Sunday afternoon?*
Je t'invite à aller à la piscine avec moi.	*I invite you to go to the pool with me.*
Tu veux prendre un Coca-Cola demain après l'école? C'est moi qui paie.	*Do you want to have a Coke with me tomorrow after school? I'll pay.*

Acceptances

Volontiers! A quelle heure est-ce qu'on se rencontre?	*Sure! At what time shall we meet?*
Avec plaisir! Tu viens me chercher? On y va dans ta voiture ou en autobus?	*Gladly! Will you pick me up? Shall we go in your car or by bus?*

Chic alors! Où est-ce qu'on se rencontre?	*Great! Where shall we meet?*

Refusals

Merci, Paul. Malheureuse-ment j'ai des devoirs à faire.	*Thanks, Paul. Unfortunately, I have homework to do.*
Merci, Marc. Mais je n'ai pas de maillot.	*Thanks, Mark, but I don't have a bathing suit.*
Je regrette, Claude. Maman veut que je rentre tout de suite après l'école. Nous avons des invités.	*I'm sorry, Claude. My mom wants me to come home right after school. We have company.*

9.5.3b   CREATING THE SITUATION

Students must be given cues as to what they are to say and how they are to react.

(1) Guided role playing: One or both students draw a slip of paper telling them how they are to react. Slips for the different roles are in separate envelopes:

DOCTOR'S VISIT

(Patient):   You have a sore throat.
(Doctor):   You discover appendicitis and send him to the hospital.

ORDERING FOOD

(Client):   Choose whatever you like.
(Friend):   You like everything your friend suggests, except the dessert. Choose something else.
(Waiter):   You are out of one of the dishes the client orders.

(2) Bartering: The class is divided into two teams: salespersons and clients. The salespersons draw a slip of paper naming the object they are to sell and giving a suggested minimum retail price. The winner is the one who gets the highest price for the object.

Variation: The clients are told to buy the object. Whoever gets it for the lowest price is the winner.

Variation: The class is divided into pairs of a salesperson and a client and are told that all negotiations must be carried out in the foreign language. When they have come to an agreement, the pair comes to the teacher and announces the price they have decided on.

If bartering becomes too serious, a time limit may have to be set.

9.5.4 Oral descriptions

Oral descriptions are most effective if the rest of the class is actively encouraged to listen to their classmates. The following techniques involve both speaking and listening:

9.5.4a   MAGAZINE CUTOUTS

For homework, each student finds a magazine cutout and prepares four sentences about it. Only known vocabulary and expressions may be used. One or more of the sentences may be inaccurate. When the class hears an inaccurate sentence, they raise their hands.

Variation: A member of the class may be called upon to correct the inaccuracies.

9.5.4b   VERBAL DESCRIPTIONS

For homework, the student prepares six statements about some object for which the foreign language equivalent is known. In class the student says the first sentence. One classmate is chosen to guess which object is being described. If he or she guesses right, another student gives a description. If the guess is wrong, the first student reads the next sentence of his or her description. Again one more guess is allowed. If no one has guessed the object at the end of the description, the student gives the correct answer.

9.5.4c   WALL CHARTS AND OTHER ILLUSTRATIONS

The teacher puts up a wall chart with four or more drawings. These are labeled (a), (b), (c), (d). A student comes to the front of the class and draws a letter from a hat. Without using gestures, he or she must describe the drawing that corresponds to the letter. When the student has finished, the class votes which one they think was described. The teacher asks, for example, "How many think it was (a)? Raise your hands."

This exercise may be made more difficult by using more complex pictures. For example, if the textbook has a colored illustration with many people, a student could be told to describe one of the people. The teacher then holds up the illustration, pointing to the people one by one. The class indicates which person they think was being described.

Drawings on the overhead projector may also be used for this type of speaking activity.

9.5.4d   GAME: TWENTY QUESTIONS

One student leaves the room while the others decide on an object in the classroom. The student comes back and has twenty questions to discover what the object is.

9.5.4e   GAME: WHAT'S MY LINE?

A student draws a slip of paper naming a profession or thinks up a profession and writes it down for the teacher. The class asks questions to guess what the profession is.

9.5.4f MEMORY GAME: PACKING MY TRUNK

One student says, "I'm going to Madrid. I'm putting a hat in my trunk." The second student repeats what the first student says and adds another object: "I'm putting a hat and a birdcage in my trunk." Each student repeats and adds. Those who forget or make mistakes must drop out of the game.

9.5.4g SLIDES

The teacher shows a few selected slides from a vacation trip to Mexico. As they are projected on the screen he or she makes a statement about each slide, using the first person:

1. En esta diapositiva estoy bajando del camión.
   In this slide I'm getting off the bus.
2. Quiero comprar un sarape. Ahora estoy regateando.
   I want to buy a serape.
   Now I'm bargaining.
3. Estoy pagando.
   I'm paying.
4. Ahora estoy comiendo un taco.
   Now I'm eating a taco.
5. En esta diapositiva estoy su- biendo la Pirámide del Sol.
   In this slide I'm climbing the Pyra- mid of the Sun.
6. Ahora estoy en la cima. ¡Caramba! ¡Empieza a llover!
   Now I'm at the top. Wow! It's begin- ning to rain.

Later the teacher shows the same slides and asks students to tell the story in the third person.

9.5.4h SUPPLEMENTARY FILM STRIPS

(1) The teacher first shows several sections of film strip No. 5 (*Deux rivières se rencontrent*)[4] and plays the accompanying tape. This is repeated as many times as necessary.

(2) The teacher shows the frames again without tape. He or she asks questions about each slide:

1. Comment s'appellent les deux fleuves qui traversent Lyon?
   What are the names of the two rivers that cut across Lyon?
2. Quels animaux voyez-vous dans le parc?
   What animals do you see in the park?
3. Qui est-ce vous voyez sur la péniche?
   Whom do you see on the barge?

(3) The teacher shows the filmstrip again without tape and calls on individual students to describe what they see.

---

[4] Peter Buckley, *A Year in France* (New York: Holt, Rinehart and Winston, 1964).

9.5.5 Strip stories

The teacher selects a short story or anecdote that has exactly the same number of sentences as there are students in the class. Each sentence is written on a separate strip of paper. (If the same story is used with several classes, the sentences may be typed on a stencil, dittoed, and then cut into strips.) The strips are randomly distributed to the students. Each student must memorize the sentence of his or her strip. Then the strips are collected. The students move around, speaking only the target language, and ask each other questions until they have reconstituted the original story. The teacher's role is merely that of facilitator; it is recommended that the teacher remain silent during the reconstruction activity.[5]

9.5.6 Prepared talks

The students are given a topic or a choice of topics for a prepared talk. They write out what they plan to say. (This written form is handed to the teacher for correction. Its main purpose is to encourage thoughtful preparation; its secondary purpose is to afford practice in writing.) In class the students give their talks. They can memorize what they have written or speak extemporaneously. They are not, however, allowed to use notes.

Prepared talks are most effective with intermediate and advanced classes. At the beginning of a school year, for example, students could prepare a short talk introducing themselves, if there are new students in the class. They might also talk about what they did during the summer.

Variation: With weaker students, the teacher might require that the written form be submitted two days in advance, so that he or she can correct and hand back the text the day before the talk is due. If the students intend to memorize certain sections of their talks, they will be memorizing the correct forms of the target language.

9.5.7 Skits

In beginning and intermediate classes, groups of five to eight students can get together to prepare a skit. The students will probably have their own ideas, but if not, the teacher can offer suggestions. When the skits are ready, they can be presented to other members of the class. The preparation of the skit might be an activity stretching over a week or two, with a quarter hour allotted for rehearsal at the end of each class period. The skits might be presented to other foreign language classes or to the language club.

In dividing the class into groups for skits, the teacher should try to put some

---

[5] Technique described by Robert E. Gibson in "The Strip Story: A Catalyst for Communication," *TESOL Quarterly* 9, no. 2 (June 1975), pp. 149–54.

good students with each group. They may serve as scribes in taking down the script accurately.

9.5.8   Stories

The teacher begins a story that the class finishes orally. This type of activity may be done with smaller groups also. Each student in turn adds a line to the plot.

Il fait nuit. Un homme grimpe à un balcon et entre à pas de loup dans une chambre à coucher. Il allume son briquet. Il voit un collier de perles sur une commode.

It's night. A man is climbing a balcony and enters a bedroom on tiptoe. He lights his lighter. He sees a pearl necklace on a dresser.

Finissez l'histoire.

Finish the story.

9.5.9   Oral games

In oral games, students are encouraged to use phrases and expressions they have been studying. The games may be done in full-class or small-group format.

9.5.9a   BECAUSE[6]

The first student describes an event: for instance, *The toast burned.* The second student adds an explanation: *Because the toaster was turned up too high.* The third student gives a probable effect: *So we all had charcoal for breakfast.*

9.5.9b   WHO AM I?

The students name well-known people from the target culture. These names, which should be familiar to the entire class, are written on cards. A card is taped to the back of each student who must ask yes/no questions of classmates until he or she discovers the hidden identity.

9.6   COMMUNICATIVE PRACTICE

It is essential that students be given the opportunity, from the earliest lessons, to use the target language to express their own ideas. At first, their responses may take merely the form of *Yes* or *No*, or *I prefer milk*, or *My favorite sport is football.*

[6] Adapted from Baltimore County Public School Teachers "Foreign Language Games," available from the ACTFL Materials Center, 2 Park Avenue, New York, N.Y. 10016, in the brochure entitled "Games for the Foreign Language Classroom."

Students should not feel that they are being forced to reveal their intimate personal thoughts and values, however. The wise teacher does not insist on a reply from a student who shows signs of reluctance. Those students who have acquired greater language skill should be given the chance to present their views more fully. Language classes are more meaningful when students feel that the teacher is listening to them and respecting their opinions.

During communicative practice, the "message" spoken by the student is all-important. The teacher corrects mistakes in pronunciation or grammar only if the student's meaning is unintelligible or ambiguous.[7]

9.6.1   Guessing games[8]

The teacher asks one student to think about something he or she has done. The rest of the class guesses what it is.

(1) Time

Teacher:	Maria, you know what time you went to bed last night? Don't tell us. We'll guess.
Carlos:	At 11 o'clock?
Maria:	No. [Earlier.]
Chang:	At 10:30?
Maria:	No. [Later.]
etc.	

(2) Birthdays

Teacher:	Armando, tell us the month of your birth, but not the day.
Armando:	March.
Teacher:	Let's guess the date.
Ingrid:	March 10th?
Armando:	No.
Paolo:	March 19th?
Armando:	No.
etc.	

9.6.2   Rank order

In a *rank order* exercise, the teacher asks students to indicate their order of preference for a series of options. Such activities are more conducive to speaking practice if they are carried out in small groups.

(1) Seasons

Which season do you like best? Rank it number one.

---

[7] For an excellent introduction to communicative practice techniques, see Virginia Wilson and Beverly Wattenmaker, *Real Communication in Foreign Language* (Upper Jay, N.Y.: Andirondack Mountain Humanistic Education Center, 1973), pp. 1–8.

[8] Elizabeth G. Joiner, "Keep Them Guessing," in *American Foreign Language Teacher* 4, no. 2 (1974), 16–18.

Which season do you like next best? Rank it number two.
Continue with ranks three and four.

Teacher: Pedro, which season did you rank number one?
Pedro: Summer.
(Optional—Teacher: Why?)

(2) Saturday night
Teacher: Let us list some of the activities one might do on a Saturday night. (With class participation, a list of four or five activities is written on the chalkboard: *watch television, go to the movies, study, listen to records, dance.*)
Teacher: Now divide into groups of four. Imagine that in each group you all are going to do the same thing this Saturday night. Which activity would you like best? Rank it number one. Rank the others from two to five.

(At the end of the discussion, each group reports on its results.)

9.6.3 Values continuum

In a *values continuum,* the teacher draws a long horizontal line on the chalkboard. Two opposite positions are indicated at each end of the line. The teacher indicates his or her position by placing a mark on the line at an appropriate point and writing his or her initials. The teacher makes a statement about the position and then gives the chalk to a student. The student similarly marks his or her position, makes a statement, and passes the chalk to a classmate.

(1) two positions
I like to be alone. ——————RV—————————— I like to be with others.

Statement: I often like to be with others, but most often I like to be alone. What about you, John, do you like to be alone or with others?

(2) three positions

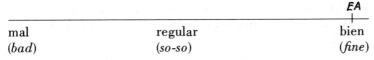

		EA
mal	regular	bien
(*bad*)	(*so-so*)	(*fine*)

Statement: Estoy bien hoy. Y   *I feel fine today. And you, Manuel,*
tú Manuel ¿cómo   *how do you feel?*
estás tú?

(3) five positions
In a five-position continuum, the statements on the board provide the students with appropriate vocabulary.

		AR		
très lentement	lentement	raisonnablement	vite	très vite
(*very slowly*)	(*slowly*)	(*properly*)	(*fast*)	(*very fast*)

Statement: Je conduis raison- nablement. Et toi, Marc, comment conduis-tu?	*I drive properly. And you, Marc, how* *do you drive?*

9.6.4 Opinion polls

The teacher finds a recent opinion poll that reflects the ideas of young people in the country where the target language is spoken. The teacher asks the class each of the questions in the poll, and a student records the responses on the board. Then the results of the class poll are compared with the results of the official poll.

Here is a sample question from a French poll:[9]

Qu'est-ce qui constitue le princi- pal attrait de l'argent pour vous?	*What does money mainly represent* *for you?*
la possibilité de loisirs (57%)	*the possibility of leisure activities*
l'indépendance (19%)	*independence*
la sécurité (22%)	*security*
le pouvoir (2%)	*power*

It is also possible to construct opinion polls on questions of local and school interest: dress code, course requirements, grades, etc.

9.6.5 Interview

The teacher writes four questions on the board. Then the class counts off: 1, 2, 3, 4, 1, 2, 3, 4, etc. The students divide into groups of four. Student #1 asks question #1 of the other three students in the group. Then student #2 asks the second question. When the "interview" has been completed, each group reports on the findings.

Here are four sample questions in English:

What color do you think of when you are hungry?
What color do you think of when you are sleepy?
What color do you think of when you are thirsty?
What color do you think of when you are cold?

[9] Taken from Jean-Paul Valette and Rebecca M. Valette, *Contacts: langue et culture françaises* (Boston: Hougton Mifflin, 1976), p. 411.

Similar questions in French or Spanish would allow beginning students to practice colors and idiomatic expressions; at the same time, the nature of the questions encourages students to listen to what their classmates say.

9.6.6 Making a survey

The teacher gives each student in the class a slip of paper with a question on it. Students are free to move around the room and ask each classmate the question on their paper. This must be done in the foreign language.

Sample questions:

1. What's your favorite food?
2. What's your favorite sport?
3. What's your favorite color?
4. How much time do you spend preparing your assignments each evening?
5. What's your favorite drink (beverage)?
6. Do you prefer to go to bed early or late?
7. Which season do you prefer?
8. When is your birthday (month only)?
9. How many brothers and sisters do you have?
10. Are you single or married?
11. Which would you rather do . . . go to a movie or read a good book?
12. Where would you rather spend your vacation . . . at the mountains or the seashore?
13. How do you prefer to travel . . . by train, bus, or plane?

After the survey has been completed, the class reassembles and the students report on their findings.

9.6.7 Categories of preference

The teacher writes the categories of TV programs on the board and asks the students to identify orally their favorite category and show.

Noticias (*News*)	Programas de variedades (*Variety shows*)
Programas Cómicos (*Comedies*)	Entrevistas y charlas (*Talk shows*)
Documentarios (*Documentaries*)	Piezas teatrales (*Plays*)
Programas policíacos (*Police stories*)	Programas para niños (*Children's programs*)

Student 1:   A mí me gustan más los   *I like comedies best.*
                 programas cómicos.

Student 2:   A mí me gustan más los   *I like police dramas best.*
                 programas policíacos.

9.7   FREE CONVERSATION

In free conversation the students assume the initiative for guiding the speaking activities. The success of such activities depends on two elements: the careful preparation by the students, and the silence of the teacher during the discussion.

Students will participate in free conversation activities if they have something to say and if they feel relatively confident about their ability to communicate. Confidence in one's speaking ability increases through practice, but the usual classroom hour does not provide the individual student with more than a few minutes of speaking time.

An excellent technique for developing oral fluency is the following:[10] Have each student buy two blank cassettes and provide access to a cassette recorder for those students who do not have one at home. For each conversation activity, ask the students to follow their reading and writing preparation with twenty minutes of extemporaneous speech on the topic. Encourage them to listen to their tapes and try to improve on their choice of words and use of structure. On the day of the conversation activity, the preparation cassette tapes are to be handed in. Later, the teacher spot checks the recordings and makes some oral comments in the second language on the second cassette. The cassettes are graded during the semester for seriousness of effort and, if desired, degree of improvement.

9.7.1   Discussion groups

Discussion initiated by students requires a point of departure. The most usual is a reading selection, but a play, film, a visit to a museum, and so on, can also serve as a springboard.

9.7.1a   PREPARATION

Each student prepares two or three questions on the reading selection for homework. These may be directly related to the text: *Why did the main character not notice that. . . .?* Discussion is more animated if opinions are solicited: *On page. . . , the author says that. . . . Do you agree?* or personal reactions asked for: *What would you have done in a similar situation?*

---

[10] Suggested by Stephan Hobbs, Choate Rosemary Hall, Wallingford, Connecticut, in a presentation at the 1976 meeting of the Connecticut Council of Language Teachers (East Hartford, October 29, 1976).

When discussions are first initiated, the teacher might give a short lecture on what types of questions can be derived from a reading passage. Even advanced students often need a review about how questions are formed.

9.7.1b WHOLE-CLASS CONVERSATION

In class the first few discussions might be carried out in a single group. Chairs are arranged in a large circle. The teacher joins the group and asks one student to begin the discussion with a question. That student may direct his or her question to anyone who wants to answer it. The greater the number of participants, the better. When the topic seems exhausted, the teacher calls on another student to ask a question. If some students are quiet, they might be singled out to give questions. Toward the end of the time allotted for conversation, the teacher should be sure to include those who have not yet said anything.

Except for encouraging participation, the teacher makes no comments or corrections during the discussion. He or she may take notes and reserve five or ten minutes at the end of the conversation to review the errors that were made.

9.7.1c SMALL-GROUP CONVERSATION

Once the students understand how the discussion is carried out, the teacher can divide the class into groups of three to five. The students take turns asking questions and giving opinions. The teacher moves from group to group, taking notes on mistakes that are being made, but saying nothing unless asked a direct question.

When time is called, the teacher briefly gives corrections to the class as a whole.

The small-group conversation technique involves all the students. It is hard to be silent in a group of three or four. Even the timid students do not mind trying to express themselves, especially if the teacher is working with another group at the time. At any given moment, the various groups might be discussing entirely different topics, even though one reading furnished the point of departure. This diversity is fine, for the aim of the conversation is self-expression, and the choice of topics is secondary.

The teacher should shift the composition of the groups from time to time, perhaps by listing the groups for the week on the class bulletin board. Conversation develops more readily if groups contain students of mixed ability and mixed interests.

9.7.2 Debates

9.7.2a TOPICS

Class debates are most effective if the topics are of interest to the students. This means that students are most fluent in discussing topics they know about, such as aspects of their native cultural and political life. Debates about aspects of the target culture are usually less lively.

Ask the students to write out subjects they would like to debate, and select debate topics accordingly. Some possibilities are:

Grades in high school should be abolished.
All students should be required to study a foreign language.
A high school dress code should be maintained.

The debate topic should be strongly worded so that it is possible to take a definite affirmative or negative stand.

9.7.2b FORMING TEAMS

Although students may be allowed to choose sides, this often results in uneven teams. It is simpler to divide the class into two sides (with students of mixed abilities on each team) and then flip a coin to see which team has first choice at selecting the affirmative or negative position.

In a French class students might be told that a French person is willing to debate either side of a topic, for fluency of expression is more important than sincerity of position.

9.7.2c PREPARATION

The teacher may hand out a ditto containing key words and expressions which relate to the topic. As homework, students jot down notes about what they might say. If teams are assigned in advance, students prepare only one side of the question. It is also possible to have students prepare both sides of the question and to divide the class into teams on the day of the debate.

9.7.2d RUNNING THE DEBATE

The class is divided into two teams. Each team meets in a "huddle" to elect a captain and to plan strategy. A point to defend is assigned to each member. The captain sees that all the members of his or her team are called on to make statements. This "huddle" may last fifteen minutes. Both teams are required to discuss strategy in the foreign language.

The debate begins with the affirmative team. Its members elaborate their position, and then the negative team is allowed to reply. The only role of the teacher is to see that all students are given a chance to participate.

The teacher makes notes of persistent errors. These are corrected during ten minutes at the end of the debate.

Many students prefer not to have an arbiter; the fun of debating is reason enough for this activity. If, however, a class wishes to appoint a judge or a jury, this should be decided before the teams are organized. The teacher may or may not be chosen to judge the debate.

9.7.3 Panel discussions

Students may be asked to prepare panel discussions on subjects relating to the foreign culture. The teacher divides the class into committees according to interests. Each group does research on its topic and later presents its findings to the class using overhead and opaque projectors.

9.7.3a THE TEACHER'S PREPARATION

Before sending a class to the library or resource center, the teacher must research the topic. Then he or she can either give the students titles of books and periodicals where they can find necessary data, or hand them the materials to read. If this preparation is not done, much class time will be wasted.

9.7.3b CLASS ORGANIZATION

One committee may work on a topic for one week, and another committee take up another topic the next week. If this system is used, the committee-of-the-week can work at the back of the classroom while the teacher works with the rest of the class. Then the class is given a written assignment while the teacher confers with the committee. The students will need guidance in selecting appropriate articles, summarizing them, and pronouncing new words.

The entire class may be divided into four or five committees. The committees work in various corners of the classroom. The teacher goes from group to group offering guidance.

outline

ten
Reading
Comprehension

For many students, reading is the one skill they may occasionally use when they have left the classroom. It is also the skill that is retained the longest. Reading is more than just assigning foreign language sounds to the written words; it requires the comprehension of what is written. Students differ in their ability to read their native language, and these same differences reappear in their ability to read a second language. Reading skills in one language are not necessarily transferred to another language and may even be inhibitory when they are. A student who reads English easily may have difficulty reading a foreign language. But the student who reads English with difficulty will surely have problems reading stories in a foreign language. The teacher must take these differences into account when teaching the reading skill.

Many ESL students are not literate in their native language. For such students, reading instruction entails an initial introduction to the concept of sound-symbol correspondences and to the written alphabet.

10.1 GENERAL CONSIDERATIONS

Reading is a developmental process. The first stage is learning sound-symbol correspondences, either directly or by reading aloud sentences and words that have been mastered orally. Then the student learns to read these same words and sentence patterns in new combinations.

From the reading of sentences, the student progresses to the reading of paragraphs and short passages. The teacher helps the student develop techniques for inferring the meanings of new words, reading for information, and increasing comprehension of structural signals.

As the number of reading experiences increases, the differences in reading rate and comprehension among the students become very apparent. It is desirable, at this point, to organize the students into reading groups; each group could then read at its level of proficiency, from very easy to advanced readings. Another approach, especially valuable in advanced classes or upper level intermediate classes, is to provide a reading program for each individual student.

Literature may be introduced as early as the first year of language instruction, if the selections are accessible to the students. Often poetry is introduced first, followed by short stories, plays, and then longer prose works. The aim of literature study is not that the students learn about authors and periods, but rather that they develop personal techniques for approaching a literary work.

The following sections of this chapter suggest ways of introducing students to the printed word and gradually bringing them to a point where they can study longer works.

10.2   INITIAL STEPS

It is possible to teach a student to read a second language aloud by beginning with sound-symbol correspondences, that is, by teaching which spellings represent which sounds. In most language courses, however, students first engage in listening and speaking activities before they are introduced to the printed word. The time elapsing between audio-lingual practice and reading aloud may range between the extremes of thirty minutes and several months. Students are taught to read entire sentences and then later are presented with sound-symbol correspondences.

The following sections offer techniques for teaching reading to students who have had prior listening and speaking practice. (For techniques of teaching sound-symbol correspondences, see Chapter 4.)

10.2.1   Reading memorized sentences

10.2.1a   OVERHEAD TRANSPARENCIES

Print on a transparency the dialog sentences out of order. Number each one. The class repeats them after the teacher. This technique prevents the students from merely parroting the dialog without looking at the spelling:

1. Allez, ne discute pas tout le temps.   *Come on, don't argue all the time.*

2. Pas question. Il y a beaucoup à faire.   *Absolutely not. There's a lot to do.*

3. Bon, Anne prépare le dessert, moi, je goûte.   *Okay, Anne will fix dessert and I'll do the tasting.*

4. Mais nous manquons toujours la fin.[1]   *But we always miss the end.*

[1] *A-LM French, Level One,* Teacher's Edition, 2d ed. (New York: Harcourt Brace Jovanovich, Inc., 1969), p. 9.

10.2.1b DITTOED SHEETS

Sentences appear on the sheet with a number above each word. Students repeat the whole sentence after the teacher models it. Then the teacher says a number, and an individual student reads the word under the number:

1	2	3	4	5	6	
Pedro	vive	en	una	casa	pequeña.	*Peter lives in a small house.*

Teacher:	Dos, Julia.	*Two, Julia.*
Julia:	Vive.	*Lives.*

NOTE: In preparing similar exercises in French, word groups linked by liaison should be numbered as one word. For example, *les amis* (*the friends*) or *j'habite* (*I live*) would be grouped as one word.

10.2.1c CUE CARDS

The teacher places cue cards for each line of the dialog on the chalkboard ledge. Above each card he or she writes the dialog line. The teacher reads each line and asks students to repeat. Then individuals are called on to read. Finally the visuals are removed and students read the lines without the help of the visuals:

Wo ist die Bibliothek?	Nicht weit.	Gut! Ich bin sehr müde,
(*Where is the library?*)	Nur über die Straße.	und diese Bücher sind
	(*Not far.*	schwer.
	Just across the	(*Good, I'm very tired*
	street.)	*and these books are*
		heavy.)

10.2.1d FLANNEL BOARD

Each word of the sentence is written on a card backed with flocking paper or flannel. The cards are scattered on the flannel board. Individual students come forward and arrange them into sentences:

en	ne	vont	ils	pas	ville	manger

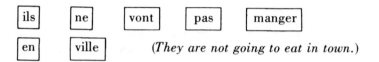

(They are not going to eat in town.)

10.2.2 New sentences with familiar words

Once students can read familiar sentences readily, they may be given the opportunity to read new sentences formed with words that they already know.

10.2.2a FLANNEL BOARD

The teacher begins by forming a sentence with just a few cards. He or she then asks who can read it. Little by little the sentences are expanded by adding additional cards (usually adjectives) and the students are asked who can read the longer sentences:

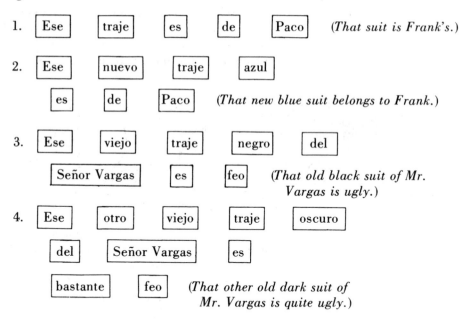

10.2.2b CUE CARDS

The teacher places along one section of the chalkboard ledge several cards with a word on each. The cards are not in correct order. He or she forms one sentence to use as a model, for example, *Heute bringt Karl einen Freund. (Today Carl is bringing a friend.)* Then he or she puts the cards back on the ledge. One by one students are called on to form other sentences:

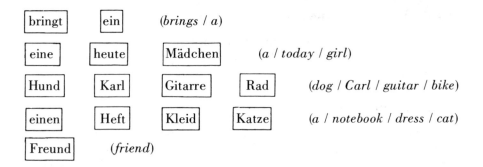

bringt | ein (*brings / a*)

eine | heute | Mädchen (*a / today / girl*)

Hund | Karl | Gitarre | Rad (*dog / Carl / guitar / bike*)

einen | Heft | Kleid | Katze (*a / notebook / dress / cat*)

Freund (*friend*)

10.2.2c POCKET CHART

The teacher prepares cards for the pocket chart that contain words familiar to the students. On the first ledge of the pocket chart, the teacher forms a question:

Où | est | le | crayon | ? (*Where is the pencil?*)

The second ledge contains cards with which plausible answers to the question may be formed:

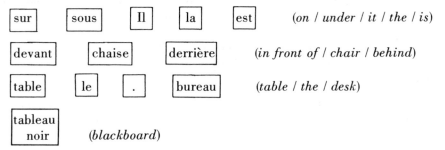

sur | sous | Il | la | est (*on / under / it / the / is*)

devant | chaise | derrière (*in front of / chair / behind*)

table | le | . | bureau (*table / the / desk*)

tableau noir (*blackboard*)

Students choose cards from this collection and place them on the third ledge in order to form an answer to the question:

Il | est | sur | la | table | . (*It is on the table.*)

Variation: The teacher puts various props in different positions in the room. He or she asks questions about them orally. Students form sentences on the pocket chart:

Teacher: Où est le cahier? *Where is the notebook?*

Student: (Places cards.)
Il est sous le bureau. *It's under the desk.*

10.2.3 Understanding sentences

The teacher writes sentences on the chalkboard for the students to read. A more rapid pace can be maintained if the sentences are prepared in advance on overhead transparencies.

10.2.3a COMMANDS

The teacher writes or projects a command and then calls on a student to execute it. *Geh an die Tafel und schreib deinen Namen (Go to the board and write your name.)* or *Va à la fenêtre, ouvre-la, et retourne à ta place. (Go to the window, open it, and go back to your seat.)*

10.2.3b QUESTIONS

The teacher writes or projects a question and asks the students to answer orally: *Quel temps fait-il? Où habitez-vous? (How's the weather? Where do you live?)*

10.2.4 Reading aloud in the language laboratory

The teacher can prepare exercises for oral reading to be used in the language laboratory or individually—with cassette recorders or a tape recorder in the classroom.

A ditto worksheet is prepared containing the selection to be read aloud. Each pause is marked by a slash line (/). The teacher records a tape on the following model:

Lisez. / Hier soir à minuit /   *Read! / Last night at midnight /*
Lisez. / Quand je suis rentré chez   *Read! / When I got back home / . . .*
 moi / . . .

In Spanish each line would be preceded by *¡Lea Ud.!* In German each line would be preceded by *Lesen Sie!*

The students take their worksheets to the lab. When they hear the command *Lisez*, they read the first segment during the first pause. Then they hear the segment read by the teacher and have another pause in which to read it once more by themselves. They hear the next *Lisez*, and read the next segment.

Students must be encouraged to read the segment aloud *before* they hear the confirmation on the tape.

10.2.5 Reading aloud in class

It is useless to have students read aloud to each other material that all have previously read. Typically such an exercise simply provides the type of pronunciation practice that could better be carried out in the language laboratory.

Meaningful practice in reading aloud is provided when the others in the class or group are unfamiliar with the material being presented. In such instances, the members of the class must listen in order to understand the message. As a follow-up activity, the reader could be asked to lay down the text and then answer content questions from others in the class. Conversely, the others in the class could be asked to provide a resume of the reading that the reader would verify and, if necessary, correct.

10.3 GUIDED READING TECHNIQUES

When the student can read aloud, guided reading activities begin. Beginning, intermediate, and advanced classes all spend a certain portion of their time on guided reading. The level of the reading material grows more difficult, but the basic classroom procedures remain the same. Passages are generally not more than one typewritten page in length.

10.3.1 Locating suitable materials

Most teachers use the reading materials provided in the textbook for guided reading practice. If the basic program does not offer sufficient materials, additional selections must be located.

10.3.1a HOMEMADE RECOMBINED NARRATIVES

The teacher should select vocabulary and structures from several chapters or units. He or she can write a short story (seven or eight sentences) using this material. This is a good technique for reviewing old lessons and for diagnosing the students' progress, especially at the beginning of the second year of language study. Here is a sample of such a story:

Este muchacho se llama Juan. Tiene quince años. Vive en la Avenida Lane, número veinte. No vive cerca de la escuela. Vive lejos de la escuela. Juan sale de casa a las ocho. Toma el autobús a las ocho y cuarto. Llega a la escuela a las ocho y media.

This boy's name is John. He's fifteen years old. He lives at 20 Lane Avenue. He doesn't live near the school. He lives far from the school. John leaves the house at 8 o'clock. He takes a bus at 8:15. He arrives at the school at 8:30.

It is recommended that such recombination narratives be written by native speakers only. It is extremely easy for a nonnative to use words and expressions that native speakers find unnatural.

The American teacher might agree to grade a set of test papers or prepare a bulletin board for the native teacher in exchange for some recombination narratives.

10.3.1b BORROWING FROM OTHER TEXTBOOKS

If the department library has copies of other textbooks, of old editions of the current textbook, or of readers, the teacher will be able to find a variety of readings. Perhaps the text might have to be slightly revised or simplified, but this is a much simpler process than writing a new passage oneself.

10.3.1c ANTHOLOGIES

Many publishers have produced anthologies of short, edited reading selections built around simple grammatical structures and a very limited vocabulary.[2] Students find it encouraging to discover that they can read and comprehend published materials.

10.3.1d STUDENT PERIODICALS

Periodicals designed for language students have short articles, written in rather simple style, which cover a wide range of topics. Each student receives a copy.

The Scholastic foreign language magazines have different magazines for the different levels of learning:

	Level I	Level II	Level III	Levels IV & Up
French:	Bonjour Ça va	Ça va	Chez Nous	Loisirs
Spanish:	Que tal El Sol	El Sol	Hoy día	
German:	Das Rad	Schuss	Der Roller	Der Roller

10.3.1e READING CARDS

André Paquette Associates produces reading cards, each of which contains a short reading followed by comprehension exercises and reading aids.[3] Each "packette" is also accompanied by a cassette that contains the spoken text of the card. The card format makes it easy for teachers to individualize the guided reading activities.

[2] See, for example, Jean-Paul Valette and Rebecca M. Valette, *Lisons: A Level One Reader* (New York: McGraw-Hill, 1968); Paul Pimsleur, *C'est la vie*, 2d ed., (New York: Harcourt Brace Jovanovich, 1975); Paul Pimsleur *Sol y Sombra*, 2d ed., (New York: Harcourt Brace Jovanovich, 1977); Paul Pimsleur and Donald Berger, *Encounters: A Basic Reader* (New York: Harcourt Brace Jovanovich, 1974).

[3] Available at 149 Franklin Street, Laconia, New Hampshire 03246.

10.3.2   Format and presentation

Guided reading means that the teacher, either directly or indirectly, is guiding the students' reading activities and focusing his or her attention on specific aspects of the reading.

10.3.2a   ACTIVITIES LED BY THE TEACHER

Activities led by the teacher may be engaged in by the entire class or by a group at a time. The material read may be in one of three formats:

(1) Overhead transparency: The teacher types the reading selection and has it transferred to a transparency. The advantage of this presentation is that the teacher has close control over what the students are reading. He or she can watch their eye movements and tell when they have finished a selection. The teacher can mask certain parts of the reading and control the rate of presentation. He or she can point out certain words and phrases and know that the students are reading precisely the part they should.

(2) Commercial materials: The teacher may guide the students in reading a paragraph or two from a textbook, reader, magazine, or other printed source. Discussion of the material is simplified if the lines are numbered. With these types of materials it is harder for the teacher to guide the class: some students may not have found the right place, while others may quickly be reading something else on the same page.

(3) Dittoed sheets: The teacher prepares a ditto of a text to be closely read. The teacher can underline certain words and expressions and perhaps number these parts for easy reference. Lines should be numbered also. The ditto sheet has the advantage that students can take notes directly on the handout; sufficient margins should be left for this purpose. If desired, questions may be placed at the bottom of the page.

10.3.2b   ACTIVITIES LED BY STUDENTS

Students may engage in guided reading individually, in pairs, or in small groups led by students. For this type of instruction, the readings are most manageable if prepared on dittos. Another possibility is the preparation of a dittoed worksheet with questions and a list of activities to accompany a reading selection in the textbook.

Another ditto may contain the answers to the questions on the worksheets. This way the students can check themselves when they have finished.

10.3.3   Sample reading exercises

The following types of reading exercises may either be performed orally, with the teacher leading the discussion, or independently, by the students. If a group of students is working together, one acts as scribe and writes down the group's answers.

In work led by the teacher, the teacher immediately corrects the students. When students lead activities, they correct their own work once they have finished the exercise. If the entire class is engaged in independent reading activities, the teacher is free to circulate and to answer questions as they arise.

10.3.3a   READING FOR STRUCTURE SIGNALS

Students tend to read the foreign language for content words rather than for structure signals. The students' attention may be focused on written grammar signals by questions of the type:

Is the author talking about one person or about several people?
  How do you know?
Has the action already taken place? How do you know?
Are the people definitely planning to do. . . ? Or are they just considering it
  as a possibility? How do you know?
Look at the pronoun *lo* in the fifth line. What does it refer to?
What is the antecedent of *qui* in line 10?
Does *lequel* in line 11 refer to *le garçon* or *la chemise?* How do you know?
What is the direct object of the verb *kaufen* in line 6?
Why did the speaker in the third paragraph use the subjunctive rather than
  the indicative?

10.3.3b   TECHNIQUES OF INFERENCE

Students should be taught how to infer meanings from paragraph context. Let us assume that the students do not know the word *maussade* (*cheerless*). If they read simply *Le temps était maussade* (*The weather was cheerless*), they cannot guess what kind of weather it is. But if they read *Le temps était triste et maussade en cette saison. Il pleuvait tous les jours* (*The weather was sad and cheerless in that season. It rained every day*), they can tell that *maussade* has a negative sense and is vaguely synonymous with *triste* (*sad*). For more on techniques of inference, see Section 7.5.3.

The students should also be guided in inferring meanings of words which are related to each other or to the students' native language. For techniques in teaching word families and recognition of cognates, see Chapter 7.

10.3.3c   PARAPHRASING

If a sentence or part of a selection seems too difficult, many students will simply skip it, hoping that they are not missing anything essential. Paraphrasing techniques make students try to grasp the meaning of a selection in its entirety.

(1) Providing paraphrases for the students: Difficult words and expressions may be glossed in the foreign language. An effective language laboratory reading exercise may be prepared as follows:

The teacher prepares a ditto of the reading, underlining the difficult words and expressions. He or she then prepares a tape script in which the difficult words are replaced by easier ones. As the students read the ditto selection in the laboratory, they hear the simplified glosses instead of the underlined expressions.

Text: El viaje que hice fue doblemente agradable para mí por el hecho de que un amigo mío, Emilio Quintani, de La Paz, quiso acompañarme de vuelta para su casa. Los dos experimentamos la misma sensación al descubrir de nuevo cosas y costumbres conocidas.

The trip I took was doubly agreeable for me because my friend, Emilio Quintani, of La Paz, wanted to accompany me when he returned to his home. We both felt the same sensation upon discovering once again the things and customs we knew.

Voice: El viaje que hice fue doblemente agradable para mí porque un amigo mío, Emilio Quintani, de La Paz, quiso acompañarme cuando volvió a su casa. Los dos sintimos la misma sensación al descubrir otra vez cosas y costumbres conocidas.[4]

NOTE: Many textbooks and readers have foreign language glosses. The teacher types up the reading and then inserts the glosses in the recorded version of the selection.

(2) Asking for paraphrases: The teacher can ask students to paraphrase difficult passages. These paraphrases are usually done in the foreign language. Occasionally it might be necessary to request an English paraphrase, but the English should simply give the gist of the text. Word-for-word translating should be discouraged.

10.3.3d METAPHRASING

Metaphrasing is a technique developed by Waldo E. Sweet for teaching students to read Latin.[5] It is equally effective with modern inflected languages such as German and Russian. In metaphrasing the student shows both the lexical and structural meanings of words as they occur in the sentence:

Wir . . .

We are doing something.

Wir werden . . .

We are *going* to do something.

---

[4] Gregory G. La Grone et al., *Hablar y Leer* (New York: Holt, Rinehart, and Winston, 1962), p. 249.
[5] See Lorraine A. Strasheim, *Teaching the Latin Student to Translate*, ERIC Focus Report No. 17 (1970). Available from ACTFL Materials Center, 2 Park Avenue, New York, N.Y. 10016.

Wir werden das Buch . . .	We are going to do something *to the book.*
Wir werden das Buch später . . .	We are going to do something to the book *later.*
Wir werden das Buch später lesen.	We are going to *read* the book later.

10.3.3e   READING FOR INFORMATION

A widely used reading technique, which should be used in conjunction with the techniques described above and not to their exclusion, is reading for information.

(1) Beginning level—simple questions: At the beginning levels the recombined readings also offer practice in both speaking (oral responses) and writing (written responses). Questions require a simple restatement of the text.

Ce garçon s'appelle Jean. Il habite rue Brun. Son père, Monsieur Dupont, est professeur de français. Jean a deux soeurs et un frère. Les quatre enfants vont à une école près de leur maison.	*This boy's name is John. He lives on Brun Street. His father, Mr. Dupont, is a French teacher. John has two sisters and a brother. The four children go to a school near their home.*

Procedure 1:	
Répondez aux questions en français:	*Answer the questions in French:*
Comment s'appelle ce garçon?	*What is the boy's name?*
Où habite-t-il?	*Where does he live?*
Qui est professeur de français?	*Who is a French teacher?*
Combien de soeurs Jean a-t-il?	*How many sisters does John have?*
Où est l'école?	*Where is the school?*

Procedure 2:	
Corrigez les phrases suivantes:	*Correct the following sentences:*
Ce garçon s'appelle Marc.	*This boy's name is Mark.*
Il habite Rue Buffon.	*He lives on Buffon Street.*
Son père est professeur d'anglais.	*His father is an English teacher.*
Jean a deux frères et une soeur.	*John has two brothers and a sister.*
Les quatre enfants ne vont pas à l'école.	*The four children don't go to school.*

(2) Intermediate and advanced level—content questions: As students progress in their reading skills, the teacher can ask questions that require the students to demonstrate their understanding of the entire selection. These questions are often asked before the student reads the passage.

The teacher distributes the reading or places it on the overhead projector. He or she says: *Je vais vous montrer (donner) une petite histoire. Lisez-la et soyez prêts à répondre aux questions suivantes: 1. Qui pleure? 2. Pourquoi cette personne pleure-t-elle? 3. Pleure-t-elle à la fin de l'histoire? Pourquoi ou pourquoi pas? Vous avez trois minutes!* (I'm going to show (give) you a little story. Read it *and be ready to answer the following questions: Who is crying? Why is that person crying? Is he/she crying at the end of the story? Why or why not? You have three minutes!)*

C'est aujourd'hui l'anniversaire de mariage des Duclos. Monsieur Duclos est stupéfait! Il avait complètement oublié que c'était l'anniversaire de son mariage.

Madame Duclos commence à pleurer. A ce moment-là, Monsieur Duclos a une idée. Il voit une belle robe dans le journal. Il donne le journal à sa femme et lui dit, "Voici ton cadeau."

Madame Duclos crie, "Un journal! Quel cadeau!"

Monsieur Duclos lui dit, "Ce n'est pas le journal, c'est la robe que je vais t'acheter." Madame Duclos embrasse son mari et lui dit, "Que tu es gentil, mon chéri!"

Today is the anniversary of the Duclos. Mr. Duclos is stupified! He had completely forgotten that it was his wedding anniversary.

Mrs. Duclos begins to cry. At that moment Mr. Duclos has an idea. He sees a beautiful dress in the newspaper. He gives the newspaper to his wife and says to her, "Here is your present."

Mrs. Duclos exclaims, "A newspaper! What a present!"

Mr. Duclos says to her, "It isn't the newspaper, it's the dress that I'm going to buy for you." Mrs. Duclos kisses her husband and says to him, "How nice you are, darling!"

The teacher may also wish to continue by asking more precise questions which can be answered by a simple rewording of the text. For example: 4. *Qu'est-ce que Monsieur Duclos voit dans le journal? 5. Quand Monsieur Duclos donne le journal à sa femme, que dit-il? 6. Que dit Madame Duclos quand elle embrasse son mari? (What does Mr. Duclos see in the newspaper? When Mr. Duclos gives the newspaper to his wife, what does he say? What does Mrs. Duclos say when she kisses her husband?)*

(3) All levels—questions initiated by students: Students can be taught to formulate their own questions before they have read the entire passage. For example, the teacher might show only the first three sentences of the story about Monsieur and Madame Duclos on the overhead: the students learn that Monsieur Duclos has forgotten his wedding anniversary. Then they are encouraged to formulate their own questions. They might wonder what the wife's reaction will be or what Monsieur Duclos will do about his oversight. Thus the following questions might be formulated by the class and written on the board: *Quelle sera la réaction de sa femme? Qu'est-ce que Monsieur Duclos va faire? (What will be the reaction of his wife? What is Mr. Duclos going to do?)*

The whole passage is then revealed on the overhead or distributed to the students. When they have finished reading, they provide the answers to their own questions.

(4) All levels—finding a title: An excellent technique for encouraging students to consider the reading passage as a whole is asking them to suggest a good title. The various suggestions are written on the chalkboard, and their merits and drawbacks are discussed. The class might want to vote on which is the best title.

10.3.4   Preparing for standardized tests

The teacher can use reading passages and items from the booklets that describe standardized tests to teach reading skills and at the same time to prepare students for tests they might be taking. The printed text of listening comprehension items can also be transformed into reading materials.

The text is put on an overhead transparency if it is short. Otherwise it is typed or reproduced on a ditto master. A transparency is prepared with the questions alone. A second overlay contains the multiple-choice responses.

Zu Beginn des neuen Schuljahres bestellte Herr Braun, der Direktor einer deutschen Mittelschule, alle Lehrer zu einer Konferenz und sagte zu ihnen: "Wir haben uns heute versammelt, um unsern neuen Kollegen, Herrn William Macy, willkommen zu heißen. Herr Macy hat in den letzten zehn Jahren in New York Deutsch und Französisch unterrichtet und wird jetzt an unserer Schule den englischen Unterricht übernehmen. Unsere Schüler erwarten mit Ungeduld ihre erste Stunde bei Herrn Macy. Sie haben allerlei über die amerikanischen Unterrichtsmethoden gehört, die so ganz anders als unsere deutschen sein sollen. Es wird unserem Kollegen nicht schwer fallen, die Begeisterung seiner Schüler zu wecken. Wir werden hoffentlich des öfteren Gelegenheit haben, mit Herrn Macy über seine Beobachtungen zu sprechen. Auch unsere Schüler sollen sich an solchen Diskussionen beteiligen. Das wird für uns alle von großem Nutzen sein. Vor allem aber hoffe ich, daß die Zusammenarbeit mit unserem amerikanischen Kollegen zu einem Gefühl von gegenseitigem Vertrauen und echter Freundschaft führen wird. Und ich nehme an, wir werden am Ende dieses Schuljahres finden, daß wir nicht so verschieden sind, wie wir geglaubt hatten."[6]

At the beginning of the new school year, Mr. Braun, the principal of a German "middle school," called all the teachers to a conference and said to them: "We have gathered today to welcome our new colleague, Mr. William Macy. During the last ten years Mr. Macy has taught German and French in New York. He is now going to take over the instruction of English at our school. Our students are impatiently awaiting their first class with Mr. Macy. They have heard much about American teaching methods, which are said to be quite different from those we use in Germany. It won't be difficult for our colleague to arouse the enthusiasm of his students. Hopefully we will have frequent opportunity to speak with Mr. Macy about his observations. Our students should also be interested in such discussions, which will be of great value for all of us. Above all, however, I hope that our cooperation with our American colleague will lead to a feeling of mutual trust and genuine friendship. I assume that at the end of the school year we will find that we are not as different as we had believed."

The students read the text. Then the teacher places the first transparency on

[6] College Entrance Examination Board, *A Description of the College Board Achievement Tests* (Princeton, New Jersey: ETS, 1962), pp. 81–82.

the overhead. The questions are asked and possible answers are discussed orally in German. When the students have answered the questions, the overlay is placed on the overhead projector. The students read the options aloud and decide which one most closely parallels the answer they themselves had given the question.

Transparency 1	Overlay
1. Was ist der Zweck dieser Zusammenkunft? (*What is the purpose of the meeting?*)	A. Die Schüler mit Herrn Macy bekanntzumachen. (*To introduce the students to Mr. Macy.*)
	B. Herrn Macy über deutsche Methoden zu informieren. (*To inform Mr. Macy about German teaching methods.*)
	C. Das Interesse der Schüler zu wecken. (*To arouse the interest of the students.*)
	D. Herrn Macy seinen neuen Kollegen vorzustellen. (*To introduce Mr. Macy to his new colleagues.*)
2. Mit welchen Gefühlen erwarten die Schüler ihren amerikanischen Lehrer? (*With what kind of feelings are the students awaiting their American teacher?*)	A. Mit Mißtrauen. (*With suspicion.*)
	B. Mit Neugier. (*With curiosity.*)
	C. Mit Furcht. (*With fear.*)
	D. Mit Bewunderung. (*With admiration.*)
3. Was denkt der Direktor über den Unterschied zwischen Deutschen und Amerikanern? (*What does the principal think about the difference between Germans and Americans?*)	A. Daß die Amerikaner praktischer sind als die Deutschen. (*That the Americans are more practical than the Germans.*)
	B. Daß die deutsche Jugend mehr Interesse am Lernen hat. (*That the German youth are more interested in learning.*)
	C. Daß der Unterschied geringer ist als man gewöhnlich glaubt. (*That the difference is smaller than one would normally believe.*)
	D. Daß der Unterschied ein gegenseitiges Verstehen unmöglich macht. (*That the difference makes a mutual understanding impossible.*)

4. Was erhofft der Direktor am meisten von der Zusammenarbeit aller Lehrer? (*What does the principal most hope for as a result of the cooperation of all teachers?*)

A. Daß sie zu dauernden Freundschaften führen wird. (*That it will lead to lasting friendships.*)

B. Daß die Schüler englische Diskussionen führen werden. (*That the students will participate in English discussions.*)

C. Daß Herr Macy deutsche Methoden lernen wird. (*That Mr. Macy will learn German teaching methods.*)

D. Daß deutsche Lehrer nach Amerika gehen werden. (*That German teachers will go to America.*)

10.3.5 Building reading speed

The teacher prepares a reading passage on an overhead transparency. The selection should be one that most of the students can read readily.

The presentation of reading is timed by the teacher in one of the following ways: (1) The entire reading is exposed for a limited amount of time only. (2) A mask reveals one line after the other. (3) Two masks, or a mask with a slot the width and breadth of a line of type, reveal only one line at a time.

After the students have quickly seen the reading, the teacher turns off the projector and asks one or two content questions.

10.4 READING LONGER SELECTIONS

When students have mastered the basic techniques of reading, they should read longer selections in addition to shorter passages used for guided reading. In fact, even the passages for guided reading will often be taken from longer articles and stories.

10.4.1 Types of materials

There are many types of reading materials. The teacher must look at available selections to check whether the contents are appropriate for the age and maturity of the students. If possible, students should be offered a choice of readings so that they may select topics which interest them.

10.4.1a READERS DESIGNED FOR SPECIFIC READING LEVELS

Some readers are written for students who have attained a specific level in their study of the foreign language. New words above the given level are glossed, usually in the foreign language. Some examples of readers of this type are:

Scherer, ed., *Reading for Meaning* (New York: Harcourt Brace Jovanovich, Inc., 1966).
Stories are based on structure and vocabulary taught in the first twenty-three units of A-LM, first edition. Available in French, German, Spanish, Russian, Italian.

Textes en Français Facile (Paris: Hachette, 1962–76) and *Collection Lire et Savoir* (Paris: Didier, 1962).
Readings are based on vocabularies of 750 words and 1300 words.

Reading and Exercise Series (Portland, Oregon: ELS International, and New York: Oxford University Press, 1973–75).
The original and adapted stories for beginning and intermediate ESL students are also accompanied with complete tape recordings and exercises.

Jarvis, Bonin, Corbin, and Birckbichler, *Connaître et se connaître* (New York: Holt Rinehart Winston, 1976)
Readings are based on vocabularies of 500, 1000 and 1500 words.

10.4.1b GRADED READERS

These readers gradually progress from easy selections to more difficult ones. New vocabulary is gradually introduced, so that the comprehension of each story depends on that of the previous one.

D.C. Heath has several series of this sort in the commonly taught languages. Houghton Mifflin publishes the Bauer-Campell series in French (Boston: Houghton Mifflin Co., 1965, 66, 70).

10.4.1c READERS WITH GLOSSES AND END VOCABULARIES

These are the standard type of readers. Most publishers offer a wide selection of readers. These typically have glosses in the native or the target language and a comprehensive end vocabulary.

10.4.1d READERS WITH INTERLINEAR GLOSSES

Interlinear readers have glosses printed above the line of text. A special grid is used which hides the glosses so that the students can see only the text. The grid is moved when necessary to reveal the glosses.[7]

10.4.1e BILINGUAL READERS

In bilingual readers the foreign language is on one page or column and English is on the other. The advantage of these books is that the student need not thumb through an end vocabulary. It is essential, however, that all classwork be con-

[7] Joseph P. Ebacher, *Programmed Reading French Series* (Englewood Cliffs, N.J.: Prentice-Hall, Inc., 1965–67).

ducted in the foreign language so that students are obliged to read the foreign language text.

10.4.2 Integrating reading and the other aspects of the language program

The teaching of reading, especially the reading of longer selections, offers a wide range of possibilities for bringing in other aspects of the foreign language program.

10.4.2a READING AND CULTURE

Almost all readings contain some cultural content. If places are mentioned, the teacher can point them out on the map. Slides and photographs might be appropriate. If the reading is going to take several days, a few students might prepare a short presentation on the region where the action takes place.

If a composer or a type of music is mentioned, an appropriate record should be played.

If an artist or work of art is mentioned, some of the works should be shown. Works of art should also be used to depict the region or the historical events under discussion (Goya's paintings and the Napoleonic wars).

If a holiday is mentioned, the traditions should be explained.

If dates or historical events or figures are mentioned, these should be briefly presented.

If social customs are part of the story, their significance should be discussed.

Individualized reading programs should contain materials from as many fields as possible: science, history, political science, architecture, mechanics, and so on. There are many possibilities in the foreign language other than literature—both in the language classroom and later in life for business or recreation.

10.4.2b READING AND WRITING

Reading and writing activities can be easily coordinated. The answering of questions and the writing of résumés are obvious examples of written work. Who, what, where, and when questions may serve as the basis of a brief synopsis of a story: 1. *¿Quién es el hombre en este cuento?* 2. *¿Qué está haciendo?* 3. *¿Dónde está?* 4. *¿Cuándo ocurre este incidente?* (*Who is the man in this story? What is he doing? Where is he? When does this incident occur?*) Other types of writing assignments may grow out of reading selections.

As a grammar exercise, a paragraph from the selection may be changed from one tense to another. Direct speech may be turned into indirect discourse, and vice versa.

Elementary and intermediate students might rewrite the opening of the story by simply changing some of the nouns and adjectives. The sentence structure stays the same, but the plot is transformed. More advanced students may write about the same incident from the point of view of another character in the story.

A story with action and dialog might be rewritten as a skit by a group of students. They could then present their version to the others in the class.

A student could rewrite the story as if it were a brief newspaper item. He or she would furnish headlines and a summary of what occurred. A longer story might be rewritten as a series of newspaper clippings, which might be arranged in a bulletin board display.

10.4.2c READING AND THE SPOKEN SKILLS

Reading selections can be used for oral practice in several ways. Traditionally this means that the teacher reads the questions in the book and the students respond. As a variation, each student might be told to write out two or three questions about the story, which he or she can address to various classmates. The teacher tries to remain in the background, unless it is necessary to encourage the more reticent members of the class to participate.

Sentences from the reading that contain difficult grammatical patterns may become models for rapid pattern drills with the teacher giving the cues.

In more advanced classes a group of students might prepare a synopsis of the reading in the form of a radio newscast. The students take turns recording the individual "news items," and the resulting tape is played to the class.

If a character in the story faces a difficult dilemma, a short debate might be organized on the pros and cons of the possible alternatives.

10.4.3 Reading groups

Not long after students begin their foreign language study, and certainly by the time they reach Level II, their individual differences, both in rate of learning and in interest, are usually very great. Some students are quite advanced, others are able to handle textbook materials at their grade level, and a few have difficulty understanding the simplest texts. Some students can look at a new word and see how it is derived; others see no relationship between one word and another. The use of reading groups enables the teacher to work with students on their own level. There are a number of different procedures that can be followed with reading groups.

(1) The teacher divides the class into groups on the basis of their demonstrated ability in reading (usually three groups for most efficient management—Group A containing the strongest students; Group B, the average ones; and Group C, the weakest). He or she gives each group a different reading selection.

To Groups A and B the teacher distributes dittoed sheets with either background material on the story or a partial synopsis (without the ending). Then he or she distributes a few guiding questions.

The teacher sits down with Group C and introduces the story orally; he or she reads the first paragraph aloud and asks questions in either English or the foreign language. Then dittoed sheets are distributed with guiding questions for the following paragraphs or pages.

By this time Group A is ready to answer the questions on their reading. The teacher sits down with them and leads a discussion. He or she distributes the next set of questions and then goes on to Group B and checks their work.

Variation: The teacher can give the written answers to the questions to one of the members of the group, who will lead the discussion in his or her place.

Group work requires much preparation on the part of the teacher. On certain days the teacher may be able to meet with only one group. When this is the case he or she should supply the other groups with as many aids as possible: vocabulary cues, word study, grammatical explanations, and guided questions.

In curriculums that use modular scheduling, team teaching, or differentiated staff, there might be interns, student teachers, or teacher aides[8] to work with smaller groups.

(2) The teacher divides the class into ability groups and gives each one the same reading material. Each group proceeds at its own rate. (See (1) for the other techniques.)

(3) The teacher allows the students to choose their own group members or a partner to work with. (See (1) for the other techniques.)

10.4.4   Individualized reading

In individualized reading, students are given freedom to select what they wish to read. Generally some teacher guidance is needed.

10.4.4a   THE TEACHER-FILE SYSTEM

The teacher compiles a list of readings in categories from very easy to very advanced and prepares a synopsis of each reading on index cards.

After the student reads the synopses he or she makes a selection and checks the choice with the teacher. If the teacher thinks it is at the appropriate level of difficulty, he or she gives approval. If not, another reading is suggested.

In a file the teacher has two sets of material to accompany each text the students read: one is a series of worksheets to guide the students through their reading, the other is a quiz to evaluate their progress.

10.4.4b   THE "CHECKER" SYSTEM

Each student keeps a notebook. At the beginning of the individualized period, students are allowed to choose what they would like to read from a list of available readings. When a student has finished a selection, he or she makes note of this in the notebook.

---

[8] The term "intern" usually refers to a person who holds a college degree, but is not yet certified to teach; he or she spends a year doing part-time teaching. A teacher's aide is usually a nonprofessional person without a college degree. A student teacher is a college student who is in a teacher training program.

The teacher calls on students one at a time after they have finished a selection. He or she asks some content questions in the foreign language and checks off that selection in the student's notebook. If the student shows an understanding of the selection, he or she is named "checker" for that selection.

On the bulletin board is kept a list of students and the selections for which they are "checker." When another student finishes a selection for which a "checker" is listed, he or she may go to that student rather than to the teacher. The "checker" asks some content questions in the foreign language and is allowed to check off the selection in the student's notebook.

Variation: The "checker" must write out the questions he or she intends to ask. The teacher has to approve the questions before the "checker" is allowed to ask them.

10.5   COMMUNICATIVE PRACTICE

Students attach much more importance to their reading if they are given the opportunity to react directly to it by voting or expressing their personal opinions. They may do so in the following ways:

10.5.1   Experience charts

The students take a trip; it could be to a museum, an antique show, a picturesque market, or simply in and around their school. When they return, they dictate to the teacher what they saw. The teacher writes the description on the overhead projector and then the class is asked to read it, chorally and individually.

In preparation for a simple trip to the first floor of the school, the teacher might ask the students to gather the following information:

1. Où est situé le bureau du directeur? l'infirmerie?

   Where is the principal's office? the infirmary?

2. Combien de portes et de fenêtres y a-t-il?

   How many doors and windows are there?

3. Décrivez les expositions (de tableaux, de trophées, de documents, etc.)

   Describe the exhibits (paintings, trophies, documents, etc.)

4. Décrivez les photographies que vous voyez aux murs.

   Describe the photographs you see on the walls.

5. Quelle est votre opinion du rez-de-chaussée? Est-il joli? assez éclairé? bien décoré?

   What is your opinion of the first floor? Is it pretty? light enough? well decorated?

10.5.2   Values questionnaires

In *values questionnaires* the students are asked to give their opinions on specific questions that imply a set of personal priorities. As a point of departure, the teacher may select an opinion poll from a newspaper or magazine. First the students are presented with the questions only, and are asked to give their personal responses. Then, the students are shown the results of the survey, and may compare their answers with those of the norm group. As a variation, the students may be asked to take the questionnaire and to administer it to five other persons as a homework assignment. On the following day, all the results are tabulated before being compared to the results reported in the original magazine.

The example that follows is a questionnaire prepared for student use. Since no responses are provided, the class might want to compare their results with those of another class in the school. The questionnaire might also be answered in small groups, and each group could report on its results.

La Conservation d'énergie[9]   *Conserving Energy*

People talk a lot these days about the need to conserve our natural resources by not using so much energy in our daily life. Consider the energy-saving activities listed here:

1. How effective do you think each one would be in reducing energy consumption? Rate them from 0 to 5 (5 = most effective).
2. How personally inconvenient would each one be? Rate them from 0 to 5 again (5 = most inconvenient).

1   2

____ ____ a. éteindre la lumière quand personne n'est dans la pièce. — *turning off the light when nobody is in the room.*

____ ____ b. baisser le chauffage et porter plus de vêtements. — *turning down the heat and wearing more clothes.*

____ ____ c. prendre des bains froids au lieu de bains chauds. — *bathing in cold rather than hot water.*

____ ____ d. organiser le transport en groupe où chacun conduit à son tour. — *organizing car pools.*

____ ____ e. marcher ou aller à bicyclette au lieu d'utiliser la voiture. — *walking or using your bicycle instead of your car.*

____ ____ f. acheter une très petite voiture. — *buying a very small car.*

____ ____ g. laver la vaisselle à la main. — *washing dishes by hand.*

____ ____ h. se lever et se coucher plus tôt. — *going to bed and getting up earlier.*

____ ____ i. ne pas utiliser de rasoir électrique. — *not using an electric razor.*

____ ____ j. ne pas utiliser de séchoir à cheveux. — *not using an electric hair dryer.*

[9] Translated from Marty Knorre et al., *Cara a cara* (New York: Holt Rinehart Winston, 1977), p. 114.

10.5.3 Self-tests

In the self-test, the student responds to a questionnaire and then analyzes his or her results in the light of an interpretation chart. Such self-tests are frequently published in popular magazines, especially youth-oriented magazines. It may be necessary to simplify some of the items if the self-test is used with beginning or intermediate students.[10] The following example has been adapted for American students of Spanish.

What kind of driver are you?
Angel o diablo?[11]   *An angel or a devil?*

Are you a demon or an angel behind the wheel? To find out, take the following test. Using the numbers 0 to 3, indicate how frequently you do or feel what the following statements suggest (0 = never, 1 = sometimes, 2 = usually, 3 = always). Then read the interpretation of your score!

_____ 1. Cuando otro coche me niega la entrada, le grito palabrotas.

When the driver of another car doesn't let me pass, I shout curse words at him.

_____ 2. Cuando el coche delante de mi se apaga y no funciona de nuevo, toco la bocina.

When the car in front of me stalls and won't start up again, I blow my horn.

_____ 3. Cuando un peatón cruza en contra de la luz, tengo ganas de atropellarlo.

When a pedestrian crosses against the light, I feel like knocking him down.

_____ 4. Cuando los conductores doblan la esquina sin indicar, me entran ganas de estrangularlos.

When drivers turn a corner without signaling, I feel like strangling them.

_____ 5. Cuando un ciclista se pone delante de mí en una calle estrecha, toco la bocina para asustarlo.

When a cyclist gets in front of me on a narrow street, I blow my horn to frighten him.

_____ 6. Cuando alguien me quita el espacio donde deseo estacionar mi coche, tengo la tentación de desinflarle las llantas.

When someone takes the place where I want to park my car, I feel tempted to let the air out of his tires.

_____ 7. Cuando un coche me sigue muy cerca, toco los frenos para asustarlo.

When a car follows me very closely, I put on my brakes to frighten him.

_____ 8. Cuando tengo prisa, siento la tentación de dar una "pasadita" a cualquier peatón.

When I'm in a hurry I get the temptation to run down any pedestrian.

_____ 9. Cuando un taxista me amenaza con la bocina, tengo ganas de robarle el taxímetro.

When a taxi driver blows his horn at me in a threatening manner, I feel like stealing his meter.

[10] Self-tests in French are available in the form of "Packettes" from André Paquette Associates, 149 Franklin Road, Laconia, N.H. 03246.
[11] Knorre et al., *Cara a cara*, pp. 160–61.

____10. Cuando los camiones bloquean toda la carretera me dan ganas de dinamitarlos.	*When buses block the entire highway I feel like dynamiting them.*

☐ TOTAL

Interpretaciones

  0–9: ¡Qué bueno es Ud.! Su corona es muy bonita, pero ¿no le molestan las alas cuando duerme?
10–19: ¿Angel o diablo? ¡Quién sabe! Depende del momento.
20–30: ¡Por Dios! ¿Es Ud. tan diabólico en todo lo que hace?

Interpretations

(*0–9:   What a good person you are! Your crown is very pretty, but don't your wings bother you when you're sleeping?*
10–19: Angel or devil? Who knows! It depends on your mood at that moment.
20–30: Good Heavens! Are you that diabolical in everything you do?)

10.6   LITERATURE IN THE CLASSROOM

Simple poems and proverbs are often introduced early in language instruction, usually to teach the sound system or to give a sampling of foreign culture. Later in the language program, longer and more difficult literary works are introduced. This section deals with selections chosen primarily for their literary value.

10.6.1   Aims in teaching literature

Before introducing a literary work to the class, the teacher must decide what his or her aims are. What does he or she expect the students to get from this particular work? Why introduce literature at all?

The primary aim is to show students many different techniques for reading and interpreting a work of literature. If students develop various approaches to literature, perhaps later they will enjoy reading literary works on their own. The aim should not be to cram their heads full of facts: names of authors, centuries, titles of works, literary movements, and the like; they can always look these things up in an encyclopedia when they need the information. But the encyclopedia cannot teach them to read—this is the role of the teacher.

The secondary aim is to reinforce certain points of grammar and items of vocabulary. In studying a work of literature the student will simultaneously be developing his or her command of the second language. Vocabulary lists might be derived from the work. Some lines of poetry could be memorized, not only for their poetic value, but also because they contain examples of grammatical patterns (such as the use of the *passé composé* in Prévert's "Le Déjeuner du Matin"). To meet this secondary aim, the teacher would do well to select contemporary works, because their structures and vocabulary will more closely parallel the type of language the student has been learning.

10.6.2 Presentation of the work

Usually the students will need to be introduced to a literary work before they can appreciate it. They may need to learn the historical background of a novel, the social conditions which the author is trying to portray in a play, the geographical setting of a story. Sometimes a short presentation of the author's life helps the student better understand a lyric poem or a semiautobiographical piece.

The following examples briefly indicate how literary works might be presented in class:

(1) *Pensativa*, by Jesús Goytortuá: The necessary background is an understanding of the causes and outcome of the Mexican Revolution of 1910 and of the status of the Church before and after the Revolution. A good source is the series *The Struggle of the Mexican People for Their Liberty*.[12] The complete teaching kit includes slides, text with tape, and tests. It contains the following titles:

The Epoch of Porfirio Díaz
Madero
Toward the Present Constitution
The Victory of the Constitutionalists

(2) *Le Petit Prince*, by Antoine de Saint Exupéry: The author's life is an interesting background.

Il était pilote. Il a eu une panne dans le désert "à mille milles de toute région habitée." Il avait perdu son petit frère (la mort du petit prince). Il aimait sa rose (sa femme). (*He was a pilot. His plane broke down in the desert a thousand miles from any inhabited region. He had lost his little brother (the death of the little prince). He loved his rose, his wife.*)

The teacher could try to find photos of Saint Exupéry as a child and as an adult (pilot) and show them with an opaque projector.[13] He or she could also show the film *Saint Exupéry*[14] for glimpses of his life and career and the sound of his voice.

(3) *El Sombrero de Tres Picos*, by Pedro Antonio de Alarcón: To create atmosphere the teacher can play excerpts of the recording *España*[15] containing The Three Cornered Hat Suite, by Falla.

[12] Wible Language Institute, 24 South Eighth Street, Allentown, Pa. 18105.
[13] Technique demonstrated by Alfred N. Smith in film, *Teaching French Literature in the Secondary School*, College of Education, Ohio State University.
[14] FACSEA, 972 Fifth Avenue, New York, N.Y.
[15] *España*, 6186, Lorraine Music Co., 23-80 48th Street, Long Island City, N.Y. 11103.

(4) *Le Bourgeois Gentilhomme*, by Molière: The necessary background is an understanding of the life of seventeenth-century bourgeois and aristocrats and of the humor in Molière's comedies. From the film *Une Journée à la Comédie Française*, the teacher can show the last scene, *"La leçon de Phonétique,"* narrated by Louis Seigner.[16]

(5) *"Der Augsburger Kreidekreis,"* by Bertolt Brecht: The necessary historical background is the Thirty Years' War. The teacher can use the AATG slide series 330.2/1 which treats the Thirty Years' War.[17]

(6) *The Old Man and the Sea* by Ernest Hemingway: The teacher presents a map of the Caribbean and locates the action of the novel. Illustrations from an encyclopedia or book on deep-sea fishing introduce the students to the fish and the type of tackle used.

10.6.3 Teaching poetry

Poetry is introduced early in the student's language learning career.[18] At first, it is primarily used as a device for improving pronunciation. Poems memorized in the first year may be reintroduced later for literary analysis.

10.6.3a SCANNING

Students may be taught the rules of traditional prosody in the language they are studying. They should be given the opportunity to apply this knowledge to the scanning of simple unfamiliar poems. Advanced students might be encouraged to try writing poetry of their own within the traditional patterns of the literature under study.

10.6.3b UNDERSTANDING THE SURFACE MEANING

Teachers often wrongly assume that students have grasped the surface meaning of the poem, that they understand the "story," or that they mentally envision the scene; they begin by lecturing on poetic images, themes, and so on. Actually, many students dislike poetry because they have never been taught to see the picture or pictures that the poet has depicted. Time spent clarifying the "story" is invaluable in bringing the students to an appreciation of poetry.

Before teaching Rilke's poem about the panther, find photographs of caged

---

[16] New York: McGraw-Hill, Inc.
[17] Available from Teaching Aid Project, NCSA/AATG Service Center, 339 Walnut Street, Philadelphia, Pa. 19106. There is no charge to AATG members, except the cost of postage and insurance. A catalogue of other slides, film strips, and tapes is available.
[18] See also G. Bording Mathieu, *Poems in Early Foreign Language Instruction*, ERIC Focus Report No. 15 (1970). Available from ACTFL Materials Center, 2 Park Avenue, New York, N.Y. 10016.

cats: tigers, lions, panthers. Let the students talk about how they would feel if they had once roamed a jungle and were obliged to spend the rest of their lives behind bars. What kind of view of life would they have? Then let the students read Rilke's poem, and they will be in a better position to grasp the meaning of the work.

Ronsard's *"Ode à Cassandre"* often seems uninteresting to students because they see in it merely a poet talking about roses. A lecture on "carpe diem" does not add to their appreciation of the work. It is more effective to put the setting in modern terms. A boy has his eye on a girl, but she is always with other people; his first objective is to get her away from the crowd. How might he do this? After students have given their suggestions for ways of handling the problem, the teacher might point out that in the sixteenth century, a good place for privacy was a remote corner of the garden. The trick was to ask the girl to come look at a special rose growing there. The boy's next problem (second verse) is to get the girl in the proper mood for what he plans to propose. He simply points out how quickly the beautiful flower wilts in the hot sun and loses its charm. It's nature's fault that we get old so quickly. In the final verse he makes the analogy explicit: How about it? How about us? We're young . . . let's make love before it's too late. Once the students understand what the poet is saying, they will be more willing to examine the poem to see how the effect was accomplished.

10.6.3c FIGURES OF SPEECH

Poems make frequent use of figures of speech. An analysis of these figures should be postponed until the students understand the poem itself. Many students have done some work in picking out such figures in their English courses, and they can apply what they know to the foreign language.

Goethe's poem *"Erlkönig"* lends itself well to a study of the technique of personification.

Students could be asked to identify the passage in which Death is speaking, the nature of its message, references that are made to it (pronouns, for example), and its physical characteristics. For example, in this part of the ballad Death is trying to woo a small boy from the arms of his father with the following words:

Willst, feiner Knabe, du mit mir gehn?	*Wilt go, then dear infant, wilt go with me there?*
Meine Töchter sollen dich warten schön;	*My daughers shall tend thee with sisterly care.*
Meine Töchter führen den nächt- lichen Reihn	*My daughters by night their glad festival keep.*
Und wiegen und tanzen und singen dich ein.	*They'll dance thee, and rock thee, and sing thee to sleep.*[19]

[19] Edgar Alfred Bowring, trans., *Poems by Goethe*, (Boston: S.E. Cassino, 1882).

10.6.3d   USE OF VOCABULARY AND STRUCTURE

The teacher may use a simplified "explication de texte" technique to help the students see how the poet's choice of words and use of tenses create a desired effect.

In teaching Prévert's "*Barbara,*" for example, the teacher would first create the two scenes: the happy prewar scene and the wartime bombings of Brest. The students would locate the poet's strong antiwar statement and its central position in the poem.

The following is a brief sample of how the teacher might focus the students' attention on the choice of adjectives, verbs, and verb tenses.[20]

(1) Le professeur aide les élèves à chercher les adjectifs et les verbes importants à la compréhension du poème.

The teacher helps the students look for the adjectives and the verbs that are important for comprehension of the poem.

Professeur: Le titre du poème est *Barbara.* Qu'est-ce que nous savons de cette jeune femme à part son nom? Cherchons les mots qui la décrivent...

The title of the poem is "Barbara." What do we know of this young woman besides her name? Let's look for the words that describe her . . .

Elèves: Souriante... épanouie... ravie... ruisselante... visage heureux.

Smiling . . . beaming . . . enraptured . . . flowing . . . a happy face.

Professeur: Excellent. Ce sont des adjectifs qui font partie d'un portrait. Cherchons maintenant les mots qui expriment ce qu'elle fait, les verbes...

Excellent. These are adjectives that are used to make a picture or a portrait. Now let's look for the words that express what she does, the verbs . . .

Elèves: Tu souriais... tu as couru vers lui... tu t'es jetée dans ses bras... tu marchais souriante...

You smiled . . . you ran towards him . . . you threw yourself into his arms . . . you were smiling while you walked . . .

(2) Le professeur pose des questions sur certains thèmes contrastés (substantifs).

The teacher asks questions about certain contrasting themes (nouns).

---

[20] Adapted from B. J. Gilliam, "Teaching French Poetry in the American Secondary School" (Ph.D. diss., Ohio State University, 1969), pp. 192–207.

Professeur:	Plus tard vous voyez le thème de la guerre— "sous cette pluie de deuil terrible et désolée." Alors on trouve des thèmes contrastés n'est-ce pas? Qu'est-ce qui contraste avec l'amour, la beauté, la jeunesse, la tendresse, la joie?	*Later you see the theme of war— "into that terrible and desolate shower of mourning." So you find contrasting themes, don't you? What contrasts with love, beauty, youth, tenderness, joy?*
		What contrasts with love, beauty, youth, tenderness, joy?
Elèves:	La violence... la haine... l'horreur... la destruction... le désespoir...	*Violence . . . hate . . . horror . . . destruction . . . despair.*

(3) Le professeur pose des questions sur la grammaire.

The teacher asks questions about the grammar.

Professeur:	Je vous ai dit que M. Prévert écrit des scénarios de film. Ce poème est un peu comme un film. Les événements du *passé* servent d'arrière plan à un *présent* qui se déroule sous nos yeux. Quels temps utilise-t-on pour exprimer des actions passées? L'imparfait et le passé composé. Qui peut nous expliquer la différence entre ces deux temps?	*I told you that Prévert writes scenarios for films. This poem is a little like a film. The events of the past serve as a backdrop for the present actions, which unfold before our eyes. Which tenses do we use to express past actions? The imperfect and the passé composé? Who can explain to us the difference between these two tenses?*
Elève:	On emploie l'imparfait pour les actions de durée imprécise.	*The imperfect is used for actions of an undetermined duration.*
Professeur:	Bien. L'imparfait est utilisé pour décrire aussi la condition, l'état, le temps, les faits accessoires à l'action principale. Et le passé composé?	*Good. The imperfect is used also to describe a situation, a condition or a set of circumstances that are subordinate to the main action. And the passé composé.*

Elève: On utilise le passé com- *The passé composé is used to express*
posé pour exprimer *a completed action that takes*
un fait précis qui a *place at a given moment.*
lieu à un moment
donné.

Professeur: Excellent. Maintenant, *Excellent. Now this half of the class*
cette moitié de la *is going to draw up a list of all the*
classe va dresser une *verbs that are used in the imperfect*
liste de tous les *in this poem. The other half will*
verbes qui se trouvent *look for all the verbs which are in*
à l'imparfait dans ce *the passé composé.*
poème. L'autre moitié
va chercher tous les
verbes qui sont au
passé composé.

10.6.3e ORAL INTERPRETATION

The teacher should try to find two or more dramatic interpretations of the poem being studied. Usually the best known poems in a language have been recorded by leading actors and speakers. Musical versions are often available. The teacher prepares a tape made up of several interpretations. Students listen to the tape independently, or in the laboratory, and write a short essay stating which version they prefer and why. They might also say that they do not like any of the interpretations and try reading the poem themselves the way they think it should sound.

10.6.4 Teaching fiction

Stories, novellas, and short novels are often introduced in high school language classes. In teaching fiction, the teacher often tends to focus entirely on the plot and to neglect literary considerations. There are a number of easy techniques which help the student to develop some skill in literary analysis once he has understood the story.

10.6.4a FINDING RECURRING THEMES

Students become more aware of recurring themes if they are actively engaged in looking for passages where these themes are expressed. The simplest way to focus students' attention on themes is to have them count references to a particular theme.

For example, in reading Camus' *L'Etranger*, the students would be asked to note all words that refer to sun, heat, and light. By the time the students reach the scene where Meursault kills the Arab, they will be aware of the effect of the

sunlight

sunlight reflected off the Arab's knife: "La lumière a giclé sur l'acier comme une longue langue étincelante qui m'atteignait au front". (*The light leaped off the steel like a long glistening tongue that hit my forehead.*)

10.6.4b POINT OF VIEW

The teacher can ask the students to uncover the point of view of a work. It may be narrated in the third person, and yet all of the scenes may be depicted as they appear to only one of the characters. Maybe the narrator plays "God" and goes inside many of his characters.

As a written exercise, the students may try to rewrite a scene from another character's point of view.

10.6.4c THE ROLE OF DESCRIPTION

Some works are heavily descriptive throughout, while others are more action-oriented. Some works begin with descriptive passages and then move to scenes with much movement and dialog.

To help the students become aware of the role of description, have them go through the story marking descriptive passages. Quantitative results may be given:

Story A: 5 pages description   10 pages action and dialog
Story B: 2 pages description   16 pages action and dialog
Story C: 7 pages description   3 pages action and dialog

The students could then list their impressions of the three stories and compare these to the quantitative analyses. Students usually prefer stories with a low proportion of descriptive passages.

The teacher could have the students look at one story again and ask them how it would read if all the description were eliminated. Would it still make sense? What role does the description play? Are some parts essential, while other parts could be cut? Which could be cut?

A similar study might be done with chapters of a longer work.

10.6.4d PLOT DIAGRAMS

Students in small groups can try to diagram the development of the story. Does the story begin with the chronological end of events and then go back to the chronological beginning and follow through consecutively? Does the story begin at the middle, with some flashbacks? Does the first half of the story cover ten months of time, and the last half cover four hours? Do conflicting interests build up and meet near the end of the work?

The diagrams may take the forms of lines and arrows. They may be shown as a time line to which are attached the various scenes or chapters. The number of pages devoted to particular episodes may be noted. Once the students are told to find a way to represent the story in a graphic fashion, they will probably come up with a variety of interpretations.

10.6.5   Teaching drama

Plays are often introduced in advanced language classes because they can be relatively short and because they are written in dialog, which the students are expected to find easy to understand. Actually, many students fail to enjoy plays because they cannot visualize the story.

10.6.5a   VISUALIZING THE ACTION

The first concern of the teacher who is presenting a play to the class must be to bring the work to life. An excellent device is the flannel board. The students read the description of the setting and design their own stage. The layout of the first scene is placed on the flannel board.

Then the students make figures to represent each character. One student may be assigned to handle the exits, entrances, and stage movements of each felt figure. If there are more students than characters, the remaining students can be put in charge of scenery and props.

Variation: The stage and characters may be drawn on acetate. The teacher moves the figures around on the overhead projector.

10.6.5b   FIGURES OF SPEECH

The text of the play may also be used as the basis of a study of figures of speech. The following examples are drawn from *La Dama del Alba* by Alejandro Casona.[21] The students are to search for metaphors and similes.

Trae un cansancio alegre arrollado a la cintura. (Act I, p. 24)
(*He wears a roll of happy lassitude tucked in his belt.*)

(A Snowstorm)
Parecía una aldea de enanos, con caperuzas blancas en las chimeneas y barbas de hielo colgando en los tejados. (Act I, p. 25)
(*It looked like a village of dwarfs, with large white caps on the chimneys and beards of ice hanging from the roofs.*)

(Laughter)
Es un temblor alegre que corre por dentro, como las ardillas por un árbol hueco. (Act I, p. 35)
(*It is a happy tremor that runs through my being, like squirrels through a hollow tree.*)

---

[21] New York: Charles Scribner's Sons, 1947.

Assignment: In the first half of Act II look for metaphors and similes about death.

(Death by drowning)

Es como una venda de agua en el alma. (Act II, p. 56)
(*It's like a bandage of water on the soul.*)

10.6.5c PLOT DEVELOPMENT

Most plays have a careful plot development, which lends itself readily to diagramming. Students can pick out the key scenes and show how other earlier scenes led up to them.

In studying French classical theater, the students can also draw several clocks to accompany the scenes of the play, in order to show that the action takes less than twenty-four hours.

10.6.5d THEMES

Drama also lends itself well to a study of themes. Students can be told to look for recurring themes and make note of them while they are reading. The teacher can ask for themes and write them on the board or on the overhead. Students can discuss the suggestions and try to decide which are most important to the play.

10.6.5e CHARACTERIZATION

Students can make lists of adjectives that the characters use to describe one another. Do the other persons see a main character the way he or she really is, or does this character, in monologs and actions, try to deceive the others?

The students may then make lists of adjectives which they themselves would use to describe the main characters in the play. Do the students' lists resemble or differ from the list derived from the play itself?

10.6.5f RECORDINGS

Recordings of plays are often available. Listening to the recording should not be a substitute for analyzing the structure of the play. However, once the play has been studied, it is often interesting to play the recording of a particular scene and to evaluate the performance of the actors.

Recordings may also be used for individual work in the laboratory. The students read the play as they listen to the recording. Often the actor's interpretation of a speech helps the student understand what is meant.

outline

11.6 WRITING LETTERS

11.7 FREE COMPOSITION

eleven
Writing

Writing may well be considered the most difficult of the language skills. People are flattered when a foreigner tries to speak their language, and they tend to tolerate a light accent and occasional awkward expressions with good grace. The speaker's personality makes a greater impression than the accuracy of his or her spoken language. But a letter is judged more severely on its purely linguistic merits. Errors in spelling and grammar are not easily excused, even if the meaning is clear and the handwriting is attractive and legible.

Many ESL students do not know how to write in their native language. Others write a language that does not use the Roman alphabet. For these students, the first step in learning to write is mastering the act of writing. For adult learners, the first goal is to acquire the degree of writing skill needed to function in American society: writing out checks, completing applications, and writing short notes.

Beyond the functional level, writing has been equated with formal education. Persons who write are expected to write correctly. In France especially, where the French language is central to the school curriculum, students are taught not only to write correct French, but to develop an individual literary style.

Obviously it takes many many years of intensive study to write a second language fluently. Even most American language teachers who read with facility the foreign language they teach do not feel qualified to express themselves in writing with the same ease as in English. Although students will not attain a high level of proficiency after only a few years of language training, they can learn how to fill out forms and how to write informal letters or short business letters.

11.1 GENERAL CONSIDERATIONS

Skill in writing begins with simple copying and ends with free self-expression. As students progress in their development of the writing skill, they will require guidance from the teacher.

284

Ability to write well grows out of prior experience in listening, speaking, and reading. If students know what the sentence they wish to write sounds like, they are well advanced on their way toward fluent written expression. They may make some spelling mistakes, but the foreign national will understand what they are trying to say. Spelling mistakes must be continually checked and corrected, if the students are to express themselves accurately. They do not see their own mistakes readily; only the teacher does.

The most serious writing problems arise when the student tries to transform a native language sentence word for word into a foreign language equivalent. At the early levels the teacher can combat this tendency by providing leading questions and cues in the target language. Assigning a written résumé or a free composition before students are ready to handle it can lead to frustration and negative learning.

The techniques that follow are samples of writing experiences from early to advanced levels.

11.2 COPYING

The first step in learning to write is copying written models. Since copying is not a very challenging activity, students become careless and make mistakes. Yet accuracy is an important feature in writing, and students should not be permitted to make mistakes that go uncorrected.

The following techniques suggest ways of maintaining students' interest in activities that require copying. After each activity, it is wise to correct the work immediately. Students exchange papers and the correct answers are placed on the overhead. If no overhead is available, the teacher may have the sentences on the chalkboard, covered with a map or chart.

11.2.1 Fill in the blanks

The students fill in the blanks by copying model sentences in their book or on a ditto:

Model: Bonjour, Jeanne. Comment vas-tu?   *Hi, Joan. How are you?*
B __ __ jour, Jea __ __ e.
Co __ __ ent va __-tu?

Model: ¿Cómo está usted?   *How are you?*
¿ __ om __ e __ __ á __ s __ ed?

Model: Was machst du heute?   *What are you doing today?*
W __ __ ma __ __ __ t d __
h __ __ t __ ?

Model: I'm so glad you could come.
I __ s __ gl __ __ __ ou
c __ __ __ d c __ __ e.

11.2.2 Noticing capitals

As the student copies the foreign sentence in each pair, he or she underlines both those letters which are capitalized in the native language and not capitalized in the foreign language, and those letters which are capitalized in the foreign language and not capitalized in the native language.[1]

There are many <u>M</u>exicans who do not speak <u>S</u>panish.
Hay muchos <u>m</u>exicanos que no hablan <u>e</u>spañol.

I shall arrive on <u>M</u>onday, <u>M</u>arch 29th.
J'arriverai le <u>l</u>undi, 29 <u>m</u>ars.

The <u>t</u>eacher sends the <u>l</u>etter and the <u>c</u>ard.
Der <u>L</u>ehrer schickt den <u>B</u>rief und die <u>K</u>arte.

11.2.3 Scrambled sentences

Sentences from the dialog are presented with the words in random order.

la balle joue Marie avec.
inglés no María practicar quiere.
die kenne Frau ich nicht.
that well interesting isn't.

the / ball / plays / Mary / with.
English / doesn't / Mary / to practice / like.
the / know / woman / I / don't.

11.2.4 Putting dialog sentences in correct order

The students rewrite a set of sentences, putting them in the correct order:

Ich gehe in die Stadt.
Darf ich mitkommen?
Wohin gehst du, Ilse?

I'm going downtown.
May I come with you?
Where are you going, Ilse?

11.2.5 Answering questions on the dialog

Stimulus: Qui dit, "Ah, tu fais du français!"?

Who says, "Ah, you're taking French!"?

[1] Thomas W. Jackson, "Developing the Writing Skill in Spanish for Native Speakers of English" (Ph.D. diss., Ohio State University, 1968). Hereafter this dissertation is cited as "Developing the Writing Skill."

Students write:	Marc dit, "Ah, tu fais du français!"	*Mark says, "Ah, you're taking French."*
Stimulus:	¿Quién dice, "No puedo. Tengo que ir a la tienda."?	*Who says, "I can't. I have to go to the store."?*
Students write:	Ana dice, "No puedo. Tengo que ir a la tienda."	*Anna says, "I can't. I have to go to the store."*

11.2.6 Line drawings

The teacher distributes a ditto sheet containing line drawings that match the basic sentences of the lesson. Students match the sentences with the appropriate pictures:

L'appartement est au quatrième étage.	*The apartment is on the fourth floor.*
Sa voiture est à côté de la maison.	*His car is next to the house.*
Si on allait au cinéma ce soir!	*What about going to the movies tonight!*

1.

Write: _____

2.

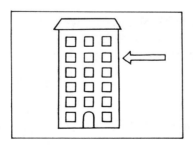

Write: _____

3.

Write: _____

11.2.7 Magazine pictures

Students bring to class magazine pictures corresponding to the basic sentences of the lesson.

(1) Students exchange pictures and write the lines of dialog on separate pieces of paper. Then they pass pictures to other classmates.

(2) The teacher puts pictures in the opaque projector. Students write corresponding lines of dialog.

11.2.8 Copying the question and the correct rejoinder

The students copy the question and follow it with the appropriate reply:

¿Tienes un lápiz azul?	*Do you have a blue pencil?*
a. No, tengo una pluma.	*No, I have a pen.*
b. Sí, una pequeña.	*Yes, a little one.*
c. No, tengo un lápiz blanco.	*No, I have a white pencil.*
Was ißt Rolf?	*What is Rolf eating?*
a. Er ist mein Freund.	*He is my friend.*
b. Er hat Apfelmus.	*He has applesauce.*
c. Er ißt Kuchen.	*He is eating cake.*

11.2.9 Matching questions and answers

The students copy questions and the appropriate replies:

¿Adónde van?	*Where are you going?*
¿Cómo estás?	*How are you?*
¿Cuántos años tienes?	*How old are you?*
¿Cuántos hermanos tienes?	*How many brothers and sisters do you have?*
Tengo quince años.	*I'm 15 years old.*
Tengo cuatro hermanos.	*I have 4 brothers and sisters.*

| Muy bien, gracias. | *Very well, thank you.* |
| A casa. | *Home.* |

11.2.10 Correcting sentences

The students change the sentences to make sense, using items from the column that follows:

Je vais à l'école en avion.	*I go to school by plane.*
Je vais en France à bicyclette.	*I go to France on a bicycle.*
Je vais à l'école le dimanche.	*I go to school on Sunday.*
Je vais à l'église le mardi.	*I go to church on Tuesday.*

en bateau	*by boat*
le dimanche	*on Sunday*
en autobus	*by bus*
à pied	*on foot*
le lundi	*on Monday*

11.2.11 Crossword puzzles

Students fill in crossword puzzles with given words:

Die Monate des Jahres heißen: Januar, Februar, März, April, Mai, Juni, Juli, August, September, Oktober, November, Dezember.
(The months of the year are: January . . . December.)

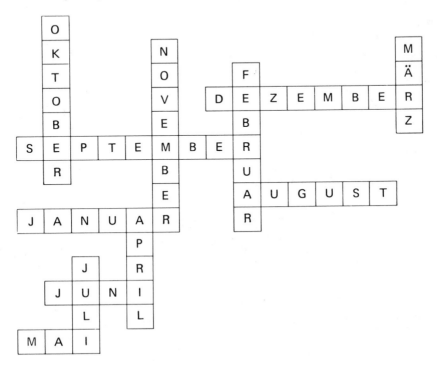

Les chiffres sont: un, deux, trois, quatre, cinq, six, sept, huit, neuf, dix.[2] (*The numbers are: one . . . ten.*)

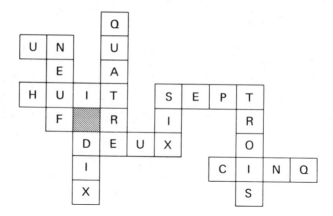

Los días de la semana son: *The days of the week are:*

Horizontal

1. domingo
   (*Sunday*)
4. miércoles
   (*Wednesday*)
5. jueves
   (*Thursday*)
6. viernes
   (*Friday*)

Vertical

2. lunes
   (*Monday*)
3. martes
   (*Tuesday*)
7. sábado
   (*Saturday*)

11.2.12   Sentence builders

The sentence builder is a chart that allows students to select the component parts of the sentence and to create a sentence that may be different from those of their classmates.

[2] Technique developed by Professor Alfred N. Smith, Department of Foreign Languages, Utah State University, for his course on the teaching of French (unpublished papers).

11.2.12a   ONLY CORRECT FORMS POSSIBLE

As students use the sentence builder in this form, they will be able to choose only correct combinations:

Marie Mademoiselle Brault	est	partie	à midi
			hier
Paul Monsieur Duroc		parti	dimanche
Les garçons Paul et Monique	sont	partis	cet été
			à Noël
Monique et Marie Les amies de Paul		parties	vers une heure

(*Marie*
Miss Brault

Paul
Mr. Duroc

The boys
Paul and Monica

Monica and Marie
Paul's girlfriends

left

at noon

yesterday

Sunday

this summer

at Christmas

around one
o'clock)

Qu'est-ce que tu vas prendre comme . . .	Je vais prendre . . .		
viande?	du bifteck du poulet		des côtelettes
légume?			des carottes des tomates
boisson?	du vin	de la bière	
dessert?	du gâteau	de la glace	des fruits

	(What kind of . . . are you going to order?	*I'll have . . .*		
meat	*beefsteak* *chicken*			*chops*
vegetable				*carrots* *tomatoes*
drink	*wine*	*beer*		
dessert	*cake*	*ice cream*	*fruit)*	

11.2.12b STUDENT SELECTS CORRECT FORMS

The student is asked to write ten sentences using the sentence builder. He or she must select the forms that may correctly be used together:

Je Jean Il Elles Paul et moi Georges et Louis	sont sommes est suis	à l'école. au salon. au musée. au café. à l'église.

I John He They Paul and I George and Louis	are is am	at school. in the living room. at the museum. at the cafe. at church.

Yo Juan El Ellos Pablo y Ana Tú María y yo	habl tom estudi compr	é amos ó aste aron	español. leche. francés. álgebra. los boletos. café. inglés. té. un coche.

I	spoke		Spanish.
			milk.
John			French.
He	took		algebra.
They			tickets.
Paul and Ann	studied		coffee.
You			English.
Mary and I	bought		tea.
			a car.

11.3   WRITING FROM DICTATION

In writing from dictation, students are closely guided by the model they hear. At a beginning level, students are already familiar with the sentences they hear dictated; their problem is one of spelling and punctuation.

11.3.1   Spot dictation: individual symbols

Spot dictation allows the teacher to focus on specific points. In the following examples, the teacher is concerned with punctuation marks and accents.

11.3.1a   MIMEOGRAPHED SHEETS

(1) The teacher writes on the board:

¿————————————————?   ¡————————————————!

Students have a mimeographed sheet with sentences, but no punctuation. As teacher reads, students fill in the marks:

__ Cuidado __	(¡ !)	*Careful*
__ Viene un camión __	(¡ !)	*A truck is coming*
__ Vive Juan en Madrid __	(¿ ?)	*Does Juan live in Madrid*
__ La maestra es bonita __	(¿ ?)	*Is the teacher pretty*

A second mimeographed sheet with answers is then distributed to the class.[3]
(2) Students have a mimeographed sheet[4] with two columns of adjectives (masculine and feminine). Students are asked to write sentences using adjectives to describe themselves: *Je suis énergique, mais je ne suis pas assez patient.* (*I am energetic, but not patient enough.*) Then they write sentences that describe their classmates: *Robert est grand.* (*Robert is tall.*), etc. Then they

[3] Jackson, "Developing the Writing Skill," p. 46.
[4] Adapted from Gilbert Jarvis et al., *Connaître et se connaître.* (New York: Holt Rinehart & Winston, 1976), p. 16.

describe the "ideal" person they would like to be: *Je désire être patient* . . . (*I want to be patient* . . .)

intelligente	intelligent	*intelligent*
énergique	énergique	*energetic*
généreuse	généreux	*generous*
réservée	réservé	*reserved*
indépendante	indépendant	*independent*
forte	fort	*strong*
modeste	modeste	*modest*
ambitieuse	ambitieux	*ambitious*
loyale	loyal	*loyal*
dynamique	dynamique	*dynamic*
irrésistible	irrésistible	*irresistible*
grande	grand	*tall*

11.3.1b OVERHEAD PROJECTOR

The teacher projects a list of words on the screen. In each word, one letter is missing. The students write the entire word as they hear it pronounced by the teacher:

Complete with *é* or *e:*

cant__	(canté)
habl__	(hable)
llam__	(llamé)
compr__	(compré)
contest__	(conteste)
escuch__	(escuche)

Complete with *ó* or *o:*

habl__	(habló)
compr__	(compro)
cant__	(canto)
contest__	(contestó)
escuch__	(escuchó)
llam__	(llamo)

The teacher then projects an overlay with the missing letters filled in.

11.3.1c TAPE RECORDING

(1) The teacher writes on the board French *é*. The students have a dittoed sheet with a list of words. They complete each word with *é* as they hear it pronounced:

caf__	C__cile
pr__sent	t__l__vision
côt__	pr__pare

(2) French *è:*

S__vres	compl__tement
l__ve-toi	s__che
m__ne	p__se

(3) French *é* or *è:*

```
H__l__ne        mis__re
t__l__graphe    pr__f__re
Th__r__se       d__sordre
```

(4) English "a":

```
f__t      r__bbit
h__ppy    __fter
__nswer   m__n
```

(5) English "ai":

```
w__t       r__ned
m__d       misl__d
br__ding   __m
```

(6) English "a" or "ai":

```
s__ling    tr__ner
s__ddle    m__nner
cont__n    b__ck
```

11.3.1d   DITTO SHEETS AND BOARD

Students have a dittoed sheet with minimal pairs; the vowel is left out in each word. The teacher writes the vowels on the board, pronounces them, and then asks the class to repeat both the long and the short varieties of these sounds: *u—ü, a—ä, o—ö* for German; *i—ee, o—oa* for English.

As each word is read, the students fill in the missing vowel:

(1) German:

```
m__chte    m__chte
   o          ö
sch__n     sch__n
   ö          o
h__tte     h__tte
   ä          a
L__ge      l__ge
   a          ä
Br__der    Br__der
   u          ü
M__tter    M__tter
   ü          u
```

(2) English:

```
b__t      b__t
  i         ee
f_____l   f__ll
  ee        i
c__t      c_____t
  o         oa
r_____d   r__d
  oa        o
```

11.3.2   Spot dictation: words

11.3.2a   WALL CHART

The teacher prepares the following wall chart.[5] He or she then distributes a sheet with missing words. The students look at the wall chart and fill in the words as the teacher reads the sentences.

(1) Spanish:

cómo	(how?)	como	(as)
cuál	(which?)	cual	(which, as)
cuánto	(how much?)	cuanto	(as much)
cuándo	(when?)	cuando	(when)
dónde	(where?)	donde	(where)
qué	(what?)	que	(that, which)
quién	(who?)	quien	(who, whom)

Parece _____ no hace nada.
_____ llega el tren?
_____ robó el dinero?

(2) English:

to (in the direction of)	too (also)
there (≠ here)	their (belonging to them)
its (belonging to it)	it's (it is)

We are going _____ Boston.
My brothers are taking _____ car.
_____ a brand new Chevrolet.

[5] Jackson, "Developing the Writing Skill", p. 43.

11.3.2b   OVERHEAD TRANSPARENCY

One student writes the dictation on the transparency in front of the class (the projector is off). The remainder of the class write at their seats.

As each sentence is completed, the teacher checks the transparency and turns the projector on. In an exercise on the agreement of past participle with preceding direct object, for example, the following sentences might be dictated:

Voilà les fleurs que j'ai achet<u>ées</u>.   *There are the flowers I bought.*
Voilà la voiture que j'ai vend<u>ue</u>.   *There is the car I sold.*
Voilà les romans que j'ai lu<u>s</u>.   *There are the novels I read.*
Voilà les lettres que j'ai reçu<u>es</u>.   *There are the letters I received.*

11.3.2c   DITTO SHEETS

Paragraph completion dictation: The teacher prepares and distributes a short mimeographed selection in which certain words have been left out. As the teacher dictates, the students fill in the blanks. (In the following examples, the verbs have been left out.)

Claude et Georges ＿＿＿＿＿ à la   *Claude and George are playing ball.*
               jouent   *George throws the ball. The ball*
balle. Georges ＿＿＿＿＿ la balle.   *falls on top of the house. Claude*
            jette   *yells "Boy, are you stupid! You*
La balle ＿＿＿＿＿ sur la maison.   *threw the ball on top of the house!*
       tombe   *Go play with the little kids!"*
Claude ＿＿＿＿＿ "Que tu es
       crie
stupide! Tu ＿＿＿＿＿ la balle sur
        as jeté
la maison! Va ＿＿＿＿＿ avec les
          jouer
enfants!"

Anoche ＿＿＿＿＿ a casa a las once.   *Last night I got home at 11:00. I took*
       llegué   *a cigarette out of my pocket and*
＿＿＿＿＿ un cigarrillo de mi bol-   *began to smoke. Suddenly, my dog*
  Saqué   *made an infernal racket, grabbed*
sillo y ＿＿＿＿＿ a fumar. De re-   *my hat, and ran away.*
      empecé
pente, mi perro ＿＿＿＿＿ un ruido
         hizo
infernal, ＿＿＿＿＿ mi sombrero
      cogió
y ＿＿＿＿＿.
  se huyó

11.3.3   Full dictation

The teacher dictates sentences, which the students write out in their entirety. This exercise is particularly difficult in French, where there are many silent letters, and in ESL, because of the many spelling irregularities of the English language.

11.3.3a   DICTATION WITH BEGINNING STUDENTS

Half the class is at the board, the others are at their seats. The first three steps precede writing:

(1) The teacher reads the short paragraph in its entirety.
(2) He or she begins again and reads only one line.
(3) Then the teacher reads short segments with backward buildup. Students repeat chorally and individually:

Teacher	Students	
al cine	(Repeat)	*to the movies*
a las tiendas o al cine		*to the shops or to the movies*
¿Quiere ir Manuel?		*Does Manuel want to go?*
¿Quiere ir Manuel a las tiendas o al cine?		*Does Manuel want to go to the shops or to the movies?*

(4) Students write the sentence.
(5) The teacher asks the class to look at a sentence on the board that is accurately written. Next, he or she asks students to make corrections.
(6) After all sentences are corrected, the teacher goes on to the next sentence and follows the same procedures.

11.3.3b   DICTATION WITH MORE ADVANCED STUDENTS

The teacher reads through the entire paragraph. Then he or she dictates each sentence slowly, pausing after word groups. The selection is read slowly a second time. Then the teacher reads the paragraph at normal speed as students read over their work. The teacher should *not* heed any requests to read sections over again. This merely leads to repeated requests for rereading and a waste of class time.

At the end of the final reading students exchange papers and put the corrected form of the dictation on the overhead. The teacher may wish to use a mask and show portions of the dictation at a time. Students correct each others' work.

11.4   PRACTICING WORD AND SENTENCE PATTERNS

When students practice word and sentence patterns, they themselves must select and write the appropriate forms. There is no written or spoken model to guide them.

11.4.1   Sentence completion

The teacher distributes a dittoed sheet with words missing. Students fill in the blanks. Then the teacher distributes an answer sheet.

In a program of individualized instruction, the students do the exercise and then get the answer sheet when they are finished. They place their corrected sheets in a folder so that the teacher can check on their progress.

(1) Write the correct form in the blanks that follow:

Qu'est-ce que, Qu'est-ce qui,   *What, Who*
   Qui est-ce que, Qui est-ce qui

1. Marc achète une montre.   *Mark buys a watch.*
   _____ Marc achète?   _____ *does Mark buy?*

2. Marie voit son ami.   *Marie sees her friend.*
   _____ Marie voit?   _____ *does Marie see?*

3. Monsieur Duclos entre le pre-   *Mr. Duclos goes into the office first.*
   mier dans le bureau.
   _____ entre le premier?   _____ *goes first?*

4. Notre école est loin du centre.   *Our school is far from the center of town.*

   _____ est loin du centre?   _____ *is far from the center of town?*

(2) Using the list of interrogatives, complete each telephone conversation with the correct form:

adónde, qué, dónde, por qué,   *where, what, where, why, when*
   cuándo[6]

1. Julio: ¿Está María Elena?   *Is Maria Elena there?*

   Luis: No, no está.   *No, she isn't.*

   Julio: Entonces, ¿_____   *Well, _____ is*
             está?   *she?*

2. Gloria: ¿No vienes porque es   *Are you not coming because it's late?*
           tarde?

   Susana: No, porque es tarde no.   *No, not because it's late.*

   Gloria: Entonces, ¿_____   *Then, _____ aren't you*
           no vienes?   *coming?*

[6] *Writing Modern Spanish*, a student manual for *Modern Spanish*, 2d ed., a project of the Modern Language Association (New York: Harcourt Brace Jovanovich, Inc., 1966), pp. 10–11.

3. Mario: ¿Llega mañana Jose-   *Is Josephine arriving tomorrow?*
           fina?
   Pedro: No, mañana no.   *No, not tomorrow.*
   Mario: Entonces, ¿_____   _____ *is she arriving?*
           llega?

11.4.2 Written pattern drills

Most pattern drills lend themselves to written exercises. The teacher may read
the cues aloud, or the students may work from the written cues.

11.4.2a SPOKEN CUES

The teacher places half the class at the chalkboard. The others work at their
seats:

Teacher's voice	Students write		
Il est beau.	Il est beau.	*He is attractive.*	*He is attractive.*
Elle	Elle est belle.	*She*	*She is attractive.*
Ils (pluriel)	Ils sont beaux.	*They (masc./ plural)*	*They are attractive.*
Elles (pluriel)	Elles sont belles.	*They (fem./ plural)*	*They are attractive.*
Es un mucha- cho guapo.	Es un muchacho guapo.	*He's an attrac- tive boy.*	*He's an attractive boy.*
muchacha	Es una muchacha guapa.	*girl*	*She's an attractive girl.*
muchachos	Son unos mucha- chos guapos.	*boys*	*They're attractive boys.*
muchachas	Son unas mucha- chas guapas.	*girls*	*They're attractive girls.*

All sentences are corrected.

NOTE: Exercises of the type shown may be personalized by referring to members of the class or to popular television stars.

11.4.2b WRITTEN CUES

Half the class is sent to the board. The others remain at their seats to write.
The teacher raises a map under which is a model sentence and a list of cues.
Students write complete sentences:

Modèle: Paul / au cinéma. Paul est   *Paul / to the movies. Paul went to the*
        allé au cinéma.   *movies.*

Maman / en ville	*Mom / downtown*
Monique et Thérèse / au concert	*Monica and Theresa / to the concert*
mes deux frères / au match de football	*My two brothers / to the football game*

11.4.3   Written situation exercises

Written situation exercises allow the students to practice new grammatical patterns and lexical items in meaningful context. The cues may be printed or dictated.

(1) Here is an example in French that focuses on the imperative forms:[7]

| Imaginez que vous avez un(e) camarade de chambre français(e) qui est sur le bord d'une dépression nerveuse. Encouragez-le(la) à garder son sang-froid! | *Imagine that you have a French roommate who is on the verge of a nervous breakdown. Encourage him(her) to keep a level head.* |

Modèles:	Il (Elle) ne se contrôle pas.	*He(She) doesn't control him(her)self.*
	Contrôle-toi!	*Control yourself!*
	Il (Elle) s'énerve.	*He(She) gets excited.*
	Ne t'énerve pas!	*Don't get excited!*

1. Il (Elle) ne se calme pas.   *He(She) doesn't calm down.*
2. Il (Elle) se dispute avec ses amis.   *He(She) argues with his(her) friends.*

(2) The following example permits the students to practice writing new vocabulary and numbers.[8]

Avec mille francs. Imagine that you have 1000 francs to spend on furniture. On the basis of the prices below and on page 302, find ten ways of spending the money.

| 500 F | 100 F | 300 F | 800 F |

[7] Taken from Jean-Paul Valette and Rebecca M. Valette, *Contacts: Langue et culture français— Cahier d'exercices* (Boston: Houghton Mifflin, 1976), p. 63.
[8] Adapted from Jean-Paul Valette and Rebecca M. Valette, *Workbook for French for Mastery, Book Two* (Lexington, Mass.: D.C. Heath, 1975), p. 47.

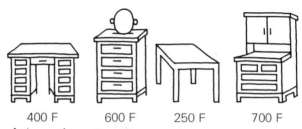

400 F   600 F   250 F   700 F

Je peux acheter dix chaises.
Je peux acheter sept chaises et un fauteuil.

(*I can buy ten chairs.*
I can buy seven chairs and one armchair.)

11.4.4 Use of world map

The teacher points to a country and asks question. Students write the reply:

Teacher:	(Points to France.)	
	Où allons-nous?	*Where are we going?*
Students:	Nous allons en France.	*We're going to France.*
Teacher:	(Points to Canada.)	
	D'où venons-nous?	*Where are we coming from?*
Students:	Nous venons du Canada.	*We're coming from Canada.*

Variation: If students are unsure of the gender of the countries, the teacher can word his or her questions as follows: *Voici la Suisse. Où sommes nous?* (Here is Switzerland. Where are we?)

11.4.5 Flash cards

The teacher prepares flash cards as follows:

front	back	
la France	français	*France / French (masc.)*
la France	française	*France / French (fem.)*
la Belgique	belge	*Belgium / Belgian*
la Belgique	belge	*Belgium / Belgian*

The teacher shows a country with a stick figure. The students write a sentence on the model: *Il est français* (*He is French*). Then the teacher turns the card over and students check their work.

The teacher can also show the nationality side of the card and ask: *Paul est français. Où habite-t-il?* (*Paul is French. Where does he live?*) Students write: *Il habite la France* (*He lives in France.*)

11.4.6 Overhead transparency

The teacher prepares a transparency with sets of paired sentences. The correct response is written on the line below the cues. Using a masking device, the teacher shows the model and the first set of sentences to be rewritten. When students have finished, the teacher slides down the mask to show the correct response. Then the mask is lowered to expose the next row of sentences.

11.4.6a RELATIVE PRONOUNS

Modèle: Voilà le garçon. Il est français.

There's the boy. He's French.

Voilà le garçon qui est français

There's the boy who is French.

1. Voilà l'autobus. Je le prends.
   Voilà l'autobus que je prends.

   There's the bus. I take it.
   There's the bus I take.

2. Voilà le roman. Vous m'en avez parlé.
   Voilà le roman dont vous m'avez parlé.

   There's the novel. You spoke to me about it.
   There's the novel you spoke to me about.

11.4.6b INDIRECT DISCOURSE

Model: Herr Benz sagte: ,,Der Volkswagen ist der billigste Wagen."
Herr Benze sagte, der VW wäre der billigste Wagen.
(*Mr. Benz said, "The Volkswagen is the cheapest car."*)
(*Mr. Benz said the Volkswagen was the cheapest car.*)

1. Meine Mutter sagte: ,,Wir haben keine Zeit."
   Meine Mutter sagte, wir hätten keine Zeit.
   (*My mother said, "We have no time."*)
   (*My mother said we had no time.*)

2. Der Mann sagte: ,,Sie sprechen nur Deutsch."
   Der Mann sagte, sie sprächen nur Deutsch.
   (*The man said, "They speak only German."*)
   (*The man said they spoke only German.*)

3. Seine Freundin sagte: ,,Es geht uns hier sehr gut.“
   Seine Freundin sagte, es ginge uns hier sehr gut.
   (*His friend said, "Things are going well for us here."*)
   (*His friend said things were going well for us here.*)

4. Er sagte: ,,Wir sind fertig.“
   Er sagte, wir wären fertig.
   (*He said, "We are ready."*)
   (*He said we were ready.*)

11.4.7 Magazine cutouts

Students bring to class magazine pictures containing two or more persons or objects that can be easily compared.

The teacher puts several pictures on the board with magnets. Students come forward to write comparative sentences underneath the pictures:

Le monsieur à gauche est plus âgé que le monsieur à droite.	*The man on the left is older than the man on the right.*
La voiture bleue est moins grande que la voiture verte.	*The blue car is smaller than the green car.*
La chica a la izquierda es más bonita que la chica a la derecha.	*The girl on the left is prettier than the girl on the right.*
El coche negro es menos grande que el coche verde.	*The black car is smaller than the green car.*

11.4.8 Native language equivalents

The teacher passes out dittoed sheets with short sentences in the native language. The students write the equivalents in the target language. Then the teacher passes out a second sheet with answers:

I like ice cream.	Me gusta el helado.
I just arrived.	Acabo de llegar.
We've got to have a record player.	Il nous faut un pickup.
I'm thinking of my friend.	Je pense à mon ami.
He doesn't like the car.	Der Wagen gefällt ihm nicht.
Does she feel warm?	Ist ihr warm?

The paired sentences may also be placed on an overhead transparency, as in Section 11.4.6. The teacher may wish to read the native-language sentences and have the students write down the foreign language equivalents.

The sentences should be kept fairly short. Translation of paragraphs and longer selections is an art that requires specialized training.

11.4.9 Using ideograms

Ideograms are simple line drawings used to represent entire sentences. Students may be asked to help develop ideograms for the basic sentences in their text-book. Through participation they become more interested in generating foreign language sentences, and they feel proud of the code they have invented.

Le garçon est très gentil.
Der Junge ist sehr nett.
El chico es muy bueno.
The boy is very nice.

Robert va à la boulangerie.
Robert geht zur Bäckerei.
Roberto va a la panadería.
Robert goes to the bakery.

11.4.10 Game: matching clauses

The teacher writes a sentence on the chalkboard: *Si vous prépariez le dîner, je ne le mangerais pas (If you prepared the dinner, I wouldn't eat it.)* or *Si Ud. cocinara, yo no comería. (If you cooked, I wouldn't eat.)*

He or she then asks each student to take several small scraps of paper. The students on one side of the room write *if* clauses starting with *vous* or *Ud.*; those on the other side write independent clauses starting with *je* or *yo*. Each piece of paper contains only one clause.

The teacher puts the scraps into two hats (one for *if* clauses, the other for independent clauses) and sends several students to the board. Each student takes a scrap from both hats and writes the results on the board. Many hilarious sentences will appear!

NOTE: The same game may be played with relative clauses: *Je déteste les hommes . . . qui travaillent beaucoup (I hate men . . . who work a lot)*; coordinate clauses: *Je reste à la maison . . . parce que je dois travailler (I stay at home . . . because I have to work)*; dependent clauses: *Je vais chez Pierre . . . pour qu'il m'aide avec mes devoirs (I go to Peter's house . . . so that he can help me with my homework)*; infinitive clauses: *On peut toujours réussir . . . sans travailler. (You can always succeed . . . without working.)*

11.4.11 Dehydrated sentences

The teacher hands out ditto sheets containing a series of model sentences. Under each sentence are segments that are to be used in forming other sentences. Students may work in pairs if desired. When they are finished they come to the teacher's desk to pick up a ditto with the correct answers and check their work:

Modelo: Roberto ha buscado el libro.	*Robert looked for the book.*
muchachos / comprar / televisión	*boys / buy / television set.*
Los muchachos han comprado la televisión.	*The boys bought the television set.*

1. Yo me lavé la cara.
   Ella / quitarse / guantes
   I washed my face.
   She / take off / gloves.

2. Ha venido para que yo lo ayude.
   llegar / sin que / tú / la / llamar
   He came so that I could help him.
   arrive / without / you / her / call

Model: Mein Bruder wohnt in Berlin.	*My brother lives in Berlin.*
Dein / Schwester / fahren / Hamburg	*Your / sister / travel / Hamburg*
Deine Schwester fährt nach Hamburg.	*Your sister travels to Hamburg.*

1. Seine Mutter kauft sich einen neuen Mantel.
   Er / sich erkälten / jeder / Winter
   His mother buys herself a new coat.
   He / get a cold / every / winter

2. Sie steht immer früh auf.
   Der Zug / abfahren / um sieben Uhr
   She always gets up early.
   The train / leave / at seven o'clock

3. Ich muss heute abend in die Stadt fahren.
   Ilse / dürfen / gehen / ins Kino
   This evening I have to travel to the city.
   Ilse / may / go / to the movies

11.4.12 Finishing sentences: communicative practice

In exercises of this sort, the students complete sentences so as to express their own ideas. The format is suggested, but the students are free in their choice of vocabulary.

À la recherche de la vie idéale[9] *Seeking the Ideal Life*

Express your own desires and wishes by completing the following sentences:

1. la famille
   family
   Un père idéal est un père qui... *An ideal father is a father who . . .*
   Une mère idéale est une mère qui... *An ideal mother is a mother who . . .*
   (Un frère, une soeur, un enfant, etc.) *(A brother, a sister, a child, etc.)*

[9] Gilbert Jarvis et al., *Connaître et se connaître* (New York: Holt Rinehart Winston, 1976), p. 200–01.

2. les gens   *people*

   Un ami idéal est un ami qui...   *An ideal friend is a friend who . . .*
   Un professeur idéal est un profes-   *An ideal professor is a professor who . . .*
      seur qui...
   (Un president, un juge, etc.)   *(A president, a judge, etc.)*

3. les situations   *situations*

   Une maison idéale est un endroit   *An ideal house is a place where . . .*
      où...
   Une université idéale est un lieu   *An ideal university is a place where . . .*
      où...
   (Une voiture, un climat, un travail,   *(Car, climate, work, etc.)*
      etc.)

11.4.13   Writing checks

Study the sample check. Then follow the instructions and complete the blank
check that is provided.

Vous venez d'acheter une bicyclette   *You just bought a bicycle at Mr. John*
   chez Monsieur Jean Béranger. Vous   *Beranger's. You paid 452 francs.*
   l'avez payée 452 francs.

11.4.14 Filling out forms

Students who plan to visit or reside in the country where the target language is spoken, and this is the case of most ESL students, need to know how to fill out forms. The teacher can try to pick up as many different forms as possible so as to provide variety and a broad range of formats. The teacher of foreign languages in the United States can try to bring back forms from travels abroad. In addition, some textbooks offer practice in filling out forms.[10]

Fiche de voyageur[11]

When you travel in France and stay at a hotel you may need to fill out a form like the one below. It is called a *fiche de voyageur*. You may fill out this card yourself or you might want to work with a classmate so you can assume the roles of the desk clerk and the traveler.

FICHE DE VOYAGEUR ——— CH. N°	Terminus Hôtel **NN R. MOREAU, PROP. Place du C^d-de-la-Motte-Rouge LA ROCHELLE Tél.: 28-77-04 - 28-22-28

NOM: ....
Name in capital letters (écrire en majuscules)

Nom de jeune fille: ....
Maiden name

Prénoms: ....
Christian names

Né le: ....à..............................
Date and place of birth

Département (ou Pays pour l'etranger): ....
Country

Profession: ....
Occupation

Domicile habituel: ....
Permanent address
....

NATIONALITÉ:
Nationality   ....

---

[10] For example, see the workbooks that accompany Jean-Paul Valette and Rebecca M. Valette, *French for Mastery* (Lexington, Mass.: D.C. Heath, 1975).
[11] Taken from Jarvis et al., *Connaître et se connaître*, pp. 26, 27.

The following are questions the desk clerk might ask the traveler when he or she fills out the form.

1. Quel est votre nom de famille? — *What's your last name?*

2. Quel est votre nom de jeune fille? (Seulement si vous parlez à une femme mariée!) — *What's your maiden name? (Only for married women!)*

3. Quels sont vos prénoms? — *What are your first and middle names?*

4. Quelle est la date de votre naissance? — *What's the date of your birth?*

5. De quel pays venez-vous? — *What country are you from?*

6. Quelle est votre profession? — *What is your profession?*

7. Quel est votre domicile habituel (c'est-à-dire, votre adresse permanente)? — *What's your home address (your permanent address)?*

8. Quelle est votre nationalité? — *What is your nationality?*

9. Avez-vous un passeport? — *Do you have a passport?*

11.5 GUIDED COMPOSITION

In a guided composition, the students write a series of connected sentences. The composition may be highly structured, as in the first examples given below. In these cases, most students will be writing exactly the same composition. When less guidance is given, the students are free to introduce an element of originality into what they are writing, but they still use known vocabulary and structures.

11.5.1 Changing a narrative to a dialog

The teacher distributes a dittoed sheet. One group of students writes the dialog on the board, the other at their seats. The teacher circulates to give assistance.

Jacques demande à Nicolas ce qu'il va faire après ses cours. Nicolas répond qu'il ne sait pas et demande à Jacques ce qu'il a l'intention de faire. Jacques dit qu'il doit aller au magasin. Il demande à Nicolas s'il veut l'accompagner. Nicolas répond qu'il est trop fatigué.

Jim asks Nicholas what he's going to do after school. Nicholas says he doesn't know, and asks Jim what he intends to do. Jim says he has to go to the store. He asks Nicholas if he wants to join him. Nicholas says he's too tired.

Ecrivez la conversation entre Jacques et Nicolas:

Write the conversation between Jim and Nicholas:

Jacques: _____
Nicolas: _____

Jacques: _____

Nicolas: _____

11.5.2   Changing a dialog into a narrative

This exercise involves the same procedure as above. The teacher distributes a dittoed sheet; one group of students goes to the board while the rest write at their seats:

Begin each sentence with either *José pregunta si . . .* or *Pedro contesta que.* *. . . (Joe asks if . . . . Peter answers that . . .)*

José: ¿Qué vas a hacer después de la escuela?	*What are you going to do after school?*
Pedro: No sé, ¿y tú?	*I don't know. What about you?*
José: Tengo que ir al centro. ¿Quieres acompañarme?	*I have to go downtown. Do you want to go with me?*
Pedro: No, gracias. Estoy muy cansado.	*No, thanks. I'm very tired.*

11.5.3   Changing the point of view

The student retells a story from another person's point of view:

Le Facteur	*The Postman*
M. Lebrun arrive chez Madame Fournier tous les matins à onze heures et demie. Il a toujours des lettres pour M. Boisseau. Quand il ne voit pas la concierge, il commence à crier. Madame le trouve pénible. Mais elle lui fait toujours une tasse de café.	*Mr. Lebrun arrives at Mrs. Fournier's house every morning at 11:30. He always has letters for Mr. Boisseau. When he doesn't see the caretaker, he begins to yell. Mrs. Fournier finds him annoying. But she always makes him a cup of coffee.*
Vous êtes le facteur. Vous racontez cette histoire:	*You are the postman. Tell the story in your own words.*
J'arrive....	*I arrive . . . .*

11.5.4   Changing the time

Passages may be rewritten to indicate past time, present time, future time:

(1) Change from the present tense to the *passé composé:*

J'invite Jean à venir chez moi. Il apporte ses nouveaux disques. On écoute tous les disques. Après, nous dînons ensemble.	*I invite John to come to my house. He brings his new records. We listen to all the records. Then we have dinner together.*

(2) Change from the past tense to the future:

Gestern bin ich in die Stadt gefahren. Ich habe mir ein Paar Schuhe gekauft. Um zwei Uhr habe ich Erika getroffen. Wir haben ein Eis gegessen. Dann sind wir ins Kino gegangen.	*Yesterday I went downtown. I bought a pair of shoes. At two o'clock I met Erica. We had ice cream. Then we went to the movies.*

11.5.5   Cued dialog

Brief cues are suggested for a dialog. Students write out the complete conversational exchange:

Au restaurant		*At the Restaurant*	
Garçon:	Désirez?	*Waiter:*	*Want?*
Client:	Spécialité?	*Customer:*	*Specialty?*
Garçon:	Biftek.		*Beefsteak.*
Client:	Alors.		*O.K.*
Garçon:	Vin?		*Wine?*
Client:	Rouge.		*Red.*

11.5.6   Cued narration

11.5.6a   DESCRIPTION BASED ON QUESTIONS

(1) Beschreiben Sie Inge! Sie ist Schülerin auf einem Gymnasium. Beantworten Sie folgende Fragen!	*Describe Inge. She is a student in high school. Answer the following questions.*

1. Wie alt ist sie?	*How old is she?*
2. Hat sie braunes Haar oder blondes?	*Does she have brown or blond hair?*
3. Welchen Sport treibt sie gern?	*What sport does she like to play?*
4. Hört sie gern Schallplatten?	*Does she like to listen to records?*

5. Was für Musik gefällt ihr?	*What kind of music does she like?*
6. Welche Fremdsprachen lernt sie?	*What foreign languages is she study-ing?*
7. Möchte sie nach Amerika reisen?	*Would she like to travel to America?*

(2) Tourist brochure (Communicative Practice)

Une promoción turística[12]   *A Vacation Brochure*

Your own hometown or area of residence could be an exotic place for someone from another part of the world. Think about where you live, and prepare a vacation brochure. In promoting your area you might want to consider the following:

1. ¿Qué hay de interés histórico? ¿edificios? ¿museos? ¿otros lugares?	*What is of historical interest? buildings? museums? other sites?*
2. ¿Hay algunos restaurantes que sirven una comida especial de la región?	*Are there restaurants that serve special regional meals?*
3. ¿Qué clase de diversión ofrece?	*What type of entertainment is available?*
a. ¿Hay lugares para deportes acuáticos?	*Are there water sports?*
b. ¿Hay una región de campo espe-cialmente atractiva para hacer camping o para montar a caballo? ¿Hay un parque nacional?	*Is there an area especially attractive for camping or horseback riding? Is there a national park?*
c. ¿Hay discotecas? ¿teatro? ¿cine?	*Are there discotheques? theaters? movies?*
d. ¿Hay lugares para jugar al béisbol (al tenis, etc.)?	*Are there baseball fields (tennis courts, etc.)?*

(3) Game—An Encounter[13]

Several students go to the board (each student needs enough space to write a composition). Each student has a copy of the questions that follow. This is a type of relay race (see Section 6.2.1e). All students invent names and adjectives for the first four guided sentences.

Here is a Spanish example:

Una muchacha fea que se llamaba Ofelia encontró a un hombre tonto que se llamaba Payaso.	*An ugly girl whose name was Ophelia met a stupid man whose name was Clown.*

Then each student moves to the right to take the place of his or her neighbor. The last student on the right moves to take the place of the first person on the left. Then, without looking at what is already above on the board, all invent answers to question 5. Then all move again and invent answers to question 6, etc. The result is usually a series of hilarious compositions.

---

[12] Marty Knorre et al., *Cara a cara*, (New York: Holt, Rinehart, and Winston, 1977), p. 30.
[13] Adapted from an article by Thomas Douglas, *Iowa F. L. Bulletin*, October, 1972.

	Un encuentro	An Encounter
1.	Una muchacha _____	A _____ girl
2.	que se llamaba _____	whose name was _____
3.	encontró a un hombre _____	met a _____ man
4.	que se llamaba _____	whose name was _____
5.	¿Dónde se encontraron?	Where did they meet?
6.	¿Qué hizo la muchacha?	What did the girl do?
7.	¿Qué hizo el hombre?	What did the man do?
8.	¿Qué dijo ella?	What did she say?
9.	¿Qué dijo él?	What did he say?
10.	¿Cuáles son las consecuencias de sus acciones?	What were the consequences of their actions?
11.	¿Qué dijo la gente?	What did people say?

11.5.6b DESCRIPTION BASED ON INSTRUCTIONS

In compositions of this type, the students are given a topic to write about plus specific instructions: vocabulary to use, tenses, types of sentences, etc.

Here are two examples in French,[14] followed by English adaptations:

(1) Les Quatre Saisons

The Four Seasons

Décrivez vos activités pendant chaque saison. Si possible, utilisez le verbe "faire" en huit expressions différentes.

Describe your activities during each season. Use at least eight different verbs.

Modèle: En automne, je vais à l'école. Quand il fait beau le weekend, je fais du football avec des amis.

In the fall, I go to school. On weekends, when the weather is nice, I play football with my friends.

(2) Excuses!

Excuses!

Imaginez que vous avez séché la dernière classe de français avec six camarades. Le professeur demande où chacun de vous était. Inventez sept excuses différentes.

Imagine you cut French class yesterday with six classmates. The teacher asks where each of you were. Invent seven different excuses.

Modèle: Je n'étais pas en classe. J'étais chez le docteur. Mon ami Paul était en ville avec sa mère. Etc.

I wasn't in class. I was at the doctor's. My friend Paul was downtown with his mother. Etc.

11.5.6c RESUME OF AN ORAL PASSAGE

Students listen to a passage on the tape recorder. The passage is played twice. Then the students write a paragraph of not more than eight sentences re-creating the passage.

[14] Taken from Valette and Valette, *French for Mastery, Book Two*, pp. 49, 140.

The teacher may want to give the first sentence and suggest additional words and phrases which might be used:

Hier après-midi Anne et Marc ont décidé d'aller au théâtre.	*Yesterday afternoon Anne and Mark decided to go to the theater.*
avoir l'occasion s'installer	*have the chance get seated*
autobus pièce	*bus play*
faire la queue applaudir	*get in line applaud*

11.5.7 Writing paragraphs

Most students need guidance in writing paragraphs. The following techniques suggest steps by which the teacher can bring the students to an awareness of what constitutes a paragraph.

11.5.7a SCRAMBLED SENTENCES

The teacher selects a well-organized paragraph from a reader or textbook. He or she writes the individual sentences on a transparency and then cuts the transparency into strips, one sentence per strip. (Note: The sentences can also be typed in a large type on a sheet of white paper and then a transparency may be made with a Thermofax machine.)

These strips of acetate are placed on the overhead in random order. The students read the sentences. Some of them might be read aloud. Then the teacher asks the students to identify the opening sentence. This sentence is placed at the top of the overhead, and the remaining sentences moved down. Gradually the students tell the teacher how to reconstitute the paragraph.

11.5.7b SEPARATING PASSAGES INTO PARAGRAPHS

The teacher selects a passage in the foreign language which is divided into a number of clearly organized paragraphs. This passage is typed in run-on fashion onto a ditto master. The teacher then numbers the lines (5, 10, 15, etc.) down the margin to make class discussion easier.

In class dittos are distributed to the students. The students, working as a whole class, in groups, in pairs, or individually, divide the passage into paragraphs. The results are compared and discussed.

11.5.7c WRITING TOPIC SENTENCES TO GIVEN PARAGRAPHS

The teacher selects two or three well organized paragraphs in which the opening sentence is clearly the topic sentence. He or she dittoes the paragraphs, leaving out the opening sentence. In class the students try to write appropriate opening sentences. The best suggestions are written on a transparency and discussed. Finally the teacher writes the author's opening sentence on the transparency.

11.5.7d WRITING TOPIC SENTENCES ON A GIVEN SUBJECT

The teacher suggests a subject, and the students write opening topic sentences. These are discussed. Sentences may be put on the board or on the overhead. The class selects two or three opening sentences (either from the ones suggested or by combining ideas). Students finish the paragraph for homework for the next day.

11.6 WRITING LETTERS

Writing letters can become a very meaningful classroom activity, especially if the letters are sent and answers received (see Section 12.5.2).

11.6.1 Teaching salutations

The teacher uses the opaque projector and letter formats. He or she shows several types of documents: business letters, formal invitations, friendly notes, announcements of weddings, births, baptisms, and funerals.

As each is shown, the teacher points out the different salutations, the layout of the document (position of addresses and salutations, indentations of paragraphs), and the closings.

He or she then shuffles the items and shows them again, covering up the salutations. The students write the salutation, and then check what they have written when the teacher uncovers the original.

11.6.2 A collective letter

Using a letter that one of the students has received from a pen pal, the teacher reads it twice to the class. Then he or she composes an answer on the board with the help of the class. The student who received the letter makes a copy at his or her seat:

Querido Carlos,

    Muchas gracias por tu carta del 22 de noviembre. La descripción de tu vida escolar me fascinó.

    Me pediste describir la mía. Entonces, aquí está:

Dear Charles,

    Many thanks for your letter of November 22. The description of your school life fascinated me.

    You asked me to describe mine. So, here it is:

The teacher gives oral cues:

¿Cuántos alumnos hay en nuestra escuela?	*How many students are in our school?*
¿Qué cursos toma Carlos?	*What courses does Charles take?*
¿Cuáles son los deportes que juegan los alumnos?	*What sports do the students play?*
¿Tenemos un buen equipo de fútbol o no?	*Do we have a good football team or not?*
¿Cuáles son los pasatiempos de los alumnos?	*What hobbies do the students have?*
¿Quiénes son los cantantes favoritos de los alumnos?	*Who are the students' favorite singing stars?*
¿A qué edad terminan los alumnos sus estudios?	*At what age do the students graduate?*
¿Qué porcentaje de los alumnos de nuestra escuela van a la Universidad?	*What percentage of the students in our school go to college?*

11.6.3 Guided individual letters

(1) The teacher distributes mimeographed sheets with blanks to be filled in by students:

1. Ich heiße _____	*My name is _____.*
2. Ich wohne _____	*I live _____.*
3. Ich bin _____ Jahre alt.	*I am _____ years old.*
4. Ich besuche die _____ (Schule) in der _____ (Straße).	*I attend _____ School on _____ Street.*
5. Ich lerne _____	*I study _____.*
6. Mein Lieblingsfach ist _____	*My favorite subject is _____.*
7. Ich spiele gern _____	*I like to play _____.*

(2) Dites à Jean que 1. vous avez été très content de recevoir sa lettre, 2. les jolis timbres vous ont beaucoup plu, 3. vous avez été navré d'apprendre son accident d'automobile, mais 4. vous êtes content qu'il n'ait pas été blessé, 5. l'équipe de football de votre école a gagné son dernier match, 6. il y aura encore un match avant la fin de la saison, 7. le prochain match sera le plus dur, et 8. que vous le décrirez dans la prochaine lettre.

Tell John that 1. you were happy to receive his letter, 2. you enjoyed the pretty stamps, 3. you were very sorry to learn about his automobile accident, but 4. you were glad he wasn't hurt, 5. the football team in your school won the last game, 6. there will be another game before the end of the season, 7. the next game will be the hardest, and 8. that you will describe it in your next letter.

11.6.4   Requesting sample products

The teacher prepares a model business letter: Have students choose a foreign company and write away for descriptive material and perhaps for sample products. Plan this project early in the year to allow for slow international surface mail.

Letters may also be sent to foreign tourist offices requesting material about regions and cities.

11.6.5   "Adopting" a child

The Spanish Club may wish to "adopt" a Spanish-speaking child through an international organization, such as Save the Children Federation. Dues and money-raising projects, together with contributions, can pay the fifteen dollars or so a month that these agencies request. It is possible to request an older child, who will be able to exchange letters with the members of the club. Spanish classes may join in the reading of the letters and the writing of replies.

It is important that the Club make provisions to continue aid over the summer months. A lump sum may be sent in June, and monthly payments resumed in September.

11.7   FREE COMPOSITION

Writing whole selections in a clear, interesting manner with no mistakes in spelling or grammar is a very complex activity. Most high school teachers consider it an unrealistic objective. Nevertheless, some aspects of free composition can be successfully achieved. If, for example, the teacher is willing to sacrifice perfection in a few of the mechanical details of writing, he or she can succeed in getting the students to express their thoughts and opinions.

Nothing is more discouraging to a student than to find his or her paper covered with red marks. Before grading a paper, the teacher needs to restate in his or her own mind the purpose of the exercise. If the goal of the composition was self-expression, the teacher should base the grade primarily on the content and secondarily on the form.

One way to help students get ready for free composition is to diagnose individual problems. Bob is told to concentrate on agreement of adjectives; Mary is asked to check the subjunctive with *croire (to believe)* and *penser (to think)*; Sue is given a review on the position of direct and indirect pronoun objects. Each student's individual problem is recorded and regularly observed. By the end of a given marking period, the specific errors should disappear.

The teacher must do all he or she can to inspire students to write. Topics must be exciting and within their realm of experience.

11.7.1   Creating situations with verbal cues

The teacher provides brief written guidelines for the composition:

(1) Breaking a date: Write what you would say over the telephone to a boy or girl with whom you had to break a date.

Expliquez que vous avez complète-ment oublié la visite de vos parents ce soir-là, que vous ne les avez pas vus depuis long-temps, que vous aviez l'intention de demander de l'argent à votre père, que vous espérez qu'elle vous pardonnerait, et que vous voulez la revoir un autre jour.	*Explain that you had completely for-gotten your parents' visit that eve-ning, that you hadn't seen them for a long time, that you intended asking your father for money, that you hoped (s)he would forgive you, and that you wanted to see (him) her another time.*
Maintenant, inventez vos propres excuses!	*Now, invent your own excuses!*

(2) English cues: Write a description in Spanish of how you and your brothers and sisters spent a rainy Saturday. Put every verb in the imperfect tense: Who was listening to records? writing letters? watching television? playing cards? washing the dog? Finally, the last sentence is in the preterite: some dreadful catastrophe occurred.

(3) Planning an outing: Look at the topic sentence. What words and expressions do you need to describe your proposed activity?

Esta tarde vamos al lago.		*This afternoon we're going to the lake.*	
la merienda	pescar	*lunch*	*to fish*
el traje de baño	los avíos de pesca	*bathing suit*	*fishing equipment*
nadar	el bote	*to swim*	*boat*
la guitarra	el termo	*guitar*	*thermos bottle*
la cámara		*camera*	

11.7.2   Creating situations with props

The teacher shows a toy pistol, a handkerchief, and a whistle. Students write a composition in which these objects play a role.

11.7.3   Creating situations with visual cues

11.7.3a   SANS PAROLES   *Without words*

The teacher distributes mimeographed sheets with a comic strip format. Students supply the narrative:

C'est un incident dans la vie de Paul (P), Sylvie (S), et Marc (M).

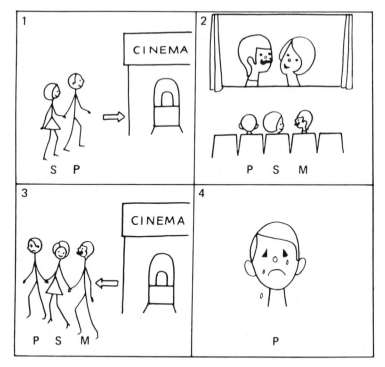

(This is an incident in the lives of Paul (P), Sylvia (S), and Mark (M).)

11.7.3b COMIC STRIP CUTOUTS

Cut out a comic strip and put it on a transparency. Blacken or remove the dialog. Students fill in the conversation on their papers.

11.7.3c BABY PHOTOS

Students exchange baby pictures and write imaginary comments to express the baby's attitudes. These are fastened with paper clips to the pictures and put in the opaque projector:

Yawning:	¡Qué aburrida está la fiesta!	*How boring this party is!*
Astonished:	¡No, hija! ¡No me digas! ¡Qué barbaridad!	*No, child! Don't say that to me! How awful!*
Crying:	¡Nunca me dejas salir con mi novia!	*You never let me go out with my girl friend!*

11.7.4 Writing a collective story

The teacher writes the beginning of the story on the board. Then, through guided questioning, he or she gets the students to dictate all but the ending.

For homework each student completes the story. The next day all share their versions of how it ended.

Ausflug ohne Badeanzug

Morgen ist Sonntag. Einige Schüler machen einen Ausflug nach dem schönen Starnberger See.

1. Was möchten sie dort machen?
2. Wer möchte mit?
3. Was soll jeder mitnehmen?
4. Wie kommen sie dorthin?
5. Wie lange dauert die Fahrt?
6. Um wieviel Uhr fahren sie ab?
7. Wo traffen sie sich?
8. Was vergißt einer?
9. Wann erfährt er es?
10. Was sagt er?
11. Was möchte er jetzt tun?
12. Was muß er nun machen?

An Excursion Without a Bathing Suit

Tomorrow is Sunday. Some students are going on an excursion to beautiful Starnberg Lake.

What would they like to do there?
Who would like to go with them?
What should each one take?
How will they get there?
How long will the trip take?
At what time will they leave?
Where will they meet?
What will one of them forget?
When will he discover it?
What will he say?
What will he want to do?
What must he do now?

11.7.5 What then? Extending a story

Students read a story and extend it beyond the author's ending.

LA PARURE
Guy de Maupassant

Madame Loisel a raconté à Madame Forestier la vie horrible qu'elle menait depuis la perte de la parure.

Madame Forestier lui a dit, "Oh! ma pauvre Mathilde! Mais la mienne était fausse. Elle valait au plus cinq cent francs."

Et puis...[15]

THE NECKLACE
Guy de Maupassant

Mrs. Loisel told Mrs. Forestier about the horrible life she led since the necklace was lost.

Mrs. Forestier said to her, "Oh, my poor Mathilde! But mine was false. It was forth five hundred francs at most."

And then . . .

[15] Camille Bauer, et al., *Lire Parler et Ecrire* (New York: Holt, Rinehart and Winston, 1964), pp. 153–57.

11.7.6 Writing a story from another character's point of view

Students read a story about a crime. The storyteller thinks he or she knows who did it and how it happened. However, there are other points of view. Students are asked to tell the story from the point of view of the accused.

La verdad es un misterio[16]	Truth Is a Mystery
Apareció en el periódico un reportaje de un accidente de avión que hubo en Guatemala hacía unos meses; era un avión pequeño en que murieron tres américanos, dos hombres y una mujer.	*There appeared in the newspaper a report of an airplane accident which had taken place in Guatemala several months previously. It was about a small plane in which three Americans died, two men and one woman.*
Del agua sacaron los restos del avión y los cuerpos destrozados de la mujer y uno de los hombres, pero el cuerpo del dueño del avión despareció.	*They took out of the water the remains of the airplane and the mutilated bodies of the woman and one of the men, but the body of the owner of the plane had disappeared.*
Según los informes ese hombre estaba vivo; fué visto en un balcón del Hotel Victoria.	*According to reports the man was alive; he was seen on a balcony of the Hotel Victoria.*
Se sabe que era un hombre muy rico pero que estaba lleno de deudas. Como tenía seguros de vida que alcanzaban a un total de más de dos millones de dólares, una compañía de seguros mandó un detective a Guatemala para buscar a ese hombre.	*It was known that the man was very rich but was deeply in debt. Since he carried life insurance that reached a total of more than two million dollars, an insurance company sent a detective to Guatemala to look for this man.*
Usted es el fugitivo. Cuente Ud. lo que ha pasado.	*You are the fugitive. Tell what happened.*

11.7.7 Writing poetry—cinquains

Students at all levels will be surprised at how easy and enjoyable it is to write short five-line poems of the cinquain variety. The teacher and the class might wish to write one or two collectively in the native language to learn the technique. Then the teacher shows the class a few in the target language. By then, the students could work together in pairs or small groups to compose their own.

1. State a subject in one word (usually a noun).
2. Describe the subject in two words (often a noun and adjective or two adjectives).
3. Describe an action about the subject in three words (often three verbs).

---

[16] Frederick Richard, "La Verdad es un Misterio," in *Spanish—Reading for Meaning* (New York: Harcourt Brace Jovanovich, Inc., 1966), pp. 109–14.

4. Express an emotion about the subject in four words.
5. Restate the subject in another single word, reflecting what you have already said (usually a noun).

Here are some examples:

ESL:

Zoo

Caged animals

Peering at me

Asking to be free

Prison

Lion

Angry beast

Killing, eating, living

They hunt you unthinkingly

King

French:

Zoo

Singes amusants

Faisant les acrobates

Une vie bien drôle

Cirque

Zoo

Funny monkeys

Acting like acrobats

A life of fun

Circus

Spanish:

Lluvia

Agua cayendo

Saltando, bailando, duchando

¡Qué alegre pareces tú!

Diversión

Rain

Falling water

Jumping, dancing, showering

How happy you seem!

Fun

part four
Beyond
Language

outline

twelve
Teaching
Culture

The word *culture* is often defined in two different ways. In one sense it is the sum total of a people's achievements and contributions to civilization: art, music, literature, architecture, technology, scientific discoveries, and philosophy. This is sometimes referred to as "culture with a big *C*." The second meaning includes the behavioral patterns or life styles of the people: when and what they eat, how they make a living, the way they organize their society, the attitudes they express toward friends and members of their families, how they act in different situations, which expressions they use to show approval and disapproval, the traditions they must observe, and so on. In the 1960s the attention of language teachers was focused on the second definition, usually called an anthropological approach or "culture with a small *c*."

Now language teachers are growing increasingly aware of the fact that a people's culture is a complex and dynamic phenomenon. Not only does every country possess a myriad of subcultures, but the international expansion of technology and communications is contributing to rapid transformations in daily life patterns. In other words, there is not *one* American culture, but many versions of American culture, ranging from rural to suburban to urban, from Black to Chicano to WASP, from blue-collar to white-collar, from teen to elderly, and so on. Village life in France in the 1970s has changed considerably from the village life of the 1950s, which was still quite similar to that of the nineteenth century. The business world of Latin America is adopting the "hora americana."

Coupled with the realization that the cultural stereotypes of the past are usually grossly simplified, if not downright inaccurate, is the rediscovery of the interrelationships between "big *C*" and "small *c*" culture. Underlying both is a set of commonly-shared values or cultural themes.[1] It soon becomes evident from looking at the school curriculum, the popular magazines and comic

[1] In his emergent model, Howard Nostrand posits twelve themes for French Culture. See Section 12.6.7.

325

books, TV programs, and transcribed interviews and conversations that the French are proud of their history, proud of their literature, proud of their language. In this sense, then, the American student must develop an awareness of French history and French literature in order to understand contemporary French attitudes.

A study of German culture reveals a people preoccupied with economic growth and stability. A knowledge of German geography is necessary if the American student wishes to understand the Germans' concern over a divided country. An awareness of German music and opera is also necessary if the American student is to understand why the people of Dresden, a city bombed out during the Second World War, rebuilt the opera house and revitalized the opera company, which played nightly to full houses, while rubble still lay in the streets and a single streetcar line provided the only transportation.

In learning about the culture of the United States, the ESL student will find that many Americans live in the present, look to the future, and seem poorly informed about the past. Yet this concern for the *here* and *now* has definite historical roots: immigrants came to America in "the pursuit of happiness," with the goal of building a good life for themselves and a better life for their children. An individual's accomplishments, rather than family background, determine his or her identity.

It is obvious that this chapter can only touch on a very few aspects of culture instruction. Indeed, the breadth of the subject calls for an entire handbook. It is hoped that the techniques and suggestions in this chapter will lead teachers to explore the many facets of the topic.

12.1 GENERAL CONSIDERATIONS

The cultural goals of the language class may be divided into four major categories: increasing student awareness of the target culture; stimulating student interest in foreign language study; developing the ability to function in the target culture; and establishing an understanding of linguistic cultural referents, cultural values, and attitudes. Each of these categories will be treated in subsequent sections of this chapter.[2]

Some teachers wonder whether the teaching of culture should be postponed until the students can study it in the foreign language. The disadvantage of waiting until the third year before introducing culture is that only about ten percent of those students who begin a foreign language ever reach that level. Culture can be taught in English from the very beginning, and it can be an integral part of all instruction rather than an added frill.

[2] Teachers of Spanish may wish to see H. Ned Seelye, ed., *Perspectives for Teachers of Latin American Culture* (Springfield, Illinois: Department of Public Instruction, 1970). All foreign-language teachers may wish to see the Foreign Culture Series, edited by Frederick I. Jenks, University Publications, Advancement Press of America, Inc., P.O. Box 07300, Detroit, Mich. 48207.

One of the concepts that students should develop in their study of a second culture is that people in various cultures respond to life's needs in a variety of different ways. The so-called American way is not the only way, nor is it the best way. It is simply the way that works best for most Americans. Other ways work best for other peoples.

Perhaps the greatest risk in teaching culture is the tendency on the part of the teacher and the students to generalize from too little data. It is essential, therefore, to discuss the way people live in big cities as well as in small country villages, the reactions of young people and those of their elders, the points of view of different ethnic groups, the attitudes of people in different socio-economic strata and in different regions.

12.2   AWARENESS OF THE TARGET CULTURE

The first step in the teaching of culture is increasing the students' awareness of the breadth and the nature of that culture. Slowly this initial awareness will translate itself into a feeling of familiarity, with the result that the culture will no longer appear "strange" and "foreign."

The development of cultural awareness consists primarily in the introduction and continued reintroduction of cultural facts of all kinds: geographical information, sociological data, historical personalities and events, contributions in the arts and the sciences, and so forth. This cultural material is not simply presented in list form for memorization. Nor is its use limited to a few cultural slide presentations the day before a vacation. It must be continually entered and reentered so that it becomes part of the students' general fund of knowledge.

Much of the presentation of culture is teacher-initiated. The teacher plans lesson activities that include cultural information and exercises built around classroom realia. Student-oriented activities, however, should not be forgotten: frequently students learn more from projects that they themselves have developed. For instance, in an intermediate Spanish class one of the Black students prepared a report, with recorded excerpts, on the African influence in Latin American music and presented it with such enthusiasm and authority that the entire class benefited greatly.

12.2.1   Evidence of foreign cultures in the United States

There are many evidences of the influence of various foreign cultures in this country. History books tell of Spanish, French, and Italian explorers, early French and Spanish settlements, Dutch and German immigrants. The history of the United States is frequently intertwined with the history of Europe, of Africa, of Asia, of Latin America. Bicentennial groups in the various cities, states and regions of the United States have published brochures stressing their multi-ethnic heritage.

At the present time our country imports a variety of ideas and goods from all parts of the world. Frankfurters and sauerkraut, spaghetti, pizza, French fries, crêpes, chili beans, tacos—all have become American foods. American movie houses show foreign films; museums hang works by foreign artists; concert halls and radio stations play music by foreign composers and orchestras; department stores sell imported goods; supermarkets carry imported foods, and so on. Signs of foreign culture are everywhere.

The role of the language teacher is to open the students' eyes to the impact foreign culture has had on American culture and to make them aware of the diversity that exists around them.

The ESL teacher can similarly stress the cultural diversity of the United States. Students from other countries can more easily identify with Americans when they realize that their own ancestors contributed to the founding and growth of the country whose language they are studying.

12.2.1a   THE AMERICAN HERITAGE

Indications of the diverse origins of the people who settled this country may be easily discovered.

(1)   Wall map

Using a large wall map of the United States, the teacher points to a few cities with foreign names and shows how to determine their origin.

Spanish: Names starting with San or Santa (Saint): many were religious missions founded in the seventeenth century, such as San José, Santa Clara.

Names starting with definite articles: Los Angeles, Las Vegas.

French: Names representing natural phenomena: Eau Claire, Fond du Lac, Presque-Isle. French names of cities: Detroit, Des Moines. Names ending in -ier, and -mont: Beaumont, Montpelier.

German: Names ending in -heim, -burg, -fort: Anaheim, Harrisburg, Frankfort.

The teacher can have the students bring a gas station map into class and make a list of all the French, Spanish, or German place names they can find.

(2)   Twin maps: game

The teacher puts up a wall map of the United States and a wall map of France or Germany. The class is divided into two teams. Team A sends a member to the map of the United States. Team B sends a member to the map of a European country. The teacher names a city to be found in both countries, such as Frankfort or Montpelier (minor spelling variations are to be ignored). The student who finds the city first makes a point for his team. The players go to the end of the line, and the next two players go to the opposite map: Team A sends a player to the European map and Team B sends a player to the United States map. The game continues until everyone has had a turn at the map.

Variation: If a player finds the city on his or her map, a point is scored. If the player then finds the same city on the other map before his or her opponent does, a second point is scored.

(3)   Drawing a map

Using a large piece of cardboard, students draw the outline of the United States, including the state boundaries, and hang it on the wall. (The quickest way to make such a map is to use the opaque projector to project the map from an atlas or other source on the blank posterboard, and to have students copy the outlines.) Students color the sections where people from the foreign countries under study have settled.

(4)   Reports

Students give reports on historical events or historical figures that link the United States to the country whose language they are studying: Ponce de León, Général de Rochambeau, Pennsylvania Dutch settlers. These reports might be correlated with units in a world history or an American history course.

12.2.1b   IMPORTS AND EXPORTS

(1)   Visit to the department store

Students take a trip to a department store and make a list of all the imported items with their prices.
Germany: cameras, Hummel figurines, Steiff toys from Nuremberg.
Spain and Mexico: mantillas, sarapes, sombreros, Maja soap, cutlery from Toledo.
France: perfume, silk scarves and ties, lace gloves, fine leather goods, and china from Limoges.
Students who own some of these articles can make a showcase display.

(2)   Visit to the supermarket

Students take a trip to a supermarket or a gourmet shop and make a list of the imported foods: Spanish olives, chorizo, and wines; French cheeses, wines, vinegar, bread, and Dijon mustard; German sausage, mustard, wines. ESL students would identify those products which are typically American: grits, corn on the cob, clam chowder.

(3)   Automobile manuals

The teacher can let interested students read manuals for European cars and encourage them to take a trip to the local dealers to examine the cars.

(4)   Advertisements in foreign journals

Students cut out advertisements from foreign magazines, promoting either American or native products. They then make a bulletin board display with

American products abroad at the top and foreign products popular in the United States at the bottom.

12.2.1c   THE PRESENCE OF ETHNIC CULTURES IN THE UNITED STATES

Foreign language teachers are becoming increasingly aware of the fact that the United States is not a monolingual country. Many of the languages taught in our classrooms are spoken not only abroad but right here in our cities and communities.[3]

(1)   Places to go

In many parts of the United States, foreign language teachers and classes do not have far to go to discover the language in use. The following suggestions are made for classes in the New York City area:[4]

Your neighborhood for foreign language signs—stores for foreign wares.
The United Nations—a consulate—a cultural center—a church.
A foreign festival or holiday celebration.
The World Trade Center.
The Port . . . for kinds of transport.
A foreign language radio, TV station, newspaper, movie, street theater, museum.
A foreign language school for adults.
An international soccer game.

(2)   Reading material

There are many foreign language newspapers, magazines, and other publications edited and produced in the United States. These periodicals treat topics of interest to Americans in the foreign language. Students can compare similar features in the foreign language publication and its American equivalent: for instance, TV schedules, movie announcements, weather reports, ads, comic pages.

In areas where there are large concentrations of groups speaking another language, one can obtain brochures of various sorts: how to get a driver's license, emergency procedures at the hospital, child care pamphlets, notices from the utility companies. These publications can be used to develop language skills, yet their very presence in the classroom heightens the students' awareness of other linguistic groups in this country.

In ESL classes, the same printed materials can be used in conjunction with

[3] Consult, for instance, Pierre Capretz, " 'The French around us' project", *AATF National Bulletin* 1, no. 3 (April 1976) pp. 10–12.
[4] Gladys Lipton, project coordinator, *New York: Multi-Speak City!* (Publication sponsored by the Economic Development Council of New York City and the New York City Board of Education; available from Open Doors, 20 West 40th Street, New York, N.Y. 10018), p. 127.

the equivalent English materials to teach the new language. At the same time, the ESL students will realize that many community services make information available in more than one language.

(3) Student notebooks

Students can be encouraged to keep notebooks (perhaps for extra credit) in which they note examples of the foreign language, or in the case of ESL students their native language, which they encounter from day to day. If desired, the actual samples of language use may form the basis of a bulletin board exhibit. The material will probably include gum wrappers with bilingual jokes, foreign words used in newspaper articles or advertisements, TV commercials or programs in which the foreign language appears, American expressions of foreign origin, etc.

12.2.2 Introduction to the foreign culture

Whereas most ESL students in the United States have at least some rudimentary ideas about this country, many American students beginning the study of a second language know very little about the countries where the language is spoken. An initial goal of instruction is to increase their awareness of the foreign culture, its breadth, and its depth.

12.2.2a CONSTRUCTION PROJECTS

Construction projects are most frequently introduced in FLES and junior high classes. The several suggestions that follow may be a point of departure for other construction ideas.

(1) Casa española

The teacher places shoe boxes in a square or rectangle to represent the walls and rooms of a house. He or she staples them together and pastes construction paper around the sides. Doors and windows can be cut in the walls facing the patio, or the sides of the boxes can be removed and furniture placed in each room.

The vocabulary for the rooms is taught as well as some information about the Roman origin of this architecture.

(2) The Brandenburg Gate

Using a photo as a model, the teacher can build a wooden gate in the school shop and paint and decorate it according to the picture. It could be large (4' × 7'), affixed to a piece of plywood, and nailed to the back of the German classroom.[5]

---

[5] Runhild E. Wessell, *Die Unterrichtspraxis* (1968), No. 1, pp. 57–60.

(3) Physical map of France

Students can make a map of France out of flour, salt, and water. This is an excellent way to learn the names and locations of the mountain ranges *les Alpes, les Pyrénées, le Massif Central, le Jura,* and *les Vosges.*

12.2.2b CLASSROOM DECORATIONS

Classroom decorations afford an unobtrusive way of initiating students to the foreign culture. The teacher should try to use all the available space for posters and displays and change the decoration every few weeks. Students will notice a change in their classroom environment. During those moments when the students' minds wander, their eyes will encounter street scenes of Berlin and castles on the Rhine. They will unconsciously be developing mental images of the country they are studying about.

(1) The classroom clock

Have an inventive student figure out a way to put the numbers 13 to 24 around the outside of the classroom clock. Even the clockwatchers in the class will be learning something about the twenty-four-hour clock as they wait for the period to end. The clock will be useful in teaching official time. A German radio announcer will say: *Sechzehn Uhr zehn (16:10).* A Mexican railroad employee will say: *El tren sale a las trece y media. (The train leaves at 13:30).* A French ticket agent will say: *Le spectacle commence à vingt heures. (The show begins at 20:00).*

(2) The class calendar

On the class calendar, mark the foreign holidays, birthdays of important historical figures, and important historical events. The class calendar may provide the opportunity for introducing some cultural material briefly at the beginning of a period otherwise devoted primarily to language-learning activities.

(3) Posters

Posters may often be obtained from travel agents and airline offices. Often the consulates of the smaller countries are more willing than those of large countries to provide posters. For posters in French, the teacher can try Belgium, Switzerland, or Quebec. For posters in Spanish, he or she can try some of the South American countries. The German Government is usually very generous in providing classroom materials.

If the teacher goes abroad, he or she can buy posters there. The teacher can also ask friends who go abroad to bring back posters. Students might have posters they would be willing to put up in the classroom during a three- or four-week period.

(4) Proverbs

The proverbs can be lettered by students taking art. Posters can then be made of them and hung around the foreign language classroom. If desired, they may be grouped thematically.[6]

(1) To show the French emphasis on individualism:

Chacun pour soi, Dieu pour tous.	*God helps those who help themselves.*
Chacun mouche son nez.	*Each one for himself.*
Chacun prêche pour son saint.	*Let everyone go to his own church.*
Charité bien ordonnée commence par soi-même.	*Charity begins at home.*

(2) To show the French feeling of *méfiance:*

La méfiance est la mère de la sûreté.	*Mistrust is the mother of safety.*
Quand le renard se met à prêcher, fais attention à ta poule.	*When the fox begins to preach, look out for your chicken.*
Chat échaudé craint l'eau froide.	*Once burned twice shy.*
Le temps est tantôt une mère, tantôt une marâtre.	*Time is sometimes a mother, and sometimes a stepmother.*
Bon nageur, bon noyeur.	*A good swimmer can also drown someone else.*

(5) The class timeline

Get two colors of ribbon and fasten a double time line around the classroom walls. Measure the length of the lines and divide by twenty-five. This gives you the length of each century, if you begin at 500 B.C. In a French class you might begin the first line with the Greeks at Nice and add subsequent important events like Caesar's conquest of Gaul, and so on. The second line is the United States time line. There is little activity there until around 1200 A.D. and the Pueblo civilizations, such as those at Mesa Verde. Different groups of students can be assigned different sections of the time line. If the classroom is used by several classes, each class might be given a section to decorate.

(6) The class bulletin board

Different groups of students may be assigned the preparation of a bulletin board display which is changed weekly. Students should be encouraged to develop their interests: stamps, coins, art, sports, racing, and so on. Especially good displays might be put in hall display cases.

[6] See Genelle Grant Morain, *French Culture: The Folklore Facet*, ERIC Focus Report No. 9 (1969). Available from ACTFL Materials Center, 2 Park Avenue, New York, N.Y. 10016.

12.2.2c INCORPORATING CULTURE IN LANGUAGE LEARNING ACTIVITIES

In presenting new vocabulary and new structures to the class, the teacher can often incorporate aspects of the target culture. It is possible, and even advisable, to use the same cultural material (such as a map or a set of pictures) several times throughout the course. In this way, the students increase their familiarity with facets of the target culture.

(1) Magazine pictures

To teach about foods in France, the teacher cuts out and mounts pictures from French magazines. These may be contrasted with pictures from American magazines. For example, the American breakfast of orange juice, fried eggs, bacon, toast, and coffee can be visually contrasted with the French breakfast of *café au lait* and bread or *croissants*. At the same time, these visuals can be used to introduce the students to the new vocabulary items.

(2) Magazine ads and titles

Attractive magazine ads can be cut out and mounted on heavy paper. These ads are then sorted as to the types of structures used in the wording: adjectives and adjective agreement; imperative forms; interrogative forms; negation; passive constructions. A recent issue of a Spanish magazine provided the following expressions using *para (for)*:

Protección para sus cabellos	*Protection for your hair*
Para una cocina modelo...	*For a model kitchen . . .*
La más completa guía para el mantenimiento de su autómovil	*The most complete guide for the maintenance of your automobile*

The titles of articles can also provide examples of specific structures. For example, titles in the form of questions illustrate the word order and punctuation in attractive type and in the format used in magazines of the target culture.

(3) Class schedule cards

Pen pals may be asked to send a copy of their schedule of courses. The teacher can place the card on an opaque projector or duplicate it on a ditto master. Students can compare, in the foreign language, a foreign student's schedule with their own.

(4) Maps

The teacher can use place names on the map to practice specific structures. This use of the map allows students to engage in meaningful language practice while developing a greater familiarity with the geography of the foreign country.[7]

---

[7] See Eberhard Reichmann, "The Map for Pattern Practice," in *German Quarterly* 38 (May 1965), pp. 345–50.

Students sit in a semicircle in front of a large map of Germany. As the teacher asks questions, he or she hands the pointer to individual students. They in turn come forward, answer the question, and point to the places they name:

Teacher: Wir sind jetzt alle in   *We are all now in Munich. We want*
             München. Wir wollen   *to take a trip. Where would you*
             eine Reise machen.   *like to travel, Mr. Smith?*
             Wohin würden Sie
             gerne reisen, Herr
             Smith.

Herr Smith: Ich würde gerne nach   *I would like to travel to Salzburg.*
             Salzburg reisen.

Other questions might be: What cities would you go through if you traveled from Bonn to Berlin? What rivers would you cross? What mountains would you see?

(5) Ditto handouts

Individual students, or pairs of students, are assigned as travel agents for a specific region or country where the foreign language is spoken. They prepare brief presentations accompanied by dittoed handouts, describing their area, its main features, attractions, and annual events. They try to convince their classmates to visit the area.

At the end of the presentations the teacher distributes a ballot listing the regions. Each student marks the three he or she wants to visit. The best travel agents are those who attracted the most tourists.

(6) Sending for products or materials

At the beginning of a school year an intermediate or advanced class might be given a lesson on business letters. As part of their written assignment, each student prepares a letter that he or she sends abroad. The letters may be sent either to a foreign company, asking for brochures and perhaps a sample product, or to various chambers of commerce, asking for illustrated descriptive material. (In France write to the *Syndicat d'Initiative* of the town. In Germany write to the *Fremdenverkehrsbüro.*)

Later in the year, when students begin getting responses, the material received may be used for reading and speaking activity as well as for cultural enrichment.

(7) Games

Classroom games, designed to encourage students to speak the target language, can be built around cultural information. The "What's my line?" format can be adapted to historical characters: one student impersonates Napoleon or Pasteur, for example, and the others ask questions to determine his line of work and his identity. Quiz games like "Jeopardy" can use questions and answers about cultural material.

12.3 USING CULTURE TO STIMULATE STUDENT INTEREST

Frequently culture is introduced into language classes to stimulate and maintain student interest in foreign languages. On an informal level, the language teacher may integrate some classroom activities with what the students are studying in other courses. This informal interdisciplinary approach may even open the way for a formal interdisciplinary course; however even if this is not the case, the approach may attract students whose primary interests lie in other areas.

12.3.1 The arts

In the area of the arts, the link between the ESL or foreign language class and the contributions of the target culture is evident.

12.3.1a MUSIC

(1) School orchestra: If some students are in the school orchestra, the teacher can ask to see the pieces they are working on. Perhaps they are playing something by a composer from the foreign country under study; if so, he or she asks for some volunteers to prepare a bulletin board display on the composer and his times.

(2) Choir: A similar project might be assigned if the choir is singing a song in the foreign language or a song composed by a composer from the country under study.

(3) Current records: Teachers who go abroad in the summer can buy some of the current hits. (Or, they can ask someone who is going abroad to buy them for them.) They can then play the records to the students and ask them to compare the songs to current American favorites. ESL students will enjoy studying lyrics to favorite American hits.

(4) Transcription of lyrics: In more advanced classes, the teacher might make available records of folk songs, traditional songs, and hit tunes. During time given to independent work, students would be encouraged to find a favorite song and try to transcribe the lyrics for the rest of the class. This project might be done in pairs or in groups of three or four. (If the classroom has only a tape recorder and no record player, the records can be duplicated on tape.)

(5) Opera: In more advanced classes, the study of a short story such as *Carmen* or *Cavalleria Rusticana* may be heightened by taking the class to a performance of the opera based on that work. If such a field trip is out of the question, the teacher could bring to class records of selected portions of the opera.

12.3.1b PAINTING

The local museum might have paintings by artists who are natives of the country under study or who resided there. To prepare students for a trip to the museum, the teacher should go there first and decide which paintings the class will see. He or she should also talk to a guide; museums often offer guided tours, lectures, and the like, free of charge. The art teacher might be willing to give a lecture with slides. The teacher could also ask the librarian for a list of books about the lives of the artists and display the book jackets on the bulletin board.

12.3.1c SCULPTURE

Sculpture becomes more meaningful to the students if they themselves try to create copies of works illustrated in art books or encyclopedias. In a unit on pre-Columbian art, junior high students could try to reproduce smaller artifacts to scale.[8] Terra cotta figures can be formed in potter's clay. Figures in gold and jade can be copied in soap sculpture, using Palmolive Gold and Green respectively.

12.3.1d DANCE

If one or more students in the French class have studied or are studying ballet, the teacher can ask them to prepare a wall chart with the French terms. Perhaps a student will be willing to demonstrate some of the steps.

In many communities, ESL students are encouraged to develop pride in the dances of their countries of origin. Haitian students who have learned native dances as part of their ESL program might be invited to perform for the French classes, and perhaps teach some of the steps. Mexican-American dance groups, similarly, could show some Mexican dances to the Spanish classes. Conversely, a school square dance group might teach steps to the ESL students.

12.3.2 Folksongs and folkdances

Folksongs and folkdances capture the spirit of a people. As the students learn the traditional lyrics and tunes, as they dance the traditional steps, they are participating in the cultural heritage of the people they are studying.

12.3.2a FOLKSONGS

(1) Many folksongs have grown around common experiences. The teacher can ask students to try to discover what types of activity might have given rise to a particular folksong. For example, if the class has sung *"Alouette,"* the teacher might ask: What is the action of the song? (The person is plucking a lark.) Why are birds plucked? (To be eaten.) What kinds of birds are eaten in the United States? The teacher would then explain that the French appreciate game and

[8] Technique suggested by Georgia Kilpatrick, Fairfield Woods Junior High School, Fairfield, Connecticut, in a presentation at the 1976 meeting of the Connecticut Council of Language Teachers (East Hartford, October 29, 1976).

that many more game birds are eaten in France than in the United States. Even though larks are no longer hunted, the French do hunt quail, partridge, pheasant, and duck.

(2) The German folksong *"Muss i' denn"* might be used to illustrate the Germans' love for the outdoors and for hiking.

(3) The ESL teacher can select American folksongs that reflect the history of the United States. "Home on the Range" presents an optimistic view of the attraction of the West and the open spaces. Working songs like "The Erie Canal," portray certain periods in the development of the country.

12.3.2b FOLKDANCES

The teacher who enjoys music and dancing might want to teach a folkdance to language students.[9] The dance might be performed for the Foreign Language Club, a school assembly, or a P.T.A. meeting.

The American square dance is of French origin. Students are often surprised to discover that *do-see-do* is really *dos-à-dos*, *al-a-mand left* is *à la main gauche*, and *promenade* is the French *promenade*.

12.3.3 Cooking

Students read cookbooks: *La Cuisine est un Jeu d'Enfants, Eating European,* and *The French Chef Cookbook.*

For language club activities they prepare: *coq au vin, une omelette aux fines herbes, une bûche de Noël,* or a continental breakfast; or *arroz con pollo, tacos, enchiladas,* Mexican wedding cookies, or hot chocolate with cinnamon sticks; or sauerbraten with potato pancakes and red cabbage. This is a good money-making activity!

ESL students, especially adult learners, might be interested in learning to read American recipes, including a presentation of the ingredients, the measurements, and the cooking instructions.

12.3.4 Celebrating foreign holidays

The teacher may wish to celebrate foreign holidays in the classroom. Some holidays may give rise to activities that involve other departments or groups in the school.

---

[9] The following sources contain many suggestions for dances and music:
Alford, Violet, *Dances of France III The Pyrenees* (New York: Crown Publishers, 1952).
Allen, Edward D., "Some Contributions of Foreign Folklore to the Secondary School Curriculum." (Unpublished Ph.D. thesis. The Ohio State University, 1954).
Duggan, Anne S., *Folk Dances of the U.S. and Mexico* (New York: A. S. Barnes, 1948).
Goldsmith's Music Shop, Inc., Language Department, 301 East Shore Road, Great Neck, N.Y. 11023.
Lawson, Joan, *European Folk Dance* (London: Pitman Publishers, 1970). (Contains dances of Spain and costume designing in Brittany.)
Lorraine Music Co., Inc., 23–80 48th Street, Long Island City, New York, N.Y. 11103.

12.3.4a PARTIES

Fasching, Mardi Gras, and *Carnaval* give students the opportunity to wear masks in spring.

Breaking the *piñata* may be an interesting project for a Spanish Club. To make a piñata: Blow up a balloon and cover it with papier-mâché. When the papier-mâché hardens, pierce the balloon and pull it out. Then decorate the shell with crepe paper, ribbons, or funny faces of people and animals. Fill it with hard candy and seal up the opening. Hang it at about eye-level. As individual students come forward, they are blindfolded and given a club. Each tries to hit the piñata and break it. If possible, put the piñata on a pulley or over a beam so that it can be moved while each person swings at it. As it breaks all dive for the candies that fall to the floor.

12.3.4b GIFTS AND CARDS

At certain times of the year it is customary to give gifts or send cards. The foreign language class might wish to take advantage of such holidays by preparing simple gifts or cards for members of the school staff: the principal and secretaries, the guidance counselors, the custodial staff, etc. The language club might select a foreign holiday to celebrate at the local hospital or old age home.

12.3.5 Pen pals

Foreign pen pals can increase student interest in language study. Individual students may have their own pen pals, or the entire class may decide to exchange letters with a class in the target country.

12.3.5a LOCATING PEN PALS

Addresses of agencies that arrange these exchanges are in the professional journals: *French Review, Hispania,* and others.

Write to post offices in foreign cities and ask for names of secondary schools. Then write to the English teachers in those schools asking them if their students would like to exchange letters with yours.

12.3.5b COMMUNICATING

Students can exchange letters, photos, tape recordings, movies, and so on. In the classroom letters can be put in an opaque projector and enjoyed by the entire class.

12.3.5c MEETING THEM LATER

When students travel abroad they can visit their pen pals—an added motivation for keeping up their correspondence.

12.4   LEARNING TO GET ALONG IN THE TARGET CULTURE

Many students study a foreign language with the intention of visiting or even residing in the country where that language is spoken. Others study ethnic languages of the United States with the idea that they might be working with minority groups in the capacity of nurses, doctors, law enforcement officers, social workers, or teachers. ESL students in the United States want to learn not only the language but the prevailing social conventions.

In order to function in the target culture, the students must be aware of outward differences in way of life patterns: greetings, telling time, eating habits, and ways of getting around.

12.4.1   Role playing

The teacher can create situations in the classroom that provide opportunities for the students to play roles. Of course, such activities are by nature highly artificial, but they can provide extra language practice and be a great deal of fun. Care must be taken to have students realize that culture is more than skin deep, and that in playing the part of a Spaniard or a Russian they are only providing a caricature of a citizen of the target culture.

Careful preparation for such activities is indispensable. The teacher must determine whether the class knows enough vocabulary, sentence structure, and dialog lines to be able to perform the assigned roles.

In the early stages of language development it is wise for the teacher to work with the class as a whole when creating dialogs for various situations. Individual members of the class dictate possible lines of dialog and the teacher writes them on the board, making corrections when necessary or casting the utterances into a more colloquial style.

Even after the class achieves a fair degree of fluency, the teacher needs to provide an orientation session in which he or she supplies essential linguistic information on verb forms, nouns, idiomatic expressions, and pronunciation.

In addition to stressing role playing, the techniques below include the use of gestures and kinesics. There is a progression from elementary to intermediate to advanced language class activities.

12.4.1a   GREETINGS

The teacher draws a series of large buildings on the board and labels them *Le Centre de la Ville* (*The Center of the City.*) She then motions for a student to approach her and says (in French or English): *I am Madame Bertrand. You are Marie Dumont. Your mother is a close friend of mine. We meet by chance downtown.* Teacher and student act out dialog as tape is played.

Mme Bertrand:	(Shakes hands with Marie.)	
	Bonjour, Marie.	*Hello, Marie.*
Marie:	Bonjour, Madame.	*Hello, Mrs. Bertrand.*
Mme Bertrand:	Comment vas-tu?	*How are you?*
Marie:	Très bien, merci. Et vous?	*Very well, thank you. And you?*
Mme Bertrand:	Très bien, merci. Comment va ta mère?	*Very well, thank you. How is your mother?*
Marie:	Bien, merci.	*Fine, thank you.*
Mme Bertrand:	Au revoir, Marie.	*Good-bye, Marie.*
Marie:	Au revoir, Madame.	*Good-bye, Mrs. Bertrand.*

The teacher then says: *Jeannette and Sylvie are good friends. They meet downtown and greet each other.* The students act out the second tape segment.

Jeannette:	Bonjour, Sylvie. (Shakes hands with Sylvie.)	*Hi, Sylvia.*
Sylvie:	Bonjour, Jeannette. Ça va?	*Hi, Jeannette. How's it going?*
Jeannette:	Bien, merci. Et toi? Ça va bien?	*Fine, thanks. And you? Are things O.K.?*
Sylvie:	Pas mal.	*Not bad.*
Jeannette:	Au revoir, Sylvie.	*See you, Sylvia.*
Sylvie:	Au revoir, Jeannette.	*See you, Jeannette.*

Successive dialogs include two teenage boys, two men, a man and a woman, and so on.

GENERALIZATION

Teacher: When two French people meet, what do they usually do?
Student: Shake hands.
Teacher: Do American teenagers generally shake hands when they meet?
Student: No.
Teacher: When do American men shake hands?
Student 1: When they are introduced.
Student 2: When they haven't seen each other for a long time.
Teacher: Do American women generally shake hands?

Student: No.

Teacher: What do you think a French person's reaction would be if you met him in the street and didn't shake his hand?

Student: He would wonder if he had done something to offend you.

Teacher: Yes. Now, look at the printed copies of typical conversations. Are *bonjour* and *au revoir* ever used alone?

Student: No.

Teacher: What are they always used with?

Student: The first name of a person, Monsieur, Mademoiselle, or Madame.

Teacher: Yes. And what is the difference between addressing an adult and one of your buddies?

Student: For adults, *vous;* for friends your own age, *tu.*

12.4.1b   INITIAL DATING CUSTOM (*EL PASEO*)

The teacher explains that girls and boys begin dating at a later age in Spanish-speaking countries than in the United States. Most schools are not mixed; there are separate boys' schools and girls' schools in most towns and cities. So, one of the best ways to see one another is on the evening or Sunday afternoon walk around the town square. The girls walk in one direction and the boys in the other; they often stare at one another and sometimes flirt. People of all ages participate and walk for hours. There are always spectators in cafés or on sidewalk benches.

The teacher "transforms" the classroom into a "plaza" and draws some buildings on the chalkboards to indicate sides of the square. Then he or she chooses a few students to serve as spectators (these are seated on the sides of the plaza). Spanish or Latin-American music played on a record player would help create atmosphere.

The boys in groups of two or more walk in one direction while groups of girls pass them in the opposite direction. All comments must be in Spanish, for example, *¡Qué guapa es!, ¡Qué ojos estupendos! ¡Qué pelo más lindo! (Boy, is she pretty! What gorgeous eyes! What beautiful hair!)* The girls, of course, pretend not to notice.

12.4.1c   TABLE MANNERS

Bring paper plates, silverware, and several pieces of bread to class. Pretend the slices of bread are pieces of meat and show the class how Europeans and Latin Americans eat it. Keep the fork in your left hand at all times and cut the meat with your right hand. Your left hand is always kept on the table. Call on various students to do the same.

In French class, bring a *porte-couteau* (knife-rest) and a *rond de serviette* (napkin-ring).

Students might also be asked, as a supplementary activity, to observe table manners in foreign movies.

12.4.1d BUYING A TRAIN TICKET

Students can learn a dialog about purchasing tickets:

AM SCHALTER IM HAUPTBAHNHOF
(At the Ticket Window at Central Station)

Herr Müller:	Zwei Karten nach Hamburg, bitte.	*Two tickets to Hamburg, please.*
Beamter:	Einfache oder Rück-fahrkarten?	*One-way or return tickets?*
Herr Müller:	Einfache, erster Klasse.	*One-way, first class.*
Beamter:	Das macht sechzig Mark neunzig.	*That will be DM 60, 90.*
Herr Müller:	Wann geht der nächste Fernschnellzug?	*When does the next long-distance express train leave?*
Beamter:	Um zwanzig Uhr zehn auf Gleis acht.	*At 20:10 on track eight.*

Variation: On a trip abroad the teacher can pick up sample train and bus schedules at train stations or tourist information centers. (A friend traveling abroad could get these also.) The actual schedules can be photostatted and transformed into ditto masters or placed on an opaque projector. Students can then play roles asking when trains leave, when they arrive, and so on. A third student can point out the cities on a wall map.

12.4.1e GESTURES AND BODY MOVEMENTS

Two people conversing in France and Spanish-speaking countries stand much closer to each other than do Americans. When students act out dialogs in front of the class, their behavior is much more authentic if they get closer to each other and imitate the gestures their teacher has taught them.

The most natural gestures are those the teacher has acquired in the foreign country. Some of the more picturesque gestures, such as those indicating eating and drinking, have a distinctly lower-class connotation.[10]

The teacher should also try to see foreign films as frequently as possible. In observing the gestures used in the films and in correlating these with the social class of the speakers, the teacher will develop a greater sensitivity of the kinesics of the foreign people.

[10] Two references on gestures are Gerard J. Brault, "Kinesics in the Classroom" in *French Review*, Vol. 36 (February 1963), and Jerald Green, *A Gesture Inventory for the Teaching of Spanish* (Philadelphia: Chilton, 1968).

Some common general gestures are listed below:

(1) Refusal or reprimand (French and Spanish): Wag the index finger of your right hand vigorously to the left and right: *Non, non! Pas de ça!* (*No, no! Not that!*)

(2) Forecasting trouble or embarrassment (French and Spanish): Jiggle vigorously your right hand in front of your chest as though you were burned by a hot iron, suck in air rapidly or make a whistling sound: *Oh, là là! Qu'est-ce que je vais prendre!* or *¡Diós mío! ¿Qué va a ser de mí?* (*Oh, boy! Will I get it!*)

12.4.1f ORDERING FOODS IN A RESTAURANT

Cut out magazine pictures of foods and paste them on individual cards. If possible, use foreign periodicals such as *Paris-Match, Parents, Arts-Ménagers, Hoy, Mañana,* and others.

After teaching the vocabulary words, the teacher asks individual students what food they would like. As each student responds, the teacher gives him or her the picture card representing that item:

Teacher:	Qu'est-ce que vous prendrez, Monsieur?	*What will you have, sir?*
Jean:	Je voudrais de la salade.	*I would like salad.*
Paul:	Je voudrais des pommes de terre.	*I would like potatoes.*
Teacher:	(Shows picture card of beverages.)	
	Et comme boisson?	*And for your beverage?*
Sylvie:	Je voudrais du lait.	*I would like milk.*
Pierre:	Je voudrais du vin.	*I would like wine.*
Antoine:	Je voudrais un Coca-Cola.	*I would like Coca-Cola.*
Thérèse:	Un café, s'il vous plaît.	*Coffee, please.*
Teacher:	(Shows picture of desserts.)	
Marc:	Je voudrais une glace.	*I would like ice cream.*
André:	Je voudrais une tarte.	*I would like a tart.*
Valérie:	Je voudrais un gâteau.	*I would like cake.*
Dominique:	Je voudrais du fromage.	*I would like cheese.*

The cards are all collected, and individual students take the teacher's place.

When everyone knows how to order the foods, the teacher creates a restaurant scene in front of the room. Two or three students become customers while the teacher takes the role of the waiter. Later, the students become waiters too.

Variation: Instead of pictures, the teacher may wish to use foreign menus. Many of the airlines and ship lines are cooperative in sending old menus to teachers who request them. Small conversation groups may work with the actual menus. For whole-class work, the teacher can Xerox the menu and make a photostatic ditto master or can put the menu on the opaque projector.

With ESL classes, the teacher can bring in menus of local restaurants, or photographs of menus at the local fast food places. Students can learn vocabulary as well as expressions used in ordering a meal.

12.4.1g GOING SHOPPING

The teacher makes artificial *peso* notes (*1, 5, 10, 50 pesos*) and cardboard *centavo* coins (5, 10, 25, 50) and gives each student these items. On the chalkboard he or she writes the sign *Comestibles (Groceries.)*

On a table in front of the room, the teacher places empty crackerboxes and tin cans on which are pasted imported labels (or home-made labels). He or she teaches solid and liquid measure: *un kilo = mil gramos, medio kilo = quinientos gramos (1 kilo = 1000 grams, ½ kilo = 500 grams.)* The teacher then explains that a *kilo* is a little more than two pounds. *Un litro* is slightly over a quart. The teacher can present a dialog such as the following:

El Dependiente:	Buenos días, señorita.	The Shop-Keeper:	Good morning, miss.
Alicia:	Buenos días, señor.	Alice:	Good morning, sir.
El Dependiente:	¿En qué puedo servirle?		What can I do for you?
Alicia:	¿Me da un kilo de azúcar, por favor?		Please give me a kilo of sugar.
El Dependiente:	Aquí está, señorita. (Hands it to her.)		Here you are, miss.
Alicia:	¿Cuánto vale?		How much is it?
El Dependiente:	Veinte pesos con diez centavos.		20 pesos and 10 centavos.
Alicia:	Aquí los tiene Ud.		Here you are.
El Dependiente:	Muchas gracias.		Thanks a lot.
Alicia:	No hay de qué.		You're welcome.

| El Dependiente: | Adiós, señorita. | *Good-bye, miss.* |
| Alicia: | Adiós, señor. | *Good-bye, sir.* |

One by one, the students come forward and buy one or two items, paying with their artificial money. (The price is always payable with one or more of the coins or bills that each student holds.)

12.4.1h   AT A CAFÉ

Films like *Quelle Chance*[11] can be excellent preparation for role playing. The film should first be shown in its entirety. Then the dialog is taught and distributed to the class.

The students learn the items sold in a café and how to ask for them:

Garçon, une glace au chocolat, s'il vous plaît.	*Waiter, chocolate ice cream, please.*
Garçon, je voudrais un vin blanc.	*Waiter, I would like white wine.*
Garçon, un paquet de Gauloises, s'il vous plaît.	*Waiter, a package of Gauloises, please.*
Garçon, l'addition, s'il vous plaît.	*Waiter, the check, please.*

Then the teacher creates a café scene in front of the class. Students take various roles.

This film shows people at their different tables in a French café. Each group orders something different. Humorous incidents follow.

12.4.1i   TRAVELING ABROAD

Slides or film strips can be used to recreate a situation likely to be encountered by a tourist abroad: going through customs, getting a taxi, checking into a hotel, renting a car, etc.[12] Students are presented with the necessary vocabulary and structures and are then asked to create variations on the basic situation. In advanced classes, students can be given instructions: for instance, one student wants to rent a simple hotel room without bath and the other student is the hotel receptionist who wants to put her into a large suite. Each student does not know the intentions of the other.

12.4.2   Understanding conventions

In order to function in the target culture, the students must understand unfamiliar conventions. Topics of this sort can be integrated into the language lessons.

[11] Chicago International Film Bureau, No. 1757, 1953.
[12] Slides of this sort may be taken by the teacher when in the target country. Kits on such topics are available commercially from EMC, 180 East Sixth Street, Saint Paul, Minn. 55101.

12.4.2a   USING THE METRIC SYSTEM

Students can be helped to learn the metric system if they see wall charts contrasting a ruler in inches with a ruler in centimeters, a map with distances in miles and kilometers, a thermometer with the numbers in Fahrenheit on one side and Celsius on the other, and a chart showing the differences between kilograms and pounds.

Communicative practice and games can be organized as the metric system is learned. Students might ask one another personal questions such as: *Combien pesez-vous? ¿Cuánto pesa Ud.?* (*How much do you weigh?*) and *Combien mesurez-vous? ¿Cuánto mide Ud.?* (*What is your height?*). The answer, of course, must be in the metric system.

Mathematics problems can be used when the students are asked to measure objects and parts of the classroom as well as areas in the school yard. A homework assignment could deal with measuring the students' rooms in square meters. Converting Fahrenheit to Celsius could also be the source of other learning activities in the language.[13]

12.4.2b   READING TIMETABLES

The teacher can collect timetables from travel agents, from personal trips in the target country, and from acquaintances who have been abroad. ESL teachers can get timetables from local airlines and bus terminals. In learning to read timetables, the students not only practice numbers and times, but they strengthen their awareness of the geographical layout of the target country.

12.4.3   Travel abroad

Some foreign language teachers take their students abroad during the summer. The following section offers some suggestions for making the trip more profitable, from a cultural point of view. (The same suggestions can also be adapted for ESL classes in the United States.)

12.4.3a   PREPARING THE STUDENTS

During the semester preceding the trip, the students can begin preparing for their experience abroad.

The students meet at least once a week with a person who knows the region. Discussion includes daily life patterns of the people—what pleases them and what offends them: *formules de politesse, fórmulas de cortesía* (*proper etiquette*). The students subscribe to a weekly regional newspaper or to magazines. They read in English or in the foreign language about the region: its geography, history, imports, exports, and folklore.

[13] Additional learning activities are suggested in Gilbert A. Jarvis, et al., *Connaître et se connaître* (New York: Holt, Rinehart and Winston, 1976), pp. 150–57.

Each student chooses a topic of personal interest. This will become his or her research project abroad. The teacher suggests themes: school life, recreation, family ties, industries, fashion, T.V. and radio programs, agriculture, and so on.

12.4.3b ACTIVITIES ABROAD

Once the group is in the foreign country, some time can be devoted to exploring outward signs of the pattern of daily life. Teams may be assigned to carry out the following projects:

(1) Visit a park for a few hours and keep a record of what takes place, who comes, how long they stay, what they wear, and so on. Take photos and record conversations, if possible. (Be sure to obtain permission.)

(2) Keep track of events at an intersection or at another part of the city.

(3) Take a local bus to the end of the line and observe the passengers: their dress, manners, and so on. Visit a city or suburb at the end of the line and take another bus back. Report on your findings.

(4) Select a shopping area in a neighborhood and make a list of the types of stores in the area.

(5) Go to a store and make a notebook of prices of items: stationery supplies, clothes, food, and so on. Compare these with prices in your community in the United States.

(6) Go to a self-service restaurant and copy the menu along with the prices. Take a flash photo of it.

(7) Take a trip to the country on a bus or train. Keep a record of the types of farming equipment and the various crops you see from the window.

NOTE: Individual students going abroad with other tours may be given a summer project and asked to report on it when they return in the fall.

12.4.3c UTILIZING THESE EXPERIENCES AFTERWARD

Students can relate their experiences to their classmates in the following ways:

(1) Make a bulletin board or showcase display of menus, ticket stubs, programs, parts of costumes, figurines, and so on.

(2) Play in the classroom or language club the tape recordings made abroad.

(3) Give a report with slides or photos of the study-tour. Find several students who have been abroad and give an entire assembly program.

12.4.4 Field trips (ESL)

The teacher prepares the students for trips to local museums, schools, factories, department stores, the Post Office, markets, restaurants, etc., by teaching them the vocabulary and sentence structures they are likely to encounter.

12.4.4a GETTING READY TO DINE IN A RESTAURANT

The teacher pays a visit to the manager of the restaurant and explains the purpose of the trip. If the restaurant is a well-known chain, there will probably be a standard menu with pictures on it. Request one or more of these menus from the manager and duplicate enough copies for your class.

Cut out pictures of foods from magazines and post them on individual cards. Drill the class thoroughly on the names of the foods and how to order them: *I would like tomato juice, veal cutlet, mashed potatoes*, etc.

Arrange the furniture in your classroom to look as much like a restaurant as possible. You may wish to bring two or three card tables to class. Then distribute the menus and take the orders. Explain that the waiter or waitress will first ask whether they want a drink and that the drink is an alcoholic beverage.

Give each student a check and explain how the tip is computed and that service is not included.

Show them how to ask for something that is not on the table, or how to point out an error to the waiter or waitress.

When the group feels confident, take them to the restaurant and have a real meal.

12.4.5   Filling out forms (ESL)

The teacher copies on overhead transparencies the following forms:

   a. Applications for drivers licenses, credit buying, and citizenship
   b. Checks
   c. Hotel registration forms

Then he or she fills them out, using the overhead projector. Dittoed copies are distributed and the class practices completing the forms.

12.5   UNDERSTANDING THE TARGET CULTURE: BEGINNING AND INTERMEDIATE CLASSES

While students are often quick to notice the existence of differences between American and foreign cultures, it is usually the teacher who must help the students see the reasons behind these differences. This section suggests ways of guiding students in an analysis of another culture.

It should be noted that the emphasis in this section lies in the techniques described and not in the specific content of each example. Cultures are changing rapidly, and specific cultural facts may quickly become outdated. The techniques themselves, however, may be adapted to present an accurate picture of the target culture at a specific time.

12.5.1 The "Socratic" method

Photos, films, radio and T.V. programs, and selected readings can be used for discussion. Through carefully planned questioning, the teacher leads the student to an understanding of the values held by the people of a foreign culture.

12.5.1a   CLASSROOM FILMS

(1) Family ties: In the film *Emilio en España*,[14] Emilio meets his cousin, Paco, in a hotel lobby. The men embrace.

Teacher: What do you think of this custom?
Student: Weird.
Teacher: Do you think the Spaniards consider it weird?
Student: I suppose not.
Teacher: Does this scene tell you anything about the way Spaniards feel toward their relatives? What would Spaniards think of the way American fathers and sons greet each other?

(2) Gauging economic status: In one film of *Parlons Français*,[15] a middle-class family lives in an eighteenth-century house.

Student: They must be poor! Such an old house!
Teacher: Does anyone know when the White House was built in Washington?
Student: About the beginning of the nineteenth century.
Teacher: Then it is old, isn't it?
Students: Yes.
Teacher: Does it look poor to you?
Students: No.
Teacher: The house that this family lives in was built in the eighteenth century. The French are proud of their history; they want to preserve their monuments and buildings from the past. Are there places in the United States that are being preserved or restored? What about Williamsburg? Georgetown? Greenfield Village? In general, do Americans tear down old houses or try to preserve them?

(3) Transportation: In Episode 13 of the film series *Toute la Bande*,[16] the Ermont family take a train from Paris to the South of France, approximately 425 miles.

Student: Why are they taking the train? I thought the family looked rich?
Teacher: What do you think of the train? How does it look?

[14] John Oller and Angel González, Chicago Encyclopedia Britannica Films, 1965.
[15] Heath de Rochemont Corp., Boston, 1961.
[16] Englewood Cliffs, N.J.: Scholastic Magazines, Inc. 1970.

Student: It's terrific. It looks new. But why don't they take a plane?

Teacher: The French railway system is excellent. It is government controlled and has about 23,000 miles of track. The trains are fast and usually depart on time. Passengers purchase tickets for either first or second class accommodations. First class cars contain comfortable upholstered seats and attractive furnishings. Most trains have dining and sleeping facilities. Many wealthy French people choose to travel by train.

12.5.1b COMMERCIAL FILMS

Foreign movies make the foreign culture accessible to students who have never traveled abroad. If you live in a big city, read the film section of the newspaper to see which movies are being shown. See the movie first before recommending it to your students. If you live in a smaller town, ask the local theaters for advance listings of the films and shorts they plan to run. Local colleges and universities often show several foreign films every year.

If the foreign film is shown in the original version with subtitles, the students will have an opportunity to hear the language spoken. But even if a dubbed version is shown, the foreign film usually is valuable in presenting a view of the foreign culture.

Before sending the students to the film, tell them to look for certain cultural signs: status symbols, behavior at table, attitude toward children, relations between young people and adults. At the next class period, allow for a short discussion of what the students noticed.

12.5.1c READINGS IN THE NATIVE LANGUAGE

Impressions of the United States, by Sophie S. Hollander,[17] is a collection of letters from native speaking Spanish students during their year in the United States.

(1) In "Pilar Attends School with the Teen-agers," Pilar is shocked that fourteen-year-old girls date. In her hometown, Córdoba, Spain, girls do not start dating before the age of eighteen.

(2) In "Margot from Colombia Takes a Job," Margot tries to emulate her classmates by getting a part-time job. She quits after the first day because she suddenly realizes that girls of her social class in Colombia do not do manual labor.

The teacher can ask the girls in the class: *Would you have taken the job? Kept it? Why not?*

---

[17] Sophie S. Hollander, *Impressions of the United States* (New York: Holt, Rinehart and Winston, 1964).

12.5.1d   TESTBOOK READINGS IN THE FOREIGN LANGUAGE

Often a textbook lesson presents a narrative or dialog that reveals much information about the value system of a particular country.[18]

(1) Georges and François are upset about arriving late for lunch at their home. Their father expects to have all his family around him when he comes home for lunch.

François: Tes excuses n'arrangent rien. Nous serons en retard pour déjeuner. Et tu connais Papa, le plus juste et le plus sévère des pères. On se met à table à midi. Tant pis pour les retardataires.

Francis: Your excuses aren't going to make things any better. We'll be late for lunch. And you know Dad, the most just and the strictest father there is. This family sits down for lunch at noon. Too bad for the latecomers.

Georges: Eh bien, la famille aura commencé à déjeuner. Papa dira, "Pas de hors d'oeuvres pour les retardataires." La belle affaire!

George: Well, the family will already be eating. Dad will say, "No hors-d'oeuvres for latecomers." What a bore!

Following the reading of this passage, the teacher leads a discussion on differences between the role of the father in France and in the United States, the importance of dining, and the custom of returning home for lunch.

(2) "Toda una Señora" from *Por Esas Españas*[19] is a vignette about an elderly widow living in genteel poverty. She does not travel because she cannot afford first-class accommodations. A rich American couple invites her on a trip. She accepts and is in her glory; she now feels she is where she belongs.

El día de su salida. . . . Doña Cipriana apareció a la puerta. Estaba vestida de negro, con guantes de seda negra, un hermoso abanico . . . y un sombrero parecido a los que llevaba la reina Victoria de Inglaterra. Pasó por entre aquella gente con toda la dignidad de una reina, saludando a derecha e izquierda. . . .

On the day of her departure . . . Doña Cipriana appeared at the door. She was dressed in black with black silk gloves, a beautiful fan . . . and a hat that looked like those worn by Queen Victoria of England. She walked past the assembled people with all the dignity of a queen, giving greetings right and left.

---

[18] Langellier, Alice and Sylvia N. Levy, *Chez les Français* (New York: Holt, Rinehart and Winston, 1969), pp. 76–77.

[19] Pedro Villa Fernández, "Toda una Señora," in *Por Esas Españas* (New York: Holt, Rinehart and Winston, 1965), p. 87.

12.5.1e   NATIVE INFORMANTS

Whenever possible, it is a good idea to invite native informants to meet with the class. Foreign students in an American high school may be asked to talk about their impressions of the United States. Puerto Rican, Cuban-American and Mexican-American students may be invited to meet with Spanish classes. Similarly, Anglo students may participate as resource persons in ESL classes. If the informant can speak both the students' native language and the target language, additional flexibility in presentation is provided.

12.5.2   Culture capsules[20]

Culture capsules are short essays that discuss one characteristic difference between the foreign culture and American culture. At Level One the culture capsule will probably be written in English. At Level Two it may be written in simple sentences in the foreign language.

The culture capsule may be accompanied with photographs or magazine pictures. A prop, such as a metro ticket, a doll in bullfighter dress, or a pair of *Lederhosen,* may also be utilized in the presentation of the culture capsule.

12.5.2a   PRESENTING HOLIDAY CUSTOMS

(1) Noël en France et aux Etats-Unis:
Nous sommes en France. C'est le vingt-quatre décembre. Dans le salon il y a une crèche et des santons. Les santons sont de petites figurines qui représentent Marie, Joseph, Jésus, les bergers, une vache et un mouton.

Christmas in France and in the U.S.A.:
We are in France. It is the 24th of December. In the living room there is a crèche and figurines. These figurines represent Mary, Joseph, Jesus, the shepherds, a cow, and a sheep.

Les enfants français mettent leurs souliers devant la cheminée. Pendant la nuit le Père Noël arrive et met des cadeaux dans chaque soulier.

French children put their shoes in front of the fireplace. During the night, Father Christmas arrives and puts gifts in each shoe.

Dans les maisons américaines il y a un grand arbre de Noël. Les enfants américains mettent leurs bas devant la cheminée. Pendant la nuit Santa Claus descend par la cheminée et met des cadeaux dans chaque bas.

In American homes, there is a large Christmas tree. American children put their stockings in front of the fireplace. During the night, Santa Claus goes down the chimney and puts gifts in every stocking.

[20] Culture capsules are now available commercially. For example, see Jane Bourque, *French Culture Capsules* (New York: Gessler Publishing, 1976); J. Dale Miller and Russell H. Bishop, *New World Culture Series: USA-Mexico* (Salt Lake City: Culture Contrasts Company, 1974); J. Dale Miller and Maurice Loiseau, *New World Culture Series; USA-France* (Salt Lake City: Culture Contrasts Company, 1974).

Visuals: Slide of French children's shoes with presents in them.
            Slide of American fireplace with stockings hanging in front of it.
Props: A French nativity scene (*une crèche avec des santons*).

(2) La Navidad en México y en los Estados Unidos:

La celebración de la Navidad es una fiesta muy importante en México y en los otros países de habla española. El dieciséis de diciembre empiezan las posadas. Las personas invitadas a una fiesta se dividen en dos grupos. Uno está delante de la puerta y el otro detrás. Los dos grupos cantan los tradicionales villancicos. El grupo que está afuera pide posada al grupo de adentro.

En la sala hay una representación en figuras de barro del Nacimiento. Las figuras representan a José, María, el niño Jesús, los tres reyes Magos, una vaca, y una oveja.

También hay una piñata llena de dulces. La piñata se rompe y los niños comen los dulces.

El veinticuatro de diciembre, a medianoche, todos van a la iglesia. Cuando regresan a su casa toman la cena de Nochebuena.

Los niños no reciben sus regalos hasta el seis de enero, día en que los tres Reyes Magos llegaron a Belén y vieron al Niño Jesús.

En los Estados Unidos las casas están decoradas con muchas luces brillantes. En la sala hay un árbol de Navidad que está cubierto de luces y de toda clase de decoraciones.

Los niños cuelgan sus medias delante de la chimenea. Durante la Nochebuena un hombre bastante viejo que se llama Santa Claus baja la chimenea y llena las medias de regalos y dulces. También pone otros regalos debajo del árbol.

El veinticinco de diciembre, en la mañana, todos corren a la sala, abren sus regalos y se ponen muy contentos.

Christmas in Mexico and in the U.S.A.:

The celebration of Christmas is a very important holiday in Mexico and in the other Spanish-speaking countries. The "posadas" begin on the 16th of December. The guests at a party are divided into two groups. One is in front of the door and the other behind it. The two groups sing the traditional Spanish carols. The group that is outside asks the inside group for shelter.

In the living room there is a nativity scene. The clay figurines represent Joseph, Mary, the Christ Child, the three wise men, a cow and a sheep.

There is also a "piñata" filled with candy. The "piñata" is broken and the children eat the candy.

The 24th of December, at midnight, everyone goes to church. When they return home, they eat the Christmas Eve meal.

The children don't receive gifts until the 6th of January, the day on which the three wise men arrived at Bethlehem and saw the Christ Child.

In the United States the houses are decorated with many bright lights. In the living room there is a Christmas tree covered with lights and all kinds of decorations.

The children hang their stockings in front of the fireplace. During the night a rather old man named Santa Claus comes down the chimney and fills the stockings with gifts and candies. He also puts other gifts under the tree.

The 25th of December in the morning, everyone runs to the living room, opens the presents and becomes very happy.

Visuals: Slide of a Mexican living room with a *piñata* hanging from the ceiling.
           Slide of an American living room with a Christmas tree.
Props: A Spanish nativity scene (*un nacimiento con las figuras de barro*).

12.5.2b PRESENTING CULTURAL VALUES

(1) The importance of bread in French life:

Le Bon Pain français[21]	Good French Bread
Les Français achètent leur pain chaque jour. Il y a même des Français qui traversent la ville pour acheter le meilleur pain. Les boulangers font du pain frais chaque jour. Le proverbe français affirme "Repas sans pain, repas de rien." Pendant la Révolution Française, la foule parisienne criait "Du pain et la Constitution." A Lyon, on criait "Le pain et l'égalité." Les Américains disent: "He is as good as gold." Les Français disent: "Il est bon comme le bon pain." Voilà des valeurs très différentes!	The French buy their bread every day. There are even French people who go across town to buy the best bread. Bakers make fresh bread daily. A French proverb affirms, "A meal without bread is a meal worth nothing." During the French Revolution, the Parisian crowds yelled, "Bread and a Constitution." In Lyon, they yelled, "Bread and Equality." Americans say, "He is as good as gold." The French say, "He is as good as good bread." These are very different values!

After reading the story, the teacher can ask questions: *Quelle sorte de pain est-ce que les Américains mangent? Est-ce que les Américains en mangent avec tous leurs repas? Quels proverbes français montrent l'importance du pain dans la vie française? (What kind of bread do Americans eat? Do Americans eat bread with all their meals? What French proverbs show the importance of bread in French life?)*

(2) Concept of time (Spanish-speaking countries):[22]

El señor Jones, hombre de negocios en Nueva York, quiere venderle su producto a una fábrica en Lima, Perú. El director de la fábrica le da cita para las diez de la mañana. El señor Jones llega a las diez en punto. La secretaria lo saluda cortésmente y le dice que se siente.	Mr. Jones, a business man from New York, wants to sell his product to a factory in Lima, Peru. The director of the factory gives him an appointment for 10:00 in the morning. Mr. Jones arrives at 10:00 sharp. The secretary greets him courteously and asks him to sit down.

[21] Henrietta Lendt, unpublished papers, The Ohio State University, 1970. It should be noted that even in this instance the French attitude toward bread has changed with the introduction of consumerism. Often bread is wasted and thrown away. People concerned with diets will eliminate bread or cut down on the amount of bread they eat.

[22] It should also be noted that the concept of time, particularly for the business community, is changing in Latin America.

Después de una hora el director llega. El señor Jones, muy irritado, le dice al director que lo había esperado una hora.	After an hour the director arrives. Mr. Jones, who is very irritated by now, tells the director that he has been waiting for him one hour.
El director, muy sorprendido por la reacción del señor Jones, no quiere comprar su producto.	The director, who is very surprised by Mr. Jones' reaction, does not want to buy the product.
El pobre señor Jones no sabía que era costumbre llegar tarde en los países de habla española.	Poor Mr. Jones was unaware that it was customary to arrive late in Spanish-speaking countries.

When the class has read the story, the teacher asks questions: *¿Por qué está irritado el señor Jones? ¿Qué costumbre ignora el señor Jones? Si lo hubiera saludado cortésmente el señor Jones al director, ¿qué habría pasado? ¿Qué habría hecho Ud.?* (*Why was Mr. Jones irritated? What custom was Mr. Jones unaware of? If Mr. Jones had greeted the director courteously, what would have happened? What would you have done?*)

(3) The importance of competitive sports in American life (ESL class):

Bob Jones, age 15, is a student at a large secondary school in the U.S.A. There are 2,500 students in his school.

It is August and his school is closed for vacation. Nevertheless, each morning he gets up early and rushes to school for football practice. His great desire is to "make the varsity squad." Only thirty boys are selected to be on the varsity squad. These boys represent the school when they play against teams in other large secondary schools.

Today, Bob is very nervous. The coach (physical education teacher) will decide which of the boys can be on the varsity squad. Before Bob left the house this morning, his father said to him, "We're counting on you, Bob." Suppose he doesn't get chosen! What will his father and mother think? How can he accept defeat when he has worked so hard to be an excellent athlete! As he thinks about his life in school during the preceding year, he realizes that his grades were not very high, but, after all, he spent every afternoon on the football field, and was too tired to study when he got home each evening.

Bob's sister Mary is 16. She is also terribly nervous today. She has spent many, many hours practicing to be a cheerleader, and today her physical education teacher will announce which six girls will be selected. Suppose she is not chosen! After all the time and effort she has given to it!

Several of the foreign exchange students in this school were talking about Bob and Mary. They wondered why these two intelligent young teenagers were willing to sacrifice good grades for activities that took time away from their studies; Mary had told them she wanted to be a doctor, and Bob said he wanted to be an engineer.

After reading the story the teacher can ask questions: *Why is Bob nervous today? If he is not selected for the varsity squad, how will his parents feel? Why is Mary nervous today? What differences do you find between typical 15 and 16 year old school boys and girls in your country and the U.S.A.?*

12.5.3   Culture assimilators

The students read a passage describing a situation in which Americans and people from another country interact. During the course of this interaction, one person or group unintentionally offends or annoys the other. What is the source of this misunderstanding? The students read four feasible explanations, and are asked to select the one they think is the true answer . . . . After making their selection, they are directed to another page to check their answer. If they are wrong, they are told why, and asked to reread the passage and select another solution.

Here is a Spanish example:

(1) Invitation to a party (for ESL students)

Juan Valera, a student from Nicaragua, is invited by his professor to a cocktail party. The invitation reads: 5:00 to 7:00. Juan arrives at 6:45 and stays till 8:00. He wonders why so few people attended the party and why his host and hostess seem less friendly than usual. What is the reason?

A. He is dressed inappropriately for a cocktail party.
B. He didn't bring flowers or a small gift.
C. His hostess has to prepare dinner for her family.
D. He didn't make enough effort to talk to the other guests.

Explanations:

A. (wrong) Americans are becoming less and less strict in their dress code, especially where students are concerned. Since you are a foreign student, your hosts would be even more understanding.
B. (wrong) You are not expected to bring flowers or a gift to a cocktail party. In the U.S.A., it is customary to bring a gift to a birthday party or send a gift to a friend on the occasion of his or her wedding.
C. (correct) Americans tend to observe time limits very carefully. When the invitation reads 5:00 to 7:00, the guests are expected to leave by 7:00 o'clock. If the hosts have children, it is very possible that they want to prepare a meal for them after the guests leave at 7:00.
D. (wrong) Although it is desirable for guests to circulate and make an effort to engage others in conversation, it is not considered improper not to do so. As a foreign student, you wouldn't be expected to initiate conversation, anyway.

(2) On a train in Germany[23]

Susan was traveling from Hamburg to Frankfurt. The train ride was rather long, so she decided to buy a ticket for a Liegewagen. It was only slightly more expensive than the regular ticket and she would be able to get a good night's sleep. When she entered the compartment, she was surprised to see four men and a lady already seated there. Since she could see no beds, she assumed

[23] This episode, prepared by Idiko Bodoni, is taken from H. Ned Seelye, *Teaching Culture, Strategies for Foreign Language Educators* (Skokie, Illinois: National Textbook Company, 1975), pp. 105–6. The chapter also includes five other examples.

that later on they would go to another compartment, with the men separate from the women. Imagine her astonishment when the porter came, folded down the seats so that they formed six bunk beds and gave everyone a pillow and a blanket! She sat upright on her bunk bed, not sleeping all night, afraid of the men. Why was Susan upset?

A. The German ticket agent had cheated her and sold her the wrong ticket.
B. She thought that she should have moved to the correct compartment and was angry at herself for not doing so.
C. She had confused the concept of a Liegewagen with that of a Schlafwagen.
D. Germans have very loose morals and she might have been the object of "improper" behavior.

Explanations:

A. (wrong) Susan had received the correct ticket for the amount of money paid and for what she had requested.
B. (wrong) All the compartments in that car were alike, and her ticket had specified this compartment.
C. (correct) Susan had confused a Liegewagen with a Schlafwagen. In a Liegewagen one does not have a private compartment with a made-up bed, and strangers ignore each other. Susan was thinking of a Schlafwagen, which is similar to the American Pullman car, when she had bought the ticket.
D. (wrong) It is a false generalization.

12.5.4 Mini-dramas

The mini-drama is a short play, usually composed of two or three scenes. Although the format may vary, the "faux-pas" is often committed in the first scene: a person of one nationality innocently behaves in a way that is offensive to someone of another nationality. In scene two, the first person discusses the dilemma with a compatriot. In the third scene, the person of the second nationality discusses the incident with one or more of his/her compatriots.

The teacher reads the mini-drama or plays a recording in which native speakers of the cultures concerned take the roles. The teacher stops the reading (or recording) of the mini-drama after each scene and asks the students whether they can explain the cause of the misunderstanding.

At the end of the skit, the teacher leads a discussion on the series of unfortunate events, and supplies data to help the students analyze the cultural conflict.

Here is a Spanish example:[24]

Explain that Lorraine (Lorena) is an American student on a study tour in Spain; she is living with a Spanish family and calls her hostess, "Mamá."

Mamá —¿Qué pasa, Lorena? Estás muy callada.   *What's the matter, Lorraine? You're so quiet.*

---

[24] Prepared by John Lett, Department of Spanish, University of Illinois.

Lorena	—Nada, nada...	*Nothing, nothing . . .*
Mamá	—Pero ¿por qué no hablas? Hace media hora que no dices nada.	*But, why aren't you talking? It's been a half hour since you said anything.*
Lorena	—Pues, la verdad es que no estoy acostumbrada a pasar dos horas o más en la comida, y me canso y me aburro un poco.	*Well, the truth is that I'm not used to spending two or more hours eating, and I'm tired and a little bored.*
Mamá	—Pero, hija, es la comida más importante del día. Hay que comer, y luego descansar para que te haga bien la digestión.	*But, daughter, it's the most important meal of the day. You must eat, and then rest so that you will digest your food well.*
Lorena	—Sí, pero ¿por qué tenemos que pasar tanto tiempo sentados a la mesa después de comer?	*Yes, but why do we have to spend so much time sitting at the table after we eat?*

(Mid-discussion) Try to identify point of conflict and develop explanatory hypotheses.

—What's the matter with Lorraine?
—Why is she bored?
—Why do Spaniards spend more time at the table than we do?
—Does our society provide a long lunch break?
—Can you go home from school to eat?
—Are stores here closed two or three hours so all employees can go home for lunch?
—Do you think there may be a difference in the importance Spaniards give to the family compared to us?

Play second half of tape (or start from beginning and play all).

Mamá	—Pues, mira, porque es la comida más fuerte del día. En ella nos reunimos toda la familia para charlar, contarnos las cosas que nos han pasado durante estas horas que hemos estados separados, y por eso la hacemos un poco más larga.	*Well, because it's the heaviest meal of the day. For this meal all the family gets together to chat and tell the things that have happened to us during the time we have been separated. That's why the meal seems a little long.*
Lorena	—Sí, mamá. Ahora comprendo mejor. ¿Me das una naranja, por favor?	*Yes, mother, now I understand better. May I have an orange, please?*
Mamá	—Toma ésta, que es la más bonita, o coge todas las que quieras.	*Take this one. It's the prettiest, or take as many as you like.*

12.5.5 Culture clusters

The *culture cluster* is a short unit that contains 3 or 4 culture capsules, questions for discussion and, finally, role-playing by the entire class. During the role-playing the teacher acts as narrator and guides the students through the simulation. The narration is usually read by the teacher. It might be a description of each phrase of the wedding ceremony with pauses so that the members of the wedding party may recite their traditional lines, e.g., *Acceptez-vous de prendre pour époux Jean Eric François Laborde? (Do you take this man for your lawfully wedded husband?) Oui, je le veux. (I do)*, etc.

Here is an example:

Un Mariage campagnard[25]   *A Country Wedding*

Format: Four self-contained culture capsules: La Cérémonie Civile, La Cérémonie Religieuse, Le Repas de Noces, Les Différences entre un Mariage Mondain et un Mariage Campagnard (*The Civil Ceremony, The Religious Ceremony, The Wedding Meal, The Differences Between a City Wedding and a Country Wedding.*)
Time: 10–15 minutes per day for four days; 45 minutes for final (fifth) day.
Level: Third or fourth.

Cultural attitudes illustrated:

1. Emphasis on system and formal structure
   Adherence to procedure at all levels: civil, religious, and social. Preoccupation with rules and regulations as manifestation of *la méfiance (distrust)*: desire to protect self through complicated network of laws and regulations.

2. Importance of *la famille, le foyer (family, home)*
   Marriage ceremony as a family observance; talk by *le maire (mayor)* to bride and groom in which he stresses the importance of establishing a new home and attendant family responsibilities; *le livret de famille (the family record book)*.

3. Humor
   L'Esprit Gaulois (Gaelic wit) as reflected in the ritual of the *"prise de la jarretière" (stealing the garter)*

Cultural symbols illustrated:

1. *L'Echarpe tricolore du maire (the mayor's tricolor sash)*: symbol of authority
2. *Le livret de famille (the family record book)*: symbol of marriage as foundation of home and family
3. *Le Registre (the register)*: symbol of the authority of the state; of permanence of marriage
4. *Les alliances (the wedding rings)*: symbol of permanence of marriage

[25] Betsy Meade and Genelle Morain, "The Culture Cluster" in *Foreign Language Annals* 6, no. 3 (March 1973), pp. 331–38.

12.5.6   Culture Learning Centers

Teachers who wish to individualize their curricula can create centers or stations in the back of their classrooms. Each center contains self-instructional materials on one broad cultural theme, such as sports, cooking, schools, weddings, crafts, etc. Students use these centers individually or in small groups. Media of all kinds can be placed in the center: film strips, slides, films, books, periodicals, and props. As the students approach the center, they see signs pointing to sets of directions on how to use the center. These directions are always accompanied by a task for the student(s) to complete.

Some sample tasks are as follows:

Mire usted las tarjetas de Navidad: ¿Cuáles son cuatro maneras de decir "Merry Christmas"?

Look at the Christmas cards. What are four ways of saying "Merry Christmas"?

A.
B.
C.
D.

Identifiez chaque article en vous servant de la liste a droite.

Using the list on the right, identify each article.

_____	1.	A. les alliances	*wedding rings*
_____	2.	B. les bans	*marriage banns*
_____	3.	C. une pièce montee	*wedding cake*
_____	4.	D. le livret de famille	*the family record book*
_____	5.	E. un faire-part de mariage	*wedding announcement*
_____	6.	F. une dragée	*wedding candy*

A French, Spanish, or German Learning Center on Christmas might look like the one on page 362.

12.6   ANALYZING THE TARGET CULTURE: ADVANCED CLASSES

In advanced language classes, the students are able to explore the target culture in greater depth. As their language proficiency increases, so does their access to sources in the target language.

12.6.1   The foreign press

The American teacher of a foreign language selects current articles from news-magazines of the target country: *Express, Paris-Match, Mañana, Der Spiegel,* etc. The teacher then finds the same subjects treated in American magazines

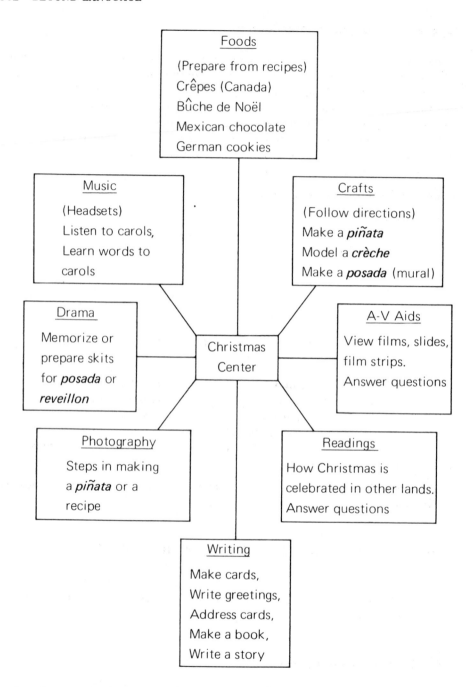

such as *Time* or *Newsweek*. The ESL teacher can reverse this technique by using the magazines or newspapers of the students' home country as a basis of comparison.

12.6.1a   COMPARING POINTS OF VIEW[26]

The class is divided into small groups, and each group is given a pair of articles. They list the differences in points of view and try to analyze the reason behind these differences. Each group presents its findings orally to the rest of the class.

12.6.1b   CLASS DEBATES

The students use the magazine articles to prepare for class debates. First they decide on a topic; then they make a list of key words and idioms from the articles. One student writes these on a ditto master so that it may be distributed to everyone in the class. The class is divided into teams, and each member prepares some arguments. The next day, the first half of the period is devoted to organizing the presentation: the teams meet separately, choose a captain, and decide which student will present which points. The second half of the period is the actual debate.

12.6.1c   STUDYING CUSTOMS[27]

Articles are selected from the foreign press which discuss table manners, dating customs, family relations, school reforms, and other customs and mores. Each group of students is given a piece of oaktag and an article to work with. The students underline salient features and prepare written comments upon them. The end result of the project is a set of posters which may be placed on the walls of the classroom.

12.6.2   The media (ESL)

The class watches a television program together with the teacher, who makes notes on vocabulary and structures that might present problems. He or she also jots down some questions to ask at the conclusion of the program. A home assignment could be to watch a certain telecast and be able to summarize it the next day in class.

A similar technique could be used with a radio program.

The teacher could preview a film at a local cinema and prepare the class for seeing it together. Teach key vocabulary and distribute dittoed sheets with a few questions to think about before viewing the film.

The local newspaper is also a good source for a learning activity in class or a homework assignment. Students could compare the American paper with those

[26] Numerous ESL exercises labeled "Points of View" and "Personal Opinions" are found in Paul Pimsleur and Donald Berger, *Encounters, A Basic Reader* (New York: Harcourt Brace Jovanovich, 1974).
[27] For many additional suggestions, see Renate Schulz, "Comparative Culture Study: An Approach Through the Printed News Media," *American Foreign Language Teacher* 4, no. 4, 1974.

in their native countries: ads, wedding announcements, the obituaries, the sports page, comics, and local, state, national, and international news coverage.

12.6.3   Cartoons

Our language is a reflection of our culture. In order to understand political, social, and economic events of the day, it is helpful to use pictorial stimuli, such as cartoons, and study the captions that accompany them.[28]

In language classes at the high intermediate and advanced levels, Jib Fowles suggests that teachers guide the discussion by asking these three questions:[29]

1. What is the factual situation?
2. What is the incongruity that would make an American laugh?
3. What is the cultural anxiety lurking behind this cartoon that is mitigated by laughter?

A good example of social unrest is a cartoon about the director of a zoo who, arriving at work one morning, finds the animals having a sit-down strike in his office.

Our uneasiness with technological advances and humanoid computers are evident in Rube Goldberg's cartoons.

An example of an incongruous situation that would make an American laugh is the cartoon in which a psychiatrist puts his patient in an electric chair instead of on a couch.

Finally, students can bring in their own cartoons and discuss them in small groups, some to be presented to the whole class.

12.6.4   Foreign visitors in the classroom

Foreign visitors in the classroom make the foreign culture seem closer, more real.

12.6.4a   FINDING A VISITOR

Contact the foreign student advisor at a nearby college or university. Check the telephone directory for clubs: *L'Alliance Française, Las Buenas Vecinas, Der Männerchor.* Speak to the minister or priest of churches that have foreign language services. Write to the local radio station that sometimes has foreign language programs. Ask students if they know of members in the community who have visitors from the foreign country or if their fathers through their busi-

---

[28] See Anthony Mollica "Cartoons in the Language Classroom," *The Canadian Modern Language Review/La Revue Canadienne des Langues Vivantes* 23, no. 4 (March 1976), pp. 424–44. This article is particularly helpful for teachers of Italian in that it provides over sixty cartoons of all sorts. French equivalents of the Italian texts are given in the footnotes.
[29] Jib Fowles, "Ho Ho Ho: Cartoons in the Language Class," *TESOL Quarterly* 4, no. 2 (1970), pp. 155–58.

ness know of foreign couples visiting the city. Sometimes the wife of a businessman will be happy to visit an American school and speak to the students. One or two students might take the visitor on a tour of the school when class is over.

12.6.4b   INTERVIEWING THE VISITOR IN ADVANCE

Before inviting foreign guests to meet your students, talk with them to determine how well they articulate (in English or in the foreign language), how receptive they would be to answering questions about their country, and whether they meet people easily or not. If they do not meet these criteria, it may be a waste of time to invite them to class.

If they do, ask them what topic they would like to discuss with the class. Then talk with them on this topic and note their vocabulary.

12.6.4c   PREPARING THE CLASS

Before native speakers arrive, describe them to the class and teach them the vocabulary they are likely to use. Ask the students what questions they would like to ask the native speakers and help them put the questions into the foreign language.

12.6.5   Interviews (ESL)

Ask the students what they have learned about Americans from personal observations. List the statements on the board. Then have the students go out and interview several Americans to confirm their assumptions.

Sample assignment:

Is it true that almost all the meals that Americans prepare at home are from cans or frozen packages?

The teacher suggests that the students ask the following questions of three Americans who had dinner at home the previous evening:

Did you have dinner at home last evening?
What did you prepare?
Was it fresh or did it come from cans and/or frozen packages?

Finally, the students bring their data to class and chart their survey on the chalkboard.

12.6.6   Controversial issues

Controversial issues are guaranteed to arouse student interest and participation. The following suggestions have been developed for ESL classes. Foreign students give their opinions of American culture as they have observed it.

12.6.6a GENERALIZATIONS

The teacher duplicates statements about Americans and asks the class to read them and react.[30] This is an effective technique for communicative practice.

Sample generalizations:

    a. Social status in the U.S.A. depends largely on an individual's wealth.
    b. Americans are very generous with their time and money.

The teacher makes two columns on the chalkboard: pro and con. The students give evidence to support their assumptions and the teacher writes their assertions in the proper column:

Pro (generous of time and money)	Con (not generous of time and money)
Miss Jones works from 8:00–5:00 Monday through Friday. Every Saturday afternoon she donates 5 hours of her time.	*My boss, Mr. Smith, pays me a minimum wage and never lets me take a day off when I need it.*

12.6.6b RANK ORDER

Ask the students to read the following qualities ascribed to Americans and then place them by rank order of importance:

generous
competitive
idealistic
materialistic
efficient
self-reliant

The teacher then charts the results on the chalkboard to see where the class stands.

12.6.6c VOTING

The teacher asks the class to vote on the following issue: Should boys and girls be permitted to start dating at age 14?

Yes _____   No _____

The teacher tallies the votes and writes the figures on the blackboard. Then the class is asked to defend their vote. The teacher puts two columns on the board: Yes and No. As the students give their reasons, the teacher writes them

[30] For analyses of American culture, see James Spradley and Michael Rynkiewich, NACIRAMA (Boston: Little Brown, 1974) and Howard Lee Nostrand, Final Report of Project OE-6-14-005, Part C: Contemporary Culture and Society of the United States, University of Washington, Seattle, 1967.

in the proper columns. Finally, the students are asked to compare dating practices in their countries with those in the U.S.A.

12.6.6d CONTINUUM

Students, one by one, go to the chalkboard and place a check mark at a point on the line that represents their point of view:

The status of women in the U.S.A.

unfairly treated	treated fairly	too privileged

Above the check mark each student writes his or her name and/or native country. If several groups from different countries are represented, each group could meet and make its own continuum. These could then be posted and the class could discuss the different points of view.

12.6.7 Cultural models

Advanced students can analyze the target culture in terms of available models. Howard Nostrand, for example, has summarized the shared patterns of a culture into a limited number of "themes":[31]

French culture: l'individualisme, l'intellectualité, l'art de vivre, le réalisme, le bon sens, l'amitié, l'amour, la famille, la religion, la justice, la liberté, la patrie.

Hispanic culture: individualism, dignidad, orientation toward persons, serenidad, beauty, leisure valued over work, human nature mistrusted, "cultura" despite "la realidad del medio," rising expectations.

In studying films or literary works or newspaper articles, the students can pick out the underlying themes. As a contrastive study, the students might try to develop a list of cultural themes that typify their native country, determining which are common to both cultures and which are different.

This thematic approach to culture might culminate in a bulletin board display depicting selected themes and their expression in anecdotes, cartoons, short literary works, advertisements, and sayings.

[31] Howard Lee Nostrand, "Levels of Sociocultural Understanding for Language Classes," in H. Ned Seelye, ed., *A Handbook on Latin America for Teachers* (Springfield, Ill.: Superintendent of Public Instruction, 1968), p. 20.

Appendix

appendix
Sample Lesson
Plans

A. ELEMENTARY GERMAN CLASS

TEXT: *A-LM German, Level One,* New 2d ed. (New York: Harcourt Brace Jovanovich, Inc. 1974), Unit 3, pp. 28–30.[1]

CLASS SIZE: Twenty-five to thirty

CLASS PERIOD: Forty minutes

EQUIPMENT:

1. Overhead projector

2. Chalkboard

3. Two magnets (if chalkboard is magnetized)

MATERIALS:

1. A transparency with line drawings and an overlay with written descriptions (see Chapter 2, pp. 13–15)

2. A paper screen with four slots and four acetate strips (see Chapter 5, p. 79)

PREVIOUS LESSONS: The class has completed Units 1 and 2 and has learned the basic dialog of Unit 3.

---

[1] The excerpts from this work are reprinted by permission of Harcourt Brace Jovanovich, Inc.

LESSON OBJECTIVES:

1. To answer questions orally in complete sentences using four present tense forms of *sein* (*to be*) correctly with eighty percent accuracy

2. To form sentences orally using a given number of German words in the proper word order with ninety percent accuracy

ACTIVITIES:

1. Warm up

2. Presentation of four forms of *sein*

   a. Third person singular

   b. Third person plural

   c. First and second persons singular

3. Songs

4. Question/answer drill on *sein*

5. Review of new material

   a. Oral

   b. Written

6. Communication activity

7. Presentation of German word order

8. Drill on German word order

PROCEDURES:

1. Warm up (five minutes)

   Using familiar vocabulary, ask questions on students' names and where they are.

Teacher: Guten Tag.	*Hello.*
Wie geht's, Peter? Hans? Inge?	*How are you, . . .*
Wie heißt du?	*What's your name?*
Heißt du Karl?	*Is your name Carl?*
Wo ist Ilse? Helga? Benno?	*Where is . . .*

2. Presentation of four forms of *sein*

  a. Third person singular

   Teach one form at a time by describing each figure and having the class repeat. Cover the rest of the transparency with a piece of paper.

Hans	Peter	Karl	Benno

Jochen	Fritz

Teacher: Hans ist groß.	*Jack is tall.*
Peter ist klein.	*Peter is short.*
Karl ist traurig.	*Carl is sad.*
Benno ist müde.	*Benno is tired.*
Jochen ist schmutzig.	*Jochen is dirty.*
Fritz ist krank.	*Fred is sick.*

   Ask questions about each boy: Wie ist Hans?   Peter?   Karl?
   (How is . . .)

   Point to each drawing and ask, Wie ist er?

   Follow the same procedure for line drawings of girls (see p. 374), on the second section of the transparency.

   Describe each figure and have the class repeat.

Teacher: Helga ist groß.	*Helga is tall.*
Inge ist klein.	*Inge is short.*
Ilse ist traurig.	*Ilse is sad.*

Helga   Inge   Ilse   Ursel

Monika   Gisela

Ursel ist müde.	*Ursula is tired.*
Monika ist schmutzig.	*Monica is dirty.*
Gisela ist krank.	*Gisela is sick.*

Ask questions about each girl: Wie ist Helga?   Wie ist sie?
(How is Helga?   How is she?)

b. Third person plural

Point to both sections of the transparency and describe two people.

Teacher: Hans und Helga
    sind groß.   *Hans and Helga are tall.*

    Peter und Inge sind
    klein.   *Peter and Inge are short.*

    Karl und Ilse sind
    traurig.   *Carl and Ilse are sad.*

Ask questions: Wie groß sind sie?   Wie sind sie?
(How tall are they?   How are they?)

c. First and second person singular

Introduce the first and second person singular in a conversation.

Teacher: Ich bin müde.   *I am tired.*

Bist du müde, Karl?	*Are you tired, Carl?*
(Antworte mit ,,ja!")	*(Answer with "yes.")*
Karl: Ja, ich bin müde.	*Yes, I am tired.*
Teacher: Bist du groß, Hans?	*Are you tall, Jack?*
Hans: Ja, ich bin groß.	*Yes, I am tall.*
Teacher: Bist du klein, Inge?	*Are you short, Inge?*
Inge: Ja, ich bin klein.	*Yes, I am short.*

3. Songs

Rounds:

,,Mein Hut, der hat drei Ecken"
(*My Hat, It Has Three Corners*)

Mein Hut, der hat drei Ecken,
Drei Ecken hat mein Hut,
Und hat er nicht drei Ecken,
Dann ist es nicht mein Hut!

,,O wie wohl ist mir am Abend"
(*Oh, How Lovely Is the Evening*)

O wie wohl ist mir am Abend,
Mir am Abend,
Wenn zur Ruh,
Die Glocken lauten,
Bim, bam, bim, bam.
Glocken lauten,
Bim, bam, bim, bam, bim, bam!

4. Question/answer drill on *sein*

Draw a two-story house with kitchen, living room, cellar, garden, and garage
on the chalkboard (see page 376).

Cut out paper figures of a boy and girl, Hans and Helga, and using magnets,
place them singly first, and then together, in the various rooms, the garden,
and the garage. Describe them in German and have the class repeat.

Teacher: Hans ist in der Küche.	*Jack is in the kitchen.*
Hans und Helga sind im Garten.	*Jack and Helga are in the garden.*

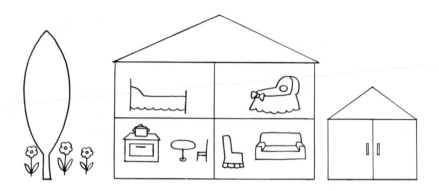

Ask questions: Wo ist Hans?   Wo sind Hans und Helga?
              (*Where is Jack?   Where are Jack and Helga?*)

5. Review of new material

   a. Oral

      Review the transparency with adjectives, using the overlay for each picture. Pronounce each sentence and have the class repeat.

Er ist groß, klein, traurig, müde . . .	*He is tall, short, sad, tired . . .*
Sie ist groß, klein, traurig, müde . . .	*She is tall, short, sad, tired . . .*
Sie sind groß, klein, traurig, müde . . .	*They are tall, short, sad, tired . . .*

   b. Written

      Distribute dittoed sheets of the new material and call on individuals to read it.

(1) Bist du müde, Peter? Ja, ich bin müde.	*Are you tired, Peter? Yes, I am tired.*
(2) Hans ist in der Küche. Helga ist im Wohnzimmer.	*Jack is in the kitchen. Helga is in the living room.*
(3) Hans und Helga sind im Garten.	*Jack and Helga are in the garden.*

6. Communication activity

Teacher introduces *glücklich (happy)*.

Ich bin nicht traurig. Ich bin glüklich.	*I am not sad. I am happy.*
Ich bin glücklich in der Schule.	*I am happy in school.*
Wo bist du glücklich? Wo bist du traurig?	*Where are you happy? Where are you sad?*
In der Schule?	*At school?*
Im Garten?	*In the garden?*
In der Garage?	*In the garage?*
In der Küche?	*In the kitchen?*
Im Wohnzimmer?	*In the living room?*

Students indicate in which of the places listed they feel happy and in which places they feel sad. If desired, students can rank their preferences.

7. Presentation of German word order

Use strips of acetate over a paper grid (see Chapter 5, p. 97).

Position 1	Position 2		
DIE BEIDEN	BIN	*the two*	*am*
ICH	PUTZEN	*I*	*are cleaning*
ER	SPIELEN	*he*	*are playing*
WIR	IST	*we*	*is*
SIE	PUTZT	*they*	*is cleaning*
	SPIELT	*(she, you)*	*is playing*
	SUCHT		*is looking for*
	SPIELE		*am playing*

Position 3   Position 4

JETZT	DAS ZIMMER	*now*	*the room*
HEUTE	TENNIS	*today*	*tennis*
MORGEN	IM GARTEN	*tomorrow*[2]	*in the garden*
	DAS AUTO		*the car*
	IN DER STUBE		*in the room*
	FUSSBALL		*soccer*
	DAS RAD		*the bicycle*
	BENNO		*Benno*
	IN DER GARAGE		*in the garage*

Move each slit up or down over the little windows to show one word in each position.

Ask for volunteers to read the sentences.

Example:    (*I am playing tennis today.*)

Then switch the strips so that the third position becomes the first and vice versa, but always be sure that the second position is never changed.

Example: 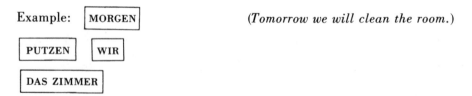   (*Tomorrow we will clean the room.*)

8. Drill on German word order

Scramble the words by taking the paper grid off the transparency, leaving the four strips of acetate entirely uncovered.

Ask the class to form as many sentences orally as possible.

---

[2] In German, the present tense is often used to indicate futurity.

HOMEWORK:

Ask the class to make a drawing of each of the following German sentences and to copy the sentences beneath their pictures.

Example: Hans und Fritz sind im Boot.
(Jack and Fred are in the boat.)

1. Das Auto ist in der Garage.   *The car is in the garage.*

2. Ich bin im Keller.   *I am in the cellar.*

3. Ilse und Monika sind traurig.   *Ilse and Monica are sad.*

4. Peter ist im Wohnzimmer.   *Peter is in the living room.*

5. Gisela ist in der Küche.   *Gisela is in the kitchen.*

6. Jochen und Karl sind groß.   *Jochen and Carl are tall.*

FOLLOW-UP FOR THE NEXT DAY

LESSON OBJECTIVE: To write complete sentences from dictation the correct present tense forms of *sein* with ninety percent accuracy.

ACTIVITIES:

1. Warm up

2. Guessing game

3. Presentation of the remaining forms of *sein*

   a. First person plural

   b. Second person plural (informal)

   c. Second person plural (formal)

4. Drill on all forms of *sein*

5. Pattern drills on tape

6. Dictation

7. Dialog review

PROCEDURES:

1. Warm up (five minutes)

   a. Personal questions using the verb *sein*:

      Bist du müde? klein?   *Are you tired? short? tall?*
      groß?

   b. Questions on transparency (adjectives):

      Wie sind Hans und Helga?   *How are Jack and Helga?*

   During the warm up, several students may put their homework drawings on the chalkboard.

2. Guessing game (five minutes)

   Ask the class to look at the chalkboard and guess which German sentence is illustrated by the drawings. Those who guess correctly may go to the chalkboard and write their answers.

3. Presentation of the remaining forms of *sein* (five minutes)

   a. First person plural

   b. Second person plural (informal)

   c. Second person plural (formal)

4. Drill on all forms of *sein* (three minutes)

   Use figures on flashcards (see Chapter 3).

5. Pattern drills on tape (five minutes)

   See Section 6, p. 31 in *AL-M German, Level One*.

6. Dictation (ten minutes)

   Use the overhead projector (see Chapter 7).

7. Dialog review (seven minutes)

   Use tapes and visuals. See *AL-M German, Level One*, p. 27.

HOMEWORK: Ask the class to bring in magazine cutouts illustrating each line of basic dialog on page 27. The students will exchange them and write the lines of dialog under each picture.

B. INTERMEDIATE SPANISH CLASS

TEXT: Brenes et al., *Learning Spanish the Modern Way, Book 2*, 2d ed. (New York: McGraw-Hill, Webster Division, 1967).[3]

CLASS SIZE: Twenty-five to thirty

CLASS PERIOD: Fifty minutes

EQUIPMENT:

1. Chalkboard

2. Overhead projector

3. Tape recorder

MATERIALS:

1. A tape recording of the narrative "El niño al que se le murió el amigo," p. 137

2. Blank transparencies

3. A set of flashcards with a pronoun on each

4. Toys or magazine cutouts of toys—marbles, a truck, a pistol, and a watch

5. Visuals to demonstrate the use of the subjunctive (Section I b)

PREVIOUS LESSONS: The teacher has presented the subjunctive and drilled the regular and irregular verbs (pp. 138–39).

LESSON OBJECTIVE: To change sentences from the present indicative to the present subjunctive, using the verbs that have been drilled in class, with ninety percent accuracy.

ACTIVITIES:

Use the subjunctive at all times.

1. Grammar review

    a. Warm up

    b. Pictorial stimuli

    c. Flashcards

    d. Written pattern drill

    e. Game—a relay race

[3] The excerpts from this work are reprinted by permission of McGraw-Hill.

2. New material

    a. Listening comprehension and word study

    b. Reading exercise

    c. Writing exercise

PROCEDURES:

1. Grammar review of Lesson 20, pp. 138–41 (twenty-five minutes)

    a. Warm up

Students decide which actions they wish their classmates to perform.

Teacher (looking at Pedro):

Quiero que Pedro vaya a la puerta.	*I want Peter to go to the door.*
(Pedro performs the action.)	
Maria, ¿qué quieres que haga Juan?	*Mary, what do you want John to do?*
Maria: Quiero que Juan escriba su nombre en la pizarra.	*I want John to write his name on the blackboard.*
(Juan performs the action.)	
Teacher: Carlos, ¿qué quieres que haga Teresa?	*Charles, what do you want Theresa to do?*
Carlos: Quiero que Teresa salga.	*I want Theresa to leave.*
(Teresa performs the action.)	

    b. Pictorial stimuli

Show a series of visuals depicting two actions, one of a child behaving in a certain way, and the other of his mother hoping he will behave in another way.

Teacher: ¡Miren Uds. este cuadro!	*Look at this picture!*

Teacher (pointing to picture
  on the left):

      Aquí está Felipe.   *Here is Philip.*

      Felipe no dice adiós.   *Philip does not say good-bye.*

      La mamá espera que   *Mama is waiting for Philip to say*
        Felipe diga adiós.   *good-bye.*

      ¿Que espera la   *What is mama waiting for?*
        mamá?

Student: La mamá espera   *Mama is waiting for Philip to say*
        que Felipe diga   *good-bye.*
        adiós.

Teacher (pointing to picture
  on the left):

      El niño no es bueno.   *The boy is not good.*

¿Qué quiere la mamá?	*What does mama want?*
Student: La mamá quiere que el niño sea bueno.	*Mama wants the boy to be good.*

Teacher (pointing to picture on the left):	
Luis no va a la escuela.	*Louis does not go to school.*
¿Que manda papá?	*What does papa order?*
Student: Papá manda que Luis vaya a la escuela.	*Papa orders Louis to go to school.*

c. Flashcards (with pronouns)

Give a model sentence and ask the class to change it as each pronoun appears.

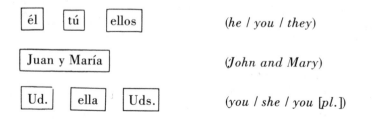

| él | tú | ellos | | *(he / you / they)* |

| Juan y María | | *(John and Mary)* |

| Ud. | ella | Uds. | | *(you / she / you [pl.])* |

(1) Teacher: Prefiero que Ud. venga.　　　　*I prefer that you come.*

　　　(Class repeats.)

　　　Flashcard: tú　　　　　　　　　　*you (sing.)*

　Class: Prefiero que tú vengas.　　　　*I prefer that you come.*

　　(One by one the other cards are shown.)

(2) Teacher: Insisto en que ella hable.　　　　*I insist that she speak.*

　　　(Class repeats.)

　　　Flashcard: ellos　　　　　　　　　*they (masc.)*

　Class: Insisto en que ellos hablen.　　　　*I insist that they speak.*

d. Written pattern drill

Dictate a model sentence for the class to write. Then give a one-word cue so that the class will rewrite the sentence making the necessary changes. One student writes the dictation on the overhead projector in front of the class. (The projector lamp is off.) The teacher corrects this example and then turns on the projector so that the class can see the correct answers.

Teacher dictates:	Students write:
Juan teme que tú lo sepas.	(same)
ella	Juan teme que ella lo sepa.
ellos	Juan teme que ellos lo sepan.
María	Juan teme que María lo sepa.
Ud.	Juan teme que Ud. lo sepa.
Uds.	Juan teme que Uds. lo sepan.
Yo	Juan teme que yo lo sepa.
John is afraid you know it.	
she	*John is afraid she knows it.*
they	*John is afraid they know it.*
Mary	*John is afraid Mary knows it.*
You	*John is afraid you know it.*

You   *John is afraid you know it.*

I   *John is afraid I know it.*

  e. Game—a relay race

Conduct the race with the boys against the girls (see Chapter 3).

Write seven pronouns on the chalkboard and ask seven boys to stand under each one.

yo   nosotros   él   tú   ellos   ella   ellas
(*I*   /   *we*   /   *he* / *you* /   *they* / *she* / *they* [*fem.*)

At the signal to begin, the boys write a sentence using these pronouns in the subjunctive. As each one finishes, he moves to the next section and writes a sentence using that pronoun. The last boy to the right takes the place of the boy on the extreme left. All continue to revolve until the board is filled with sentences.

Example: yo   *I*

      El quiere que yo   *He wants me to leave.*
      salga.

Then the girls take their turn.

The team that has the largest number of correct sentences wins.

2. New material—the narrative "El niño al que se le murió el amigo," p. 137 (twenty-five minutes)

  a. Listening comprehension and word study

Before playing the tape, ask the class two questions:

  (1) ¿Quién se murió?   *Who died?*
  (2) ¿Qué dijo la madre al fin   *What did the mother say at the end*
      del cuento?   *of the story?*

Before playing the tape the second time, ask the class two more questions:

  (1) ¿Qué juguetes tenía el   *What toys did the boy have?*
      niño?
  (2) ¿Qué hacía el niño toda   *What did the boy do all night?*
      la noche?

Continue the exercise with a word study.

1) Give the Spanish word for each toy as you pick it up and have the class repeat.

    Es un camión, un reloj,   *It is a truck, a watch, a pistol.*
    una pistola.

Then take each toy and question the class.

¿Qué es esto?   *What is this?*

2) Draw on the chalkboard two figures to illustrate growth.

A

B

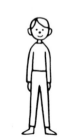

¡Miren Uds. el cuadro B!   *Look at picture B.   John has grown,*
Juan ha crecido, ¿ver-   *hasn't he?*
dad?

3) Give the class another interpretation of *crecido*.

Otra interpretación de   *Another interpretation of* grown *is*
crecido es *más viejo* o   older *or* more mature.
más hombre.

4) Review the parts of the body by pointing to them.

¿Qué son?   *What are they?*

Son las manos, las rodillas,   *They are the hands, the knees, the*
los codos, los brazos.   *elbows, the arms.*

b. Reading exercise

Let the class read the narrative silently. Then, for today's group work, divide the class into three sections.

Group A reads fluently. Their assignment is a guided composition on the narrative.

Group B reads at a normal speed. Their assignment is to answer the textbook questions: p. 10, a; p. 160, b and c.

Group C reads slowly and with difficulty. The teacher spends the last ten minutes with them explaining sections of the story and answering questions. Their assignment is to complete a worksheet containing true/false and completion exercises.

c. Writing exercise

Worksheets

Group A (guided composition):

Write the narrative in the first person, as though it happened to you, and use the past tense.

(1) Al levantarse, ¿adónde fue Ud.?	*Upon getting up, where did you go?*
(2) ¿A quién buscó Ud.?	*Whom were you looking for?*
(3) ¿Qué le dijo su madre?	*What did your mother say to you?*
(4) ¿Por qué volverá su amigo?	*Why will your friend return?*
(5) ¿Por qué no quería Ud. entrar a cenar?	*Why didn't you want (wish) to come in and have supper?*
(6) ¿Comó pasó Ud. la noche?	*How did you spend the night?*
(7) ¿Qué hizo Ud. con los juguetes?	*What did you do with the toys?*
(8) ¿Cuándo volvió Ud. a casa?	*When did you return home?*
(9) ¿Qué le dijo su madre?	*What did your mother say to you (tell you)?*
(10) ¿Qué se le compró?	*What was bought for you?*

Group B (see assignment on page 387)

Group C:

1) Read the following sentences. Write T if the sentence is true, F if it is false. Rewrite all the false sentences and make them true.

Samples:

(a) Una mañana el niño fue a buscar al amigo.	*One morning the boy went to look for his friend.*
(b) La madre le dijo, "El amigo no se murió."	*The mother said to him (told him), "The friend did not die."*
(c) El amigo volverá porque los juguetes están allí.	*The friend will return because the toys are there.*
(d) Su mamá lo llamó y el niño entró a cenar.	*His mother called him and the boy came in to have supper.*

2) Fill in the missing words.

Samples:

(a) El niño fue a _____ al amigo.	*The boy went to _____ the friend.*
(b) El reloj no _____.	*The watch does not _____.*

(c) Pasó buscándolo toda
   la _____.

He spent the whole _____
   looking for him.

(d) "¡Cuánto ha _____
   este niño!"

"How much this boy has _____*!"*

FOLLOW-UP FOR THE NEXT DAY

ACTIVITIES:

1. Warm up

2. Check assignments

3. Grammar study

4. Presentation of geography and history lesson, "La Otra América," pp. 145–47

5. Group work on "La Otra América"

PROCEDURES:

1. Warm up (five minutes)

   Discuss the narrative, p. 137. Hold a question and answer period.

2. Check assignments (ten minutes)

   Group A: Sit with them and ask one or two individuals to read their compositions.

   Group B: Distribute a dittoed sheet with the answers to the questions. Students check their papers.

   Group C: Put answers on the overhead projector. Students check their papers. When the students are finished with one transparency, they put on the second.

3. Grammar study

   a. Generalization on the subjunctive (five minutes)

   b. Dehydrated sentences, using the overhead projector, on the present progressive, p. 145 (five minutes)

   Juan está bajando.

   John is coming down.

   /niños/estar/correr/

   /boys/to be/to run/

4. Presentation of the geography and history lesson, "La Otra América," p. 145–47 (ten minutes)

   Use a map of South America.

5. Group work on "La Otra América" (fifteen minutes)

The entire class reads the lesson, pp. 145–47.

The teacher meets with Groups A and B to discuss the reading.

HOMEWORK:

Group A: Students are to read supplementary articles on South America from *El Sol* and do the exercises following them.

Group B: Students choose one country in South America and write about it as though they lived there. Distribute a worksheet with guided questions such as, What nation is north of your country? South? East? West? What rivers are in your country? What are the major cities in your country?

Group C: Students receive a blank map of South America and are asked to fill in the places that were mentioned in the lesson.

C. ADVANCED FRENCH CLASS

TEXT: Bauer, C., et al., *Le Français, Lire, Parler et Ecrire* (New York: Holt, Rinehart and Winston, 1964), pp. 6–7.[4]

CLASS SIZE: Twenty-five to thirty

CLASS PERIOD: Fifty minutes

EQUIPMENT:

1. Overhead projector

2. Tape recorder

3. Record player

4. Slide projector

MATERIALS:

1. A transparency with the outline of the state of Texas, drawn to the same scale as a map of France, and an overlay with the outline of France in red and the following cities: Paris, Lille, Saint-Brieuc, Tarascon, Avignon, and Marseille

2. The record *Songs and Dances of France* #491 (Lorraine Music Co., 23-80 48th St., Long Island City, New York)

---

[4] The excerpts from this work are reprinted by permission of Holt, Rinehart and Winston.

3. A tape recording (made by a native speaker if possible) of the paraphrases found in Section I b

4. A dittoed sheet of the paraphrases in Section I b

5. Slides of la Cannebière, le Vieux Port, Provençal costumes, la pétanque, red tile roofs, Breton costumes, Breton architecture, Saint-Brieuc (if possible)

ACTIVITIES:

1. Presentation of reading lesson

    a. Summary

    b. New vocabulary

    c. Grammar review

2. Group and individual work

PROCEDURES:

1. Presentation of reading lesson (twenty-five minutes)

    a. Summary of passage with books closed (fifteen minutes)

Teacher: La France n'est pas gigantesque comme les Etats-Unis. Voici la carte du Texas (transparency and overhead projector). Et voici la carte de la France (overlay). Lequel des deux est le plus grand, le Texas ou la France?

France is not gigantic like the United States. Here is a map of Texas. And here is a map of France. Which is bigger, Texas or France?

Student: Le Texas. *Texas.*

Teacher: Très bien. *Very good.*

(Remove map of Texas and keep map of France on the projector.)

Teacher: Aux Etats-Unis les distances sont

In the United States, distances are great, but the inhabitants look

grandes, mais les habitants se ressemblent d'une région à une autre. Il est par exemple difficile de distinguer un habitant de Baltimore d'un citoyen de Los Angeles.

alike from one region to the next. For instance, it is difficult to distinguish an inhabitant of Baltimore from an inhabitant of Los Angeles.

En France il y a une grande différence entre l'habitant de Marseille et celui de Saint-Brieuc.

In France there is a big difference between an inhabitant of Marseille and an inhabitant of Saint-Brieuc.

(Point to these cities.)

Marseille est situé en Provence. Saint-Brieuc se trouve en Bretagne.

Marseille is located in Provence. Saint-Brieuc is located in Brittany.

Voici quelques vues de Marseille.

Here are some pictures of Marseille.

(Show le Vieux Port and la Cannebière.)

Qu'est-ce que vous voyez sur les diapositives?

What do you see on the slides?

Class: La mer, des bateaux . . .

The sea, boats . . .

Teacher: Bien. Maintenant, regardez ces vues de la région. Décrivez les toits.

Good. Now look at these pictures of the region. Describe the roofs.

(Show slides of Provence.)

Student 1: Ils sont rouges.

They are red.

Student 2: Ce sont des toits   *The roofs are made of _____.*
        de _____ ?

Teacher: De tuiles.   *Tiles.*

Use the same procedure for slides of Brittany. Show slides or dolls with Provençal or Breton costumes.

Teacher: Les Français ne   *French people no longer wear these*
        portent plus ces   *costumes every day, but you can*
        costumes tous les   *sometimes see them in certain folk-*
        jours, mais on les   *lore celebrations. The music of*
        voit quelquefois   *Brittany is different from that of*
        dans certains   *Provence.*
        spectacles folk-
        loriques. La mu-
        sique de la
        Bretagne est dif-
        férente de celle
        de la Provence.

(Play a selection from the record.)

        Quels instruments   *What instruments do you hear?*
        entendez-vous?

Student 1: Un tambour et un   *A drum and a pipe. (Provence)*
        fifre. (Provence)

Teacher: Bien. En Bretagne   *Good. In Brittany, they play the bag-*
        on joue de la cor-   *pipe. Why are there such big dif-*
        nemuse. Pourquoi   *ferences among the regions of*
        est-ce qu'il y a de   *France?*
        si grandes dif-
        férences entre les
        régions françaises?

Student 1: La France est un   *France is an old country.*
        pays ancien.

Student 2: Autrefois il n'y   *In the past, there were not many*
        avait pas beau-   *means of communication between*
        coup de moyens   *the regions.*
        de communi-
        cation entre les
        régions.

Teacher: Oui. Au treizième
siècle ces régions
étaient presque
des pays indé-
pendants, avec
leur propre gou-
vernement et leurs
traditions.

*Yes. In the thirteenth century, these
regions were almost independent
countries, with their own govern-
ments and their traditions.*

Même aujourd'hui
les gens qui sont
nés dans le même
quartier de Lille,
Marseille ou
Saint-Brieuc con-
sidèrent les autres
français un peu
comme des étran-
gers. On appelle
cette sorte de par-
ticularisme "l'es-
prit de clocher."
Voici un clocher.

*Even today, people who are born in
the same section of Lille, Marseille or Saint-Brieuc consider
other French people a little bit like
foreigners. This type of village
parochialism is called "belfry
spirit." Here is a belfry.*

(Draw a belfry on the chalkboard.)

Le clocher symbo-
lise le village ou le
petit quartier où
tous les gens pas-
sent leur exist-
ence. Ils sont unis
par des liens
étroits.

*The belfry symbolizes the village or
the neighborhood where all the
people spend their existence. They
are united through close bonds.*

b. New vocabulary (seven minutes)

Distribute a dittoed sheet with several difficult sentences taken from the
reading. The new words and expressions are underlined.

Ask the class to read the sentences silently.

Play a tape recording with easier words, those already known by the class,
that replace the more difficult new ones.

(1) Sheet: Quand on regarde
la carte des
Etats-Unis, on a
de la peine à
comprendre. . . .

*When one looks at a map of the
United States, one has trouble
understanding . . .*

Tape: Quand on regarde la carte des Etats-Unis, on comprend difficilement. . . .

When one looks at a map of the United States, one has difficulty understanding . . .

(2) Sheet: Chacun a <u>son</u> <u>caractère bien</u> <u>tranché.</u>

Each has its carefully delineated character.

Tape: Chacun a une personnalité bien marquée.

Each has its distinct personality.

(3) Sheet: Cet amour <u>des</u> <u>siens.</u>

This love of one's own people.

Tape: Cet amour de sa famille.

This love of one's family.

(4) Sheet: Ce n'est pas par hasard si l'<u>émis-</u> <u>sion</u> "Intervilles" a remporté un triomphe à la télévision.

It is not by accident that the "Intervilles" show was successful on television.

Tape: Ce n'est pas par hasard si le programme "Intervilles" a remporté un triomphe à la télévision.

It is not by accident that the program "Intervilles" was successful on television.

(5) Sheet: Et <u>par surcroît,</u> c'était <u>fort</u> joyeux.

And in addition, it was extremely happy.

Tape: Et de plus, c'était très joyeux.

And moreover, it was very happy.

(6) Sheet: L'esprit de clocher est détestable quand il est un esprit <u>de morgue</u> <u>et de dédain.</u>

Village parochialism is bad when it reflects a spirit of lifelessness and disdain.

Tape: L'esprit de clocher
est détestable
quand il est un
esprit de supéri-
orité désagré-
able.

*Village parochialism is bad when it
reflects a spirit of unpleasant
superiority.*

(7) Sheet: Il est <u>fécond</u> au
contraire, et
plein de res-
sources . . .

*It is fruitful, on the contrary, and
full of resources . . .*

Tape: Il est productif au
contraire, et
plein de res-
sources . . .

*It is productive, on the contrary, and
full of resources . . .*

Distribute a second dittoed sheet with the original sentences and their
paraphrases. Give the class several minutes to review them.

c. Grammar review (three minutes)

Use subjunctive sentences from the text as models for pattern drills.

(1) Modèle: Le professeur dit,
"Il faut que les Mar-
seillais aient un accent."
Vous allez répéter la
phrase. Ensuite le pro-
fesseur dit "vous."
Vous dites, "Il faut que
vous ayez un autre ac-
cent."

*The teacher says: "People from Mar-
seille have to have an accent."
You are going to repeat the sentence. Then the teacher says
"you." You say: "You have to have
another accent."*

Commencez.

Begin.

Le Professeur

Les Elèves

Il faut que vous ayez un autre
accent.
(*You have to have another
accent.*)

(Repeat.)

les Lillois
(*People from Lille*)

Il faut que les Lillois aient un autre
accent.
(*People from Lille have to have another accent.*)

les Norvégiens
(*Norwegians*)

Il faut que les Norvégiens aient un
autre accent.

(Norwegians have to have another accent.)

nous
(We)

Il faut que nous ayons un autre accent.
(We have to have another accent.)

tu
(You)

Il faut que tu aies un autre accent.
(You have to have another accent.)

(2) Modèle: Le professeur dit, "Cela n'empêche pas que l'on s'aime bien." Les elèves répètent. Le professeur dit, "On s'amuse." Les elèves disent, "Cela n'empêche pas que l'on s'amuse."

The teacher says: "That doesn't prevent us from liking one another." The students repeat. The teacher says: "We have fun." The students say: "That doesn't prevent us from having fun."

Commencez.

Begin.

Le Professeur

Les Elèves

On va au cinéma.
(We go to the movies.)

Cela n'empêche pas que l'on aille au cinéma.
(That doesn't prevent us from going to the movies.)

On fait son travail.
(We do our work.)

Cela n'empêche pas que l'on fasse son travail.
(That doesn't prevent us from doing our work.)

On sort ensemble.
(We go out together.)

Cela n'empêche pas que l'on sorte ensemble.
(That doesn't prevent us from going out together.)

On boit quelque chose.
(We drink something.)

Cela n'empêche pas que l'on boive quelque chose.
(That doesn't prevent us from drinking something.)

2. Group and individual work (twenty-five minutes)

For today's lesson, divide the class into three groups.

Group A will prepare a debate. Ask those students who are fluent and those who like to speak French to join this group.

Group B will write a composition. Ask those students who are able to write compositions and who like to write them to join this group.

Group C will answer oral and written questions on the reading selection. These students will probably have less skill in speaking and writing than those in Groups A and B.

a. Group A—Debate

See Chapter 5.

Distribute the following worksheet:

1) Lisez les pages 6 et 7.	*Read pages 6 and 7.*
2) Proposition: "L'esprit de clocher" est typiquement américain aussi. Il faut prendre un parti. Etes-vous pour ou contre? Paul Johnson va organiser les équipes. Dites-lui quelle équipe vous avez choisie. Les membres de chaque équipe vont exposer leurs arguments.	*Resolved: Village parochialism is also typically American. You must take sides. Are you for or against? Paul Johnson will organize the teams. Tell him which team you have selected. The members of each team will present their arguments.*
3) Vocabulaire: la compétition	*Vocabulary:* *competition*
une société industrielle	*industrial society*
une population mobile	*mobile population*
l'influence de la télévision	*the influence of television*
l'individualisme (individualiste)	*individualism (individualist)*
"Chacun pour soi"	*"Every man for himself"*
l'esprit des pionniers	*pioneer spirit*
nos ancêtres	*our forefathers*
le système d'entraide (aide mutuelle)	*the system of helping one another (mutual assistance)*
l'esprit civique	*civic spirit*

l'amitié   *friendship*

les voisins   *neighbors*

(The teacher may supply other vocabulary when requested.)

4) Distribute questions for both sides of the argument to guide the debators.

Est-ce que le rythme de la vie actuelle nous laisse le temps de créer des liens d'amitié?

Does the pace of life today leave us the time to develop friendships?

Est-il vrai que les Américains sont si sociables qu'ils se font des amis très facilement?

Is it true that Americans are so sociable that they make friends very easily?

Est-ce que vous seriez triste de quitter vos amis si vos parents décidaient de déménager?

Would you be sad to leave your friends if your parents decided to move away?

Est-ce que vous êtes indifferent(e) à la ville ou au quartier que vous habitez?

Do you feel indifferent towards the city or neighborhood where you live?

b. Group B—Written composition

See Chapter 7.

Distribute the following worksheet:

1) Lisez les pages 6 et 7.

Read pages 6 and 7.

2) Imaginez que vous êtes en France et que vous écrivez une lettre à un de vos camarades américains. Dans votre lettre d'environ cent mots vous décrivez "l'esprit de clocher" et les différences régionales que vous avez trouvées en France. Suivez les directives en basant vos phrases sur la lecture des pages 6 et 7.

Imagine that you are in France and that you are writing a letter to one of your American friends. In your letter of about 100 words, you describe village parochialism and the regional differences you have found in France. Follow the instructions below and base your information on the reading on pages 6 and 7.

Cher/chère ——————,   *Dear . . .*

Expliquez à votre cama-
rade la différence qu'il y a
entre les distances en
Amérique et en France.

*Explain to your friend the differ-
ence between distances in the United
States and in France.*

Dites-lui dans quelles
circonstances les Français
éprouvent un grand senti-
ment pour la patrie.

*Tell him/her under which circum-
stances the French people show a
patriotic spirit.*

Dites-lui comment s'ap-
pelle l'autre patriotisme
local et les adjectifs qu'on
emploie pour le décrire.

*Tell him/her the name one gives to
local patriotism and the adjectives
used to describe it.*

Expliquez-lui comment
l'esprit de clocher ressem-
ble à l'attitude des mem-
bres d'une famille les uns
envers les autres.

*Explain to him/her how the village
parochialism mirrors the attitude
that members of the family have
toward one another.*

Décrivez-lui les différ-
ences qui existent entre les
Marseillais et les Lillois.

*Describe the differences between
the people from Lille and those from
Marseille.*

Expliquez-lui l'im-
portance d'un match de
football entre l'équipe de
Lille et celle de Marseille.

*Explain to him/her the importance
of a soccer game between the team
from Lille and the one from
Marseille.*

Dites-lui le nom d'une
émission qui a remporté un
triomphe à la télévision et
expliquez-lui pourquoi.

*Tell him/her the name of the popu-
lar TV program and explain its
popularity.*

Expliquez-lui dans
quelles circonstances
l'esprit de clocher est
détestable.

*Explain to him/her under which
circumstances village parochialism
is bad.*

Dites-lui ce qu'il y a de
bon dans l'esprit de clocher
(quand il est fécond).

*Tell him/her the good side of vil-
lage parochialism (when it is productive).*

Bien à toi,   *Best wishes,*

c. Group C—Oral and written work

Spend fifteen minutes with the group and read each paragraph aloud. Explain difficult words, giving synonyms, antonyms, and definitions in French or English. Finally, ask questions on each paragraph.

Sample (the first two paragraphs)

Read:

Quand on regarde la carte des Etats-Unis, on a de la peine à comprendre ce qu'un habitant de Baltimore peut avoir de commun avec un citoyen de Los Angeles. Près de trois mille kilomètres séparent leurs deux villes. La distance est moindre de Paris à Moscou.

When one looks at the map of the United States, one has difficulty understanding what an inhabitant of Baltimore can have in common with an inhabitant of Los Angeles. About three thousand kilometers separate their two cities. The distance from Paris to Moscow is smaller.

Pourtant, l'homme de Baltimore et celui de Los Angeles sont unis par des liens étroits. Ils appartiennent à une même nation, ils jouissent d'une même liberté, ils payent les même impôts. Si les Etats-Unis font la guerre, ils combattent sous le même uniforme.

Nevertheless, the man from Baltimore and the man from Los Angeles are closely united. They belong to the same country, they enjoy the same liberty, they pay the same taxes. If the United States go to war, they wear the same uniform.

Teacher: Regardez la première phrase. Cherchez un synonyme de citoyen.

Look at the first sentence. Find a synonym for "citoyen."

Student: Habitant.

"Habitant."

Teacher: Très bien.

Teacher: Combien de kilomètres séparent Baltimore et Los Angeles?

How many kilometers separate Baltimore and Los Angeles?

Teacher: Prononcez "des liens étroits."

Cela veut dire "by close bonds." Par quoi est-ce que l'homme de Baltimore et celui de Los Angeles sont unis?	*Pronounce "des liens étroits." This expression means "by close bonds." How are the man from Baltimore and the man from Los Angeles united?*
Student: Par des liens étroits.	*By close bonds.*
Teacher: A quoi est-ce qu'ils appartiennent?	*What do they belong to?*
Qu'est-ce qu'ils payent?	*What do they pay?*
Si les Etats-Unis font la guerre, qu'est-ce que ces hommes portent?	*If the United States goes to war, what do these men wear?*

Distribute the same questions, this time in written form, to be completed for homework. The students may start answering them during the last ten minutes of the hour.

Spend the last ten minutes with Group A, listening to their arguments for tomorrow's debate, supplying vocabulary, and correcting errors.

Do not work with Group B at all today. Spend fifteen minutes with them tomorrow on their compositions. Several compositions will be put in the opaque projector and read collectively.

HOMEWORK:

Group A: The students have two notebooks. They are to do the following assignment in one of the notebooks to hand it in the next day.

While the teacher corrects this assignment, he or she can give another one to be written in the second notebook.

Exposez par écrit cinq arguments en faveur de votre position et soumettez-les moi demain. Soyez prêts à les présenter oralement en classe.	*Prepare in writing five arguments in support of your position and turn them in tomorrow. Be ready to present them orally in class.*

Minimum acceptable performance: Each student should present his or her arguments with eighty percent accuracy.

Group B: Complétez votre lettre   *Complete your letter for tomorrow.*
        pour demain.

        Minimum acceptable performance: Each student should attain ninety-five percent accuracy in spelling and grammar.

Group C: Ecrivez des réponses aux   *Write out the answers to the ques-*
        questions.   *tions.*

        Minimum acceptable performance: Each student should answer with ninety percent accuracy in spelling and eighty percent accuracy in grammar.

FOLLOW-UP FOR THE NEXT DAY

PROCEDURES:

1. Collect notebooks from Group A.

Have them corrected by the following day.

2. Debate (twenty-five minutes)

The students present their arguments. If they cannot recall a word or have difficulty finishing a sentence, the teacher may help them and members of their team.

Do not interrupt the debaters to correct their French. Instead, take careful notes to use for discussion during the last ten minutes of the class period.

3. Correct compositions for the entire class (fifteen minutes)

Members of Group B put their compositions on the opaque projector. Errors are corrected collectively.

4. Group work (ten minutes)

Group A: Discuss with the students the major errors in grammar, vocabulary, and pronunciation that were made during the debate.

Group B: Students make corrections on their compositions.

Group C: Students check the answers to their homework assignment with the overhead projector.

D. ELEMENTARY ESL CLASS

TEXT: Sheeler, Willard D., *Elementary Course in English*, Book Two (Portland, Oregon: English Language Services and Washington Educational Research Associates, Inc., 1974).[5]

[5] The excerpts from this work are reprinted by permission of English Language Services and Washington Educational Research Associates, Inc.

CLASS SIZE: Twenty-five to thirty students

CLASS PERIOD: Fifty minutes

EQUIPMENT: Overhead projector

MATERIALS:

1. A set of flash cards with magazine cutouts to teach and drill adjectives.

2. A transparency with line drawings for eliciting comparative sentences.

3. A blank overlay for writing sentences describing the drawings in #1.

4. A transparency with a sentence builder using "more" or "less."

5. A transparency with line drawings for eliciting sentences in the superlative.

6. A blank overlay for writing sentences describing the drawings in #5.

7. A transparency with a sentence builder using "the most" and "the least."

8. A transparency containing sentences with irregular comparatives and super-latives: better, best, worse, worst.

9. A transparency showing orthographic changes: y → ie, easy – easier – easiest.

PREVIOUS LESSONS: The class has completed Units 18–24 of the text. Unit 19 contains drills on the objectives of color, size, shape, and condition.

LESSON OBJECTIVE: To produce comparative and superlative sentences orally and in writing with ninety percent accuracy.

ACTIVITIES:

1. Warm up

2. Presentation of the forms of the comparative on an overhead transparency.

3. Oral pattern drill on the comparative.

4. Presentation of the forms of the superlative on an overhead transparency.

5. Oral pattern drill on the superlative.

6. Small group work—Communicative practice.

PROCEDURES:

1. Warm up

   Vocabulary review of adjectives

   a. Teacher displays the cue cards, one by one, and asks the class to describe them. Students say: *That girl is pretty. That man is tall. That car is old. That house is modern.* Etc.

b. Teacher asks class if anyone can think of a person who is tall, famous, intelligent, pretty, etc. Students may refer to their classmates if they wish.

2. New material

a. Teacher shows transparency with drawings for teaching the comparative. (Spaces are left below each set so that the teacher can write the sentence(s) dictated by the class, on the overlay.)

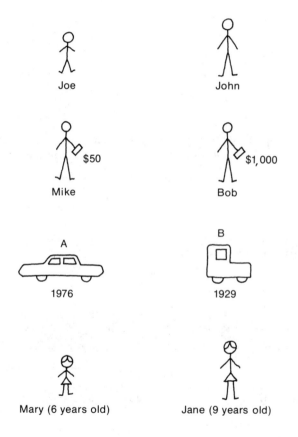

b. Pattern drill

Teacher: tall

Class: Jack is taller than Bill.

Teacher	Class
fat	Jack is fatter than Bill.
thin	
small	
short	
mean	
nice	
slow	
clean	
dirty	
smart	
dumb	

c. Teacher shows transparency with sentence builder, pronounces a few model sentences and asks the class to practice producing others orally.

This man is
This book is   more
This chair is   less

intelligent
important
comfortable
expensive
beautiful
difficult
interesting
capable

than   that one.

d. Generalization: Teacher shows the following transparency:

I	II
Jack is <u>tall</u>.	Jack is <u>taller</u> than Bill.
Fred is <u>short</u>.	Fred is <u>shorter</u> than Bob.
Jane is <u>smart</u>.	Jane is <u>smarter</u> than Joe.
Mary is <u>nice</u>.	Mary is <u>nicer</u> than Jane.

III	IV
Jack is <u>intelligent</u>.	Jack is more <u>intelligent</u> than Bob.
Fred is <u>interesting</u>.	Fred is more <u>interesting</u> than Bill.
Jane is <u>beautiful</u>.	Jane is more <u>beautiful</u> than Mary.
Sue is <u>capable</u>.	Sue is more <u>capable</u> than Lisa.

TEACHER'S QUESTIONS:

1. Look at the underlined words in Column I. How many syllables do you find in each word?

2. When you use these words in comparative sentences (Column II) what ending do you add?

3. Now look at the underlined words in Column III. How many syllables do you find in each word?

4. When you use these words in comparative sentences (Column IV), what other word must you put before each adjective?

    e. Teacher shows transparency with drawings for teaching the superlative and follows some procedures used for the comparative lesson.

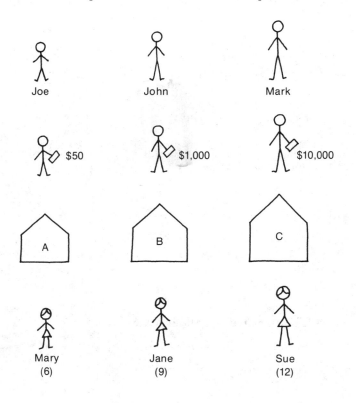

f. Teacher gives class sentence builders using *better, worse, the best,* and *the worst.*

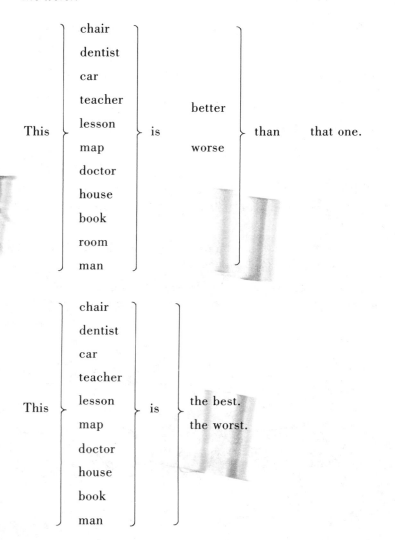

| This | { chair, dentist, car, teacher, lesson, map, doctor, house, book, room, man } | is | { better, worse } | than | that one. |

| This | { chair, dentist, car, teacher, lesson, map, doctor, house, book, man } | is | { the best., the worst. } |

g. Teacher shows transparency with orthographic changes. Only the first three examples are completed. The class dictates the other changes and the teacher writes them in.

	Comparative	Superlative
easy	easier than	the easiest
funny	funnier than	the funniest

| lonely | lonelier than | the loneliest |

pretty

ugly

lazy

3. Small Group Work—Communicative Practice

Divide the class randomly into groups of three. Each group is to find the answers to the following questions:

Who is the tallest?

Who is the youngest?

Who is the richest today?   (each person counts the money he or she is carrying)

Then the class reassembles and the groups report their findings.

HOMEWORK:

Group A: Students create original sentences.

Write your opinion of the following people or objects by using comparatives or superlatives.

Example; A. The *Ohio State University*
The Ohio State University has the best football team in the country.
B. *American children*
American children are more independent than European children.

1. American women

2. American food

3. The city where we now are

4. American men

5. The President of the United States

6. The Secretary of State

7. American T.V. programs

8. American houses

9. American films

10. Your English teacher

Group B: Students write an exercise.

> Change each adjective to its opposite and rewrite the sentence (use another piece of paper).

> Example: Mary is the tallest girl in the class. → Mary is the shortest girl in the class.

1. This is the worst room in the house.

2. I think my English is better than yours.

3. That table is older than mine.

4. Jack is the smartest boy in the class.

5. He married the most beautiful girl in the world.

6. I think that boy is faster than his brother.

7. This lesson is more difficult than that one.

8. This car is cheaper than yours.

9. Mr. Jones is the oldest teacher in our school.

10. Today's lesson is shorter than yesterday's.

11. Her house is smaller than his.

12. I think my country is more beautiful than yours.

13. This problem is simpler than that one.

14. This machine is the most modern in the factory.

15. Her sister is the most intelligent student in the class.

16. Marguerite is the richest woman I know.

17. The earliest you can leave is 6:00.

18. He is the laziest student I know.

19. John is more athletic than Steve.

20. I am healthier than you.

Group C: Students write Exercises 1, 2 and 3 on pages 134 and 135 in the textbook.

FOLLOW-UP FOR THE NEXT DAY

Groups B and C will be given dittoed sheets with the correct answers so that they may check their assignments. Meanwhile, the teacher is rapidly checking or spot-checking the original sentences written by Group A.

Then the entire class listens to the sentences composed by Group A and indicates whether or not they agree. This becomes the basis for a conversation class.

Index

Index

I 45
J 6